Frontiers in Data Science

Chapman & Hall/CRC Big Data Series

SERIES EDITOR
Sanjay Ranka

AIMS AND SCOPE
This series aims to present new research and applications in Big Data, along with the computational tools and techniques currently in development. The inclusion of concrete examples and applications is highly encouraged. The scope of the series includes, but is not limited to, titles in the areas of social networks, sensor networks, data-centric computing, astronomy, genomics, medical data analytics, large-scale e-commerce, and other relevant topics that may be proposed by potential contributors.

PUBLISHED TITLES
FRONTIERS IN DATA SCIENCE
Matthias Dehmer and Frank Emmert-Streib

BIG DATA OF COMPLEX NETWORKS
Matthias Dehmer, Frank Emmert-Streib, Stefan Pickl, and Andreas Holzinger

BIG DATA COMPUTING: A GUIDE FOR BUSINESS AND TECHNOLOGY MANAGERS
Vivek Kale

BIG DATA : ALGORITHMS, ANALYTICS, AND APPLICATIONS
Kuan-Ching Li, Hai Jiang, Laurence T. Yang, and Alfredo Cuzzocrea

BIG DATA MANAGEMENT AND PROCESSING
Kuan-Ching Li, Hai Jiang, and Albert Y. Zomaya

BIG DATA ANALYTICS: TOOLS AND TECHNOLOGY FOR EFFECTIVE PLANNING
Arun K. Somani and Ganesh Chandra Deka

BIG DATA IN COMPLEX AND SOCIAL NETWORKS
My T. Thai, Weili Wu, and Hui Xiong

HIGH PERFORMANCE COMPUTING FOR BIG DATA
Chao Wang

NETWORKING FOR BIG DATA
Shui Yu, Xiaodong Lin, Jelena Mišić, and Xuemin (Sherman) Shen

Frontiers in Data Science

Edited by
Matthias Dehmer
Frank Emmert-Streib

CRC Press is an imprint of the
Taylor & Francis Group, an **informa** business

CRC Press
Taylor & Francis Group
6000 Broken Sound Parkway NW, Suite 300
Boca Raton, FL 33487-2742

Printed on acid-free paper

International Standard Book Number-13: 978-1-4987-9932-4 (Hardback)

Visit the Taylor & Francis Web site at
http://www.taylorandfrancis.com

and the CRC Press Web site at
http://www.crcpress.com

Contents

About the Editors **vii**

Contributors **ix**

1 **Legal aspects of information science, data science, and Big Data** **1**
Alessandro Mantelero and Giuseppe Vaciago

2 **Legal and policy aspects of information science in emerging automated environments** **47**
Stefan A. Kaiser

3 **Privacy as secondary rule, or the intrinsic limits of legal orders in the age of Big Data** **69**
Bart van der Sloot

4 **Data ownership: Taking stock and mapping the issues** **111**
Florent Thouvenin, Rolf H. Weber, and Alfred Früh

5 **Philosophical and methodological foundations of text data analytics** **147**
Beth-Anne Schuelke-Leech and Betsy Barry

6 **Mobile commerce and the consumer information paradox: A review of practice, theory, and a research agenda** **171**
Matthew S. Eastin and Nancy H. Brinson

7 **The impact of Big Data on making evidence-based decisions** **191**
Rodica Neamtu, Caitlin Kuhlman, Ramoza Ahsan, and Elke Rundensteiner

8 **Automated business analytics for artificial intelligence in Big Data@X 4.0 era** **223**
Yi-Ting Chen and Edward W. Sun

9 The evolution of recommender systems: From the beginning to the Big Data era **253**
Beatrice Paoli, Monika Laner, Beat Tödtli, and Jouri Semenov

10 Preprocessing in Big Data: New challenges for discretization and feature selection **285**
Verónica Bolón-Canedo, Noelia Sánchez-Maroño, and Amparo Alonso-Betanzos

11 Causation, probability, and all that: Data science as a novel inductive paradigm **329**
Wolfgang Pietsch

12 Big Data in healthcare in China: Applications, obstacles, and suggestions **355**
Zhong Wang and Xiaohua Wang

Index **371**

About the Editors

Matthias Dehmer studied mathematics at the University of Siegen, Siegen, Germany and earned his PhD in computer science from the Technical University of Darmstadt, Darmstadt, Germany. Afterward, he was a research fellow at Vienna Bio Center, Austria, Vienna University of Technology, and University of Coimbra, Portugal. He obtained his habilitation in applied discrete mathematics from the Vienna University of Technology. Currently, he is a professor at UMIT—The Health and Life Sciences University, Austria. His research interests are in data science, Big Data, complex networks, machine learning, and information theory. He has published more than 220 publications in applied mathematics, computer science, data science, and related disciplines.

Frank Emmert-Streib studied physics at the University of Siegen, Germany, and earned his PhD in theoretical physics from the University of Bremen, Bremen, Germany. He was a postdoctoral fellow in the United States before becoming a faculty member at the Center for Cancer Research at the Queen's University Belfast, UK. Currently, he is a professor in the Department of Signal Processing at Tampere University of Technology, Finland. His research interests are in the field of computational biology, data science and analytics in the development and application of methods from statistics, and machine learning for the analysis of Big Data from genomics, finance, and business.

Contributors

Ramoza Ahsan
Worcester Polytechnic University
Worcester, Massachusetts

Betsy Barry
Emory University
Atlanta, Georgia

Amparo Alonso-Betanzos
Universidade da Coruña
A Coruña, Spain

Nancy H. Brinson
University of Texas at Austin
Austin, Texas

Verónica Bolón-Canedo
Universidade da Coruña
A Coruña, Spain

Yi-Ting Chen
National Chiao Tung University
Hsinchu, Taiwan

Matthew S. Eastin
University of Texas at Austin
Austin, Texas

Alfred Früh
Universität Zürich
Zürich, Switzerland

Stefan A. Kaiser
Independent Researcher
Wassenberg, Germany

Caitlin Kuhlman
Worcester Polytechnic University
Worcester, Massachusetts

Monika Laner
Fernfachhochschule Schweiz
Brig, Switzerland

Alessandro Mantelero
Polytechnic University of Turin
Turin, Italy

Noelia Sánchez-Maroño
Universidade da Coruña
A Coruña, Spain

Rodica Neamtu
Worcester Polytechnic University
Worcester, Massachusetts

Beatrice Paoli
Fernfachhochschule Schweiz
Brig, Switzerland

Wolfgang Pietsch
Technische Universität München
Munich, Germany

Elke Rundensteiner
Worcester Polytechnic University
Worcester, Massachusetts

Beth-Anne Schuelke-Leech
University of Windsor
Windsor, Ontario, Canada

Jouri Semenov
Fernfachhochschule Schweiz
Brig, Switzerland

Edward W. Sun
KEDGE Business School
Talence, France

Florent Thouvenin
Universität Zürich
Zürich, Switzerland

Beat Tödtli
Fernfachhochschule Schweiz
Brig, Switzerland

Giuseppe Vaciago
University of Insubria
Varese, Italy

Bart van der Sloot
Tilburg University
Tilburg, the Netherlands

Zhong Wang
Beijing Academy of Social Sciences
Beijing, China

Xiaohua Wang
Chinese Academy of Sciences
Beijing, China

Rolf H. Weber
Universität Zürich
Zürich, Switzerland

Chapter 1

Legal aspects of information science, data science, and Big Data[*]

Alessandro Mantelero

Giuseppe Vaciago

Introduction: The legal challenges of the use of data 2
Data collection and data processing: The fundamentals of data protection regulations 4
The European Union model: From the Data Protection Directive to the General Data Protection Regulation 6
Use of data and risk-analysis 10
Use of data for decision-making purposes: From individual to collective dimension of data processing 17
Data-centered approach and socio-ethical impacts 21
Multiple-risk assessment and collective interests 23
The guidelines adopted by the Council of Europe on the protection of individuals with regard to the processing of personal data in a world of Big Data 25
Data prediction: Social control and social surveillance 29
Use of data during the investigation: Reasonable doubt versus reasonable suspicion 30
Big Data and social surveillance: Public and private interplay in social control 31
The EU reform on data protection 35
References 36

[*]Alessandro Mantelero, Polytechnic University of Turin, is the author of sections "Introduction: The legal challenges of the use of data" and "Use of data for decision-making purposes: From individual to collective dimension of data processing." Giuseppe Vaciago, University of Insubria, is the author of section "Data prediction: Social control and social surveillance."

Introduction: The legal challenges of the use of data

There are many definitions of Big Data, which differ depending on the specific discipline. Most of the definitions focus on the growing technological ability to collect, process, and extract new and predictive knowledge from a bulk of data characterized by a great volume, velocity, and variety.*

However, in terms of protection of individual rights, the main issues do not only concern the volume, velocity, and variety of processed data, but also the analysis of data, using software to extract new and predictive knowledge for decision-making purposes. Therefore, in this contribution, the definition of Big Data encompasses both Big Data and Big Data analytics.†

The advent of Big Data has suggested a new paradigm in social empirical studies, in which the traditional approach adopted in statistical studies is complemented or replaced by Big Data analysis. This new paradigm is characterized by the relevant role played by data visualization, which makes it possible the analysis of real-time data streams to get their trajectory and predict future trends possible [3]. Moreover, large amounts of data make it possible to use unsupervised machine-learning algorithms to discover hidden correlations between variables that characterize large datasets.

This kind of approach, which is based on the emerging correlations among data, leads social investigation to adopt a new strategy, in which there are no preexisting research hypotheses to be verified through empirical statistical studies. Big Data analytics suggest possible correlations, which constitute *per se* the research hypothesis: data show the potential relations between facts or behavior. Nevertheless, these relations are not grounded on causation and, for this reason, should be further investigated using the traditional statistical method.

Assuming that data trends suggest correlations and consequent research hypotheses, at the moment of data collection only very general research hypotheses are possible, as the potential data patterns are still unknown. Therefore, the specific purpose of data processing can be identified only at a later time, when correlations reveal the usefulness of some information to detect specific aspects. Only at that time, the given purpose of the use of information becomes evident, also with regard to further analyses conducted with traditional statistical methods [4].

---

*The term "Big Data" usually identifies extremely large datasets that may be analyzed computationally to extract inferences about data patterns, trends, and correlations. According to the International Telecommunication Union, Big Data are "a paradigm for enabling the collection, storage, management, analysis, and visualization, potentially under real-time constraints, of extensive datasets with heterogeneous characteristics" [1].

†This term is used to identify computational technologies that analyze large amounts of data to uncover hidden patterns, trends, and correlations. According to the European Union Agency for Network and Information Security, the term Big Data analytics "refers to the whole data management lifecycle of collecting, organizing, and analysing data to discover patterns, to infer situations or states, to predict and to understand behaviors" [2].

On the other hand, there are algorithms, such as supervised machine-learning algorithms, that need a preliminary training phase. In this stage, a supervisor uses data training sets to correct the errors of the machine, orienting the algorithm toward correct associations. In this sense, supervised machine-learning algorithms require a prior definition of the purpose of the use of data, identifying the goal that the machine should reach through autonomous processing of all available data.

In this case, although the purpose of data use is defined in the training phase, the manner in which data are processed and the final outcome of data mining remain largely unknown. In fact, these algorithms are black boxes and their internal dynamics are partially unpredictable.*

Both data visualization and machine-learning applications pose relevant questions in terms of Big Data processing, which will be addressed in the following sections. How is it possible to define the specific purpose of data processing at the moment of data collection, when the correlations suggested by analytics are unknown at that time? If different sources of data are used in machine training and running learning algorithms, how can data subjects know the specific purpose of the use of their information in given machine-learning applications?

These questions clearly show the tension that characterizes the application of the traditional data protection principles in the Big Data context. But this is not the only crucial aspect: the very notion of personal data is becoming more undefined. Running Big Data analytics over large datasets could make it difficult to distinguish between personal data and anonymous data, as well as between sensitive data and nonsensitive data.

Various studies have demonstrated how information stored in anonymized datasets can be partially reidentified, in some cases without expensive technical solutions [5–12]. This suggests going beyond the traditional dichotomy between personal and anonymous data and representing this distinction as a scale that moves from personal identified information to aggregated data. Between these extremes, the level of anonymization is proportional to the effort, in terms of time, resources and costs, which is required to reidentify information.

Finally, with regard to sensitive data, Big Data analytics make it possible to use nonsensitive data to infer sensitive information, such as information concerning religious practices extracted from location data and mobility patterns [13].

Against this background, the existing data protection regulations and the ongoing proposals [14,15] remain largely focused on the traditional main pillars of the so-called fourth generation of data protection laws [16]: the *notice*

*See, e.g., Zhang M., "Google Photos Tags Two African-Americans As Gorillas Through Facial Recognition Software," *Forbes*, July 1, 2015. http://www.forbes.com/sites/mzhang/2015/07/01/google-photos-tags-two-african-americans-as-gorillas-through-facial-recognition-software/#36b529227b63 (accessed March 23, 2016).

and consent model (i.e., an informed, freely given, and specific consent) [17–21],* the purpose limitation principle [24,25], and the minimization principle.

For this reason, the following sections investigate the limits and criticisms of the existing legal framework and the possible options to provide adequate answers to the new challenges of Big Data processing. In this light, this chapter is divided into three main sections.

The first section focuses on the traditional paradigm of data protection and on the provisions, primarily in the new EU General Data Protection Regulation (Regulation (EU) 2016/679, hereafter GDPR), that can be used to safeguard individual rights in Big Data processing.

The second section goes beyond the existing legal framework and, in the light of the path opened by the guidelines on Big Data adopted by the Council of Europe, suggests a broader approach that encompasses the collective dimension of data protection. This dimension often characterizes Big Data applications and leads to assess the ethical and social impacts of data uses, which assume an important role in many Big Data contexts.

The last section deals with the use of Big Data to anticipate fraud detection and to prevent crime. In this light, the new Directive (EU) 2016/680† is briefly analyzed.

Data collection and data processing: The fundamentals of data protection regulations

Before considering the different reasons that induce the law to protect personal information, it should be noted that European legal systems do not recognize the same broad notion of the right to privacy that exists in U.S. jurisprudence.‡ At the same time, in the European countries, data protection laws do not draw their origins from the European idea of privacy and its related case law.

---

*See Articles 6 and 7, Regulation (EU) 2016/679 of the European Parliament and of the Council of April 27, 2016 on the protection of natural persons with regard to the processing of personal data and on the free movement of such data, and repealing Directive 95/46/EC (General Data Protection Regulation). Differently, in the United States, the traditional approach based on various sectorial regulations has underestimated the role played by user's choice, adopting a market-oriented strategy. Nevertheless, the guidelines adopted by the U.S. administrations in 2012 [14] seem to suggest a different approach, reinforcing self-determination [8,22,23].

†Directive (EU) 2016/680 on the protection of natural persons with regard to the processing of personal data by competent authorities for the purposes of the prevention, investigation, detection or prosecution of criminal offences or the execution of criminal penalties, and on the free movement of such data, and repealing Council Framework Decision 2008/977/JHA.

‡With regard to the notion of right to privacy (and in brief), in the United States the right to privacy covers a broad area that goes from informational privacy to the right of self-determination in private life decisions. On the other hand, in European countries, this right mainly focuses on the first aspect and is related to media activities [26–31].

European data protection regulations, since their origins in the second half of the last century, focused on information regarding individuals, without distinguishing between public or private information [32]. Compared with the right to privacy, the issues regarding the protection of personal data have been more recently recognized by law, both in the United States and Europe [33]. This dates from the 1960s, whereas the primitive era of the right to privacy was at the end of the nineteenth century, when the penny press assumed a significant role in limiting the privacy of the people belonging to upper classes [34].

In the light of the above, the analysis of the fundamentals of data processing should start from the effects of the computer revolution that happened in the late 1950s. The advent of computers and its social impact led to the first regulations on data protection and posed the first pillars of the architecture of the present legal framework.

The first generations of data protection regulations were characterized by a national approach. They were adopted in different times by national legislators and were different with regard to the extension of the safeguards provided and the remedies offered.

The notion of data protection was originally based on the idea of control over information, as confirmed by the literature of that period [35–37]. The migration from dusty paper archives to computer memories was a Copernican revolution which, for the first time in history, permitted the aggregation of information about every citizen that was previously spread over different archives [38].

The first data protection regulations were the answer to the rising concern of citizens about social control, as the new big mainframe computers gave governments [16,38–41] and large corporations the opportunity to collect and manage large amount of personal information [16,42]. In this sense, the legal systems gave individuals the opportunity to have a sort of countercontrol over the collected data [16,38,43].

The purpose of the regulations was not to spread and democratize power over information but to increase the level of transparency about data processing and safeguard the right to access to information. Citizens felt they were monitored, and the law gave them the opportunity to know who controlled their data, which kind of information was collected, and for which purposes.

The mandatory notifications of new databases, registration, licensing procedures, and independent authorities [16,44] were the fundamental elements of these new regulations. They were necessary to know who had control over information and to monitor data processing. Another key component was the right to access, which allows citizens to ask data owners about the way in which information is used and, consequently, about the exercise of their power over information. Finally, the entire picture was completed by the creation of *ad hoc* public authorities to safeguard and enforce citizen's rights, exercise control over data owners, and react against abuses.

In this model, there was no space for individual consent, due to the economic context of that period. The collection of information was mainly made by public entities for purposes related to public interests, was mandatory, and there was no space of autonomy in terms of negotiation about personal information. At the same time, personal information did not have an economic value for private companies: data about clients and suppliers were mainly used for operational functions regarding the execution of company activities.

Another element that contributed to exclude the role of self-determination was the lack of knowledge, the extreme difficulty for ordinary people to understand the use, and the mode of operation of mainframes. The computer mainframes were a sort of modern God, with sacral attendants, a selected number of technicians who were able to use this new equipment. In this scenario, it did not make sense to give citizens the chance to choose, as they were unable to understand the way in which their data were processed.

In conclusion, during the 1970s and the first part of the 1980s of the last century, legislators laid the foundations for data protection regulations in many European countries and outside Europe, as a result of the technological and social changes of that period. These first regulations defined the initial core of data protection (i.e., transparency, rights to access, and data protection authorities), which is still present in the existing legal framework.

The European Union model: From the Data Protection Directive to the General Data Protection Regulation

The period from the mid-1980s to the 1990s was characterized not only by the rising of a uniform approach to data protection regulation among the members of the European Union, but also by a change in the regulatory paradigm, due to the new technological, social, and economic scenarios.

Home computers entered the market in the late 1970s to become common during the 1980s. This was the new era of distributed computers, in which a lot of people bought a personal computer to collect and process information.

The big mainframe computers became the small desktop personal computers, with a relatively low cost. Consequently, the computational capacity was no longer an exclusive privilege of governments and big companies but became accessible to many entities and consumers.

This period witnessed another transformation involving direct marketing, which was no longer based on the concept of mail order and moved toward computerized direct marketing solutions.* The new forms of marketing were based on customer profiling and required extensive data collection to apply

*Although direct marketing has its roots in mail order services, which were based on personalized letter (e.g., using the name and surname of addressees) and general group profiling (e.g., using census information to group addressees in social and economic classes), the use of computer equipment increased the level of manipulation of consumer information and generated detailed consumer's profiles [45,46].

data mining software. The main purpose of profiling was to suggest a suitable commercial proposal to any consumer.

This was an innovative application of data processing driven by new purposes. Information was no longer collected to support supply chains, logistics, and orders, but to sell the best product to each user. As a result, the data subject became the focus of the process, and personal information acquired an economic and business value, given its role in sales.

These changes in the technological and business frameworks created new requests from society to legislators, as citizens wanted to have the chance to negotiate their personal data and gain something in return.

Although the new generations of the European data protection laws placed personal information within the context of fundamental rights,* the main goal of these regulations was to pursue economic interests related to the free flow of personal data. This is also affirmed by the Directive 95/46/EC,† which represents both the general framework and the synthesis of this second wave of data protection laws.‡

However, the roots of data protection remained in the context of personality rights. Therefore, the European approach is less market-oriented than it happens in other legal systems. The directive also recognizes the fundamental role of public authorities in protecting data subjects against unwilled or unfair exploitation of their personal information for marketing purposes.

Both the theoretical model of fundamental rights, based on self-determination, and the rising data-driven economy highlighted the importance of user consent in consumer data processing. Consent does not only represent an expression of choice with regard to the use of personality rights by third parties but is also an instrument to negotiate the economic value of personal information.

In this new data-driven economy, personal data cannot be exploited for business purposes without any involvement of data subjects. It is necessary that individuals become part of the negotiation, as data are no longer used mainly by government agencies for public purposes but also by private companies with monetary revenues [49,50].

---

*See Council of Europe, Convention for the Protection of Individuals with regard to Automatic Processing of Personal Data, opened for signature on January 28, 1981 and entered into force on October 1, 1985. http://conventions.coe.int/Treaty/Commun/QueVoulezVous.asp?NT=108&CL=ENG (accessed February 27, 2014); OECD, Annex to the Recommendation of the Council of 23rd September 1980: Guidelines on the Protection of Privacy and Transborder Flows of Personal Data. http://www.oecd.org/internet/ieconomy/oecdguidelinesontheprotectionofprivacyandtransborderflowsofpersonaldata.htm#preface (accessed February 27, 2014).

†Directive 95/46/EC of the European Parliament and of the Council of 24 October 1995 on the protection of individuals with regard to the processing of personal data and on the free movement of such data [1995] OJ L281/31.

‡The EU Directive 95/46/EC has a dual nature, as it was written on the basis of the existing national data protection laws, in order to harmonize them, but at the same time it also provided a new set of rules. See the recitals in the preamble to the Directive 95/46/EC [47,48].

Effective self-determination in data processing, both in terms of protection and economic exploitation of personality rights, cannot be obtained without adequate and prior notice.* For this reason, the *notice and consent* model† added a new layer to the existing paradigm based on transparency and access [17].

Finally, it is important to highlight that, during the 1980s and 1990s, data analysis increased in quality, but its level of complexity was still limited. Consequently, consumers were able to understand the general correlation between data collection and related purposes of data processing (e.g., profiling users, offering customized services, or goods). At that time, informed consent and self-determination were largely considered as synonyms, but this is changed now, in the Big Data era.

The advent of Big Data analytics has created a different economic and technological scenario, with direct consequences on the adequacy of the legal framework adopted to safeguard personal information. The new environment is mainly digital and characterized by an increasing concentration of information in the hands of a few entities, both public and private.

The role played by specific subjects in the generation of data flows is the main reason for this concentration. Governments and big private companies (e.g., large retailers, telecommunication companies) collect huge amounts of data while performing their daily activities. This bulk of information represents a strategic and economically relevant asset, as the management of large databases enables these entities to assume the role of gatekeepers with regard to the information that can be extracted from the datasets. They are able to keep information completely closed or to limit access to the data, perhaps to specific subjects only or with regard to circumscribed parts of the entire collection.

Not only governments and big private companies acquire this power but also the intermediaries in information flows (e.g., search engines, Internet providers, data brokers, and marketing companies), which do not generate information but play a key role in circulating it.

There are also different cases in which information is accessible to the public, both in raw and processed form (e.g., open datasets, online user-generated contents). This only apparently diminishes the concentration of power over information, as access to information is not equivalent to knowledge [51].

A large amount of data create knowledge if the data holders have the adequate interpretation tools to select relevant information, to reorganize it, to place the data in a systematic context, and if there are people with the required skills to define the design of the research and give an interpretation to the results generated by Big Data analytics [3,15,52,53]. Without these skills, data only produce confusion and less knowledge in the end, with information interpreted in an incomplete or biased way. For these reasons, the availability

*The notice describes how the data are processed and the detailed purposes of data processing.

†See Articles 2(h), 7(a) and 10, Directive 95/46/EC.

of data is not sufficient in the Big Data context [54,55]. It is also necessary to have the adequate human and computing resources to manage it.

In this scenario, control over information does not only regard limited access data, but can also concern open data [56,57], over which the information intermediaries create an added value by means of their instruments of analysis. Given that only few entities are able to invest heavily in equipment and research, the dynamics described earlier enhance the concentration of power over information, which increases due to the new expansion of Big Data.

Under many aspects, this new environment resembles the origins of data processing, when, in the mainframe era, technologies were held by a few entities and data processing was too complex to be understood by data subjects. Nevertheless, there are important differences that may affect the possible evolution of this situation, in terms of a diffused and democratic access to information.

The new data gatherers do not base their position only on expensive hardware and software, which may become cheaper in the future, or is based on the growing number of experts able to give an interpretation to the results of data analytics. The fundamental element of this power is represented by the large databases they have. These data silos, which are considered the goldmine of the twenty-first century, do not have free access, as they represent the main or the side effect of the activities conducted by their owners, due to the role that they play in creating, collecting, or managing information.

For this reason, in the Big Data context, it seems quite difficult to imagine the same process of *democratization* that happened with regard to computer equipment during the 1980s [58]. The access to large databases is not only protected by legal rights, but it is also strictly related to the peculiar positions held by data holders in their market and to the presence of entry barriers.

Another aspect that characterizes this new form of concentration of control over information is the nature of the purposes of data collection: data processing is no longer focused on single users (profiling), but it increased by scale and it is trying to investigate attitudes and behaviors of large groups and communities, up to entire countries. The consequence of this large-scale approach is the return of the fears about social surveillance, which characterized the mainframe era.

Against this background, the GDPR does not change the main pillars of the previous regulatory model. Therefore, personal data are still primarily protected by individual rights; the *notice and consent* model remains an important legal ground for data processing, and the principles of purpose limitation and data minimization are reaffirmed.

Despite this traditional approach, which seems to be partially inadequate in the Big Data context, the GDPR shows a partial shift of the regulatory focus from data subject's self-determination to accountability of the controller and persons involved in data processing. In this sense, accountability represents the core of the new EU data protection framework and an important element to tackle the potential negative impacts of the use of data analytics [59].

More specifically, accountability is based on the data protection impact assessment, the role played by data protection officers and, when required by law, the prior assessment process conducted by data protection authorities. In this sense, compared with the previous Data Protection Directive, the GDPR undoubtedly moves toward a risk-based approach.

Nevertheless, this transition is still incomplete. Elements of the previous model focused on data subjects that coexist with the new approach, but without a complete redraft of the architecture defined in the 1990s, it seems to be difficult to address the social and technological challenges of Big Data.

Use of data and risk-analysis

Regarding risk management in data processing, it is worth pointing out that risk can be considered, in a broad sense, as any negative consequence that can occur when personal data are processed, regardless of the fact that these consequences might produce damage or prejudice to individual rights and freedoms.

In this sense, data subjects that use social networks expose themselves to the risk of being profiled [60], of having their information shared with third parties, of being tracked for commercial purposes, and so on. None of these consequences are against the law, as those are detailed in terms and conditions and privacy policies by service providers and accepted by users, on the basis of the *notice and consent* model.

In these cases, it seems that there is no relevant risk for the safeguard of data subjects' rights, as individuals can assess the consequences of data processing and have freely expressed their consent. Nevertheless, legal and sociological studies have clearly demonstrated that users are usually unaware of the consequences of providing their consent, as they do not read long and technical notices or are not able to completely understand these descriptions and imagine their practical consequences [61–65]. Moreover, in many cases, power imbalance and social lock-in drastically reduce any effective freedom of choice.

As a consequence of these constraints, users frequently accept some forms of data processing without any prior risk/benefit analysis and are unaware of the consequences. This shows the limits of the traditional *notice and choice* paradigm [66,67], which are more evident in the context of Big Data analytics, in which it is difficult to describe the "specific" purposes of data processing [Article 6(1)(a) GDPR] at the moment of data collection, due to the transformative use of data made by data controllers [68].*

---

*In this light, it is also difficult to comply with the provisions of Article 4 of the GDPR, which qualifies data subject's consent as "freely given, specific and informed." According to the Article 29 Data Protection Working Party, "to be specific, consent must be intelligible: it should refer clearly and precisely to the scope and the consequences of data processing" [17].

In this sense, with respect to the broad notion of risk-concerning data processing, the GDPR maintains the important roles played by self-determination of data subjects and transparency, recognized by law in the last decades. The European legislator seems to be unaware of the weaknesses of this approach, where the formal transparency of terms and conditions combined with users' behavior [61] provide data controllers with the *notice and consent* model, an easy way to lawfully exploit personal data in an extensive manner.

On the other hand, a narrower notion of risk can be adopted, which focuses on "material or nonmaterial damages" that prejudice the "rights and freedom of natural persons." This notion has been adopted in the GDPR to define the risk-based approach (Recital 75 GDPR). According to the regulation, when a risk of prejudice exists and cannot be mitigated or excluded, data processing becomes unlawful, despite the presence of any legitimate grounds, such as the data subject's consent.

Recital n. 75 of the GDPR provides a long list of cases in which data processing is considered unlawful. Moreover, this recital does not limit these hypotheses to the security of data processing but also takes into account the risk of discrimination and "any other significant economic or social disadvantage."

This notion of risk impact, which is echoed in the Article 35 of the GDPR, represents an important step in the direction of an impact assessment of data processing [69] that is no longer primarily focused on data security (see Article 32 GDPR) and evolves toward a more robust and broader Privacy, Ethical, and Social Impact Assessment (PESIA).* Moreover, the attention to the economic and social implications of data uses assumes relevance in the Big Data context, in which analytics are used in decision-making processes and may have negative impacts that affect individuals in terms of discrimination rather than in terms of data security.†

In line with the risk-based approach, the new provisions of the GDPR reinforce the accountability of data controllers that, according to Article 24, are liable when they do not "implement appropriate technical and organizational measures" to tackle the risks mentioned in the regulation (see also Article 83(4) GDPR). These measures should be implemented from the earliest stage of data processing design, embedding them in the processing, according to the data protection by design approach (Article 25 GDPR).

In the light of the above, regarding transparency, rights to access, and data protection authorities, which are the founding pillars of data protection regulation, and the further element of the data subject's consent, the new regulation

---

*See sections "Multiple-risk assessment and collective interests" and "The guidelines adopted by the Council of Europe on the protection of individuals with regard to the processing of personal data in a world of Big Data." Regarding the PESIA model, see also the H2020 project "VIRT-EU: Values and ethics in Innovation for Responsible Technology in Europe." http://www.virteuproject.eu/ (accessed December 21, 2016).

†See section "Data-centered approach and socio-ethical impacts."

sheds light on the accountability of data controllers. Although accountability principles were already present in the first data protection regulations, in which the duties of transparency and the role played by data protection authorities increased data controllers' accountability, in the Directive 95/46/EC, there was not a general process of risk-assessment, with specific consequences in terms of accountability.

Before the new regulation, there were only national provisions or best practices regarding the privacy impact assessment [69], but no uniform risk-based approach. This goal has now been reached in the GDPR by means of a set of rules that concern the role played by risk analysis, the data protection impact assessment, the prior consultation of data protection authorities, and the data protection officer (Articles 35, 36, and 37 GDPR).

In more detail, the risk-based model defined by the GDPR is articulated in three different levels of assessment. The first is required by Article 24 GDPR, and implicitly by Article 35(1). This is a general assessment of "the risk of varying likelihood and severity for rights and freedoms of natural persons," which defines the level of the potential negative impact of data processing.

When this first assessment shows that the processing "is likely to result in a high risk to the rights and freedoms of natural persons" (Article 35 GDPR), the controller should carry out a formal data protection impact assessment. Moreover, there is a list of cases in which high risk is presumed (Article 35(3) GDPR). This is an open list, due to the fact that data protection authorities may add further cases (Article 35(4) GDPR), according to the margin of maneuver recognized in several provisions by the regulation to national authorities or legislators.

Nevertheless, the idea of a list of high-risk cases, as well as of cases excluded from the impact assessment (Article 35(5) GDPR), raise doubts about the feasibility of this categorization. In this sense, an *ex ante* general definition of the presumed level of risk seems to be in conflict with the idea of risk-assessment, which is necessarily context based.

Moreover, the cases of high risk are described using indefinite notions, such as "large scale" data processing (Article 35(3)(b) and (c) GDPR). In this regard, Recital n. 91 may be of help to clarify the meaning of this provision, as it states that the impact assessment "should in particular apply to large-scale processing operations which aim to process a considerable amount of personal data at regional, national or supranational level and which could affect a large number of data subjects." Nevertheless, the recital does not explain when an amount of data is deemed "considerable" and why, in the digital global context, the amount of data should refer to territorial dimensions (regional, national, or supranational).

Finally, in the absence of any scale, the general notion of *high risk* remains quite indefinite. Recital n.77 identifies a series of bodies and instruments that can provide guidance as regards the "identification of the risk related to the processing, their assessment in terms of origin, nature, likelihood and severity," but, at the moment, the framework remains uncertain.

These criticisms seem to have a limited impact on the field of Big Data analytics, as the majority of applications fall within the cases listed in Article 35(3) GDPR, in which high risk is presumed. Nevertheless, it is worth pointing out that analytics can be used in contexts in which the evaluation of personal aspects is not necessarily "systematic and extensive," as they may focus only on a specific subset of attributes or on a given cluster of persons.

Pursuant to Article 35(3), the use of Big Data analytics usually requires a prior data protection impact assessment. This procedure is defined by Article 35(7), in line with the traditional model of risk-assessment, which is primarily a prior evaluation of the potential negative outcomes of a process, product, or activity, and a consequent identification of the measures that should be adopted to avoid or, at least, mitigate the identified risks.*

This procedure can be divided into three different stages: analysis of the process (Article 35(7)(a) GDPR), risk-assessment (Article 35(7)(b) and (c) GDPR), and definition of the measures envisaged to address the risks (Article 35(7)(d) GDPR). It is worth pointing out that the stage concerning the risk-assessment includes two different kinds of evaluation: assessment of the "necessity and proportionality" of data processing, and assessment of the "risks to the rights and freedoms of data subjects." These two evaluations are correlated and consequent, as disproportional or unnecessary data processing cannot be put in place and, in this case, there is not any further question about the impact on individual rights and freedoms. On the other hand, when the principles of necessity and proportionality are respected, further investigation is needed to assess the specific balance of interests that the use of data implies.

According to the principles and values framed in the European Chart of Fundamental Rights of the European Union, this balance of interests is not a mere risk/benefit analysis, but a comparison between interests that are different and may have a different hierarchical order.† In this sense, the data protection impact assessment is not in line with the risk-based theories [70] that suggest the adoption of a risk/benefit approach instead of a risk-mitigation approach.‡

---

*According to the traditional paradigm of risk-assessment, data controllers should be able to demonstrate compliance with the Regulation on the basis of the assessment results (Article 35(7)(d) GDPR) and should periodically review these results, due to the possibility of a change in the nature and severity of the risks over the time (Article 35(11) GDPR).

†See European Court of Justice, May 13, 2014, Case 131/12, *Google Spain SL, Google Inc. v Agencia Española de Protección de Datos (AEPD), Mario Costeja González.* http://curia.europa.eu/juris/document/document.jsf?text=&docid=152065&pageIndex=0&doclang=EN&mode=lst&dir=&occ=first&part=1&cid=980962 (accessed June 16, 2016).

‡According to the risk/benefit approach, the assessment should be based on the comparison between the amount of benefits and the sum of all risks, without any distinction regarding the nature of risks and benefits. In this sense, for instance, economic benefits may prevail over individual rights. On the other hand, the risk mitigation approach assumes that some interests (e.g., fundamental rights) are prevailing and cannot be compared with other interests that have a lower relevance. As a consequence, the risk mitigation approach focuses on the potential prejudice for fundamental rights and suggests adequate measures to reduce this risk or, where feasible, to exclude it.

When data protection impact assessment "indicates that the processing would result in a high risk in the absence of measures taken by the controller to mitigate the risk," data controllers must consult the supervisory authority prior to the start of processing activities (Article 36(1) GDPR). According to Recital n. 84 of the GDPR, the absence of measures to mitigate the risk is evaluated taking into account the "available technology and costs of implementation."

It is worth pointing out that the reference to the costs and the available technology, also present in the provisions concerning security risk (Recital n. 83 and Article 32(1) GDPR) and data protection by design (Article 25(1) GDPR), represents an important opportunity to put the principle of proportionality into practice in the context of risk mitigation. Therefore, these provisions reduce the risk of an excessive burden for data controllers due to the implementation of the risk-assessment model.

When a data protection impact assessment indicates that processing would result in a high risk in the absence of measures taken by the controller to mitigate the risk, data controllers should consult the supervisory authority prior to the start of processing activities (Recital n. 94 GDPR).*

According to Article 36(2) GDPR, when the supervisory authority is of the opinion that the intended processing would infringe the regulation, the authority "shall [. . .] provide written advice to the controller and, where applicable to the processor, may use any of its powers referred to in Article 58." Given the powers given to supervisory authorities by Article 58, this means that there are two options as follows: (1) The assessment is not satisfactory, and the data controller has not adequately identified or mitigated the risk; (2) the assessment has been conducted in a correct manner, but there are no measures available to mitigate the risk. In the first case, the supervisory authority orders the controller or processor "to bring processing operations into compliance with the provisions of this Regulation, where appropriate, in a specified manner" (Article 58(2)(d) GDPR), whereas, in the second case, the authority imposes "a temporary or definitive limitation including a ban on processing" (Article 58(2)(f) GDPR).

Finally, minor aspects concerning the risk-based approach regard the role played by the data protection officer, whose main tasks are to provide advice to the controller or the processor of their obligations (included the data protection impact assessment), and to monitor compliance with legal provisions concerning data protection and with the privacy policies of the controller or processor (Article 39(1) GDPR). In the performance of these tasks, the data protection officer must "have due regard to the risk associated with processing operations, taking into account the nature, scope, context, and purposes of

*The model of prior consultation is built on the concept of prior checking, which was already present in Article 20 of the Directive 95/46/EC.

processing" (Article 39(2) GDPR). Therefore, the risk-assessment represents one of the main criteria that should drive the action of the data protection officer.

The new provisions about risk-assessment represent an important evolution in the direction of a risk-based approach in data protection and, in this sense, may offer an adequate solution to the potential negative outcomes of the use of Big Data analytics. The main limit of these provisions lies in the link to the purposes of data processing.*

Although the assessment should necessarily be related to the use of data for a specific purpose, there is a problem due to the fact that, according to Article 5(1)(b) GDPR, data processing purposes should be "specific, explicit, and legitimate" and defined at the moment of data collection, which contrast with the transformative use of data made by private and public bodies by means of Big Data analytics.

For these reasons, a better design of the impact assessment should not focus on the initial purpose of data collection, but on each specific data use that is put in place by the data controller after data collection. In this regard, it should be noted that, at the moment, this result is achieved by data controllers circumventing the provisions on purpose limitation. They collect personal data on the basis of broad series of different purposes and then, if they have already adopted procedures of impact assessment, evaluate case-by-case the potential impact on data protection, with regard to each different use of information for a given purpose.

Against this background, a different perspective can be adopted, which expressly accepts the idea that data are collected for multiple purposes, defined only broadly at the beginning of data processing. This model focuses on the different specific uses of collected information and the prior assessment of the potential risks of each use.

This kind of approach, if adopted by the legislator, will be more efficient and consistent with the transformative use of data made by companies in the Big Data context, as well as with the level of self-determination of the data subjects [66,71]. In this sense, a more extensive use of the legitimate interest as legal grounds [24] may complete this model. Companies may enlist users in data processing without any prior consent, provided they give notice of the results of the assessment, which should be supervised by data protection authorities (licensing model), and provide an opt-out option [66].

It might be noted that the suggested approach undermines the chances for users to negotiate their consent, but the strength of this objection is reduced by the existing limits to self-determination described above. In the majority

*See Article 35(1) GDPR ("Where a type of processing in particular using new technologies, and taking into account the nature, scope, context and purposes of the processing, is likely to result in a high risk to the rights and freedoms of natural persons") and 35(7)(b) ("[The assessment shall contain at least] an assessment of the necessity and proportionality of the processing operations in relation to the purposes").

of the cases, the negotiation is reduced to the alternative *take it or leave it.* A prior assessment conducted under the supervision of independent authorities, the use of legitimate interest as legal ground, and the adoption of an opt-out model seem to offer more guarantees to users than an apparent, but inconsistent, self-determination based on *notice and consent* and on the opt-in model.

On the other hand, remaining focused on the existing legal framework defined by the Regulation 2016/679, a different option [71] may be to limit Big Data uses to statistical purposes, which benefit from an explicitly permitted reuse of data (Articles 5 (1) and 89, GDPR). Nevertheless, in this case, using analytics for decision-making purposes directly affecting a particular individual would be outside the field of statistical purposes and also violate the restrictions on automated individual decision making, including profiling. In this sense, the GDPR "can be seen as a stepping stone, pointing toward the need to evolve data protection beyond the old paradigm, yet not fully committed to doing so" [71].

The model of data management defined by the new Regulation does not completely address the new challenges of use of Big Data analytics in data processing [24,71]: the new provisions do not provide an effective transparency of data processing (obscure notices, impact assessment not publicly available), but only a higher level of accountability.

Moreover, the risk-mitigation approach adopted by the Regulation seems still to be far from the idea of a multiple and participative risk-assessment. Although Recital n. 75 recognizes the risk of discrimination and "any other significant economic or social disadvantage," the provisions of the Regulation do not offer an adequate framework for the assessment of this kind of negative outcome.

With regard to the use of Big Data analytics in decision-making processes, important questions arise about the ethical and social values that should be taken into account, as well as the role that the different social stakeholders can play in assessing the impact of data uses.* In conclusion, the European Union seems to be insecure in moving its steps away from the traditional model of data protection, whereas other international bodies are trying to offer a more courageous answer to the challenges of the data age.

In this sense, the new guidelines on Big Data of the Council of Europe seem to be aware of the limits of the traditional principles governing data protection and open to a broader risk-assessment, which takes into account the social and ethical impacts of data uses and recognizes the benefits of a participatory model based on the multistakeholder approach.†

---

*See section "The guidelines adopted by the Council of Europe on the protection of individuals with regard to the processing of personal data in a world of Big Data."

†See section "Multiple-risk assessment and collective interests."

Use of data for decision-making purposes: From individual to collective dimension of data processing

The new scale of data processing of Big Data applications and the use of analytics in decision-making processes pose new questions about data protection. As Big Data make it possible to collect and analyze large amounts of information, data processing is no longer focused on individual users, and this sheds light on the collective dimension of the use of data.

In the Big Data environment, general strategies are adopted on a large scale and on the basis of representations of society generated by algorithms, which predict future collective behavior [3,25,55,64]. These strategies are then applied to specific individuals, given the fact that they are part of one or more groups generated by analytics [3,56,72].

The use of analytics and the adoption of decisions based on group behavior rather than on individuals are not limited to commercial and market contexts. They also affect other important fields, such as security and social policies, where a different balance of interest should be adopted, given the importance of public interest issues.* One example of this is provided by predictive policing solutions such as *PredPol* [73–77].

This *categorical* approach characterizing the use of analytics leads policymakers to adopt common solutions for individuals belonging to the same cluster generated by analytics. These decisional processes do not consider individuals *per se*, but as a part of a group of people characterized by some common qualitative factors.

In this sense, the use of personal information and Big Data analytics to support decisions exceeds the boundaries of the individual dimension and assumes a collective dimension [78], with potential harmful consequences for some groups [79,80]. In this sense, prejudice can result not only from the well-known privacy-related risks (e.g., illegitimate use of personal information, data security) but also from discriminatory and invasive forms of data processing [15,81,82].

The dichotomy between individuals and groups is not new, and it has already been analyzed with regard to the legal aspects of personal information. Nonetheless, the right to privacy and the right to the protection of personal data have been largely safeguarded as individual rights, despite the social dimension of their rationale.

The focus on the model of individual rights is probably the main reason for the few contributions by privacy scholars on the collective dimension of privacy and data protection. Hitherto, only few authors have investigated the notion of group privacy. They have represented this form of privacy as the privacy of the facts and ideas expressed by the members of a group in the group environment or in terms of protection of information about a group [37,83,84].

*See also section "Data prediction: social control and social surveillance."

On the other hand, collective data protection does not necessarily concern facts or information referring to a specific person, as with individual privacy and data protection. Nor does it concern clusters of individuals that can be considered as groups in the sociological sense of the term. In addition, collective rights are not necessarily a large-scale representation of individual rights and related issues [85]. Finally, collective data protection concerns non-aggregative collective interests [86], which are not the mere sum of many individual interests.*

The importance of this collective dimension [78] depends on the fact that the approach to classification by modern algorithms does not merely focus on individuals, but on groups or clusters of people with common characteristics (e.g., customer habits, lifestyle, online and offline behavior). Data gatherers are mainly interested in studying groups' behavior and predicting this behavior, rather than in profiling single users. Data-driven decisions concern clusters of individuals and only indirectly affect the members of these clusters. One example of this is price discrimination based on age, habits, or wealth.

The most important concern in this context is the protection of groups from potential harm due to invasive and discriminatory data processing. In this sense, the collective dimension of data processing is mainly focused on the use of information [66,70], rather than on secrecy [83,84] and data quality.

Regarding the risk of discrimination, this section does not focus on the unfair practices characterized by intentional discriminatory purposes, which are generally forbidden and sanctioned by law [87,88],† but on the involuntary forms of discrimination in cases in which Big Data analytics provide biased representations of society [89,90].

For example, in 2013, a study examined the advertising provided by Google AdSense and found statistically significant racial discrimination in advertisement delivery [91,92]. Similarly, Kate Crawford has pointed out certain *algorithmic illusions* [93,94] and described the case of the City of Boston and its StreetBump smartphone app to passively detect potholes [95].‡

Another example is the Progressive case, in which an insurance company obliged drivers to install a small monitoring device in their cars to receive the

---

*Contra Vedder [81], who claims that the notion of collective privacy "reminds of collective rights," but subjects of collective rights are groups or communities. Conversely, the groups generated by group profiling are not communities of individuals sharing similar characteristics and structured or organized in some way. For this reason, Vedder uses the different definition of "categorial privacy."

†See Article 14 of the Convention for the Protection of Human Rights and Fundamental Freedoms; Article 21 of the Charter of Fundamental Rights of the European Union; Article 19 of the Treaty on the Functioning of the European Union; Directive 2000/43/EC; Directive 2000/78/EC.

‡In this case, the application had a signal problem, due to the bias generated by the low penetration of smartphones among lower income and older residents. While the Boston administration took this bias into account and solved the problem, less-enlightened public officials might underestimate such considerations and make potentially discriminatory decisions.

company's best rates. The system is considered as a negative factor driving late at night but did not take into account the potential bias against low-income individuals, who are more likely to work night shifts, compared with late-night party-goers, "forcing them [low-income individuals] to carry more of the cost of intoxicated and other irresponsible driving that happens disproportionately at night" [76].

These cases represent situations in which a biased representation of groups and society results from flawed data processing* or a lack of accuracy in the representation. This produces potentially discriminatory effects as a consequence of the decisions taken on the basis of analytics.

On the other hand, the decision to put in place different treatment of different situations may represent an intentional and legitimate goal for policy makers, in line with the rule of law. This is the case of law and enforcement bodies and intelligence agencies, which adopt solutions to discriminate between different individuals and identify targeted persons. Here, there is a deliberate intention to treat given individuals differently, but this is not unfair or illegal providing it is within existing legal provisions. Nonetheless, as in the previous case, potential flaws or a lack of accuracy may cause harm to citizens.†

Discrimination, in terms of the different treatment of different situations, also appears in commercial contexts to offer tailored services to consumers. In this case, in which the interests are of a purely private nature, commercial practices may lead to price discrimination [99,100] or the adoption of different terms and conditions depending on the assignment of consumers to a specific cluster [56,99,101,102].

Thus, consumers classified as "financially challenged" belong to a cluster "[i]n the prime working years of their lives [...] including many single parents, struggl[ing] with some of the lowest incomes and little accumulation of wealth." This implies the following predictive viewpoint, based on Big Data analytics and regarding all consumers in the cluster: "[n]ot particularly loyal to any one financial institution, [and] they feel uncomfortable borrowing money and believe they are better off having what they want today as they never know what tomorrow will bring" [56]. It is not hard to imagine the potential discriminatory consequences of these classifications with regard to individuals and groups.

These forms of discrimination are not necessarily against the law, especially when they are not based on individual profiles and only indirectly affect

*This is the case of the errors that affect the E-Verify system, which is used in the United States to verify if a new worker is legally eligible to work in the United States [76,96].

†For instance, criticisms have been raised with regard to the aforementioned predictive software adopted in recent years by various police departments in the U.S. Criticisms also concern the use of risk assessment procedures based on analytics coupled with a categorical approach (based on typology of crimes and offenders) in U.S. criminal sentencing [97,98].

individuals as part of a category, without their direct identification.* For this reason, existing legal provisions against individual discrimination might not be effective in preventing the negative outcomes of these practices, if adopted on a collective basis. Still, such cases clearly show the importance of the collective dimension of the use of information about groups of individuals.

From a data protection perspective and in the European Union, such data analysis focusing on clustered individuals may not represent a form of personal data processing, as the use of categorical analytics methodologies does not necessarily make it possible to identify a person, and group profiles can be made using anonymized data.† This reduces the chances of individuals taking action against biased representations of themselves within a group or having access to the data-processing mechanisms, as the anonymized information used for group profiling cannot be linked to them [88,104–106]. However, it has been observed that "once a profile is linked to an identifiable person—for instance in the case of credit scoring—it may turn into a personal data, thus reviving the applicability of data protection legislation" [72].

It should be noted that, as group profiling based on analytics is used to take decisions affecting a multiplicity of individuals, the main target of data processing is not the data subject, but the clusters of people created by Big Data gatherers. In this light, the interests that assume relevance are primarily supraindividual and collective [86].

In general terms, collective interests may be shared by an entire group without conflicts between the views of its members (aggregative interests) or with conflicts between the opinions of its members (non-aggregative interests) [86,107]. If the group is characterized by non-aggregative interests, the collective nature of the interest is represented by the fundamental values of a given society (e.g., environmental protection).

With regard to data protection, the notion of collective non-aggregative interests seems to be the best way to describe the collective dimension of the use of personal information. In this sense, although individuals may have different opinions about the balance between the conflicting interests,‡ there are some collective priorities concerning privacy and data protection that are of relevance to the general interest. Here, the rationale for collective data protection is mainly focused on the potential harm to groups caused by extensive and invasive data processing.

---

*Regarding the decisions that affect an individual as member of a specific cluster of people, it should be noted that in many cases, these decisions are not based solely on automated processing [82]. In this sense, credit scoring systems have reduced but not removed human intervention on credit evaluation. At the same time, classifications often regard identified or identifiable individuals [103].

†On the limits of anonymization in the big data context, see section "Introduction. The legal challenges of the use of data."

‡In this sense, an extensive group profiling for commercial purposes can be passively accepted, considered with favor or perceived as invasive and potentially discriminatory. The same divergence of opinions and interests exists with regard to government social surveillance for crime prevention and national security, in which part of the population is in favor of surveillance, due to concerns about crime and terrorism.

Data-centered approach and socio-ethical impacts

Privacy and data protection are context-dependent notions, which vary from culture to culture and across historical periods [37,104,108,109]. In the same way, the related collective dimensions are necessarily influenced by historical and geographical variables and are the result of actions by policymakers. For these reasons, it is impossible to define a common and fixed balance between collective data protection and conflicting interests.

There are jurisdictions that give greater priority to national and security interests, which in many cases prevail over individual and collective data protection; meanwhile, in some countries, extensive forms of social surveillance are considered disproportionate and invasive. Therefore, any balancing test must focus on a specific social context in a given historical moment [110]. As has been pointed out in the literature [111], defining prescriptive ethical guidelines concerning the values that should govern the use of Big Data analytics and the related balance of interests is problematic.

Given such variability, from a theoretical perspective, a common framework for a balancing test can be found in the values recognized by international charters of fundamental rights. These charters provide a baseline from which it is to identify the values that can serve to provide ethical guidance and define the existing relationships between these values [111].

In addition, the context-dependent framework of values and the relationship between conflicting interests and rights needs to be specified with regard to the actual use of Big Data analytics. In Europe, for instance, commercial interests related to credit score systems can generally be considered compatible with the processing of personal information, providing that data are adequate, relevant, and not excessive in relation to the purposes for which it is collected.* Even so, specific Big Data analytics solutions adopted by some companies for credit scoring purposes may lead to a disproportionate scrutiny of consumers' private life. The same reasoning can also be applied to smart mobility solutions, which can potentially lead to extensive social surveillance. This means that a prior case-by-case risk-assessment is necessary to mitigate the potential impact of these solutions on data protection and individual freedoms.

This "in-context" balance of conflicting interests is based on an impact assessment that, in the presence of complex data collection and processing systems, should not be conducted by consumers or companies but must entail an active involvement of various stakeholders. Against this background, an important aspect of the protection of collective interests relating to personal information is the analysis of the existing conflicting interests and the representation of the issues regarding the individuals grouped in clusters by data gatherers.

---

*See Articles 18 and 20 of the Directive 2014/17/EU. See also Article 8 of the Directive 2008/48/EC on credit agreements for consumers and repealing Council Directive 87/102/EEC.

Here, it is useful to briefly consider the fields in which the group dimension of data protection is already known in more traditional contexts that are not characterized by extensive data collection and use of analytics. For instance, labor law recognizes this collective dimension of rights and the dualism between individuals and groups.* Under certain circumstances, trade unions and employees' representatives may concur in taking decisions that affect the employees and have an impact on data protection in the workplace.

Collective agreements on these decisions are based on the recognition that the power imbalance in the workplace means that, in some cases, the employee is unaware of the implications of employer's policies (e.g., employers' workplace surveillance practices). Moreover, in many cases, this imbalance makes it difficult for employees to object to the illegitimate processing of their data.

Entities representing collective interests (e.g., trade unions) are less vulnerable to power imbalance and have a broader vision of the impact of the employer's policies and decisions. It should also be noted that the employer's unfair policies and forms of control are often oriented toward discriminatory measures that affect individual workers, even though they are targeted at the whole group.

This collective representation of common interests is also adopted in other fields, such as consumer protection and environmental protection. These contexts are all characterized by a power imbalance affecting one of the parties directly involved (employees, consumers, or citizens). Furthermore, in many cases, the conflicting interests refer to contexts in which the use of new technologies makes it hard for users to be aware of the potential negative implications.

The same situation of imbalance often exists in the Big Data context, where data subjects are not in a position to object to discriminatory uses of personal information by data gatherers. Data subjects often do not know the basic steps of data processing, and the complexity of the process means that they are unable to negotiate their information and are not aware of the potential collective prejudices that underlay its use.† This is why it is important to recognize the role of entities representing collective interests, as it happens in the earlier cases.

Employees are part of a specific group, defined by their relationship with a single employer; therefore, they are aware of their common identity and have mutual relationships. By contrast, in the Big Data context, the common attributes of the group often only become evident in the hands of the data gatherer.

Data subjects are not aware of the identity of the other members of the group, have no relationship with them, and have a limited perception of their collective issues [112,113]. Furthermore, these groups shaped by analytics have a variable geometry, and individuals can shift from one group to another.

---

*See for example, Italian Statute of the Workers' Rights, Articles 4 and 8, Act 300, May 20, 1970.

†See section "Introduction. The legal challenges of the use of data."

This does not undermine the idea of representing collective data protection interests. On the contrary, this atomistic dimension makes the need for collective representation more urgent. However, it is hard to imagine representatives appointed by the members of these groups, as is instead the case in the workplace.

In this sense, there are similarities with consumer law, where there are collective interests (e.g., product security, fair commercial practices), but the potential victims of harm have no relationship to one another. Thus, individual legal remedies must be combined with collective remedies.* Examples of possible complementary solutions are provided by consumer law, where independent authorities responsible for consumer protection, class action lawsuits, and consumer associations play an important role.

In the field of Big Data analytics, the partially hidden nature of the processes and their complexity probably make timely class actions more difficult than in other fields. For instance, in the case of a product liability, the damages are often more evident making it easier for the injured people to react. On the other hand, associations that protect collective interests can play an active role in facilitating reaction to unfair practices and, moreover, they can be involved in a multistakeholder risk-assessment of the specific use of Big Data analytics.

The involvement of such bodies requires specific procedural criteria to define the entities that may act in the collective interest.† This is more difficult in the context of Big Data, in which the groups created by data gatherers do not have a stable character. In this case, an assessment of the social and ethical impact of analytics often provides the opportunity to discover how data processing affects collective interests and thus identify the potential stakeholders.

Multiple-risk assessment and collective interests

How collective interests should be protected against discrimination and social surveillance in the use of Big Data analytics is largely a matter for the policymakers. Different legal systems and different balances between the components of society suggest differing solutions. Identifying the independent authority charged with protecting collective interests may therefore be difficult.

Many countries have independent bodies responsible for supervising specific social surveillance activities, and other bodies focused on antidiscrimination actions [114]. In other countries, this responsibility is spread across various authorities, which take different approaches, use different remedies, and do not necessarily cooperate in solving cases with multiple impacts.

Meanwhile, a central element in the risk-assessment of Big Data analytics is the analysis of data processing, which is the factor common to all these

---

*The same approach has been adopted in the realm of antidiscrimination laws [114,115].

†See also Article 80 GDPR.

situations, regardless of the potential harm to collective interests. For this reason, data protection authorities can play a key role in the risk-assessment processes, even if they are not focused on the specific social implications (e.g., discrimination).

On the other hand, if we take a different approach that takes into consideration the various negative effects generated by the use of Big Data (discrimination, unfair consumer practices, social control, etc.), we should involve multiple entities and authorities. Nevertheless, the end result may be a fragmented and potentially conflicting decision-making process that may underestimate the use of data, which is the common core of all these situations [95].

Furthermore, data protection authorities are accustomed to addressing collective issues and have already demonstrated that they do consider both the individual and the wider collective dimension of data processing. Focusing on data protection and fundamental rights, they are also well placed to balance the conflicting interests around the use of data.

The adequacy of the solution is also empirically demonstrated by important cases decided by data protection authorities concerning data-processing projects with significant social and ethical impacts. These cases show that decisions to assess the impact of innovative products, services, and business solutions on data protection and society are not normally on the initiative of the data subjects, but primarily on that of data protection authorities, who are aware of the potential risks of such innovations. Based on their balancing tests, these authorities are in a position to suggest measures that companies should adopt to reduce the risks discussed here and to place these aspects within the more general framework of the rights of the individual, as a single person and as a member of a democratic society.

The risk assessment represents the opportunity for group issues to be identified and addressed. Thus, bodies representing collective interests should not only partially exercise traditional individual rights on behalf of data subjects but also exercise other autonomous rights relating to the collective dimension of data protection. These new rights mainly concern participation in the risk-assessment process, which should take a multistakeholder approach.*

Against this background, data protection authorities may involve in the assessment process the various stakeholders that represent the collective interests affected by specific data-processing projects [111,116].† This would lead to the definition of a new model in which companies that intend to use Big Data analytics would undergo an assessment prior to collecting and processing data.

---

*The extent of the rights conferred upon the different stakeholders in the protection of collective privacy is largely a matter for policymakers to decide and would depend on the nature and values of the different sociolegal contexts.

†A different assessment exclusively based on the adoption of security standards or corporate self-regulation would not have the same extent and independency. This does not mean that, in this framework, forms of standardization or coregulation cannot be adopted.

The assessment would not only focus on data security and data protection but also consider the social and ethical impacts relating to the collective dimension of data use in a given project.* This assessment should be conducted by third parties and supervised by the data protection authorities.† Once this multiple-impact assessment is approved by data protection authorities, the ensuing data processing would be considered secure in protecting personal information and collective interests.

Although data protection authorities are already engaged to some degree in addressing the collective dimension, the suggested solution would lead to a broader and deeper assessment, which would become mandatory. This proposal is therefore in line with the view that a licensing scheme might "prove to be the most effective means of ensuring that data protection principles do not remain 'law-in-book' with respect to profiling practices" [44,104].

The guidelines adopted by the Council of Europe on the protection of individuals with regard to the processing of personal data in a world of Big Data

Although the guidelines provided by the Council of Europe on the basis of the Convention 108 on data protection have not the same impact of the regulation (EU) 2016/679, in terms of efficacy and direct application, they represent an interesting set of rules that, for some aspects, shows a new manner to address the issues concerning the use of Big Data analytics.

Before briefly examining the previsions of the "Guidelines on the protection of Individuals with Regard to the Processing of Personal data in a World of Big Data" (hereafter Guidelines) adopted by the Council of Europe,‡ the nature and the peculiarity of these guidelines should be highlighted.

Within the framework of the Convention 108, the guidelines are practical and operative instructions provided by the Council of Europe to member states. They are primarily addressed to data controllers and data processors, to facilitate the effective application of the principles of the Convention in

---

*In the Big Data context, another important aspect is the transparency of the algorithms used by companies [55,64,82,88,90]. See Articles 13 (2)(f), 14 (2)(f), and 15 (1)(h) GDPR, which recognize data subject's right to receive "meaningful information about the logic involved."

†The entire system will work only if the political and financial autonomy of data protection authorities from governments and corporations is guaranteed. Moreover, data protection authorities would need new competence and resources in order to bear the burden of the supervision and approval of these multiple-impact assessments. For these reasons, a model based on mandatory fees—paid by companies when they submit their requests for authorization to data protection authorities—would be preferable [66]. It should also be noted that, in cases of large-scale and multinational data collection, forms of mutual assistance and cooperation may facilitate the role played by data protection authorities in addressing the problems related to the dimensions of data collection and data gatherers.

‡The guidelines are available https://rm.coe.int/CoERMPublicCommonSearchServices/DisplayDCTMContent?documentId=09000016806ebe7a.

specific sectors.* Nevertheless, unlike the guidelines previously adopted by the Council of Europe, which concerned specific contexts or issues, these guidelines focus on the use of a given technology (Big Data) and are not sector specific.†

The awareness of the critical issues posed by the new forms of data processing based on analytics characterizes the entire text of the Guidelines. Therefore, the principles of the Convention 108 are interpreted to provide adequate solutions, taking into account "the given social and technological context" and "a lack of knowledge on the part of individuals" with regard to Big Data applications.‡

In this light, the effective safeguard of the individual's "right to control his or her personal data and the processing of such data"§ is placed in the context of Big Data uses, in which processes of collection and analysis of data are characterized by complexity and obscurity [64].

For this reason, the Guidelines do not consider the notion of control as merely circumscribed to individual control (such as in the *notice and consent* model) but adopt a broader idea of control over the use of data, according to which "individual control evolves in a more complex process of multiple-impact assessment of the risks related to the use of data."¶

This leads to go beyond the individual dimension of data protection and investigate aspects that concern the relations among individuals and the society at large. In this light, potential prejudices are not only restricted to the well-known privacy-related risks (e.g., illegitimate use of personal information, data security) but also include other prejudices that may concern the conflict with ethical and social values [15,82], in line with the Privacy, Ethical, and Social Impact Assessment model (PESIA) mentioned above.**

Nevertheless, the assessment concerning the impact of the use of data on ethical and social values is more complicated than the traditional data protection assessment. Moreover, although individual rights concerning data

*See Section II (Scope) of the Guidelines.

†These guidelines do not provide an authoritative definition of Big Data, as there are many definitions of Big Data, which differ depending on the specific discipline. The Guidelines cover both Big Data and Big Data analytics.

‡See Section I (Introduction) of the guidelines. See also Section II (Scope) of the guidelines ("Given the nature of Big Data, the application of some of the traditional principles of data processing [e.g., minimization principle, purpose specification, meaningful consent, etc.] may be challenging in this technological scenario. These guidelines therefore suggest a tailored application of the principles of the Convention 108, to make them more effective in practice in the Big Data context").

§See Section I (Introduction) of the guidelines. See also the Preamble of the Draft modernized Convention for the Protection of Individuals with Regard to the Processing of Personal Data ("Considering that it is necessary to secure the human dignity and protection of the human rights and fundamental freedoms of every individual and [...] personal autonomy based on a person's right to control of his or her personal data and the processing of such [personal] data").

¶See the previous footnote.

**See section "Use of data and risk-analysis."

processing are generally recognized by different national regulations and international conventions, as well as data security, and data management best practices are commonly diffused among data controllers, the values that should inspire the use of data are more indefinite and context based, changing from a community to another. This makes more complicated to identify a benchmark for these values that can be used in the ethical and social risk-assessment.

This point is clearly addressed in the section "Introduction. The legal challenges of the use of data" of the fourth part (Principles and guidelines) of the Guidelines. First, the section urges both data controllers and data processors to "adequately take into account the likely impact of the intended Big Data processing and its broader ethical and social implications." Second, it recognizes the relative nature of the social and ethical values and, in this sense, the Guidelines require that data uses should not be in conflict with the "ethical values commonly accepted in the relevant community or communities and should not prejudice societal interests, values and norms."

Although the Guidelines recognize the difficulties in defining the values that should be taken into account in the social and ethical assessment, they do not renounce to define some practical steps to identify these values. Therefore, they suggest, "the common guiding ethical values can be found in international charters of human rights and fundamental freedoms, such as the European Convention for the Protection of Human Rights."

Given the context-dependent nature of social and ethical assessment and the fact that international charters may only provide high-level guidance, the Guidelines combine this general suggestion with a more tailored option that is represented by "ad hoc ethics committee."* These committees, which already exist in practice, should identify the specific ethical values to be safeguarded with respect to a given use of data, providing more detailed and context-based guidance for risk assessment.

The Guidelines put the risk-assessment process in the broader context of the precautionary approach, which should characterize any new application of technology that may produce potential risks for individuals and society.† In this light, the Guidelines require data controllers to adopt preventive policies to adequately address and mitigate the potential risks related to the use of Big Data analytics.‡

*See Guidelines, IV.1.3 ("If the assessment of the likely impact of an intended data processing described in section IV.2 highlights a high impact of the use of Big Data on ethical values, data controllers could establish an ad hoc ethics committee, or rely on existing ones, to identify the specific ethical values to be safeguarded in the use of data").

†See Guidelines, IV.2.1 ("Given the increasing complexity of data processing and the transformative use of Big Data, the Parties should adopt a precautionary approach in regulating data protection in this field").

‡See Guidelines, IV.2.2. This is consistent with the provision of the Modernized Convention, which focuses both on risk analysis and the design of data processing "in such a manner as to prevent or minimise the risk of interference with [...] rights and fundamental freedoms." See Article 8bis (2) of the Draft modernised Convention for the Protection of Individuals with Regard to the Processing of Personal Data.

According to the general theory on the risk-based approach, the assessment process is divided into the following four different stages:* (1) identification of the risks, (2) analysis of the potential impact of the identified risks, (3) identification of the solutions to exclude or mitigate the risks, and (4) continuous or periodical monitoring of the effectiveness of the solutions provided.†

This is the traditional scheme that characterizes risk-assessment. Here, the most innovative aspect concerns the broader range of interests considered in the assessment process, which goes beyond the traditional notion of data protection. In this sense, the right to nondiscrimination and the social and ethical impacts of data processing activities assume specific relevance.

Given the complexity of this assessment and the different aspects that should be taken into account, it cannot be conducted only by experts in data protection law but requires external auditors with specific and multidisciplinary skills. In this light, these guidelines require that the risk-assessment "should be carried out by persons with adequate professional qualifications and knowledge to evaluate the different impacts, including the legal, social, ethical and technical dimensions."‡ Moreover, the collective dimension of the potential impact of the use of data leads to encourage a multistakeholder approach that gives voice to the different groups of persons that may be affected by a given use of data.§

Due to the complexity of this assessment and the continuous evolution of both the potential risks and the measures to tackle them, data protection authorities may play a relevant role in supporting data controllers, providing information about the state-of-the-art of data-processing security methods, and providing detailed guidelines on the risk-assessment process.¶

From the data subject's perspective, a better understanding of the purposes of data processing can come from the analysis of the way in which data uses impact on individuals and society. In this light, the disclosure of the results of the different impacts mentioned above should become part of the duties of transparency of data controllers, to increase individuals' awareness about their choices concerning personal information.**

With regard to the level of disclosure that should characterize the publicity of the impact assessment, the Guidelines, according to the suggestion of legal scholars [66,111], clarify that the public availability of the result of the assessment should be made "without prejudice to secrecy safeguarded by law." Therefore, in the presence of such secrecy, data controllers "shall provide

*See Guidelines, IV.2.5.

†See Guidelines, IV.2.9. Moreover, data controllers shall document the assessment and these solutions (Guidelines, IV.2.10).

‡See Guidelines, IV.2.6.

§See Guidelines, IV.2.7 ("With regard to the use of Big Data which may affect fundamental rights, the Parties should encourage the involvement of the different stakeholders (e.g., individuals or groups potentially affected by the use of Big Data) in this assessment process and in the design of data processing").

¶See Guidelines, IV.2.8.

**See Guidelines, IV.3.2 and 3.3.

any sensitive information in a separate annex to the risk-assessment report." Anyway, although this annex is not public, it may be accessed by supervisory authorities.*

Minor provisions of these guidelines concern the by-design approach† and data subject's consent. With regard to the latter and the *notice and consent* model, the Guidelines highlight that the notice should be comprehensive of the outcome of the assessment process and "might also be provided by means of an interface that simulates the effects of the use of data and its potential impact on the data subject, in a learn-from-experience approach."‡ Moreover, consent cannot be considered freely given when "there is a clear imbalance of power between the data subject and the Data Controllers or Data Processors, which affects the data subject's decisions with regard to the processing."§

Finally, the Guidelines devote a section to the role of the human intervention in Big Data–supported decisions,¶ reaffirming that the use of Big Data "should preserve the autonomy of human intervention in the decision-making process." In this light, when decisions based on Big Data might affect individual rights significantly or produce legal effects, a human decision-maker should, upon request of the data subject, "provide her or him with the reasoning underlying the processing, including the consequences for the data subject of this reasoning." In the same vein, the autonomy of decision makers should be preserved and, on the basis of "reasonable arguments," they should be allowed the freedom not to rely on the result of the recommendations provided using Big Data.

Data prediction: Social control and social surveillance

Big Data prediction promises incredible opportunities to anticipate fraud detection and to prevent crime but, at the same time, its use could also threaten fundamental legal rights such as privacy and due process [68].

Law enforcement agencies [73], secret services [117], doctors, lawyers,** accountants [55], and judge†† are using Big Data predictive analytics solutions

*See Guidelines, IV.3.2.

†See Guidelines, IV.4.

‡See Guidelines, IV.5.1.

§See Guidelines, IV.5.3. In these cases, data controller "should demonstrate that this imbalance does not exist or does not affect the consent given by the data subject."

¶See Guidelines, IV.7.

**See ROSS, the first Artificially Intelligent Lawyer at the following Url: http://www.rossintelligence.com; see IBM Watson, at the following Url: http://www-03.ibm.com/innovation/us/watson.

††A recent experiment demonstrates that artificial intelligence has been used to predict decisions of the European Court of Human Rights (ECtHR) to 79% accuracy. Further information at: http://www.legalfutures.co.uk/latest-news/robot-judge-ai-predicts-outcome-european-court-cases.

as they are well aware of how these tools can be useful and/or profitable especially in a society increasingly preoccupied with the concepts of risk and public protection [118]. However, new technologies enhance preemptive profiling of individuals as the combination of predictive strategies and increased surveillance allow for more targeted profiles.

Kerr and Earle identified three categories of Big Data prediction: consequential, preferential, and preemptive prediction.

Consequential prediction is, in a general terms, an attempt to anticipate the likely consequences of a person's action. Usually, this is the kind of prediction used by a lawyer to show to the client a realistic scenario of her defense strategy.

Preferential prediction is mostly used by private players (iTunes Genius or Amazon Recommendation engine represents two significant examples), and it uses anticipatory algorithms based on social media intelligence to predict what kind of service a user will find interesting.

Preemptive predictions assess the likely consequences of allowing or disallowing a person to act in a certain way. In contrast to consequential or preferential predictions, preemptive predictions do not usually adopt the perspective of the actor. Preemptive predictions are mostly made from the standpoint of the state, a corporation, or anyone who wishes to prevent or forestall certain types of action. Preemptive predictions are not concerned with an individual's actions but with whether an individual or group should be permitted to act in a certain way. Examples of this technique include a no-fly list used to preclude possible terrorist activity on an airplane, or analytics software used to determine how much supervision parolees should have based on predictions of future behavior [118]. This latter form of prediction could considerably threaten the concept of the fundamental rights in any democratic constitution. Ferguson correctly questioned if a computer program that predicts the probability of future crime locations could change Fourth Amendment protections in the targeted area. Furthermore, are data-driven *hunches* more reliable than personal *hunches* traditionally deemed insufficient to justify reasonable suspicion?

Use of data during the investigation: Reasonable doubt versus reasonable suspicion

The new reality, which has been briefly described in the previous section, simultaneously undermines the protection that reasonable suspicion provides against stops and potentially transforms reasonable suspicion into a means of justifying those same stops.

Reasonable suspicion in the United States is a legal standard of proof that is less than probable cause, the legal standard for arrests and warrants, but more than an *unparticularized suspicion*; it must be based on *specific and articulable facts*, "taken together with rational inferences from those facts," and the suspicion must be associated with the specific individual.

In Europe, the article 5 of the Convention on the Human Rights states that "everyone has the right to liberty and security of person. No one shall be deprived of this liberty save in the following cases and in accordance with a procedure prescribed by law [...]." This means that a *reasonable suspicion* presupposes the existence of facts or information that would satisfy an objective observer that the person concerned may have committed an offence.* Therefore, a failure by the authorities to make a genuine inquiry into the basic facts of a case, to verify whether a complaint was well founded, disclosed a violation of Article 5 §1 (c) of the European Convention on Human Rights.†

To better understand the consequence of the principle of reasonable suspicion in the Big Data scenario, it could be helpful a practical example. Suppose police are investigating a series of robberies in a particular neighborhood having in their patrol cars a facial recognition software, connected to the database of the arrest photos, which scans people on the street.

Suddenly, there is a match with a suspected person. The suspect's personal information scrolls across the patrol car's computer screen—prior to robbery arrests and robbery convictions. The officer then searches additional sources of third-party data, including the suspect's GPS location information for the last six hours, or license plate records that tie the suspect to pawn shop trades close in time prior to robberies and—obviously—social media information. The police now have particularized, individualized suspicion about a man who is not doing anything overtly criminal.

Can this aggregation of individualized information be sufficient to justify interfering with a person's constitutional liberty?‡ This question, and more, will be raised by the use of any predictive policing strategy.

Big Data and social surveillance: Public and private interplay in social control

The interaction between public and private in social control could be divided into two categories, both of which are significant with regard to data protection. The first concerns the collection of private company data by government with surveillance and social control purpose, whereas the second is the use of judicial authorities of instruments and technologies provided by private companies for organizational and investigative purposes.

---

*ECHR, Ilgar Mammadov v. Azerbaijan, §88; Erdagöz v. Turkey, §51; Fox, Campbell and Hartley v. the United Kingdom, §32.

†ECHR, Stepuleac v. Moldova, §73; Elçi and Others v. Turkey, §674.

‡All these investigative instrument could be used on the basis of the following principle: law enforcement officers may access many of these records without violating the Fourth Amendment, under the theory that we can claim no reasonable expectation of privacy in information we have knowingly revealed to third parties.

With regard to the first category and especially when the request is made by governmental agencies, the issue of the possible violation of fundamental rights becomes more delicate. The Echelon Interception System [119] and the Total Information Awareness program [120] are concrete examples that are not isolated incidents, but undoubtedly the National Security Agency (NSA) case has clearly shown how could be invasive the surveillance in the era of global data flows and Big Data. To better understand the NSA case, it is quite important to have an overview of the considerable amount of electronic surveillance legislation that, particularly in the wake of 9/11, has been approved in the United States and, to a certain extent, in a number of European countries.

The most important legislation is the Foreign Intelligence Surveillance Act (FISA) of 1978* which lays down the procedures for collecting foreign intelligence information through the electronic surveillance of communications for homeland security purposes. The section 702 of FISA Act amended in 2008 extended its scope beyond interception of communications to include any data in public cloud computing as well. Furthermore, this section clearly indicates that two different regimes of data processing and protection exist for U.S. citizens and residents on the one hand, and non-U.S. citizens and residents on the other. More specifically, the Fourth Amendment is applicable only for U.S. citizens as there is an absence of any cognizable privacy rights for *non-U.S. persons* under FISA.

Thanks to FISA Act and the amendment of 2008, U.S. authorities had the possibility to access and process personal data of EU citizens on a large scale via, among others, the NSA's warrantless wiretapping of cable-bound internet traffic (UPSTREAM) and direct access to the personal data stored in the servers of U.S.-based private companies such as Microsoft, Yahoo, Google, Apple, Facebook, or Skype (PRISM), through cross-database search programs such as X-KEYSCORE. U.S. authorities have also the power to compel disclosure of cryptographic keys, including the secure sockets layer (SSL) keys used to secure data in transit by major search engines, social networks, webmail portals, and Cloud services in general (BULLRUN Program) [121].

Even if the FISA Act is the mostly applied and known legislative tool to conduct intelligence activities, there are other relevant pieces of legislation on electronic surveillance. One needs only to consider the Communications Assistance for Law Enforcement Act of 1994,† which authorizes the law enforcement and intelligence agencies to conduct electronic surveillance by requiring that telecommunications carriers and manufacturers of telecommunications equipment modify and design their equipment, facilities, and services to ensure that they have built-in surveillance.

*Foreign Intelligence Surveillance Act (50 U.S.C. §1801–1885C).

†See Communications Assistance for Law Enforcement Act (18 USC §2522).

Truthfully, the surveillance programs are not only in the United States. In Europe, the Communications Capabilities Development Program has prompted a huge amount of controversy, given its intention to create a ubiquitous mass surveillance scheme for the United Kingdom in relation to phone calls, text messages and e-mails, and extending to logging communications on social media. On June 2013, the so-called program TEMPORA showed that UK intelligence agency Government Communications Headquarters has cooperated with the NSA in surveillance and spying activities [122]. These revelations were followed in September 2013 by reports focusing on the activities of Sweden's National Defense Radio Establishment. Similar projects for the large-scale interception of telecommunications data has been developed by both France's General Directorate for External Security and Germany's Federal Intelligence Service.

Even if it seems that EU and U.S. surveillance programs are similar, there is one important difference: in the European Union, under data protection law, individuals have always control over their own personal data, whereas in the United States, the individuals have a more limited control once the user has subscribed to the terms and condition of a service.*

Other than government agencies' monitoring activities, the second category regarding the use by judicial authorities of private tools for investigative purposes has two interesting examples.

The first is the *PredPol*† software initially used by the Los Angeles police force and now by other police forces in the United States (Palm Beach, Memphis, New York, Chicago, Minneapolis, and Dallas). Police Chief (ret.) William J. Bratton and the Los Angeles police department (LAPD) are credited with envisioning the PredPol, whereas Charlie Beck, chief of LAPD since 1977, wrote in 2009, "what can we learn from Wal-Mart and Amazon about fighting crime in a recession? Predictive policing leverages advanced analytics to enable information-based approaches to law enforcement tactics, strategy, and policy, enhancing public safety and changing outcomes. Advanced analytics tools, techniques, and processes support meaningful exploitation of public-safety data necessary to turn data into knowledge and guide information-based prevention, thwarting, mitigation, and response."

Predictive policing, in essence, cross-checks data, places, and techniques of recent crimes with disparate sources, analyzing them and then using the results to anticipate, prevent, and respond more effectively to future crime. Even if the software house created by PredPol declares that no profiling activities are carried out, it becomes essential to carefully understand the technology used to anonymize the personal data acquired by the law-enforcement database.

*See United States v. Miller (425 U.S. 425 [1976]). In this case the United States Supreme Court held that the "bank records of a customer's accounts are the business records of the banks and that the customer can assert neither ownership nor possession of those records." The same principle could be applied to an Internet Service Provider.

†See PredPol, Predictive Policing Software available at www.predpol.com/.

This type of software is bound to have a major impact in the United States on the conception of the protection of rights under the Fourth Amendment, and more specifically on concepts such as *probable cause* and *reasonable suspicion* that in future may come to depend on an algorithm rather than human choice [73].

The second example is Geofeedia software.* This software maps a given location, such as a certain block within a city or even an entire particular metropolitan area, and searches the entire public Twitter and or Facebook feed to identify any geolocated tweets in the past days within that specific area. This application can provide particularly useful data for the purpose of social control. One can imagine the possibility to have useful elements (e.g., IP address) to identify the subjects present in a given area during a serious car accident or a terrorist attack.

From a strictly legal standpoint, these social control tools may be employed by gathering information from citizens directly due to the following principle of public: "Where someone does an act in public, the observance and recording of that act will ordinarily not give rise to an expectation of privacy" [123].

In the European Union, although this type of data collection frequently takes place, it could be in contrast with European Court of Human Rights (ECHR) case law that, in the *Rotaru vs. Romania* case,† ruled that "public information can fall within the scope of private life where it is systematically collected and stored in files held by the authorities." As O'Floinn [124] observes, "Non-private information can become private information depending on its retention and use. The accumulation of information is likely to result in the obtaining of private information about that person."

In the United States, this subject has been addressed in the case *People v. Harris*;‡ the New York County District Attorney's Office sent a subpoena to Twitter, Inc. seeking to obtain the Twitter records of user suspected of having participated in the *Occupy Wall Street* movement. Twitter refused to provide the law enforcement officers with the information requested and sought to quash the subpoena. The Criminal Court of New York confirmed the application made by the New York County District Attorney's Office, rejecting the arguments put forward by Twitter, stating that tweets are, by definition, public, and that a warrant is not required to compel Twitter to disclose them. The District Attorney's Office argued that the *third party disclosure* doctrine put forward for the first time in the *United States v. Miller* was applicable.§

*See https://geofeedia.com/. The ACLU of California has recently obtained records showing that Twitter, Facebook, and Instagram provided user data access to Geofeedia, a developer of a social media monitoring marketed to law enforcement as a tool to monitor activists and protesters. More information at: https://www.aclunc.org/blog/facebook-instagram-and-twitter-provided-data-access-surveillance-product-marketed-target.

†See Rotaru v. Romania (App. No. 28341/95) (2000) 8 B.H.R.C. at [49].

‡See 2012 NY Slip Op 22175 [36 Misc 3d 868].

§See United States v. Miller (425 U.S. 425 [1976]).

The EU reform on data protection

In addition to the GDPR, the new directive on the protection of individuals with regard to the processing of personal data by competent authorities (DPI) establishes some protection against a possible *violation* of *EU citizens' privacy.*

The goal of this directive is to ensure that "in a global society characterized by rapid technological change where information exchange knows no borders," the fundamental right to data protection is consistently protected.[*]

The founding principles of this directive, which are shared with the previous directives referred to, are twofold

1. First, there is the need for *fair, lawful, and adequate data processing* during criminal investigations or to prevent a crime, on the basis of which every data must be collected for specified, explicit, and legitimate purposes and must be erased or rectified without delay.[†]
2. Then there is the obligation to make a clear distinction between the various *categories of the possible data subjects* in a criminal proceeding (persons with regard to whom there are serious grounds for believing that they have committed or are about to commit a criminal offence, persons convicted, victims of criminal offense, and third parties to the criminal offence).

For each of these categories, there must be a different adequate level of attention on data protection, especially for persons who do not fall within any of the categories referred previously.[‡]

These two principles are of considerable importance, although their application on a practical level will be neither easy nor immediate in certain member states. This is easily demonstrated by the difficulties encountered when either drafting practical rules distinguishing between several categories of potential data subjects within the papers on a court file, or attempting to identify the principle on the basis of which a certain court document is to be erased.

In addition to these two general principles, the provisions of the directive are interesting and confirm consolidated data protection principles. Suffice to mention here, the prohibition on using measures is solely based on automated processing of personal data that significantly affect or produce an *adverse legal effect* for the data subject,[§] as well as the implementation of

---

[*] See DPI, explanatory Memorandum, (SEC(2012) 72 final).

[†] Art. 4, DPI and Art. 4b, Directive 2016/280 of the European Parliament and of the Council on the protection of individuals with regard to the processing of personal data by competent authorities for the purposes of prevention, investigation, detection or prosecution of criminal offences or the execution of criminal penalties, and the free movement of such data, available at: http://eur-lex.europa.eu/legal-content/EN/TXT/HTML/?uri=CELEX:32016L0680&from=EN.

[‡] Art. 5, DPI.

[§] Art. 9a, DPI.

data protection by design and by default mechanisms to ensure the protection of the data subject's rights and the processing of only those personal data.*

Furthermore, the directive entails the obligation to designate a data protection officer in all law-enforcement agencies to monitor the implementation and application of the policies on the protection of personal data.†

These principles constitute a significant limitation to possible data mining of personal and sensitive data collection by law enforcement agencies. If it is true that most of these provisions were also present in the Recommendation No. R (87) of Council of Europe and in the Framework Decision 2008/977/JHA, it is also true that propelling data protection *by design* and *by default* mechanisms and measures could encourage data anonymization and help one to avoid the indiscriminate use of automated processing of personal data.

References

[1] ITU. 2015. Recommendation Y.3600: Big data—Cloud computing based requirements and capabilities. http://www.itu.int/itu-t/recommendations/rec.aspx?rec=12584 (accessed July 23, 2016).

[2] ENISA. 2015. Privacy by design in big data: An overview of privacy enhancing technologies in the era of big data analytics. https://www.enisa.europa.eu/publications/big-data-protection/at_download/fullReport (accessed June 15, 2016).

[3] Bollier, D. 2010. The promise and perils of big data. Aspen Institute, Communications and Society Program. http://www.aspeninstitute.org/sites/default/files/content/docs/pubs/The_Promise_and_Peril_of_Big_Data.pdf (accessed February 27, 2014).

[4] Paparrizos, J., White, R.W., and Horvitz, E. 2016. Screening for pancreatic adenocarcinoma using signals from web search logs: Feasibility study and results. *Journal of Oncology Practice* 12(8): 737–744.

[5] Golle, P. 2006. Revisiting the uniqueness of simple demographics in the US population. In Juels, A. (Ed.), *Proceedings of the 5th ACM Workshop on Privacy in Electronic Society*. New York: ACM.

---

*Art. 19, DPI.

†Art. 30, DPI.

[6] Narayanan, A., and Felten, E.W. 2014. No silver bullet: De-identification still doesn't work. http://randomwalker.info/publications/no-silver-bullet-de-identification.pdf (accessed March 25, 2015).

[7] Narayanan, A., Huey, J., and Felten, E.W. 2015. A precautionary approach to big data privacy. http://randomwalker.info/publications/precautionary.pdf (accessed April 4, 2015).

[8] Ohm, P. 2010. Broken promises of privacy: Responding to the surprising failure of anonymization. *UCLA Law Review* 75(6): 1701–1777.

[9] Sweeney, L. 2000. Foundations of privacy protection from a computer science perspective. *Proceedings of the Joint Statistical Meeting, AAAS*, Indianapolis, IN. http://dataprivacylab.org/projects/disclosurecontrol/paper1.pdf (accessed January 24, 2015).

[10] Sweeney, L. 2000. Simple demographics often identify people uniquely. Pittsburgh, PA: Carnegie Mellon University, Data Privacy Working Paper 3. http://dataprivacylab.org/projects/identifiability/paper1.pdf (accessed January 24, 2015).

[11] Sweeney, L. 2015. Only you, your doctor, and many others may know. *Technology Science*, September 29. http://techscience.org/a/2015092903 (accessed November 28, 2015).

[12] United States General Accounting Office. 2011. Record linkage and privacy. Issues in creating New Federal Research and Statistical Information. http://www.gao.gov/assets/210/201699.pdf (accessed December 14, 2013).

[13] Mantelero, A. 2015. Data protection, e-ticketing and intelligent systems for public transport. *International Data Privacy Law* 5(4): 309–320.

[14] The White House. 2012. A consumer data privacy in a networked world: A framework for protecting privacy and promoting innovation in the global digital economy. http://www.whitehouse.gov/sites/default/files/privacy-final.pdf (accessed June 25, 2014).

[15] The White House, Executive Office of the President. 2014. Big data: Seizing opportunities, preserving values. http://www.whitehouse.gov/sites/default/files/docs/big_data_privacy_report_may_1_2014.pdf (accessed December 26, 2014).

[16] Mayer-Schönberger, V. 1997. Generational development of data protection in Europe? In Agre, P.E., and Rotenberg, M. (Eds.), *Technology and Privacy: The New Landscape*. Cambridge, MA: MIT Press.

[17] Article 29 Data Protection Working Party. 2011. Opinion 15/2011 on the definition of consent. http://ec.europa.eu/justice/policies/privacy/docs/wpdocs/2011/wp187_en.pdf (accessed February 27, 2014).

[18] Article 29 Data Protection Working Party. 2014. Opinion 06/2014 on the notion of legitimate interests of the data controller under Article 7 of Directive 95/46/EC. http://ec.europa.eu/justice/data-protection/article-29/documentation/opinion-recommendation/files/2014/wp217_en.pdf (accessed February 27, 2014).

[19] Brownsword, R. 2009. Consent in data protection law: Privacy, fair processing and confidentiality. In Gutwirth, S., Poullet, Y., De Hert, P., de Terwangne, C., and Nouwt, S. (Eds.), *Reinventing data protection?* Dordrecht, the Netherlands: Springer.

[20] European Commission, Directorate-General Justice, Freedom and Security. 2010. Comparative study on different approaches to new privacy challenges, in particular in the light of technological developments: Working Paper No. 2: Data protection laws in the EU. The difficulties in meeting challenges posed by global social and technical developments. http://ec.europa.eu/justice/policies/privacy/docs/studies/new_privacy_challenges/final_report_working_paper_2_en.pdf (accessed July 5, 2014).

[21] Van Alsenoy, B., Kosta, E., and Dumortier, J. 2014. Privacy notices versus informational self-determination: Minding the gap. *International Review of Law, Computers, & Technology* 28(2): 185–203.

[22] Cranor, L.F. 2012. Necessary but not sufficient: Standardized mechanisms for privacy and choice. *Journal on Telecommunications and High Technology Law* 10: 273–307.

[23] Richards, N.M., and King, J.H. 2014. Big data ethics. *Wake Forest Law Review* 49: 339–432.

[24] Moerel, L. 2014. *Big Data Protection: How to Make the Draft EU Regulation on Data Protection Future Proof.* Tilburg, the Netherlands: Tilburg University. http://www.debrauw.com/wp-content/uploads/NEWS%20-%20PUBLICATIONS/Moerel_oratie.pdf (accessed October 15, 2016).

[25] Rubinstein, I.S. 2013. Big data: The end of privacy or a new beginning? *International Data Privacy Law* 3(2): 74–87.

[26] Henkin, L. 1974. Privacy and autonomy. *Columbia Law Review* 74(8): 1419–1433.

[27] Murphy, R.S. 1996. Property rights in personal information: An economic defense of privacy. *Georgetown Law Journal* 84: 2381.

[28] Parent, W.A. 1983. A new definition of privacy for the law. *Law & Philosophy* 2(3): 305–338.

[29] Wacks, R. 1980. The poverty of "privacy." *Law Quarterly Review* 96: 73–78.

[30] Wacks, R. 1980. *The Protection of Privacy.* London: Sweet & Maxwell.

[31] Zimmerman, D.L. 1983. Requiem for a heavyweight: A farewell to Warren and Brandeis's privacy tort. *Cornell Law Review* 68(3): 291–367.

[32] Costa, L., and Poullet, Y. 2012. Privacy and the regulation of 2012. *Computer Law & Security Review* 28(3): 254–262.

[33] Secretary's Advisory Committee on Automated Personal Data Systems. 1973. Records, computers and the rights of citizens. http://epic.org/privacy/hew1973report/ (accessed February 27, 2014).

[34] Schudson, M. 1978. *Discovering the News. A Social History of American Newspaper.* New York: Basic Books.

[35] Breckenridge, A.C. 1970. *The Right to Privacy.* Lincoln, NE: University of Nebraska.

[36] Solove, D.J. 2008. *Understanding Privacy.* Cambridge, MA: Harvard University Press.

[37] Westin, A.F. 1970. *Privacy and Freedom.* New York: Atheneum.

[38] Schwartz, P.M. 2013. The E.U.-US privacy collision: A turn to institutions and procedures. *Harvard Law Review* 126: 1966–2009.

[39] Brenton, M. 1964. *The Privacy Invaders.* New York: Coward-McCann.

[40] Miller, A.R. 1971. *The Assault on Privacy Computers, Data Banks, Dossiers.* Ann Arbor, MI: University of Michigan Press.

[41] Packard, V. 1964. *The Naked Society.* New York: David McKay.

[42] Bennett, C.J. 1992. *Regulating Privacy: Data Protection and Public Policy in Europe and the United States.* Ithaca, NY: Cornell University Press.

[43] Agre, P.E., and Rotenberg, M. (Eds.). 1997. *Technology and Privacy: The New Landscape.* Cambridge, MA: MIT Press.

[44] Bygrave, L.A. 2014. *Data Privacy Law. An International Perspective.* Oxford, UK: Oxford University Press.

[45] Petrison, L.A., Blattberg R.C., and Wang, P. 1997. Database marketing. Past, present, and future. *Journal of Direct Marketing* 11(4): 109–125.

[46] Solove, D.J. 2001. Privacy and power: Computer databases and metaphors for information privacy. *Standford Law Review* 53(6): 1393–1462.

[47] Poullet, Y. 2006. EU data protection policy. The Directive 95/46/EC: Ten years after. *Computer Law & Security Review* 22(3): 206–217.

[48] Simitis, S. 1995. From the market to the polis: The EU directive on the protection of personal data. *Iowa Law Review* 80(3): 445–469.

[49] European Data Protection Supervisor. 2014. Privacy and competitiveness in the age of big data: The interplay between data protection, competition law and consumer protection in the Digital Economy. https://secure.edps.europa.eu/EDPSWEB/webdav/site/mySite/shared/Documents/Consultation/Opinions/2014/14-03-26_competitition_law_big_data_EN.pdf (accessed February 27, 2014).

[50] OECD. 2013. Exploring the economics of personal data: A survey of methodologies for measuring monetary value. http://www.oecd-ilibrary.org/docserver/download/5k486qtxldmq.pdf?expires=1403110041&id=id&accname=guest&checksum=1F20BE8EB6E36BA2F7D94A175C5FB089 (accessed February 27, 2014).

[51] Gurstein, M. 2011. Open data: Empowering the empowered of effective data use for everyone? *First Monday* 16(2). http://firstmonday.org/ojs/index.php/fm/article/view/3316/2764 (accessed September 4, 2013).

[52] Boyd, D., and Crawford, K. 2012. Critical questions for big data: Provocations for a cultural, technological, and scholarly phenomenon. *Information, Communication, & Society* 15(5): 662–679.

[53] Cohen, J.E. 2013. What privacy is for. *Harvard Law Review* 126(7): 1904–1933.

[54] Dwork, C., and Mulligan, D.K. 2013. It's not privacy and it's not fair. *Standford Law Review Online* 66: 35–40.

[55] Mayer-Schönberger, V., and Cukier, K. 2013. *Big Data. A Revolution That Will Transform How We Live, Work and Think.* London: John Murray.

[56] Federal Trade Commission. 2014. Data brokers: A call for transparency and accountability. https://www.ftc.gov/system/files/documents/reports/data-brokers-call-transparency-accountability-report-federal-trade-commission-may-2014/140527databrokerreport.pdf (accessed February 27, 2014).

[57] Marton, A., Avital, M., and Blegind Jensen, T. 2013. Reframing open big data. *ECIS 2013 Proceedings*, Utrecht (*AISeL 2013*).

[58] Hartzog, W., and Selinger, E. 2013. Big data in small hands. *Standford Law Review Online* 66: 81–88.

[59] Article 29 Data Protection Working Party. 2012. Opinion 01/2012 on the data protection reform proposals. http://ec.europa.eu/justice/data-protection/article-29/documentation/opinion-recommendation/files/2012/wp191_en.pdf (accessed March 29, 2015).

[60] Article 29 Data Protection Working Party. 2013. Advice paper on essential elements of a definition and a provision on profiling within the EU General Data Protection Regulation. http://ec.europa.eu/justice/data-protection/article-29/documentation/other-document/files/2013/20130513_advice-paper-on-profiling_en.pdf (accessed March 29, 2015).

[61] Acquisti, A., Brandimarte, L., and Loewenstein, G. 2015. Privacy and human behavior in the age of information. *Science* 347(6221): 509–514.

[62] Brandimarte, L., Acquisti, A., and Loewenstein, G. 2010. Misplaced confidences: Privacy and the control paradox. *Ninth Annual Workshop on the Economics of Information Security.* http://www.heinz.cmu.edu/~acquisti/papers/acquisti-SPPS.pdf (accessed February 27, 2014).

[63] Calo, R.M. 2013. Against notice skepticism in privacy (and elsewhere). *Notre Dame Law Review* 87(3): 1027–1072. http://scholarship.law.nd.edu/ndlr/vol87/iss3/3 (accessed February 27, 2014).

[64] Pasquale, F. 2015. *The Black Box Society. The Secret Algorithms That Control Money and Information.* Cambridge, MA: Harvard University Press.

[65] Turow, J., Hoofnagle, C.J., Mulligan, D.K., and Good, N. 2007. The federal trade commission and consumer privacy in the coming decade. *ISJLP* 3: 723–749. http://scholarship.law.berkeley.edu/facpubs/935 (accessed February 27, 2014).

[66] Mantelero, A. 2014. The future of consumer data protection in the E.U. Rethinking the “notice and consent” paradigm in the new era of predictive analytics. *Computer Law & Security Review* 30(6): 643–660.

[67] Ohm, P. 2013. Branding privacy. *Minnesota Law Review* 97: 907–989.

[68] Tene, O., and Polonetsky, J. 2012. Privacy in the age of big data. A time for big decisions. *Standford Law Review Online* 64: 63–69. http://www.stanfordlawreview.org/sites/default/files/online/topics/64-SLRO-63_1.pdf (accessed March 14, 2013).

[69] Wright, D., and De Hert, P. (Eds.). 2012. *Privacy Impact Assessment.* Dordrecht, the Netherlands: Springer.

[70] Cate, F.H., and Mayer-Schönberger, V. 2013. Data use and impact. *Global Workshop.* The Center for Information Policy Research and the Center for Applied Cybersecurity Research, Indiana University. http://cacr.iu.edu/sites/cacr.iu.edu/files/Use_Workshop_Report.pdf (accessed February 27, 2014).

[71] Mayer-Schönberger, V., and Padova, Y. 2016. Regime change? Enabling big data through Europe's data protection regulation. *Columbia Science & Technology Law Review* XVII: 315–335.

[72] Hildebrandt, M. 2006. Profiling: From data to knowledge. The challenges of a crucial technology. *Datenschutz und Datensicherheit* 30(9): 548–552.

[73] Ferguson, A.G. 2012. Predictive policing: The future of reasonable suspicion. *Emory Law Journal* 62(2): 259–325. http://law.emory.edu/elj/_documents/volumes/62/2/articles/ferguson.pdf (accessed January 29, 2014).

[74] Mantelero, A., and Vaciago, G. 2014. Social media and big data. In Akhgar, B., Staniforth, A., and Bosco, F. (Eds.), *Cyber Crime & Cyber Terrorism. Investigator's Handbook.* Waltham, MA: Elsevier.

[75] Perry, W.L., McInnis, B., Price, C.C., Smith, S.C., and Hollywood, J.S. 2013. *Predictive Policing: The Role of Crime Forecasting in Law Enforcement Operations.* The RAND Corporation. http://www.rand.org/content/dam/rand/pubs/research_reports/RR200/RR233/RAND_RR233.pdf (accessed March 10, 2015).

[76] Rieke, A., Robinson, D., and Yu, H. 2014. Civil rights, big data, and our algorithmic future. A September 2014 report on social justice and technology. http://bigdata.fairness.io/wp-content/uploads/2014/09/Civil_Rights_Big_Data_and_Our_Algorithmic-Future_2014-09-12.pdf (accessed March 10, 2015).

[77] van Brakel, R., and De Hert, P. 2011. Policing, surveillance and law in a pre-crime society: Understanding the consequences of technology based strategies. *Journal of Police Studies* 20(3): 163–192.

[78] Mantelero, A. 2017. From group privacy to collective privacy: towards a new dimension of privacy and data protection in the big data era. In Taylor, L., Floridi, L., and van der Sloot, B. (Eds.), *Group Privacy: New Challenges of Data Technologies.* Dordrecht, the Netherlands: Springer.

[79] Boyd, D., Levy, K., and Marwick, A. 2014. The networked nature of algorithmic discrimination. In Peña Gangadharan, S., Eubanks, V., and Barocas, S. (Eds.), *Data and Discrimination: Collective Essays.* Open Technology Institute and New America. http://www.newamerica.org/downloads/OTI-Data-an-Discrimination-FINAL-small.pdf (accessed April 14, 2015).

[80] Crawford, K., Faleiros, G., Luers, A., Meier, P., Perlich, C., and Thorp, J. 2013. Big data, communities and ethical resilience: A framework for action. http://www.rockefellerfoundation.org/app/uploads/71b4c457-cdb7-47ec-81a9-a617c956e6af.pdf (accessed April 5, 2015).

[81] Vedder, A.H. 1997. Privatization, information technology and privacy: Reconsidering the social responsibilities of private organizations. In Moore, G. (Ed.), *Business Ethics: Principles and Practice.* Sunderland: Business Education Publishers.

[82] Zarsky, T.Z. 2013. Transparent predictions. *University of Illinois Law Review* 4: 1503–1569.

[83] Bloustein, E.J. 1977. Group privacy: The right to huddle. *Rutgers-Camden Law Journal* 8(2): 219–283.

[84] Bloustein, E.J. 1978. *Individual and Group Privacy.* New Brunswick, NJ: Transaction Books.

[85] Capotorti, F. 1992. Are minorities entitled to collective international rights? In Dinstein, Y., and Tabory, M. (Eds.), *The Protection of Minorities and Human Rights.* Dordrecht, the Netherlands: Martinus Nijhoff Publishers.

[86] Newman, D.G. 2004. Collective interests and collective rights. *American Journal of Jurisprudence* 49(1): 127–163.

[87] Ellis, E., and Watson, P. 2015. *EU Anti-Discrimination Law.* 2nd ed. Oxford, UK: Oxford University Press.

[88] Schreurs, W., Hildebrandt, M., Kindt, E., and Vanfleteren, M. 2010. Cogitas, ergo sum. The role of data protection law and non-discrimination law in group profiling in the private sector. In Hildebrandt, M., and Gutwirth, S. (Eds.), *Profiling the European Citizen. Cross-Disciplinary Perspective.* Dordrecht, the Netherlands: Springer.

[89] Burnbaum, B. 2003. Insurers' use of credit scoring for homeowners in Ohio: A report to the Ohio civil rights commission. https://www.researchgate.net/publication/265217840_Insurers'_Use_of_Credit_Scoring_for_Homeowners_Insurance_In_Ohio_A_Report_to_the_Ohio_Civil_Rights_Commission (accessed June 28, 2015).

[90] Citron, D.K., and Pasquale, F. 2014. The scored society: Due process for automated predictions. *Washington Law Review* 89: 1–33.

[91] Bosker, B. 2013. Google's online ad results guilty of racial profiling, according to new study. *The Huffington Post*, May 2, 2013. http://www.huffingtonpost.com/2013/02/05/online-racial-profiling_n_2622556.html (accessed March 27, 2015).

[92] Sweeney, L. 2013. Discrimination in online ad delivery. *Communications of the ACM* 56(5): 44–54.

[93] Crawford, K. 2013. Algorithmic illusions: Hidden biases of big data. *Presentation at Strata 2013.* https://www.youtube.com/watch?v=irP5RCdpilc (accessed March 15, 2015).

[94] Crawford, K. 2013. The hidden biases in big data. *Harvard Business Review*, April 1. https://hbr.org/2013/04/the-hidden-biases-in-big-data (accessed January 29, 2015).

[95] Lerman, J. 2013. Big data and its exclusions. *Standford Law Review Online* 66: 55–62.

[96] National Immigration Law Center. 2013. Verification nation. www.nilc.org/document.html?id=957 (accessed January 29, 2015).

[97] Administrative Office of the United States Courts—Office of Probation and Pretrial Services. 2011. An overview of the federal post conviction risk assessment. http://www.uscourts.gov/uscourts/FederalCourts/PPS/PCRA_Sep_2011.pdf (accessed January 29, 2015).

[98] U.S. Department of Justice—Criminal Division, Office of the Assistant Attorney General. 2014. Annual letter. http://www.justice.gov/criminal/foia/docs/2014annual-letter-final-072814.pdf (accessed January 29, 2015).

[99] Executive Office of the President of the United States-Council of Economic Advisers. 2015. Big data differential pricing. https://www.whitehouse.gov/sites/default/files/docs/Big_Data_Report_Nonembargo_v2.pdf (accessed March 25, 2015).

[100] Rosenblat, A., Randhava, R., Boyd, D., Peña Gangadharan, S., and Yu, C. 2014. Data & civil rights: Consumer finance primer. http://www.datacivilrights.org/pubs/2014-1030/Finance.pdf (accessed March 15, 2015).

[101] Dixon, P., and Gellman, R. 2014. The scoring of America: How secret consumer scores threaten your privacy and your future. http://www.worldprivacyforum.org/wp-content/uploads/2014/04/WPF_Scoring_of_America_April2014_fs.pdf (accessed March 10, 2015).

[102] Lambert, T.C. 1999. Fair marketing: Challenging pre-application lending practices. *Georgetown Law Journal* 87: 2182.

[103] Article 29 Data Protection Working Party. 2010. Opinion 2/2010 on online behavioural advertising. http://ec.europa.eu/justice/policies/privacy/docs/wpdocs/2010/wp171_en.pdf (accessed March 29, 2015).

[104] Bygrave, L.A. 2002. *Data Protection Law. Approaching Its Rationale, Logic and Limits.* The Hague, the Netherlands: Kluwer Law International.

[105] Koops, B.-J. 2014. The trouble with European data protection law. *International Data Privacy Law* 4(4): 250–261.

[106] Rauhofer, J. 2014. Round and round the garden? Big data, small government and the balance of power in the information age. University of Edinburgh School of Law, Research Paper Series 2014/06. http://papers.ssrn.com/sol3/papers.cfm?abstract_id=2389981 (accessed March 15, 2015).

[107] Finnis, J. 1984. The authority of law in the predicament of contemporary social theory. *Notre Dame Journal of Law, Ethics, & Public Policy* 1: 115–137.

[108] Nissenbaum, H. 2010. *Privacy in Context. Technology, Policy, and the Integrity of Social Life.* Stanford, CA: Stanford University Press.

[109] Whitman, J.Q. 2004. The two western cultures of privacy: Dignity versus liberty. *Yale Law Journal* 113(6): 1151–1221.

[110] Bygrave, L.A. 2004. Privacy protection in a global context. *A Comparative Overview. Scandinavian Studies in Law* 47: 319–348.

[111] Wright, D. 2011. A framework for the ethical impact assessment of information technology. *Ethics and Information Technology* 13(3): 199–226.

[112] Gandy, O.H. Jr. 2000. Exploring identity and identification in cyberspace. *Notre Dame Journal of Law, Ethics, & Public Policy* 14(2): 1085–1111. http://scholarship.law.nd.edu/ndjlepp/vol14/iss2/10 (accessed July 10, 2015).

[113] Hildebrandt, M., and Gutwirth, S. (Eds.). 2010. *Profiling the European Citizen. Cross-Disciplinary Perspective.* Dordrecht, the Netherlands: Springer.

[114] European Commission. 2013. Developing anti-discrimination law in Europe. The 28 EU Member States, the Former Yugoslav Republic of Macedonia, Iceland, Liechtenstein, Norway and Turkey compared. http://www.non-discrimination.net/content/media/Developing%20Anti-Discrimination%20Law%20in%20Europe%20EN%2029042014%20WEB.pdf (accessed March 28, 2015).

[115] Farkas, L. 2014. Collective actions under European anti-discrimination law. *European Anti-Discrimination Law Review* 19: 25–40.

[116] Citron, D.K. 2008. Technological due process. *Washington University Law Review* 85(6): 1249–1313.

[117] Van Dijck, J. 2014. Datafication, dataism and dataveillance: Big data between scientific paradigm and ideology. *Surveillance & Society* 12: 197–208.

[118] Kerr, I., and Earle, J. 2013. Prediction, preemption, presumption: How big data threatens big picture privacy. *Stanford Law Review Online* 66: 65.

[119] European Parliament. 2001. Report on the existence of a global system for the interception of private and commercial communications (ECHELON interception system). http://www.fas.org.

[120] DARPA. 2002. Total Information Awareness Program (TIA). System Description Document (SDD), Version 1.1. http://epic.org/privacy/profiling/tia/tiasystemdescription.pdf.

[121] Bigo, D., Carrera, S., Hernanz, N., Jeandesboz, J., Parkin, J., Ragazzi, F., and Scherrer, A. 2013. The US surveillance programmes and their impact on EU citizens' fundamental rights. *Study for the European Parliament, PE 493.032.*

[122] Brown, I. 2013. Expert witness statement for big brother watch and others re: Large-scale internet surveillance by the UK. *Application No: 58170/13 to the European Court of Human Rights.* http://papers.ssrn.com/sol3/papers.cfm?abstract_id=2336609 (accessed December 21, 2016).

[123] Gillespie, A. 2009. Regulation of internet surveillance. *European Human Rights Law Review* 4: 552–565.

[124] O'Floinn, M., and Ormerod, D. 2011. Social networking sites RIPA and criminal investigations. *Criminal Law Review* 10: 766–789.

Chapter 2

Legal and policy aspects of information science in emerging automated environments

Stefan A. Kaiser*

Introduction 48
Sectoral approach 50
Government and military 50
Commercial and industrial 52
Science 54
Activity approach 56
Information collection 57
Characteristics 57
Automated information collection 57
Affected rights 57
Legal issues 57
Information processing 58
Characteristics 58
Automated information processing 58
Affected rights 59
Legal issues 59
Information storage and distribution 59
Characteristics 59
Automation 59
Affected rights 60
Legal issues 60
Automation of physical devices—Internet of Things 61
Characteristics 61
Automation and autonomy 62
Affected rights 62
Legal issues 62
Conclusion 64
References 66

*LLM (McGill), stefanakaiser@aol.com

The current chapter represents the author's personal opinion and shall not be attributed to any organization with which he is affiliated.

Introduction

Information science has many new frontiers. The legal and policy implications are one of them, and automated environments are another. Information science* uses a broad range of methods, especially from the domains of mathematics, statistics, and computer applications, to extract knowledge from information. Information or data† are the substances researched by these methods. Large amounts of data or information are required to efficiently use mathematical and statistical methods for generating meaningful results. This leads to another buzz word frequently used today: Big Data.

Different definitions of Big Data put the emphasis on different aspects, several thereof on quantitative dimensions such as volume, velocity, and variety—the three "Vs" [5]. This is not surprising, because it is already implied by the literal meaning of *big*. This quantitative perspective does not support any legal analysis, because it does not touch the content of the information and what it implies in regard to people, who are the subjects of law and whose rights and interest need to be protected. Historically, the accumulation of information is nothing new, since the humans invented the skill of writing and collected the writings in libraries. The destruction of the ancient libraries of Alexandria and Constantinople still let us wonder about information available to early high cultures. Moving further ahead from the quantitative elements, some definitions of Big Data include veracity [5] to highlight the quality, certainty, and trustfulness of data. From a legal viewpoint, veracity is more important than the classical three "Vs," as legal determinations need to be based on evidence. Not every information in a database suffices the quality required in law, but there must be evidence that it mirrors facts of the physical world. Nevertheless, the classical three Vs even combined with veracity do by themselves not establish legally relevant facts for the legal relationships between humans.

Other definitions of Big Data take a different methodological path by strongly concentrating on the implications of computer science and technology. To that end, they center around the size and complexity of the datasets and the technologies as the tools and techniques that are used to process a sizable or complex dataset [5]. Such technology-driven definitions do neither support any legal analysis.

Considering these definitions of Big Data, what are lawyers looking for? For the study of the legal and policy aspects, we need to establish parameters that distinguish between activities that affect the rights, in one way or

*For more precise definitions of information science, see for example References [1–3] referenced after https://www.asist.org/about/information-science/.

†"Data" is generally understood as a basic piece of (raw or non-analyzed) fact, whereas the term "information" is used for a more refined, processed, or analyzed product generated from data.

another, and thus raise legal issues. For example, privacy and the protection of intellectual property rights are crucial legal principles affecting information science. It is hence advisable to take a sectoral approach depending on the different user groups or sectors and their culture of information sharing or restriction. This sectoral approach needs to distinguish between the following sectors because they use information in different ways with different intentions and with different legal effects:

- Government and military,
- Commercial and industrial,
- (Information) science.

This is not the only purpose of this chapter. The expansion of information technologies from the virtual to the real world raises additional legal and policy challenges. Critical infrastructures in sectors such as energy, transport, water, banking, healthcare, industry, and military increasingly depend on networked automation. At the moment, we see these technologies also spreading to personal and domestic applications. The *Internet of Things* is a term that is frequently used to portray these developments. However, the information and uses are diverse and result in different sensitivities. To look at these aspects, an activity approach needs to be taken to differentiate between the different kinds of activities and the degree of automation. This activity approach needs to distinguish between:

- Information collection,
- Information processing, analysis, storage, and distribution and finally
- The automation of physical processes and machinery based on information inputs.

Before moving on further, it must be borne in mind that the laws relating to information and data are national or, within the European Union regional, at best. Therefore, any examination of the legal implications in this chapter can only be of a generic nature and cannot reflect details that result from the diversity and fragmentation of law. This fragmentation is an additional complication, which cannot be fully explained in this chapter. For easier understanding, but without prejudice to other national privacy and data protection laws, this chapter refers more generally to the European Union's General Data Protection Regulation [6].*

*Even though this Regulation will be uniformly binding within EU Member States, it can lead to a degradation of the level of protection in States, whose national protection was more stringent.

Sectoral approach

The use of information and the legal vulnerabilities depend on the sector in question and the related sharing culture. The purpose and sharing culture of each of the sectors leads to the legal issues and the affected rights.

Government and military

Governments and a broad range of public entities use information for administration and national and international security. National security covers not only police and law enforcement but also national secret service activities. The military uses information as part of their intelligence, surveillance, and reconnaissance activities and their command and control. For proactive purposes, such as the prevention of safety and security incidents and crises, government and the military use information for establishing situational awareness in a broad range of scenarios. Other governmental uses are for infrastructure, urban planning, and public services.

Historically, government and political leaders have been collecting and retaining information for the perseverance of their rule and power. This restrictive information practice is the opposite of sharing. A similar restrictive access regime is typically applied today for the purpose of national and international security with the secret service being at the pinnacle of secrecy. Access to and exchange of such security sensitive information is very limited. Nevertheless, governments may enter into national and international intergovernmental arrangements on a reciprocal basis for strategic purposes. The existence of such arrangements is often kept secret as well. Significantly, even at the national level, sharing among agencies of the same government cannot be taken for granted. The distribution and export of military products and dual use goods are likewise restricted under national export control regulations that impose strict limitations on manufacturers and traders.* The use of geospatial data from open sources for governmental intelligence purposes is currently leading to new measures of counter geospatial intelligence, or *counter geo-int*† because the open source information can be manipulated.

Governmental practice and interpretation of the protection of security relevant information differs broadly, and it can easily blur with the preservation of rule and power. This practice displayed by a government is linked to the state of democracy, separation of powers, and the rule of law.

---

*The Wassenaar Arrangement is an international regime to facilitate the international transfer of military and dual use goods among participating States in order to contribute to regional and international security, see [7].

†Robert Cardillo, Director of the U.S. National Geospatial-Intelligence Agency (NGA), referred to by Reference 8.

Outside of the security area, governments may be a lot more open, for example, on the field of infrastructure, urban planning, and public services. For higher transparency of governmental activities, some states have established freedom of information policies in one way or another, which find their limits again in matters of national and international security.

The information collected and evaluated by governments has first of all an effect on the nationals and the individuals in the territory. It is internationally recognized that personal and personalized information of individuals requires legal protection. This protection is a human right and serves not only as a defense of humans against the authority of a state,* similar to an individual's rights of access to justice, but also as a defense against the misuse of personal data by other natural and legal persons. In national legal systems, the protection against the informational exploitation of an individual's rights may also be referred to as privacy† or right of informational self-determination.‡ Broadly speaking, these legal concepts follow the principles that personal data§ have to be processed lawfully, fairly, transparently, and accurately, limited to the legitimate purpose and not to exceed the scope that is necessary for that purpose¶ and, typically, with a heightened protection of specially sensitive categories of personal data.**

Governmental collection and evaluation of information does not only affect the rights and freedoms of individuals but also of legal persons. In regard to commercial and industrial entities, the sensitive areas do not relate to personal aspects in the narrow sense, but to industrial and intellectual property.

Even though privacy and data protection are concepts for the protection of the individual and companies against public and private misuse of personal information, they are not absolute defenses. Governments rather have

---

*See for example [9], Article 7 (Respect for private and family life): *Everyone has the right to respect for his or her private and family life, home and communications;* Article 8 (Protection of personal data): *1. Everyone has the right to the protection of personal data concerning him or her. 2. Such data must be processed fairly for specified purposes and on the basis of the consent of the person concerned or some other legitimate basis laid down by law. Everyone has the right of access to data that has been collected concerning him or her, and the right to have it rectified. ....*

†In common law, the right of privacy refers to a broader concept than the protection of personal data: *the right to be let alone; the right of a person to be free from unwarranted publicity* [10].

‡In Germany, the right of information self-determination was established by a decision of the Federal Constitutional Court in 1983 [11] and entails the (freedom) right of every natural person to determine the use and disclosure of his personal and personalizable data, see [12].

§"Personal data" means any information relating to an identified or identifiable natural person, see definition of Article 4 (1) of Reference 6.

¶See for example Article 5 of Reference 6.

**See for example Article 9 of Reference 6, which gives special protection to racial or ethnic origin, political opinions, religious or philosophical beliefs, trade-union membership and genetic/biometric data to identify a natural person's health, sex-life, or sexual orientation.

to balance the public interest in regard to safety and security as opposed to the privacy and data protection of the affected natural and legal persons.

To maintain their privacy and data protection rights, it must be assured that the affected person is informed* of and consents† to the collection, analysis, storage, and distribution of personal data, or it is authorized for other lawful purposes.‡ National public laws are to insure this level of protection. In the European Union, however, the Data Protection Directive [13] that established the minimum standards for the national legislation of the Member States will be replaced by a new General Data Protection Regulation [6] to enter into effect on May 25, 2018 with directly binding effect in all Member States.

Highly critical is the borderline between the legitimate interest of governments to collect and analyze personal information for fighting crime and terrorism and, on the other hand, the data protection of individuals.§ The indiscriminate collection of and access to personal information that is neither limited in scope and purpose to the fighting of crime, nor in advance being reviewed by a court or independent authority, finds its limits in the data protection of individuals.¶

Commercial and industrial

Commercial and industrial entities seek to protect their intellectual and industrial property to safeguard their business and to maintain their competitive advantage. For the purpose of marketing, they protect information of their customers, their consumption, and product interests. For the analysis of markets and trends, they collect and analyze information about individuals and their consumption and interests.

---

*See for example Articles 12 and 13 of Reference 6 on transparent information, communication, and modalities for the exercise of the data subject and the information to be provided where personal data have not been obtained from the data subject.

†See for example Articles 6 and 7 of Reference 6 on the lawfulness of processing and the conditions for consent. Article 4 (11) of Reference 6 defines consent as *any freely given, specific, informed and unambiguous indication of the data subject's wishes by which he or she, by a statement or by a clear affirmative action signifies agreement to the processing of personal data relating to him or her.*

‡For example, for the performance of a contract or the protection of a vital interest of the affected person, or for compliance with a legal obligation of the data processor or the public interest, see Article 6 of Reference 6.

§See for example Article 10 of Reference 6 on the processing of personal data relating to criminal conviction and offences.

¶The European Court of Justice (ECJ) has in December 2016 ruled that competent national authorities are precluded to access retained data, *where the objective pursued by that access, in the context of fighting crime, is not restricted solely to fighting serious crime, where access is not subject to prior review by a court or an independent administrative authority, and where there is no requirement that the data concerned should be retained within the European Union* [14].

Commercial and industrial entities primarily follow a restrictive policy on information. Intellectual property,* and trade secrets are central elements of protecting their products. Information obtained from customers is used to position themselves on the market and to improve their market position. As such, information on customers and potential customers is used like a trade secret. However, commercial entities may also engage in the trade or exchange of technical information and personal information of their users, either for generating an additional revenue stream or within strategic partnership arrangements.

Some practices of commercial businesses may appear as if they were embracing an information-sharing culture, but in fact they are not. For example, social media and internet entertainment can be used for marketing purposes but are masked as a free utility for the users with the ultimate goal to collect personal information of them and their habits. A more strategic approach is followed, when commercial entities provide, for example, their own software products as free open source products, to establish technical de facto standards and, in the long run, to increase their market position.

Players in the commercial and industrial sector seek to protect their own intellectual and industrial property. When they collect, analyze, and distribute personal information of customers, they can affect those customers' privacy rights.

For the collection, analysis, storage, and distribution of personal information, the consent of the affected person or right holder needs to be obtained under national privacy and data-protection legislation.† Of course, national legislation differs from country to country, or may not exist at all.

In the commercial and industrial sector, this consent is often asked for by the terms and conditions of commercial entities or on their websites by confirming a pop-up window with the terms and conditions by a mouse click. This is legally critical for several reasons. Prospective users typically do not read all the fine print or the lengthy texts on a website. Website terms of use are often written in a way that the consent is implicitly given upon the use of the website. Such terms and conditions are typically far-reaching and can include future and hidden activities, such as the analysis, storage, and distribution of information for purposes and in ways that cannot be comprehended at the moment of their collection. In the commercial sector, in which personal information of (potential) customers is considered as a business asset, the consent is often not obtained on the basis of transparent information. This shortcoming falls under the broader area of (the lack of) consumer protection. Similar to privacy or data protection, consumer protection is internationally highly fragmented, as the underlying private law regimes differ widely, whereas the

*Patents grant their holder protection rights within the jurisdiction of the patent authority, but all details of the technical innovation are publicly disclosed, and hence do *not* keep the patented novelty secret. Protection of software is primarily achieved through copyright. Patent protection of software is disputed, see [15].

†To that end the principles on consent apply as described above.

internet serves as a global information platform and market place. On this global marketplace, domestic commercial practices of U.S. entities paved the way for global internet businesses, despite more stringent data and consumer protection legislation in other countries.

Another issue arises for the protection of products created by automated information analysis, because copyright protection requires human input and creativity. As this is absent in automated products, the protection of products of automated processes including automated information analysis raises additional questions.

Science

Analysis of large amounts of data and data sharing for scientific purposes is a common practice in many areas such as genomics, earth science, and astronomy. The purpose of science in collecting, analyzing, storing, and distributing information is scientific research and analysis, especially by mathematical and statistical methods. In a broad sense, it is about an increase in knowledge and partly also to obtain situational awareness of factual events. The applied methodology is not merely a discovery and understanding of the already existing information, albeit hidden in the large quantities of information inherent to Big Data. It is rather about deriving *new* information by means of statistical and mathematical methods as a deductive conclusion from the collected data. The context and structure of information is an important contributor to this possibility of generating information beyond the meaning of the sum of all individual datasets. This is the role of *metadata*, which is "structured information that describes, explains, locates, or otherwise makes it easier to retrieve, use, or manage an information resource. Metadata is often called data about data or information about information" [16]. In contrast to structural metadata, typically created to structure an archive of collected data, descriptive metadata can also describe the context of the creation, collection, processing, or storage of data.* The patterns embedded in metadata allow automated (software driven) methods to efficiently analyze huge amounts of data. Data patterns cannot substitute the meaning and analysis of the data content, but in many instances the analysis of the patterns found in metadata can lead to conclusions or predictions for a specific purpose—with less time and effort.

What does all that imply? That the total amount of information contained in a bulk of information, call it Big Data, is more than the information contained in the sum of the individual datasets. This is the information that scientists wish to derive from numerous sources, even though collected and stored by various agencies. But not all players are from the scientific field.

---

*See, for example, the metadata for geographic information as defined in Reference 17, which provides information about the *identification, the extent, the quality, the spatial and temporal aspects, the content, the spatial reference, the portrayal, distribution, and other properties of digital geographic data and services.*

Government, military, commercial, and industrial entities focus on different aspects and have different interests.

In contrast to the governmental and military and the commercial and industrial sectors, the hallmark of science is an open information sharing culture as a corollary of the scientific freedom. Even though science is not intended to generate commercial benefits or to constitute a means of governmental control or of national or international security, there can be no doubt that science indirectly can have an effect on the other sectors. Scientific knowledge forms not only the basis for technological progress but can also become instrumental for governmental and military endeavors. Likewise, the government and military and the commercial and industrial sectors may compete in the collection of the same information intended to be used for scientific purposes. This can limit the access of scientists to obtain information from the other two sectors and lead to a fragmentation of available information in a given field.

The collection, analysis, storage, and distribution of information for exclusively scientific purposes does typically not interfere with other rights, unless there is an overlap with security, privacy, and intellectual and industrial property. In the analysis of Big Data such overlaps frequently occur, as not only the scientific sector has an interest in it and as not only scientific bodies collect it. At this point, metadata play an important role. Descriptive metadata that define the context of the creation, collection, processing, or storage of data are a key for information science, especially when such metadata reflect the process information of automated creation, collection, processing, and storage. If such metadata are erased or modified, intentionally or unintentionally, the data context gets lost or is distorted.

Metadata may be modified for various reasons. For example, for the protection of privacy, medical, genetic, and biometrical information needs to be pseudonymized for legal reason, when using this information for scientific purposes unrelated to the health of the affected individual. Pseudonymization is a technical and organizational design measure to be followed by a data controller to ensure that personal data cannot be attributed to an identified or identifiable natural person.* This modification of (meta)data is imposed for legal reasons, but depending on the way how the pseudonymization is undertaken can have adverse effects on the usability of the data for scientific purposes.

An example relates to data for tracking the population of space debris in orbit, which endangers space traffic. These data are collected from different sources from different countries derived from different types of sensors. The biggest data distributors are military and governmental, most notably the United States and Russia, but also private space operators contribute data.†

*See for example Articles 25 1. and 4 (5) of Reference 6.

†For more details on the roles of the United States, Russia, Europe, and China see [18]. Satellite operators cooperate for the purpose of space situational awareness in the Space Data Association, a nongovernmental, nonprofit association founded in 2009 by Intelsat, Inmarsat, and Eutelsat [18].

The amount of data may not reach the quantities considered as Big Data today, but it may exceed the capabilities of the individual space faring nations, so that only a collaborated effort leads to a realistic situational picture. The common interest has moved space actors to share data, but there are limitations. For reasons of (national) security, military and governments are reluctant to disclose the highest precision of their data and unabridged metadata. These metadata are essential for making high precision prediction of possible in-orbit collisions [19]. An interesting role in this effort takes Celestrak [20] a free service, open to all, provided by T.S. Kelso that includes predicted conjunctions in orbit based on data collected from available sources including metadata. Finkleman has characterized Celestrak as a centralized data pool architecture that "adds value through independent analysis and trusted independent information" [19].

What can we learn from these examples? We need to find solutions in delimiting functional interest zones for the analysis of Big Data to allow all sectors with their different interests and information retention and sharing cultures to coexist. Clearly, any such solution cannot be simple and needs to be tailored to the specific nature of the data pools in question. One organizational solution could be a trusted agent, such as Celestrak. By analysis of data from different sources, with different quality, structure, and metadata, the data pool becomes reliable. In the end, the success of this concept is directly linked to the trust in that service provider.

What else can be done? Standardization of metadata can help, similar to the way it is applied to geographic information [17]. But as there are also legally valid reasons for altering metadata, for example, for the protection of personal data, mechanisms such as pseudonymization also need to follow a standardized pattern. Metadata modified in a standardized way can help one to form reliable and trusted data pools originating from different sources.

Activity approach

Another approach leads us to the use of information depending on the activity and automation. Information collection, analysis, storage, and distribution fall into the sphere of the information or virtual world. Their purpose is to gather knowledge, to achieve situational awareness, or to undertake research or analysis, depending on the sector. To understand the legal issues and rights affected by these activities, we need to look at their characteristics and their level of automation. The automation of physical machinery adds a new dimension, when it is based on information inputs, which have a direct effect in the physical or real world. The purpose of information in these automated environments is the control of physical processes.

Information collection

Characteristics

Collection is the starting point of all information processing. The sources from which information is collected become increasingly diverse. Long gone are the times, when most inputs were directly entered by humans. External sources, such as a plethora of sensors and cameras, can provide information that is distributed over the internet and other networks. The information that can be retrieved from the virtual world has not only been growing exponentially and provides countless opportunities for new informational compositions but also bears the risk of nonauthenticated or false content. Mobile devices such as smartphones have become popular tools for the collection of information with social media serving as platforms, very often without the consent of the individual or right holder whose image, information, or work is collected.

Automated information collection

The automated collection of information results from the connectivity with the virtual world. Sources are not only dedicated sensors including webcams but also the feedback from networked machinery in industry, commerce and domestic applications, such as the refrigerator that becomes part of the Internet of Things. In the area of security, we can see an increase in automated data collection with closed circuit television, body scanners, and other sensors in connection with recognition tools, such as face recognition, license plate recognition, and voice recognition. Sensors on remote sensing satellites and drones also serve for the automated collection of information. The automated collection of information may not always be apparent and can indeed be hidden behind other functionalities, for example, smartphone games can be used to take images and geolocate them by the inbuilt satellite navigation functionality, not only of the player himself, but also of his social environment. Other everyday internet devices are search engines and providers of message and other services that record and analyze the communication behavior of their users and use this information either to enhance their business models or to the sell the derived information.

Affected rights

The collection of personal information can violate the privacy of individuals and the intellectual and industrial property, if the collector has not obtained the consent of the affected person or of the right holder.

Legal issues

For the automated or nonautomated collection of personal information, the consent of the affected person or right holder needs to be obtained under the governing national privacy or data protection legislation, even though the extent of the collection and future applications and purposes are unknown, especially in the governmental and in the commercial and industrial sectors.

Information processing

Characteristics

Information processing consists of different stages including, but not limited to, formatting, analysis, authentication, geolocation, and identification. Formatting typically is a conversion of information into another machine-readable format, so that information that originates from different sources can be combined or used together. Authentication can involve diverse steps for verifying information, originating from unknown or nonverified sources, typically be comparing it with verified information in terms of consistency and plausibility. Geolocation is a methodology normally used for geographic information systems (GIS), by which information is attributed to a certain location (and possibly also time). High spatial and temporal resolution often also allows attributing information to a person or a legal entity.

At the moment a person is identified, this information is attributed to a person and becomes personal information with the implications on the protection of privacy or data protection. Profiling of natural persons is an enhanced form of such analysis of personal information and becomes especially sensitive, when the profiling touches aspects such as personal performance and behavior, the economic situation of the person, his or her location, the sexual, religious and political orientation, and affiliation and his or her health, including genetic and biometric information.

Automated information processing

Information analysis is increasingly undertaken by automated processing. Instead of an individual human intervention, automated processes can analyze data following prearranged patterns. This largely accelerates and increases the overall volume of analysis. However, it can also result in systematic deficiencies of the analyzed work products, if the source information is unprecise or not authenticated, for example, when metadata are missing that provide the context of the source information.

Automated authentication, geolocation, and especially identification can lead to an attribution of information to a natural person and therefore make the automated product to become personal data. Voice and face recognition are such automated processes, which typically affect the privacy rights and data protection of individuals.

The automated creation of new, nonpersonal information products can have other implications. Commercial entities that create information products by automated means are not eligible for copyright protection, because copyright, just like a patent, requires a creative human act, not just an automated process.

Affected rights

Just like the collection of information, its analysis also can violate the privacy of individuals and the intellectual and industrial property rights, if the affected person or right holder has not consented to the analysis in question.

Legal issues

Again, like for the collection of information, it can be difficult to verify, whether the consent of the affected person or right holder had been obtained for the given analysis, even if its purpose and scope was not yet known at the time of the consent.

As the intellectual property protection requires human input, those who seek legal protection for their automatically generated information products cannot rely on existing regimes like copyright.

Information storage and distribution

Characteristics

Traditionally, the distribution of personal, intellectual, commercial, and industrial information has been a sensitive issue, because information may reach recipients beyond the authorized circle of user, as defined by the owner's intent and purpose. The internet, or more generally the online connectivity, has aggravated the problem of distributing information past the limits authorized by the owner. The same applies to decentralized storage of information, as the storing of information in the *cloud* becomes increasingly popular. The *cloud* means that the storage of information is accomplished on unknown servers of third parties, as opposed to traditional local storage media. The same trend can be seen in cloud computing, which provides internet-based processing and analysis capabilities, rather than on local processors and memories. One can therefore say that the scope of the distribution of information has been widening, as the activities of storage, processing, and analysis have left the traditional confines of the local computer. Storage and analysis have started to blur with information distribution, possibly allowing third parties controlling the *cloud* to access information, all without the knowledge and consent of the affected person and right holder.

Automation

Automation has been widely advanced in the area of information distribution. Network protocols direct information packages to the destination, without giving the ordinary sender any information about the international routing. The same is true for cloud storage and computing. The user has no idea, in which his or her information is stored or processed, on whose hardware, what are the security safeguards and who has access.

Affected rights

Just similar to the collection and the analysis, the storage and distribution of information can violate the privacy of individuals and the intellectual and industrial property, if the affected person or right holder has not consented to the analysis in question.

Legal issues

The distribution of information over networks does not only possibly infringe upon the rights of affected persons and right holders, but it poses multiple issues in regard to cross-border jurisdiction and enforcement. Despite the attempts made to harmonize national privacy and data protection regimes, the level of protection still largely varies from state to state. This is also the result of different cultural perceptions; for example, those who feel that the mere possession of information entitles them to use it without restrictions as opposed to the privacy rights of individuals and the owners of intellectual property.

Cross-border enforcement becomes a problem in the case of criminal acts committed over networks and cyberattacks. States can enforce actions only within their jurisdiction, which is typically defined territorially or linked to its nationals. But as the distribution of packet switched information, and also the cloud storage and processing is dispersed over networks around the entire globe, it is difficult to locate information, its storage, and processing for the purpose of enforcement.

Even if the location of storage and processing can be found, it is difficult, if not impossible, to identify a natural person to whom this activity can be attributed. In light thereof, measures of enforcement bodies, if necessary, become impossible.

This raises some important questions. Can activities undertaken over the internet be attributed to States and make them responsible? If so, States would be compelled to undertake measures against malicious activities of their nationals or originating from network infrastructure in their territories in order to avoid being held responsible for such acts. Unfortunately, public international law does generally *not legally* attribute acts of nationals to their State of nationality and make these States legally responsible,* unless an organ of that State or a representative undertook that act.

Nevertheless, Jason Healey has proposed to step beyond the *attribution fixation* and to make States responsible for cyberattacks originating from their territory. Recognizing that States do not have the same level of effective control

*This is also reflected in Reference 21, Annex, Article 11.

A noteworthy exception to this rule is Art. VI of Reference 22: *States Parties to the Treaty shall bear international responsibility for national activities in outer space ... whether such activities are carried on by governmental agencies or by non-governmental entities, and for assuring that national activities are carried out in conformity with the provisions set forth in the present Treaty. The activities of non-governmental entities in outer space ... shall require authorization and continuing supervision by the appropriate State Party to the Treaty.*

over that portion of the cyber infrastructure in their territory as, for example, over other physical devices within their national territory, their responsibility for cyberattacks should rather imply that States stop these attacks, clean up the cyber environment and cooperate with other States in their investigations [23]. As it seems possible to pinpoint at least the country of origin of a cyber-attack*—but not the individual attacker—an international public order for cyber space should be established that requires States to police and supervise their national portions in international cooperation in the case of the most serious misuses and attacks. States may be hesitant, because the required level of transparency may unveil their governmental activities in cyber space. State supervision can also be critical, when it is exercised extensively and interferes with the freedom of speech and access to information. Nevertheless, a regime built on State responsibility can be a way of lifting the cover of anonymity for criminal acts committed through cyber space. Of course, this is not a purely legal endeavor, but a policy driven value judgment for the creation of a new public order.

Automation of physical devices—Internet of Things

Characteristics

The automation of physical devices reaches beyond the automation of the collection, analysis, storage, and distribution already discussed. It comprises the command and control of physical machinery based on information inputs. Generally referred to as the *Internet of Things* it links information networks with the physical world, by exchanging information between automated physical devices and information networks. Most notably, the automation of physical *smart* devices allows to control physical features, sensors, and actuators through remote control by providing information over networks. In this context, connectivity is used not only for the transmission of command and control inputs, but also to downstream information originating from the *smart* device and thus to become another source for generating Big Data. The networked automation of physical devices spans over all sectors, including governmental and military or industrial and commercial and affects critical infrastructures of energy, transport, water, banking, healthcare, and manufacturing industry.† Increasingly critical is the spreading to personal and domestic applications, such as vehicles and homes.

* "While it's very difficult in cyber to have a 'smoking gun', so to speak, the clear paths back into servers and other mechanical devices inside of the Chinese sovereign domain remain a constant problem for us [the U.S. defense establishment]." Vice Chairman of the U.S. Joint Chiefs of Staff James Cartwright [24] at p. 153.

† States are sponsoring national initiatives on such networked, information driven industries, called "Industrie 4.0" in Germany, the "Factory of the Future" in France and Italy, and Catapult centers in the United Kingdom [25].

Automation and autonomy

A further step in automating physical devices is autonomy, a term especially used in robotics and for unmanned vehicles. It describes the ability of automated physical devices to perform tasks through their own logic processing based on preprogrammed algorithms and to react to situations based on information inputs. As autonomous operations are not dependent on remote control, they can be performed without connectivity to information networks. Nevertheless, information necessary for situational awareness may not only be derived from sensors, but also from connected networks, so that autonomous devices can be connected to information networks as well.

Affected rights

The automation of physical devices and the Internet of Things show that the effects of processed information are not limited to the information as such. The range of affected rights is reaching farther than the protection of privacy, copyright, and intellectual property. It is about the protection of fundamental rights, including the protection of life, bodily integrity, and property.* In automated environments, failures and malicious interference can result in the same effects as kinetic failures or assaults. Even though the means are different, the effects can be the same.

Legal issues

One of the principle legal issues in automated environments is the responsibility for automated systems and autonomous actions. This may sound trivial, as law is to regulate the social relations between subjects of law—natural and legal persons, whereas technology, machinery, or information processing are not legal subjects. It is the purpose of law to establish rules about how natural and legal persons handle such technologies. Human responsibility for applying technology, automated processes, and autonomous (robotic) actions is one of the cornerstones of law relating to technology. The underlying concept is simple. Humans shall not be allowed to deny their responsibility, when they engage technology.

As simple as this principle may sound, when physical devices are automated through information technologies, it becomes increasingly difficult to implement it. The reasons are a cultural divide and industrial and commercial practices during the last two decades.

The automation of physical devices is at the junction of two technological cultures: traditional (mechanical) engineering and information technologies. Mechanical engineering has a long-standing safety culture. It is the goal to

*See Articles 3, 17 of Reference 26. See also Article 2 (Right to life) of Reference 27 and Article 1 (Protection of property) of Reference 28.

release products only when they are mature and have zero or very little tolerance for defects. Big efforts are undertaken for testing and improving a product. Contrary thereto, it is a common practice in the software industry to release products quickly and fix problems later on by issuing updates. The speed of the quick market release takes priority over quality. From the outset, there was no safety mindedness in the information technology (IT) industry. In the worst-case information of the user was lost, in which case the IT industries put the onus on the users and inform them about the need to make data backups. This way, the IT industry has been trying to create a no-risk business model. At the same time, it allows quicker product cycles, higher revenue through more generations of products sold, and less engineering time and expenditure on quality and product safety precautions.

But that is not all. The business model of the IT industry also had an impact on user expectations and contractually limited the rights of users by one-sided contract and licensing terms. Originating in the United States, software warranty limitations and disclaimers that might have been held up in U.S. jurisdictions became the worldwide commercial standard, when the U.S. software business practices became the worldwide benchmark of the industry. Today it appears generally accepted that software products have limited or disclaimed warranties, even if the general private law rules on product warranty do not allow such limitations. Consumers have become used to the experience that their personal computers freeze or crash from time to time and that no plausible cause can be found. Instead, *shut-down and restart* has become part of the skill set of any participant in today's information culture who desires to resolve a computer problem.

The automation of physical devices through networked information systems changes the scene. A business practice that is deemed normal by many for information systems does not suffice for physical machinery. The safety culture of traditional (mechanical) engineering needs to be maintained, also for automated physical devices that mate information technologies and mechanical machinery.

For end-consumers, the legal aspects of this issue can at least partly be accommodated by existing product liability laws. Who sustains personal injury, death or loss of or damage to personal property due to a defective product has a compensation claim against the manufacturer and component manufactures without having to proof fault.* However, product liability laws do not solve all issues. They typically focus on private consumers and do not apply to loss of or damage to commercial property and loss of profit.† They neither establish a precautionary regime for preventing damage, nor do they create a safety culture for automated physical devices. Product liability rules

*See for example the preamble and Articles 1 and 4 of Reference 29. As a Directive, it is subject to implementation into national laws by the Member States.

†See for example Art, 9 (b)(i),(ii) of Reference 29.

furthermore do typically not apply to (information) services* and hence leave the product risk to the manufacturer of the integrated final physical product who cannot seek recourse against the information provider, should a defect originate in the information sphere.

Other issues of automated physical devices have been raised in the context of armed conflict. How do autonomous weapons systems interact and comply with the rules of armed conflict? When such a weapon system activates itself and targets objects and persons without any human intervention based on preprogrammed algorithms, this raises questions about the proper application of the principles of proportionality and distinction and about the command responsibility for the engagement of such systems [30].

Finally, the discussion of legal issues of automated environments may in the future lead to special rules about the engagement of robotics, the responsibility for these technologies and a necessary safety and security regime. This reminds of the robot rules of science fiction writings of Isaac Asimov† that seek to prevent robots to harm humans, bestow humans with the ultimate decision power over automated and autonomous processes, and seek to prevent humans to misuse this technology for harming other humans. Albeit these rules stem from science fiction novels, the practical developments of automated physical devices in recent years necessitate paying attention to such type of rules in the not too distant future.

Conclusion

A sectoral approach to the use of Big Data shows different information restrictions and sharing cultures in the governmental/military, commercial/industrial, and scientific sectors. As long as these sectors collect, process, and store their information separately, they may not encounter legal problems, provided they comply with the rules for the protection of personal information and intellectual and property rights. When these sectors share their information across sectoral borders, legal issues arise. If in the

---

*See for example Articles 2 and 3 1. of Reference 29, which defines product as *all movables* and producer as "the manufacturer of a finished product, the producer of any raw material or the manufacturer of a component part"—all definitions that do not apply to services or the provision of information.

†The three *laws* are mentioned for example in Reference 31:

1. A robot may not injure a human being or, through inaction, allow a human being to come to harm.
2. A robot must obey the orders given it by human beings except where such orders would conflict with the First Law.
3. A robot must protect its own existence as long as such protection does not conflict with the First or Second Laws.

arena of Big Data information originating from different sectors are joined, for whatever reason and purpose, embedded personal data can be distributed to unauthorized users. Also in this instance the legal protections for personal data and intellectual property need to be maintained. Rules exist to pseudonymize identified and identifiable data and to limit personal profiling—albeit not in all countries, because the legal rules on data protection and privacy are fragmented. Aside from the political endeavor to create a worldwide harmonized regime for data protection—not realistic in the foreseeable future, it is necessary to create standards for the format, the processing, and modification of metadata. Metadata are the tool for making datasets comparable and compatible, even if they originate from different sources and have undergone different kinds of processing. An example is pseudonymization. As the protection of personal data requires in certain instances that data are pseudonymized, it needs to be done in a standardized fashion to maintain the uniformity of the metadata. It may be a long way to reach this goal, but the processing of metadata could be supported by the following organizational arrangements: agents to undertake the processing of metadata (e.g., to pseudonymize it) or to safeguard the quality of data and their metadata. In the end, it is all a matter of trust.

The impact of automation spans across all areas of activities: information collection, processing, storage, distribution, and finally the automation, possibly the autonomy, of physical devices based on information inputs. This automation and autonomy of devices and machinery reaches into the physical sphere and can thus affect fundamental rights of life, the bodily integrity of persons and their property. The legal bottom line is clear. There must be human responsibility for any kind of automated or autonomous physical devices, and users must be protected against deficiencies of that technology. Located at the juncture of traditional mechanical engineering and the IT industry, the automation and autonomy of physical devices unfortunately suffers from the cultural divide between these two industries. The IT industry does not share the safety culture and reliability of mechanical engineering. With a growing segment of automated and autonomous physical devices, just think of autonomous passenger vehicles, neither the low product quality nor reliability of the IT industry is acceptable. Therefore, it will be inevitable to establish rules for IT products, integrated or stand-alone, on safety, security, quality, and reliability. Even though the end-consumer can resort to existing product liability laws in the case of damage, the IT industry may attempt to escape liability to the detriment of manufacturers of physical components. These deficiencies need to be readjusted for automated and autonomous physical devices. Sooner or later, rules for autonomous processes—robot rules—need to follow. When information controls physical devices autonomously, not only human responsibility is essential, but also minimum design and operational requirements for safeguarding the rights for life, bodily integrity and property. In automated and autonomous environments, information technologies reach new frontiers.

References

[1] Borko, H., Information science: What is it? *American Documentation*, 1968, 19, 3.

[2] Williams, M. E., Defining information science and the role of ASIS, *Bulletin of the American Society for Information Science*, 1987/1988, 14(2), 17–19.

[3] Saracevic, T., *Information Science*, 2009, in Bates, M. J. (Ed.), *Encyclopaedia of Library and Information Sciences* (3rd ed.), New York, Taylor & Francis Group, pp. 2570–2585. https://www.asist.org/about/information-science/.

[4] Ward, J. S. and Barker, A., *Undefined by Data: A Survey of Big Data Definitions.* https://arxiv.org/pdf/1309.5821.pdf (last access June 23, 2017).

[5] European Union, Regulation of the European Parliament and of the Council (EU 2016/679) on the protection of natural persons with regard to the processing of personal data and on the free movement of such data and repealing Directive 95/46/EC.

[6] Wassenaar arrangement on export controls for conventional arms and dual-use goods and technologies, final declaration of 19 December 1995 and related instruments. www.wassenaar.org (last access June 23, 2017).

[7] DiMascio, J., Future analysis, *AW&ST*, January 9–22, 2017, p. 22.

[8] Charter of fundamental rights of the European Union, 2012/C 326/02.

[9] Black, H. C., *Black's Law Dictionary* (5th ed.), St. Paul, MI, West Publishing, 1979.

[10] German Federal Constitutional Court in 1983, BVerfGE 65,1.

[11] Simitis, S., *Die informationelle Selbstbestimmung—Grundbedingung einer verfassungskonformen Informationsordnung*, NJW 1984, 398 pp.

[12] European Union, Directive 95/46/EC of the European Parliament and of the Council of 24 October 1995 on the protection of individuals with regard to the processing of personal data and on the free movement of such data.

[13] European Union, European Court of Justice (ECJ), Cases C-203/15 and C-698/15.

[14] World Intellectual Property Organization, *Patenting Software.* http://www.wipo.int/sme/en/documents/software_patents_fulltext.html (last access June 23, 2017).

[15] National Information Standards Organization, *Understanding Metadata*, p. 1. http://www.niso.org/publications/press/UnderstandingMetadata.pdf (last access June 23, 2017).

[16] International Standardization Organization (ISO), Standard 19115. http://www.iso.org/iso/iso_catalogue/catalogue_ics/catalogue_detail_ics.htm?csnumber=53798 (last access June 23, 2017).

[17] Kaiser, S. A., Legal and policy aspects of space situational awareness, *Space Policy*, 2015, 31, 5–12.

[18] Finkleman, D., Sharing space data by design, *67th International Astronautical Congress*, Guadalajara, Mexico, September 26–30, 2016, IAC-16, D5,4,5,x31844.

[19] Celestrak, http://celestrak.com (last access June 23, 2017).

[20] International Law Commission, *Draft Articles on Responsibility of States for Internationally Wrongful Acts*, UN Doc. A/RES/56/83 (2001).

[21] Treaty on principles governing the activities of states in the exploration and use of outer space, including the moon and other celestial bodies, January 27, 1967, 610 U.N.T.S. 205.

[22] Healey, J., *Beyond Attribution: Seeking National Responsibility for Cyber Attacks*, Atlantic Council, Issue Brief, January 2012. http://www.atlanticcouncil.org/images/files/publication_pdfs/403/022212_ACUS_NatlResponsibilityCyber.PDF (last access June 23, 2017).

[23] United States 112th Congress, 2nd Session (November 2012), *Activities' in 2012 Annual Report to Congress of the U.S.-China Economic and Security Commission, Section II, China's Cyber Activities*, pp. 149–151. http://www.uscc.gov/sites/default/files/annual_reports/2012-Report-to-Congress.pdf (last access June 23, 2017).

[24] European Union, European Parliament, Briefing September 2015, Industry 4.0 Digitalisation for productivity and growth. http://www.europarl.europa.eu/RegData/etudes/BRIE/2015/568337/EPRS_BRI(2015)568337_EN.pdf (last access June 23, 2017).

[25] Universal Declaration of Human Rights, GA res. 217A (III), UN Doc A/810 at 71 (1948).

[26] Convention for the protection of human rights and fundamental freedoms, Rome, 4.XI.1950.

[27] Protocol to the convention for the protection of human rights and fundamental freedoms, Paris, 20.III.1952.

[28] European Union, Product liability directive (85/374/EEC of 25 July 1985).

[29] International Law Association, Study Group Interim Report 2014, *Challenges of the 21st Century Warfare, The Conduct of Hostilities and International Humanitarian Law*, pp. 12–14.

[30] Asimov, I., *Runaway*, New York, Street & Smith, Astounding Science Fiction, 1942.

Chapter 3

Privacy as secondary rule, or the intrinsic limits of legal orders in the age of Big Data

Bart van der Sloot*

Introduction 69
Privacy, Big Data, and the need for intrinsic limits on legal orders 72
Hart's positivist and liberal position 79
Law and morality 79
The rules of change 81
The rule of adjudication 83
Conclusion 88
Privacy as intrinsic limit on legal orders 88
Necessities of life 89
Individual autonomy 92
Positive freedom 97
Conclusion 103
Wrap-up: Privacy as secondary rule 103
References 107

Introduction

Mark Twain, in his short story *My Debut as a Literary Person*, recounts the tail of a boat crew stranded on a desolate spot of land. After a few days, the men become desperate as proper food is lacking and the captain and the two passengers start scraping boot leather and wood and make a pulp of the scrapings by moistening them with water. The sailors, however, did not make pulp but started to eat strips of leather from old boots, with chips from the butter cask. When one of the mates was asked afterward about the

*Bart van der Sloot is senior researcher at the Tilburg Institute for Law, Technology, and Society (TILT), Tilburg University, Netherlands. E-mail: b.vdrsloot@uvt.nl. Room M 719, PO Box 90153, 5000 LE Tilburg, Netherlands. Tel: +31 13 466 3515.

affair, he remembered that the boots were old and full of holes, and he added thoughtfully that they were the holes that digested the best [1]. It is to such stories that legal positivists jokingly refer to indicate the positions natural law scholars: They always prefer the gaps over the legal order itself [2].

Legal positivists, at their turn, have always struggled with intrinsic limits of legal orders. They refer to these limits as *gaps*, as the silence of the law (silentium legis) or simply deny the possibility of legal *gaps* by holding that everything that is not prescribed by law must be deemed legal. Still, most, if not all, legal positivists are concerned with upholding the rule of law and protecting citizens from overarching legal orders. Hart's position on legality, for example, is very complex and ambiguous [3] and the proper limit of laws and legal orders is a recurrent topic in much of his texts. This chapter will explore Hart's ambiguous position mainly on the basis of his discussions with Devlin, and it will compare his stance with the approach he adopted in other texts, such as in *The Concept of Law,* and in his arguments with Lon Fuller.

In the Hart–Fuller debate and *The Concept of Law,* Hart defended the view that legal orders are not limited by a prelegal *outer morality*, imposed by nature or some divine being, or by what Fuller called an *inner morality*, the principles of the rule of law. Although Hart thought moral considerations to be important and held the principles of legality high, he argued that legal orders could be called legal orders even if they did not respect these principles. In other writings, such as in the famous Devlin–Hart debate, Hart defended the view that the law should be bound by limits and respect citizen's privacy. He adopted the classic liberal position that the state had no business to regulate conduct in private, except in which harm was done. Especially, Hart argued against Devlin, immorality as such, as in the case homosexual conduct, could not be a reason for criminal prosecution.

These two strands in Hart's work, which are both infused by utilitarianism, have mostly been reconciled by referring to the fact that Hart defended on the one hand that law and morals *could* be separated, the position of legal positivists, and on the other hand that law and morals *should* be separated, the liberal position that harm should be regarded as the only legitimate basis for state interference. Not in the last place, this is due to the fact that Hart himself framed his dispute with Devlin in terms of the question: "Ought immorality as such to be a crime?" [4, p. 4]. Although there are many arguments to support this distinction, there are others that suggest that these two positions sometimes overlap. Already, Fuller complained that he often found it difficult to determine whether Hart thought "the distinction between law and morality simply 'is,' or is something that 'ought to be' " [5, p. 631]. Indeed, there are some instances in which liberalism infused Hart's position as a legal positivist and vice versa. Many disagreements with Lord Devlin, for example, were not so much about what law ought to do, on what grounds legal orders should criminalize actions, and about the question whether states ought to respect the privacy of its citizens, but about positivist presumptions.

The current chapter will explore the overlaps between Hart's attack on Devlin and his writings as a positivist and argue that there are reasons to believe that the protection of the private sphere, for Hart, is not only something that governments ought to do, but that legal orders must do. This is important because the current privacy paradigm is focused on the individual in multiple ways. In short, it grants natural persons a subjective right to invoke their right before court when they feel that their private interests have been infringed. This is problematic because in the age of Big Data, there are simply so many data collection processes going on that it becomes impossible for an individual to assess each and every time whether a data processing initiative contains his data, if so, whether the data processing is correct and if not, go to court. Moreover, even if an individual goes to court, it is increasingly difficult to specify how a Big Data initiative has harmed the specific interests of that individual. For example, what concrete negative effect did the mass data collection by the National Security Agency (NSA) have on the ordinary American or European citizen? The point is that what is at stake with these types of processes is often not the individual interest of particular citizens, but rather the abuse of power by the state as such.

Seeing privacy as an intrinsic limit on governmental policies could provide a theoretical foundation for such an alternative approach to privacy regulation, in which privacy protection is aligned in part to the principles of the rule of law, which the state needs to respect as a minimum condition for exercising power, even if there are no concrete individual interests at stake. This might ameliorate privacy protection, because right now, it is often difficult to address more systematic and systemic privacy infringements. These infringements do not directly affect a personal interest or undermine an individual right by a specific person. That is why the rights-based approach to privacy often is unable to provide satisfying answers to modern privacy questions. Consequently, many authors have tried to find alternatives for the rights-based approach to privacy, in which the focus is not on the individual, his rights and his interests, but on the actor, the one engaging in a privacy infringement. The problem is, however, finding a suitable ground and theoretical basis for such an approach. This chapter will argue that such a basis may be found in the legal positivist writing of H.L.A. Hart.

The current chapter will argue, in short, that such a theoretical foundation can be found in the work of H.L.A. Hart. First, this chapter will elaborate a bit further on why this discussion is of relevance for the current privacy debate (section "Privacy, Big Data and the need for intrinsic limits on legal orders"). After that, the chapter will proceed with the first main argument (section "Hart's positivist and liberal position") that runs as follows: Hart's attack on Devlin was based partially on the suggestion that law and morals could be separated (section "Law and morality"); Devlin's position conflicted with Hart's rules of changes, spelled out in *The Concept of Law* as one of the minimum conditions of legal orders (section "The rules of change"); and with Hart's positivist account on the proper position of the judiciary (section "The rule of adjudication"); followed by a small conclusion (section "Conclusion"). Then, this chapter will proceed with the second main argument (section "Privacy as intrinsic limit on legal orders"), which is that there are intrinsic limits on legal orders in Hart's writings and that they relate to elements of the right to privacy, such as physical privacy (section "Necessities of life"); informational privacy (section "Individual autonomy"); and decisional privacy (section "Positive freedom"); followed by a small conclusion (section "Conclusion"). Finally, the wrap-up will argue that the minimum conditions of legal orders could ameliorate the current protection of privacy (section "Wrap-up: Privacy as secondary rule").

Privacy, Big Data, and the need for intrinsic limits on legal orders

It is impossible to give an exhaustive overview of the current privacy regulation in Europe.* Instead, this section will focus on the protection of the right to privacy in the most dominant discourse, namely that of the European Convention on Human Rights, Article 8, which contains the right to privacy. This description focuses on the approach of the European Court of Human Rights when dealing with cases under this article, but the general point, namely that the right to privacy is interpreted as a subjective right of natural persons to protect their individual interests, holds true for most privacy doctrines in Europe. Under the European Convention, the right to privacy is focused on the individual in many ways. To successfully submit an application, a complainant must of course have exhausted all domestic remedies; the application should be submitted within the set time frame, and it must fall under the competence of the court. But more importantly, the applicant needs to demonstrate a personal interest, that is, individual harm following from the violation complained of. This is linked to the notion of ratione personae, the question whether the claimant has individually and substantially suffered from a privacy violation, and in part to that of ratione materiae, the question whether the interest said to be interfered falls under the protective scope of the right to privacy. This focus on individual harm and individual interests brings with it that certain types of complaints are declared inadmissible by the European Court of Human Rights, which means that the cases will not be dealt with in substance.†

The so-called *in abstracto* claims are in principle declared inadmissible. These are claims that regard the mere existence of a law or a policy, without necessarily having any concrete or practical effect on the claimant. "Insofar as

---

*This section is partly based on References 6 and 7.

†http://www.echr.coe.int/Documents/Admissibility_guide_ENG.pdf.

the applicant complains in general of the legislative situation, the Commission recalls that it must confine itself to an examination of the concrete case before it may and may not review the aforesaid law *in abstracto*. The Commission therefore may only examine the applicant's complaints insofar as the system of which he complains has been applied against him."* A priori claims are rejected as well, as the Court will usually only receive complaints about injury that has already materialized. *A contrario* claims about future damage will in principle not be considered. "It can be observed from the terms 'victim' and 'violation' and from the philosophy underlying the obligation to exhaust domestic remedies provided for in Article 26 that in the system for the protection of human rights conceived by the authors of the Convention, the exercise of the right of individual petition cannot be used to prevent a potential violation of the Convention: in theory, the organs designated by Article 19 to ensure the observance of the engagements undertaken by the Contracting Parties in the Convention cannot examine—or, if applicable, find—a violation other than a posteriori, once that violation has occurred. Similarly, the award of just satisfaction, that is, compensation, under Article 50 of the Convention is limited to cases in which the internal law allows only partial reparation to be made, not for the violation itself, but for the consequences of the decision or measure in question which has been held to breach the obligations laid down in the Convention."†

Hypothetical claims regard damage that might have materialized, but about which the claimant is unsure. The court usually rejects such claims because it is unwilling to provide a ruling on the basis of presumed facts. The applicant must be able to substantiate his claim with concrete facts, not with beliefs and suppositions. The European Court of Human Rights (ECtHR) will also not receive an actio popularis, a case brought up by a claimant or a group of claimants, not to protect their own interests, but to protect those of others or society as a whole. These types of cases are better known as class actions. "The Court reiterates in that connection that the Convention does not allow an actio popularis but requires as a condition for exercise of the right of individual petition that an applicant must be able to claim on arguable grounds that he himself has been a direct or indirect victim of a violation of the Convention resulting from an act or omission which can be attributed to a Contracting State."‡

Furthermore, the court has held that applications are rejected if the injury claimed following from a specific privacy violation is not sufficiently serious, even though it does fall under the scope of Article 8 European Convention on Human Rights (ECHR). This can also be linked to the more recent introduction of the so-called *de minimis* rule in the convention, which provides that a claim will be declared inadmissible if "the applicant has not suffered

---

*ECmHR, Lawlor v. the United Kingdom, application no. 12763/87, July 14, 1988.

†ECmHR, Tauira and others v. France, application no. 28204/95, December 4, 1995.

‡ECtHR, Asselbourg and 78 others and Greenpeace Association-Luxembourg v. Luxembourg, application no. 29121/95, June 29, 1999.

a significant disadvantage."* With environmental issues, for example, it has been ruled that if the level of noise is not sufficiently high, it will not be considered an infringement on a person's private life or home.† Similarly, although data protection partially falls under the scope of Article 8 ECHR, if only the name, address, and other ordinary data are recorded about an applicant, the case will be declared inadmissible, because such "data retention is an acceptable and normal practice in modern society. In these circumstances, the Commission finds that this aspect of the case does not disclose any appearance of an interference with the applicants' right to respect for private life ensured by Article 8 of the convention."‡ Moreover, an interference might have existed that can be substantiated by the applicant and that was sufficiently serious to fall under the scope of Article 8 ECHR. Still, if the national authorities have acknowledged their wrongdoing and provided the victim with sufficient relief and/or retracted the law or policy on which the violation was based, the person can no longer claim to be a victim under the scope of the convention [8,9].

Then, there is the material scope of the right to privacy, Article 8 ECHR. In principle, it only provides protection to a person's private life, family life, correspondence, and home. However, the court has been willing to give a broader interpretation. As discussed in the introduction, it has held, *inter alia*, that the right to privacy also protects the personal development of an individual; it includes protection from environmental pollution and may extend to data protection issues.§ Still, what distinguishes the right to privacy from other rights under the convention, such as the freedom of expression, is that it only provides protection to individual interests. Although the freedom of expression is linked to personal expression and development, it is also connected to societal interests, such as the search for truth through the market place of ideas and the well-functioning of the press, a precondition for a liberal democracy. By contrast, Article 8 ECHR, in the dominant interpretation of the ECtHR, only protects individual interests, such as autonomy, dignity, and personal development (in literature, scholars increasingly emphasize a public dimension of privacy). Cases that do not regard such matters are rejected by the court.¶

This focus on individual interests also had an important effect on the types of applicants that are able to submit a complaint about the right to privacy. The convention, in principle, allows natural persons, groups of persons, and

---

*Article 35 paragraph 3 (b) ECHR.

†ECmHR, Trouche v. France, application no. 19867/92, September 1, 1993. ECmHR, Glass v. the United Kingdom, application no. 28485/95, October 16, 1996.

‡ECmHR, Murray v. the United Kingdom, application no. 14310/88, December 10, 1991.

§See among others: ECtHR, Leander v. Sweden, application no. 9248/81, March 26, 1987. ECtHR, Amann v. Switzerland, application no. 27798/95, February 16, 2000. ECtHR, Rotaru v. Roemenia, application no. 28341/95, May 4, 2000. See also: http://www.echr.coe.int/Documents/FS_Data_ENG.pdf.

¶See for one of the earliest examples of the broadening scope of Article 8 ECHR: ECmHR, X. v. Iceland, application no. 6825/74, May 18, 1976.

legal persons to complain about an interference with their rights under the convention. Indeed, the court has accepted that, under certain circumstances, churches may invoke the freedom of religion (Article 9 ECHR) that press organizations may rely on the freedom of expression (Article 10 ECHR) and that trade unions are admissible if they claim the freedom of assembly and association (Article 11 ECHR). However, because Article 8 ECHR only protects individual interests, the court has said that, in principle, only natural persons can invoke a right to privacy. For example, when a church complained about a violation of its privacy by the police in relation to criminal proceedings, the commission found that "[t]he extent to which a non-governmental organization can invoke such a right must be determined in the light of the specific nature of this right. It is true that under Article 9 of the Convention a church is capable of possessing and exercising the right to freedom of religion in its own capacity as a representative of its members and the entire functioning of churches depends on respect for this right. However, unlike Article 9, Article 8 of the Convention has more an individual than a collective character []."* This led the commission to declare the complaint inadmissible, a line that has been confirmed in the subsequent case law of the court and that it is willing to leave only in exceptional cases.† Groups of natural persons claiming a Convention right are also principally rejected by the court and the possibility of interstate complaints (Article 33 ECHR) is seldom practiced [11]. This leaves only the individual to submit a complaint about a breach of the right to privacy.

Consequently, the current privacy paradigm focuses largely on the individual, his interests, and his subjective right to protect those individual interests. In the field of privacy, the notion of harm has always been problematic as it is often difficult to substantiate what harm has been caused by a particular violation; what harm, for example, follows from entering a home or eavesdropping on a telephone conversation when neither objects have been stolen nor private information has been disclosed to third parties? Even so, the traditional privacy violations (house searches, telephone taps, etc.) are clearly demarcated in time, place, and person, and the effects are, therefore, relatively easy to define. In the current technological environment, with developments such as Big Data, however, the notion of harm is becoming increasingly problematic. An individual is often simply unaware that his or her personal data are gathered by either fellow citizens (e.g., through the use of smartphones), by companies (e.g., by tracking cookies), or by governments (e.g., through covert surveillance). Obviously, people who are unaware of their data being gathered will not invoke their right to privacy in court.

Even if people were aware of these data collections, given the fact that data gathering and processing is currently so widespread and omnipresent and

*ECmHR, Church of Scientology of Paris v. France, application no. 19509/92, January 9, 1995.

†See among others: ECtHR, Stes Colas Est and others v. France, application no. 37971/97, April 16, 2002. See in more detail: B. van der Sloot [10].

will become even more so in the future, it will quite likely be impossible for them to keep track of every data processing that includes (or might include) their data to assess whether the data controller abides by the legal standards applicable, and if not, to file a legal complaint. Moreover, if individuals go to court to defend their rights, they have to demonstrate a personal interest, that is, personal harm, which is a particularly problematic notion in Big Data processes: what concrete harm has data gathering by the NSA done to ordinary American or European citizens? This also shows the fundamental tension between the traditional, legal, and philosophical discourse and the new technological reality, whereas the traditional discourse focuses on individual rights and individual interests; data processing often affects a structural and societal interest and, in many ways, transcends the individual.

Finally, under the current privacy and data-protection regimes, the balancing of interests is the most common way to resolve cases. In a concrete matter, the societal interests served with the data gathering, for example, wiretapping someone's telephone because they are suspected of committing a murder is weighed against the harm that wiretapping does to their personal autonomy, freedom, or dignity. However, the balancing of interests becomes increasingly difficult in the age of Big Data, not only because the individual interest involved in a particular case is hard to substantiate but also because the societal interest at the other end is increasingly difficult to specify. It is mostly unclear, for example, in how far the large data collections by intelligence services have actually prevented concrete terrorist attacks. This balance is even more difficult if executed on an individual level, that is, how the collection of the personal data of this individual (as a nonsuspected person) has ameliorated national security. The same holds true for CCTV cameras hanging on the corners of almost every street in some cities; the problem here is not that one specific person is being recorded and that data about this identified individual are gathered, but rather that everyone in that city is being monitored and controlled. Perhaps more important is the fact that, with some of the large-scale data collections, what appears to be at stake is not a relative interest, which can be weighed against other interests, but an absolute interest. For example, the NSA data collection is so large, has been conducted over such a long time span, and includes data about so many people that it may be said to simply qualify as abuse of power. Abuse of power is not something that can be legitimated by its instrumentality toward a specific societal interest; it is an absolute minimum condition of having power.

Consequently, the current rights-based approach to privacy protection is inadequate when applied to Big Data processes. Significantly, in recent cases, the European Court of Human Rights seems to have acknowledged this fact and seems to be willing to adjust its own approach to privacy protection. In some exceptional cases, mostly regarding mass surveillance, the ECtHR has been willing to accept *in abstracto* claims. Although the court has done so for years without explicitly acknowledging the fact that, in exceptional cases, it is prepared to relax its individualized approach to privacy; it has finally made this unequivocally clear in two recent cases: *Szabó & Vissy** and especially *Zakharov.*† In *Zakharov*, the ECtHR argued as follows: "[T]he Court accepts that an applicant can claim to be the victim of a violation occasioned by the mere existence of secret surveillance measures, or legislation permitting secret surveillance measures, if the following conditions are satisfied. First, the court will take into account the scope of the legislation permitting secret surveillance measures by examining whether the applicant can possibly be affected by it, either because he or she belongs to a group of persons targeted by the contested legislation or because the legislation directly affects all users of communication services by instituting a system in which any person can have his or her communications intercepted. Second, the court will take into account the availability of remedies at the national level and will adjust the degree of scrutiny depending on the effectiveness of such remedies. As the court underlined in *Kennedy*, in which the domestic system does not afford an effective remedy to the person who suspects that he or she was subjected to secret surveillance, widespread suspicion, and concern among the general public that secret surveillance powers are being abused cannot be said to be unjustified. In such circumstances, the menace of surveillance can be claimed in itself to restrict free communication through the postal and telecommunication services, thereby constituting for all users or potential users a direct interference with the right guaranteed by Article 8. There is therefore a greater need for scrutiny by the court and an exception to the rule, which denies individuals the right to challenge a law *in abstracto,* is justified. In such cases, the individual does not need to demonstrate the existence of any risk that secret surveillance measures were applied to her. By contrast, if the national system provides for effective remedies, a widespread suspicion of abuse is more difficult to justify. In such cases, the individual may claim to be a victim of a violation occasioned by the mere existence of secret measures or of legislation permitting secret measures only if he is able to show that, due to his personal situation, he is potentially at risk of being subjected to such measures."‡

Although this development seems laudable in terms of concrete protection, the question is how this approach relates to the dominant approach to privacy cases, as discussed earlier. What is left for the court to assess in *in abstracto* cases is the mere quality of laws and policies as such, and the question is whether this narrow assessment is still properly addressed under a human rights framework. The normal assessment of the court revolves around, roughly, three questions that are as follows: (1) Has there been an infringement of the right to privacy of the claimant? (2) Is the infringement prescribed by law? and (3) Is the infringement necessary in a democratic society in terms of, *inter alia*, national security—that is, does the societal interest in this particular case outweigh the individual interest (balancing test). Obviously, the first question does not apply to *in abstracto* claims because there

*ECtHR, Szabó and Vissy v. Hungary, application no. 37138/14, January 12, 2016.
†ECtHR, Roman Zakharov v. Russia, application no. 47143/06, December 4, 2015.
‡Zakharov, §171.

has been no infringement with the right of the claimant. The third question is also left untouched by the court, because it is impossible, in the absence of an individual interest, to weigh the different interests involved. This means of course that another of the court's principles, namely that it only decides on the particular case before it, is also overturned.

Even the second question—whether the infringement is prescribed by law—is not applicable as such, as there is no infringement that is or is not prescribed by law. Although the court regularly determines in cases, *inter alia*, whether the laws are accessible, whether sanctions are foreseeable, and whether the infringement at stake is based on a legal provision; this does not apply to *in abstracto* claims. There is often a law permitting mass surveillance (that is exactly the problem), and these laws are accessible and the consequences are foreseeable (in the sense that everyone will be affected by it). Rather, it is the mere quality of the law as such that is assessed; the content of the law, the use of power as such, may be deemed inappropriate. The question of abuse of power can of course be addressed by the court, though not under Article 8 ECHR, but under Article 18 of the convention, which specifies: "The restrictions permitted under this Convention to the said rights and freedoms shall not be applied for any purpose other than those for which they have been prescribed." But, as the court has stressed, this provision can only be invoked if one of the other convention rights are at stake. Reprehensible as the abuse of power may be, there are arguments for saying that it is only proper to address this question under a human rights framework if one of the human rights contained therein will be or has been violated by the abuse. The court cannot assess the abuse of power as such (a doctrine that it also applies to, inter alia, Article 14 ECHR, the prohibition of discrimination).

However, what is assessed in cases in which *in abstracto* claims regarding surveillance activities have been accepted is precisely the use of power by the government as such, without a specific individual interest being at stake. Accepting *in abstracto* claims and assessing the legality and legitimacy of laws as such seems to diverge in essence from the approach the ECtHR has taken to the right to privacy for a long time. No individual interests of natural persons are the core of these types of cases, but general interests in relation to the legitimacy and legality of laws. The cases are not about individual rights, but more on the intrinsic limits on legal orders, with respect to, inter alia, the abuse of power. The problem is that the theoretical foundation for such an approach is lacking.

The current chapter develops such a theoretical basis by turning to legal positivism. The reason for this choice is that legal positivism, in contrast to natural rights defenders, has traditionally opposed intrinsic limits of laws and legal orders. Although natural rights theories have stressed that laws and legal order that violate inalienable human rights may be deemed illegitimate or invalid, legal positivist usually claim that a law is a law, even if its content is immoral or undesirable. Consequently, if it can be shown that even for legal positivists, there are certain absolute and inviolable principles that can never be infringed, such as with respect to the safeguards against the abuse of power and for the respect of individual autonomy; the case for intrinsic limits on legal orders is much stronger than when reference is only made to natural law philosophies. It is impossible to give a general account of legal positivism; that is, why this chapter will focus on one of the most prominent defenders of this branch of legal philosophy, namely H.L.A. Hart.

Hart's positivist and liberal position

This section will discuss Hart's approach to the right to privacy, individual autonomy, and the respect for the private sphere. The defense of these aspects is common to liberal politicians and philosophers alike. Hart's position has consequently often been interpreted as sprouting primarily from his political opinions. This would mean that his defense of these aspects would rely on his personal opinion about what the legal order should prohibit or not, how far it should go or not in enforcing the rules in the private sphere, and so on. This section will argue, however, that Hart's position and his defense of the different aspects of the right to privacy is based to a considerable extent not on his views as a liberal, but on his position as a legal positivist. Many of his arguments rely on the description of what laws and legal orders are, not on what they should be.

Law and morality

This section will briefly touch upon the debate between Hart and Fuller on the separability of law and morality and show that this debate was revived when Devlin and Hart discussed the Wolfenden report, which proposed to ban the criminalization of homosexual conduct [12]. (1) Hart's classic argument as a legal positivist will be indicated by briefly recounting the position he took in *The Concept of Law* and *Positivism and the Separation of Law and Morals.* (2) Fuller's response on this matter will be discussed by reference to his reply to the latter article in *Positivism and Fidelity to Law* and his book *The Morality of Law.* (3) It will be argued that Devlin, in his defense for a prohibition on homosexual conduct in *The Enforcement of Morals*, relied in part on the thesis that law and morals were inseparable. (4) Hart, in *Law, Liberty, and Morality,* rejected the criminalization of homosexual conduct between consenting adults in private in part on the basis of a reformulation of his positivist position.

1. It is not necessary to discuss in depth about Hart's position as a legal positivist, as its general assumptions are well known. Hart, building on the utilitarian doctrine of Bentham and Austin, suggested that laws and morals are separable. It is important to note that Hart did not suggest

that legal orders and morality, as a matter of fact, are detached or that they should be separated [13, p. 601]. Hart's position could be best described as a separability thesis, which is the claim "that there exists at least one conceivable rule of recognition (and therefore on possible legal system) that does not specify truth as a moral principle among the truth conditions for any proposition of law" [14]. The thesis that law and morals are separable, at least in theory, is mainly targeted at defenders of the natural law doctrine, who suppose that there is a prelegal morality, either installed by nature or by God, to which the legal order must commit itself. Hart contended, for example, that bad laws, such as those of the Nazi regime, were in fact laws, though they may be immoral [15].

2. Fuller, against Hart, argued that there are minimum qualities that laws must abide by. These were not prelegal moral norms, such as natural law philosophers would suggest, but what he called standards of the *inner morality* of law. These were in fact elements of the rule of law, such as the requirement that laws must be clear, general, noncontradictory, followable, publicized, stable, and nonretroactive [16]. Fuller argued that legal orders must not be merely approached as factual objects, but as purposive enterprises. Legal orders are made by men for a purpose, and they aim at certain general, societal goals. Furthermore, legal orders, as such, are installed to ensure order. As an end in itself and as an instrument to reach these societal goals, laws must abide to the minimum standards of the rule of law. Without respecting this *inner morality*, among others, citizens cannot take into account the norms the laws provide, because they do not know them and cannot follow them. Consequently, neither can law bring order nor can the societal goals be reached [17]. Hart's opposition to this suggestion, namely that these principle are not moral principles but principles of efficient legal orders, will be analyzed in a later section.

3. As opening statement to his argument that society had a right to criminalize homosexual conduct, Devlin argued that, in fact, many of the legal doctrines in law reflected some sort of morality. The penalization of rape, he argued, could be legitimately seen as a reformulation of the Millian harm principle, as this was conducted against the will of the victim and caused harm.* With the prohibition of murder or euthanasia, however, a different aspect played a role. Even if a person consented to being murdered, the murderer would commit a crime. "Euthanasia or the killing of another at his own request, suicide, attempted suicide and suicide pacts, dueling, abortion, incest between brother and sister, are all acts which can be done in private and without offence to others and

* "That the only purpose for which power can be rightfully exercised over any member of a civilized community, against his will, is to prevent harm to others."

need not involve the corruption or exploitation of others" [18, p. 7;19]. Similarly, Devlin argued, there are many concepts in family law that are based on moral sentiments, such as the protected status of marriage and the prohibition of polygamy. He argued that in many instances, the function of the law is "simply to enforce a moral principle and mothering else" [18, p. 7].

4. Hart reclaimed his positivist position on this point and argued that it was possible to separate laws and morals. First, he denied that the only explanation for the examples cited by Devlin was the enforcement of morals. With reference to Mill, Hart distinguished policies that were inspired by the concern to make the subject happier (paternalism), and policies that were inspired simply by the fact that in the opinion of others certain conduct would be right (the enforcement of morals). Hart argued that the examples suggested by Devlin could also be seen as a matter of paternalism. "The rules excluding the victim's consent as a defence to charges of murder or assault may perfectly well be explained as a piece of paternalism, designed to protect individuals against themselves" [4, p. 31].

Second, Hart argued that even if these examples were based on moral sentiments, this proves nothing. "The importance of this feature of the question is that it would plainly be no sufficient answer to show that in fact in some society—our own or others—it was widely regarded as morally quite right and proper to enforce, by legal punishment, compliance with the accepted morality. No one," Hart continues, "who seriously debates this question would regard Mill as refuted by the simple demonstration that there are some societies in which the generally shared morality endorses its own enforcement by law, and does so even in those cases where the immorality was thought harmless to others" [4, pp. 17–18]. Hart argued that even if Devlin was right in suggesting that the examples he gave regarded in fact the enforcement of morality and even if Devlin could show that most or even all societies enforced morality, this does not prove a necessary connection.*

The rules of change

The last section showed that part of Hart's attack on Devlin was based on a reformulation of his positivist suggestion that law and morality are separable, at least in principle. This section will build on that position and argue that Hart not only defended the separability thesis in his debate with Devlin, but also the so-called rules of change. (1) Devlin's argument in *The Enforcement of Morals* is that societies can be defined by the shared morality at a given

*Hart also attacked Stephen, who he felt had already put forward much of the arguments proposed by Devlin [20]. Hart's attack on this point is also often based on a reformulation of his positivist stance. See among others: H. L. A. Hart [4, p. 34] and further.

moment in time. (2) Hart's reply in *Law, Liberty, and Morality* is that it does not follow from this fact that this particular morality must be maintained in absolute form. (3) It will be argued that this reply can be understood as a restatement of one of his three secondary rules, namely the rules of change that he defended in *The Concept of Law.*

1. Devlin suggested that not only societies have always based legislation on morality but also that there is a theoretical connection between law and morality, both because a society means, by definition, the commonality of moral sentiments, and because societies would dissolve without the enforcement of popular morality for "society is not something that is kept together physically; it is held by the invisible bonds of common thought" [18, p. 10]. Devlin argued that the morality that law enforces must be popular morality, which he understood as the reasonable beliefs of the larger part of society, excluding totally irrational beliefs such as that homosexuality caused earthquakes [18, pp. 8–10], but including the belief that homosexuality is a moral perversion.*

2. Hart denied his claim on three accounts. First, he argued that popular morality could survive even without it being enforced. He argued, on the one hand, that even if laws did not codify a certain commonly shared belief or feeling, this common opinion was perfectly well capable of surviving. If homosexual conduct was not criminalized and punished, for example, society at large could still retain the idea that it was a morally corrupted act. The other way around, Hart argued that although a prohibition could lead to the abstention of certain conduct, this "contributes nothing to the general sense that these practices are morally wrong" [4, p. 68]. Thus, even if the connection between society and upholding popular morality is a necessary one, the connection to law (enforcement) is not. Second, he argued that there is no empirical evidence to suggest that societies who do not enforce popular morality dissolve. Hart attacked Devlin, who had compared actions against popular morality to treason, by holding that there is no evidence "to show that deviation from accepted sexual morality, even by adults in private, is something which, like treason, threatens the existence of society" [4, p. 50].

   Finally, Hart defended the need for change, instead of preservation of popular morality, as society cannot only survive individual divergences from its prevalent morality, but profit from them [4, p. 71]. Hart referred to Devlin's position in which he "appears to move from the acceptable proposition that *some* shared morality is essential to the existence of any society to the unacceptable proposition that a society is identical with its morality as that is at any given moment of its history, so that a change in its morality is tantamount to the destruction of a society." Hart agreed with the first statement, as society could quite plausible

*Devlin also believed that it is rational for humans to live in communities [18, p. 25].

be seen as "a body of men who hold certain moral views in common. But the latter proposition is absurd. Taken strictly, it would prevent us saying that the morality of a given society had changed, and would compel us instead to say that one society had disappeared and another one taken its place. But it is only on this absurd criterion of what it is for the same society to continue to exist that it could be asserted without evidence that any deviation from a society's shared morality threatens its existence" [4, p. 51–52].

3. Why it is absurd to Hart to hold such views as Devlin did, he never made explicit. The most plausible suggestion is that it would conflict with one of his secondary rules. In *The Concept of Law*, Hart distinguished between primary and secondary rules. Primary rules are the laws and legal regulations as every society has them, which differ from state to state. Secondary rules are the necessary (nonlegal) preconditions of every legal order. Hart specified three of these secondary rules: the rule of recognition, the rules of change, and the rules of adjudication. The simplest form of a rule of change "is that which empowers an individual or body of persons to introduce new primary rules for the conduct of the life of the group, or of some class within it, and to eliminate old rules" [21, p. 95]. The rules of changes are necessary, Hart believed, to prevent societies from becoming *static*, that is, from merely enforcing one set of primary rules without changing the laws over time [21, p. 92]. This would be catastrophic to society, he argued, because changes in sentiments could not be reflected in the primary rules, and laws could not adapt to new circumstances. From this perspective, it is clear why the suggestion that a society is identical with its morality as that is at any given moment of its history, so that a change in its morality is tantamount to the destruction of a society, would be absurd to Hart. This would lead to a static society and would make the rules of change redundant. Part of what Hart found *absurd* in Devlin's suggestions is that it would conflict with the very minimum principles for legal orders he spelled out as a positivist. It seems clear that Hart's attack on Devlin was not merely inspired by the fact that societies *ought* not to remain static, but that this would be in violation of one of the preconditions of legal orders.

The rule of adjudication

This section will argue that another secondary rule, that of adjudication and the position of the judge in Hart's positivist account of legal orders, was at stake in his disagreement with Devlin. Consequently, his views as a positivist again infused his liberal arguments. (1) Hart's view on the judiciary in *The Concept of Law* and *Positivism and the Separation of Law and Morals* and (2) Fuller's reaction in the *Positivism and Fidelity to Law* will be highlighted briefly. (3) Devlin's suggestion that although laws might prohibit homosexual conduct, even in private, it should be left to the discretion of the jury to decide whether in specific cases, the rules should be enforced, will be contrasted with (4) Hart's position in *Law, Liberty, and Morality.*

1. In *The Concept of Law,* Hart regarded as one of the three secondary rules, the rule of adjudication. This rule was necessary to tackle the defect of "the *inefficiency* of the diffuse social pressure by which the rules are maintained. [] It is obvious that the waste of time involved in the group's unorganized efforts to catch and punish offenders, and the smouldering vendettas which may result from self-help in the absence of an official monopoly of 'sanctions,' may be serious" [21, p. 93]. The rule of adjudication ensures that it is clear to all who has the power to decide over disputes, on what grounds, within which limits and to what extent. It is thus closely connected to the rule of recognition, which specifies that there must be an authoritative way to determine the outcome and application of rules in specific cases [21, p. 97].

   In *Positivism and the Separation of Law and Morals,* Hart discussed at length the position of the judge. Two examples have become quite well known: that of the grudge informer and of a rule prohibiting vehicles into a public park. The latter example was used to discuss the matter of legal interpretation: what is a vehicle and what falls under its definition? Hart argued that in general, words, such as vehicle, have some standard instances in which no doubt exists about their application [22]. "There must be a core of settled meaning, but there will be, as well, a penumbra of debatable cases in which words are neither obviously applicable nor obviously ruled out" [13, p. 607]. Obviously, in these matters, judges need to interpret the rules, their aims, purposes, and meaning, and there can be discussion and indeed legitimate differences in the way rules are applied. But Hart suggests that this is only a discussion about the *correct* way to interpret the rules, which he regards as inevitable; this is something different from saying that judges have to take recourse to their private moral opinion to determine the right outcome of the case. Legal positivist have always argued for a closed legal order, in which judges cannot rely on extralegal morality, such as their private opinion, to interpret laws.

   The case of the grudge informer built on a famous example used by Gustav Radbruch [23], which regarded a German woman during the Nazi period who had notified the local authorities about the anti-Nazi remarks her husband had made to her when he returned home from the battle-front, who was then sentenced by a Nazi court.* After the war, the woman was charged with the illegal depravation of her husband's liberty, and she argued that she was obliged to do so under Nazi laws. However, the postwar court rejected her claim and argued that the statue on

*See on this topic amongst others: T. Mertens [24] and D. Dyzenhaus [25].

which she based the legitimacy of her actions "was contrary to the sound conscience and sense of justice of all decent human beings" [13, p. 619]. Hart, to the contrary, held that a law might be a law, even though it is a bad law. He did not so much oppose the punishment of the woman for her actions but thought that it should not be a matter of judiciary discretion to decide on the moral quality of laws and argued that such a conviction should have been based on a law. Although a retroactive law to this course was clearly an evil, it could be called the lesser of two evils. "Odious as retrospective criminal legislation and punishment may be, to have pursued it openly in this case would at least have had the merits of candour. It would have made plain that in punishing the woman a choice had to be made between two evils, that of leaving her unpunished and that of sacrificing a very precious principle of morality endorsed by most legal systems" [13, p. 619].

2. Fuller disagreed with Hart on both points. Regarding the case of the grudge informer, although agreeing with Hart that the best solution might have been to enact a retroactive law, he argued that, in truth, it was very dubious whether the Nazi laws could be called laws and be considered binding. He referred to the existence of secret laws, which was not published, were vague, unstable, and so on.* These laws consequently failed to meet the minimum conditions he set out for legal orders. Consequently, the laws and the legal order as such failed to meet their goal, that is, to provide action guidance to German citizens. That is why Fuller disagreed with Hart's statement that although the provisions may have promoted morally perverted goals, they were still legal provisions. According to Fuller, the fact that the laws violated the *inner morality* of the law meant that they could not be called laws or only partially so.

   Against the suggestion of Hart that judges should settle cases only by deliberating on the true meaning or correct interpretation of a rule in a specific matter, instead of taking recourse to judge-made law, Fuller argued that there are a number of cases in which the distinction between the core and the penumbra is difficult to uphold and others in which there is no *right* or objectively justifiable answer. What, he asked, if vehicles were prohibited in the park, but "local patriots wanted to mount on a pedestal in the park a truck used in World War II, whereas other citizens, regarding the proposed memorial as an eyesore, support their

*Fuller also thought that the law in the case of the grudge informer has been incorrectly applied on the private domain by the Nazi court. "This question becomes acute when we note that the act applies only to *public* acts or utterances, whereas the husband's remarks were in the privacy of his own home. Now, it appears that the Nazi courts (and it should be noted, we are dealing with a special military court) quite generally disregarded this limitation and extended the act to all utterances, private or public." "Is Professor Hart prepared to say that the legal meaning of this statute is to be determined in the light of this apparently uniform principle of judicial interpretation?" [5, p. 654].

stand by the 'no vehicle' rule?" [5, p. 663]. Would this fall within the core or the penumbra? What if, he continues, a rule made it a misdemeanor to sleep in any railway station and two persons were brought to a judge, a tramp who had brought his blanket and pillow to the station but had been arrested before he could catch sleep, and another person who, waiting for a delayed train, had dozed off? [5, p. 664]. Fuller's critique on Hart's envisaged proper role of the judiciary and the possibility to abstain from judge-made law, based on extra-legal morality, are of course explored more elaborately in Dworkin's work on hard cases [26].

3. Devlin denied principally that "there is a private realm of morality into which the law cannot enter" [18, pp. 9–10], as the Millian harm-principle could not provide an adequate rule for separating the private from the public domain because it was impossible "to settle in advance exceptions to the general rule or to define inflexibly areas of morality into which the law is in no circumstances to be allowed to enter" [18, p. 13]. Devlin denied that there were places, such as the home, which could be principally excluded from the reach of laws. This, Devlin combined with the suggestion that there are no theoretical limits on the legislation against immorality and concluded that were no necessary limits on legal orders [18, p. 14].

   But Devlin did not believe that laws should be enforced at all times at the cost of anything. Devlin argued for the criminalization of homosexual conduct, because he felt that "homosexuality is usually a miserable way of life and that it is the duty of society, if it can, to save any youth from being led into it. I think that duty has to be discharged although it may mean much suffering by incurable perverts who seem unable to resist the corruption of boys. But if there is no danger of corruption," he added, "I do not think that there is any good the law can do that outweighs the misery that exposure and imprisonment causes to addicts who cannot find satisfaction in any other way of life. Punishment will not cure and because it is haphazard in its incidence I doubt if it deters" [18, p. 5].

   Police forces, he suggested, may only restrictively enter the private domain and thus many instances of illegal conduct would pass unnoticed [18, p. 18]. Neither, Devlin said, must the law always be enforced if illegal conduct was discovered. Rather, he argued, judges and juries are often quite hesitant, and rightly so, to convict people for illegal actions that were conducted in private without causing harm [18, p. 21]. Consequently, Devlin suggested that although laws, codifying popular morality, might criminalize homosexual conduct, juries, also voicing popular morality, might in concrete circumstances choose not to convict perpetrators.

4. Hart never targets this suggestion of Devlin directly but does refer to the chilling effect that such a practice might have because people do not

know beforehand whether they will be convicted or not. Moreover, Hart rejects the approach taken by Devlin on the ground that it would lead to legal provisions that are left unenforced most of the time, either because the criminal conduct is not detected or because the law is not applied, which he found undesirable.* More importantly, he targets Devlin's suggestion on the basis that it would lead to the situation in which judges or juries would take recourse to their own moral sentiment to determine the outcome of the case, instead of applying the legal regulation. Hart does so by referring to the case of Shaw v. Director of Public Prosecutions, which regarded Shaw's publication of nude photographs of prostitutes as advertisement in the *Ladies Directory,* for which he was charged for publishing an obscene article, living on the earnings of prostitutes and for conspiring to corrupt public morals through the publication. Hart cites the following statement of one of the judges in length:

> When Lord Mansfield, speaking long after the Star Chamber had been abolished, said that the Court of King's Bench was the custos morum of the people and had the superintendency of offences contra bonos mores, he was asserting, as I now assert, that there is in that Court a residual power, in which no statute has yet intervened to supersede the common law, to superintend those offences that are prejudicial to the public welfare. Such occasions will be rare, for Parliament has not been slow to legislate when attention has been sufficiently aroused. But gaps remain and will always remain as no one can foresee every way in which the wickedness of man may disrupt the order of society. Let me take a single instance to which my noble and learned friend, Lord Tucker, refers. Let it be supposed that at some future, perhaps, early, date homosexual practices between adult consenting males are no longer a crime. Would it not be an offence if even without obscenity, such practices were publicly advocated and encouraged by pamphlet and advertisement? Or must we wait until Parliament finds time to deal with such conduct? I say, my Lords, that if the common law is powerless in such an event, then we should no longer do her reverence. But I say that her hand is still powerful and that it is for Her Majesty's Judges to play the part which Lord Mansfield pointed out to them [27].

*He seems, for example, critical about the American practice on "the inclusion among their statute of much legal lumber in the form of penal provisions no longer enforce" [4, p. 7].

Hart criticizes this conception of the judges as the *custos morum* of the people, on the basis of which they could act independently of the legal rules enacted by parliament and substitute or supplement parliamentary laws, on the basis of moral considerations, by judge-made laws. "The particular value which they sacrificed is the principle of legality which requires criminal offences to be as precisely defined as possible, so that it can be known with reasonable certainty beforehand what acts are criminal and what are not. As a result of Shaw's case, virtually any cooperative conduct is criminal if a jury consider it *ex post facto* to have been immoral" [4, p. 12]. Like in Shaw's case, Devlin's proposal would result in a wide discretion of judges and juries, marginalize the position of the legislator, and facilitate judge-made law, devised on the basis of their private moral sentiments.

Conclusion

So far the following has been shown: (1) That a part of the debate between Hart and Devlin was not so much about whether immoral conduct *ought* to be criminalized, but whether it is necessary to do so. Furthermore, Devlin's suggestions conflict with Hart's positivist writings on the (2) necessity for societies to have rules that allow for change in their set of primary rules and (3) the position of the judge and the rejection of judge-made law. These statements do not prove the point that Hart believed in the intrinsic (necessary) limitations of the law. Argument (1) only proves that Hart believed that it was not necessary to enforce moral sentiments, not that it was necessary to abstain from it. Argument (2) holds that it is impossible for societies to strictly enforce and maintain their moral sentiments at a particular moment in time, but not that it cannot (temporarily or partially) enforce popular morality. Argument (3) goes against the specific way in which Devlin thought the prohibition of homosexual conduct should be enforced, but there are many other ways to do so that might be in compliance with Hart's minimum standards of legal orders. The next section will proceed the argument that Hart did in fact accept a number of intrinsic limits on legal orders.

Privacy as intrinsic limit on legal orders

The following three subsections will argue that Hart did actually propose a number of necessary, intrinsic limits to legal orders. It will be suggested that these principles would nowadays be approached as matters of privacy. It is important to stress that it is not the goal of this chapter to give an exhaustive overview of different privacy theories, nor to subscribe to one or another approach of privacy protection. Rather, it shows that there are intrinsic limits on laws and legal orders in Hart's work, and that these limits are similar to those proposed by scholars defending the right to privacy. Three examples will be given to illustrate this point.* In the three following sections, the following points will be made: (1a) In certain privacy theories, the private domain is described as providing a place for people to discuss, experience, or hide the *necessities of life* and (1b) that the respect for these necessities provides the first intrinsic limit on legal orders in Hart's writings (section "Necessities of life"). (2a) Respect for the informational privacy is seen by many as a precondition for the autonomy of citizens and (2b) in Hart's system, the autonomous citizen is a minimum condition for legal orders (section "Individual autonomy"). (3a) Decisional privacy is often connected to the capacity of humans to pursue their preferred form of positive freedom, and (3b) the respect for the decisional capacity of humans is a minimum condition for legal orders in Hart's writings (section "Positive freedom").

Necessities of life

(1a) One of the theories that has been historically influential is the private domain functions as a place where the *necessities of life* can be hidden. For centuries, man has been regarded as half-god half-animal, with the *divine* capacities of rationality, speech, and moral reflection and the natural necessity to eat, drink, sleep, defecate, and, arguably, have sex. Although the public domain was dominantly reserved for the former functions of human life, the latter were banned to the private domain. In public, men could be free, whereas in private, they were unfree, bound by the necessities of their animal descend.† Hannah Arendt, among others, has tried to provide a reformulation of this aspect of privacy, in her thoughts on the political action [30, p. 30]. In this philosophy, the household is regarded as prepolitical, as a sphere of bare life, where justice and laws have no meaning as justice is only relevant in which man has a choice to do or abstain from certain conduct [30, p. 34].

Although the idea of an absolutely separated sphere is no longer feasible, in privacy literature, the principled separation of the private domain from the public, until reasons are provided that legitimate interferences (e.g., signals to suggest the use of violence), reserves a dominant position.‡ This branch of physical privacy can also be found in most legal orders, in which it is protected as a matter of bodily integrity and the sanctity of the home. For example, the European Convention on Human Rights provides that everyone has the right to respect his home and that there shall be no interference by a public authority with the exercise of this right except such as is in accordance with the law and is necessary in a democratic society in the interests of national security,

*These relate to the tripartite division of privacy theories made in Reference 28, p. 9.

†Among others, such a formulation of the private sphere may be found in Aristotle's Politica [29].

‡See for a full oversight of the different privacy theories: D. J. Solove [31].

public safety, or the economic well-being of the country, for the prevention of disorder or crime, for the protection of health or morals, or for the protection of the rights and freedoms of others.* It should also be recalled that in most, if not all, legal orders, there are laws that ban bodily activities, such as sleep, defecation, and sex, from the public domain.†

A private domain, such as the house, separated from the public domain in which laws and justice are applied, according to this branch of privacy theory, is essential because it is necessary to retract bodily actions from rules that presuppose choice. It might perhaps be argued that there is no logical connection between the necessities of life and the respect for privacy. Perhaps, theoretically, one could envisage a society in which all defecation, eating, drinking, and sex were done in public and legally allowed. It is, however, a fact of life and a historical (and perhaps social) datum that such a society has never existed. Even in the most communal societies, sexual activities are often committed in private, in the dark, and in silence, and even in societies where communal defecation is accepted, separate locations are reserved for this practice, and there are social norms that guarantee at least the suggestion of a personal space, such as pretending to not hear the other while he is having sex or defecating [32]. The public domain is the sphere of solidarity and choice; there are certain natural drifts that are not rational, which humans exercise no control over. These are consequently beyond the reach of law, which presupposes choice and a free will.

(1b) One of Fuller's minimum qualities of legal orders was that laws must be followable. For Hart too, this element played an important role. In his *Concept of Law,* he specified, besides the three secondary rules, a couple of minimum conditions of legal orders, namely that laws must be general, that legal orders must contain restrictions on the free use of violence, theft, and deception, "to which human beings are tempted but which they must, in general, repress, if they are to coexist in close proximity to each other" [21, p. 91], and that in general, the laws must be obeyed [21, p. 92]. This latter point is reformulated when Hart argues that there are "two minimum conditions necessary and sufficient for the existence of a legal system. On the one hand, those rules of behavior which are valid according to the system's ultimate criteria of validity must be generally obeyed, and, on the other hand, its rules of recognition specifying the criteria of validity and its rules of change and adjudication must be effectively accepted as common public standards of official behavior by its officials. The first condition is the only one which private citizens *need* satisfy: they may obey each 'for his part only' and from any motive whatever; though in a healthy society they will in fact often accept these rules as common standards of behavior and acknowledge an obligation to obey them, or even trace this obligation to a more general obligation to respect the constitution" [21, pp. 116–117].

---

*Article 8 ECHR.

†See also Article 2 & 3 ECHR.

Devlin, as has already been explained, argued for the criminalization of homosexual conduct but did not feel that the provisions should be enforced at the cost of anything. Hart had difficulties with this approach, because it would mean that legal regulations would in many instances not be obeyed. This critique relied on the specific way Devlin suggested to enforce such a provision. But on a more abstract level, without a victim and without the state being able to constantly control the private domain, it is unlikely that much of the homosexual *offenses* would come to the attention of the police. It is very unlikely that if person A and B would conduct illegal homosexual practices in private, one of them would go to the police as he would admit the illegal conduct himself. Moreover, as a matter of proof, in the unlikely circumstance that person A did go to the police, person B could simply deny that such practice had taken place, and the police would have insufficient evidence for subsequent actions. As a consequence, laws would remain mostly a dead letter.

There is another reason to believe that such regulations would not be obeyed, namely that it is impossible for people to successfully repress their natural instincts. "Unlike sexual impulses," Hart suggests, "the impulse to steal or to wound or even kill is not, except in a minority of mentally abnormal cases, a recurrent and insistent part of daily life. Resistance to the temptation to commit these crimes is not often, as the suppression of sexual impulses generally is, something which affects the development or balance of the individual's emotional life, happiness, and personality" [4, p. 22]. On other occasions in *Law, Liberty, and Morality,* Hart distinguishes between the enforcement of morals and the enforcement of sexual morality and made reference to the "difficulties involved in the repression of sexual impulses" [4, p. 22].

Although Hart stressed that internalization of rules and the coercion of laws through chilling effects are not only a valuable, but an indispensable aspect of law enforcement, with regard to sexual morals, he questioned their beneficial effects [4, p. 43]. It should be underlined that, for example, a rule only validating monogamous, heterosexual marriages is different for two reasons. One, it does not regard the natural inclination as such, but only the way in which it is publicly recognized. Two, it leaves open one (very common) way of publicly recognizing a sexual relationships. This is of course different for the prohibition of homosexual conduct, which does regard the restriction of sexual instincts as such and does not (realistically) leave open a legitimate way to explore and use sexual freedom.*

A substantive part of the population has homosexual inclinations, and these inclinations cannot be suppressed. This conflicts with Hart's requirement that in a valid legal order, the laws must be followed by most of the people most of the time, as a prohibition of homosexual conduct would lead to significant disobedience. This also holds true for the other *necessities of life.* A law prohibiting the intake of water and other fluids would surely not be obeyed by the bulk of the people most of the time. People would rather risk punishment

*See for similar remarks: H. L. A. Hart [4, p. 43].

than choose a certain death. It would also be clearly absurd if a society must, as a minimum condition, pose restrictions on violence and murder but, at the same time, would be at liberty to effectively kill its entire population.

The necessities of life may thus safely be called one of the intrinsic limits of legal orders in Hart's philosophy. Again, it should be stressed that there is no absolute connection between this fact and the respect for the private domain. Theoretically, it would be possible to say that the intake of fluids is prohibited everywhere (including the private domain), except for in the central park. Even if this were a feasible way to formulate rules, the fact would remain that people would surely be inclined to break the law in private areas over which the state has limited control and the state would have to pursue the impossible task of subjecting the private domain in total to public scrutiny to avoid mass disobedience.* Moreover, for sexual activities, it would be dubious whether people would accept the rule to only copulate in the central park. Given the fact that legal positivists determine whether a law is a law not on the basis of moral considerations, such as natural law philosophers propose, but on the basis of the question of whether the law is followed and respected or not, laws can simply not lay down severe restriction with respect to the necessities of life nor fully subsume the private sphere.

Individual autonomy

(2a) One of the constant arguments in privacy theory is the suggestion that the protection of privacy is necessary for the development of autonomous individuals. Already Mill, in the wake of Humboldt, thought the state should respect certain limits to allow every individual to develop his personal identity to the fullest. This was not only essential to the personal happiness of the citizens, but the diversity in characters and pluriformity in opinions was considered a necessary precondition for prosperous and thriving societies. Humboldt, for example, suggested that the true end of man "is the highest and most harmonious developments of his powers to a complete and consistent whole. Freedom is the first and indispensable condition which the possibility of such a development presupposes; but there is besides another essential—intimately connected with freedom, it is true—a variety of situations" [33]. Mill, although rephrasing this ideal in utilitarian terms, admitted "it must be utility in the largest sense, grounded on the permanent interest of man as a progressive being. Those interests, I contend, authorize the subjection of

*Even if, with a reference to Hart's remarks about the Nazi laws, one might argue that laws could be called laws if they lead to the mass death of subjects, there are limits to these laws. The rule "It is prohibited to drink fluids," including the private domain must be monitored and enforced with some rigor. This needs to be done by the public officials, who by necessity must be alive to enforce the rules. Thus, the rule must be "Except for officials, it is prohibited to drink fluids." Even if such rule would not conflict with Hart's minimum demand of laws as generally formulated, it would be conflicting with Hart's conceptualization of legal orders to only have public officials and no citizens.

individual spontaneity to external control, only in respect to those actions of each which concern the interest of other people" [34].

Theories that link the respect for privacy to the development of autonomous individuals are dominant in the current privacy debate. They are defended predominantly by liberal scholars, who focus on the notion of control and informed consent of the individual. For example, Beate Roessler has built a theory around the argument that respect "for a person's privacy is respect for her as an autonomous subject" [28, p. 117]. The suggestion in these theories is that without privacy, there is no possibility for the subject to develop his own identity. If a person is constantly subjected to and scrutinized by legal and societal norms, he becomes indoctrinated and follows the rules and laws in a sheep-like manner. Only when the individual can freely experiment, develop his ideas, and engage in self-reflection, unhindered or controlled by third parties, can the individual develop his personal identity and become fully autonomous.*

This focus on control and autonomy has been predominantly, though not exclusively, developed in privacy theories that focus on the processing of and control over personal information. This entails the possibility of "controlled self-presentation and self-disclosure," forms of reputation management and the selection of those persons having access to certain personal details. Such theories take as presumption the right or moral claim of the individual to control, limit, and restrict the use of personal data. Alan Westin has for example defined privacy as the claim of individuals "to determine for themselves when, how, and to what extent information about them is communicated to others" [36]. This is linked, according to Westin, to the idea that persons should be able to shape, maintain, and alter their identity in different groups in different ways.† "The individual's sense that it is he who decides when to 'go public' is a crucial aspect of his feeling of autonomy. Without such time for incubation and growth, through privacy, many ideas and positions would be launched into the world with dangerous prematurity []" [36]. Consequently, a double correlativity is coined, privacy is necessary for individual autonomy and individual autonomy is necessary for a well-functioning democracy and a flourishing society.

(2b) The same concerns are prominent in the work of Hart. It should be recalled that in his debate with Fuller, Hart did not oppose the principles of the rule of law. He did argue against Fuller that these principles should not be regarded as moral standards, but as instruments to an effective legal order.‡ It is well known that Hart sometimes made bold statements about the necessity of respecting the autonomy or person's in legal orders. One of the more salient remarks is built on the earlier quoted suggestion of Hart that

*Critical about the relationship between autonomy and privacy is among others: E. L. Beardsley [35].

†Reference is often made to E. Goffman [37].

‡Famously, he compared it with the art of poisoning and begged the question whether efficiently murdering a person could be truly called the inner morality of poisoning [38].

legal orders have two minimum conditions, namely that most of the private citizens obey the primary rules most of the time and that the secondary rules must be effectively accepted as common public standards of official behavior by its officials, who appraise critically their own and each other's deviations as lapses [21, pp. 116–117]. With regard to the latter aspect, which Hart calls the internal point of view, he adds that in an "extreme case the internal point of view with its characteristic normative use of legal language ('This is a valid rule') might be confined to the official world. In this more complex system, only officials might accept and use the system's criteria of legal validity. The society in which this was so might be deplorably sheeplike; the sheep might end in the slaughter-house. But there is little reason for thinking that it could not exist or for denying it the title of a legal system" [21, p. 117].

Apart from this rhetoric, Hart did actually accept a number of preconditions safeguarding the autonomy of individuals as intrinsic limits of legal orders. First of all, it must be concluded that as a minimum, state officials must retain some sort of autonomy and reflexive understanding of the primary rules and secondary rules and be able to critically appraise their own and each other's behavior. It also follows from the rules of change that there must be at least one person or a group that is capable of grasping the essence of the primary rules at a given moment in time, has an understanding of the changes occurring in society, and has the capacity to change the rules accordingly. But it seems to follow from his discussion with Devlin, which Hart thought that there should actually be a quite substantial group with a different opinion than the *communis opinio*, to be able to prevent the moral community from becoming static. Similarly, it follows from the rule of adjudication that there must be a group of people who understand the meaning and essence of the primary rules and are capable of applying them to specific cases. They cannot merely act in a sheep-like manner by applying rules on cases one on one. Public officials must consequently be able to critically reflect both on the primary and on secondary rules of the legal order.

Second, it must be recalled that Hart suggested in *The Concept of Law* that as another minimum condition, legal orders must contain rules restricting the free use of violence, theft, and deception. This, to Hart, is necessary because people living together are tempted to do those things and must repress those temptations if they want to coexist in close proximity to each other. The basis of Hart's suggestion never becomes clear. Somewhat more elaborate is his remark in *Social Solidarity and the Enforcement of Morality,* in which he revisits Devlin's argument that societies must by necessity enforce morality. Hart here suggests that "the common morality which is essential to society, and which is to be preserved by legal enforcement, is that part of its social morality which contains only those restraints and prohibitions that are essential to the existence of any society of human beings whatever. Hobbes and Hume have supplied us with general characterizations of this moral minimum essential for social life: they include rules restraining the free use of violence and minimal forms of rules regarding honesty, promise keeping, fair dealing, and property" [39]. Although he feels that Devlin does not refer to this kind of morality, Hart does accept that the respect for such a common morality is a minimum quality of legal orders.

Hart does not elaborate further on this point, but significantly, in contrast to the remark in *The Concept of Law,* he includes elements of private law, such as property, honesty, fair dealing, and especially promise keeping, which needless to say, are the basis of all contract law. It is not the place here to answer the question whether it is absolutely impossible to speak of someone being *honest* or *fair* if he is a sheep-like, nonautonomous person, though it seems clear that these terms are difficult to reconcile. The protection of promise keeping, however, seems to ascertain that Hart does require some minimum form of autonomy. To promise one sack of grain in return of 100 dollar requires individual autonomy, the capacity to reflect upon one's desires, and to commit to certain terms and conditions of negotiation. The protection of respect for promise keeping presupposes the capacity of individuals to act autonomously, as surely laws cannot go so far as to prescribe in detail what individuals must promise. Enabling private contracts and protecting promise keeping are essentially different from the prohibition of murder and theft. The latter prevents certain actions and restricts the choices of individuals; the former not only facilitates the autonomous dealing of private citizens but also presupposes it.

Third and finally, Hart has written numerous works in the area of criminal law, especially about attribution and responsibility and the requirement of *mens rea.* It should be noted that this issue was also on Hart's mind when attacking Devlin. In *Law, Liberty, and Morality,* he opposed the criminalization of homosexual conduct because it did no harm to others. Hart, as a utilitarian, had in other writings already suggested that he preferred punishment that had regard for the effects and denounced with force retributive criminal theories. In *Law, Liberty, and Morality,* he argued not only against retributive theories but held furthermore that a "theory which does not attempt to justify punishment by its results, but simply as something called for by the wickedness of a crime, is certainly most plausible, and perhaps only intelligible, where the crime has harmed others and there is both a wrongdoer and a victim" [4, p. 59]. He continues that even the most faithful adherents of utilitarianism were inclined to feel that those responsible for the Auschwitz and Buchenwald crimes should be punished because what they did was wrong and not merely because of the beneficial future consequences of such punishment. "But," Hart stresses, "the strength of this form of retribution is surely dependent on there being a victim as well as an offender; for where this is the case, it is possible to conceive of the punishment as a measure designed to prevent the wrongdoer prospering when his victim suffer or have perished" [4, pp. 59–60].

It should be noted that although Hart had on many occasions opposed retributive theories, his argument here is not only about the best possible system of criminal punishment, but about the basic legitimacy of it. Hart argues that in the case of homosexual conduct, retributive theories that propose to punish people merely on the basis of a violation of the common moral sentiment, not on the basis of revenge for some harm inflicted by them, what remains is "the implausible claim that in morality two blacks make a white: that the evil of suffering added to the evil of immorality as its punishment makes a moral good" [4, p. 60]. Consequently, Hart's argument is that retributive theory applied on sexual morals is not only objectionable but is totally without foundation and indeed unintelligible. This is not yet to say that Hart would argue that legal orders cannot, as a matter of fact, apply such a system of punishment in their criminal law, but the argument does transcend the debate about the most appropriate foundation for criminal law and punishment. In his works on criminal law, there are many arguments to be found, which suggest that Hart attached great weight to the victim requirement, the concept of responsibility and *mens rea* in criminal systems. These concepts are of course linked to "a group of other protections (e.g., against retroactive, secret, and vague laws) that are afforded by the ideal known as the rule of law. It is through this ideal that the mental element in crime is connected with individual freedom" [40].

Hart, in writings on criminal law, proposed as a minimum for criminal punishment, that there must be some element of responsibility, accountability, or guilt for the harm inflicted. The autonomous person, capable of making choice and being responsible for his own actions, presupposes that law must not only see humans as mere Cartesian automata, who may be directed through stimuli and incentives, but as responsible agents capable of and accountable for their own choices. Hart, to this course, suggests that we "must cease to regard the law simply as a system of stimuli goading the individual by its threats into conformity. [] Consider the law not as a system of stimuli but as what might be termed a *choosing* system, in which individuals can find out, in general terms at least, the costs they have to pay if they act in certain ways. [T]he conception of the law simply as goading individuals into desired courses of behavior is inadequate and misleading; what a legal system that makes liability generally depend on excusing conditions [such as ignorance or insanity] does is to guide individuals' choices as to behavior by presenting them with reasons for exercising choice in the direction of obedience, but leaving them to choose" [41].

Consequently, criminal law and punishment must not only be seen as giving stimuli or incentives for individuals, they must also, as a minimum, enable and respect the choice of individuals, although it might still try to influence that choice. Individuals must retain a form of autonomy and some control over their own lives to possibly be responsible for a criminal act of have a *guilty mind.* This point is stressed again when, in his essay *Problems of Philosophy of Law* for the Encyclopedia of Philosophy, Hart writes about the rule of law and emphasizes that these "requirements and the specific value which conformity with them imparts to laws may be regarded from two different points of view. On the one hand, they maximize the probability that the conduct required by the law will be forthcoming, and on the other hand, they provide individuals whose freedom is limited by the law with certain information and assurances which assist them in planning their lives within the coercive framework of the law. This combination of values may be easily seen in the case of the requirements of generality, clarity, publicity and perspective operation. For the alternative to control by general rules of law is orders addressed by officials to particular individuals to do or to abstain from particular actions; and although in all legal systems there are occasions for such particular official orders, no society could efficiently provide the number of officials required to make them a main form of social control" [42].

Hart thus argues that such rules of law are not only instrumental to efficient law enforcement and coercion, they are also a minimum quality for legal orders because without any understanding on the part of its citizens about the purpose and essence of the rules, it would be undoable to enforce the law. Moreover, respecting a minimum form of autonomy is essential to the legal order seen as a *choosing* system, in which individuals can find out, in general terms at least, the rules that apply to them and their conduct and incorporate these matters in their decisions. Consequently, Hart did not only believe that the respect for the private sphere and the private opinions of individuals is essential for citizens to be or become autonomous and independent, as discussed in the previous section; he also makes clear that the autonomy of citizens is a precondition for a legal order.

Positive freedom

(3a) A third and final example of approaches to privacy might be found in theories that focus on what is commonly called *decisional privacy*. It relates to the freedom not so much to control certain aspects of one's life, but to engage in acts, to exert a form of positive freedom. This form of privacy may be found in many legal orders and different branches of law. The classic example is the case of Roe v. Wade, in which the Unites States Supreme Court decided that the right to abortion was protected as a part of the right to privacy under the American constitution. Judge Blackmun, on behalf of the court, held that the although the constitution did not explicitly mention any right of privacy, in previous cases, the court had been prepared to recognize a right of personal privacy by reference to the first, fourth, fifth, ninth, and tenth amendment. "These decisions make it clear that only personal rights that can be deemed 'fundamental' or 'implicit in the concept of ordered liberty,' are included in this guarantee of personal privacy. They also make it clear that the right has some extension to activities relating to marriage; procreation; contraception; family relationships; and childrearing and education. This right of privacy [] is broad enough to encompass a woman's decision whether or not to terminate her pregnancy."*

*Case references have been excluded from the citation. Supreme Court of the United States, 410 U.S. 113, Roe v. Wade, No. 70-18 Argued: December 13, 1971—Decided: January 22, 1973. http://www.law.cornell.edu/supct/html/historics/USSC_CR_0410_0113_ZO.html.

Decisional privacy is not only reflected in many legal traditions, it is also well established in privacy literature; although there, it is not so much linked to specific acts, such as abortion, procreation, and childrearing, but to the positive freedom of human agents as such. Already, Warren and Brandeis formulated "the right to privacy, as a part of the more general right to the immunity of the person,—the right to one's personality" [43]. This has spurred the question what privacy protects, separate from other commonly accepted rights, as it can be argued that it is through freedom of speech, control over property, and right to vote, amongst others, that a person experiences his individuality and develops his personality. The suggestion in this respect is that the right to privacy is linked to the right of a person as a person. Stanley I. Benn has for example argued "that a general principle of privacy might be grounded on the more general principle of respect for persons. By a *person* I understand a subject with a consciousness of himself as agent, one who is capable of having projects, and assessing his achievements in relation to them. To *conceive* someone as a person is to see him as actually or potentially a chooser, as one attempting to steer his own course through the world, adjusting his behavior as his apperception of the world changes, and correcting course as he perceives his errors" [44].

The damage suffered from a privacy violation lies both in ignoring the wishes of a person as rational chooser and in undermining his capacity to be a rational chooser, as the world around him changes without his knowledge or consent. Benn refers extensively to the dangers of surveillance, as both violate a person's wish to keep matters private, annuls zones of unfettered creation, and experiment and alters the world around the person without his knowledge. For example, Benn suggests, covert observation or spying is "objectionable because it deliberately deceives a person about his world, thwarting, for reasons that *cannot* be his reasons, his attempts to make a rational choice." It is important to note that the right to privacy in this sense is not so much seen in terms of the effective control and autonomy that a person can assert, as is prominent in informational privacy. The respect for decisional privacy is respecting a person as a person, as an agent engaging in certain activities and pursuing forms of positive freedom.*

(3b) Hart, like Fuller and Devlin for that matter, did not reserve a special position for the protection of individual, subjective rights. Hart believed that utilitarianism and fundamental rights were principally at odds [46]. In his essay *Utilitarianism and Natural Rights,* for example, he referred to the difference between Bentham, who argued fervently against the existence of prelegal rights, and Mill, who thought they could be compatible with utilitarianism. Hart believed the latter "was mistaken, for in the last resort there is an unbridgeable gap between pure Unitarianism, for which the maximization of the total aggregate general welfare or happiness is the ultimate criterion of value, and a philosophy of basic human rights, which insists on the priority

*See further on this point: S. I. Benn [45].

of principles protecting, in the case of each man, certain aspects of individual welfare and recognizing these as constraints on the maximizing aggregative principle of Utilitarianism" [47].

Although Hart objected to prelegal rights, Hart did believe societies have to respect citizens' rational capacity and ability to pursue forms of decisional freedom. In his debate with Devlin, Hart made two important statements: (1) Societies ought not to legislate on the basis of morality. (2) The private domain has a separate position from the public domain. Upon this latter point, Devlin had referred to Mill's own struggle with the question of defining harm. Mill suggested that societies might have a legitimate interest to regulate certain public indecencies—private actions, such as suicide, and actions conducted in private, such as heavy drinking—as this might have effects on public behavior, such as with alcohol infused violence. In similar vein, Devlin suggested that it is not theoretically possible to distinguish the private from the public, not only because private actions might have effects on other persons but also because it might influence society as a whole. "You may argue that if a man's sins affect only himself it cannot be the concern of society. If he chooses to get drunk every night in the privacy of his own home, is anyone except himself the worse for it? But suppose a quarter or a half of the population got drunk every night, what sort of society would it be? You cannot set a theoretical limit to the number of people who can get drunk before society is entitled to legislate drunkenness" [18, p. 14].

Hart, in *Law, Liberty, and Morality*, held that the recognition of individual liberty as a value involves, "as a minimum, acceptance of the principle that the individual may do what he wants, even if others are distressed when they learn what it is that he does—unless, of course, there are other good grounds for forbidding it. No social order which accords to individual liberty any value could also accord the right to be protected from distress thus occasioned" [4, p. 47]. He added that the regulation of public indecencies must not be confused with moral-based legislation. "Sexual intercourse between husband and wife is not immoral, but if it takes place in public it is an affront to public decency. Homosexual intercourse between consenting adults in private is immoral according to conventional morality, but not an affront to public decency, though it would be both if it took place in public. But the fact that the same act, if done in public, could be regarded both as immoral and as an affront to public decency must not blind us to the difference between these two aspects of conduct and to the different principles on which the justification of their punishment must rest" [4, p. 45]. Sexual conduct may be banned from the public domain, irrespective of it being heterosexual or homosexual, as societies need rules to ensure an orderly collective sphere, but society should not prohibit conduct in private merely upon the prevailing moral sentiment of the majority.

More importantly, however, Hart attacked Devlin's claim that society has a *right* to pass judgments on matters of morals and has a *right* to use the weapon of law to enforce it, even if it regards private conduct [18, pp. 7–8].

Hart comes back to this claim a number of times in *Law, Liberty, and Morality,* for example, when he contends that Devlin's arguments are related to morality in a dual way: They question whether the enforcement of morality is itself morally justified [4, p. 17]. What is important here, Hart argues, is that "Lord Devlin's principle that a society may take the steps required to preserve its organized existence is not itself tendered as an item of English popular morality, deriving its cogency from its status as part of our institutions. He puts it forward as a principle, rationally acceptable, to be used in the evaluation or criticism of social institutions generally. And it is surely clear that anyone who holds the question whether a society has the 'right' to enforce morality, or whether it is morally permissible for any society to enforce its morality by law, to be discussable at all, must be prepared to deploy some such general principles of critical morality" [4, pp. 19–20].

The moral right of a society to legislate on the basis of morality has thus posed itself by Devlin as an objectively or rationally determinable principle, not something that follows itself from the popular morality of the community. But Hart strongly opposes this view. When, at the end of his book, he regards the principle of democracy, he states for example that it is "fatally easy to believe that loyalty to democratic principles entails acceptance of what may be termed moral populism: the view that the majority have a moral right to dictate how all should live. This is a misunderstanding of democracy that still menaces individual liberty" [4, p. 79]. Although Hart believes that the rule of the majority is the best governmental principle, it should not be posed as a right of society to impose moral based legislation that is "beyond criticism and must never be resisted" [4, p. 79].

Hart made the exact same argument that society cannot claim a right to enforce (popular) morality, some 10 years earlier in his essay *Are there any natural rights?,* in which he famously proposed that there might be one natural right, namely the right of equal freedom, which "all men have if they are capable of choice; they have it *qua* men and not only if they are members of some society or stand in some special relation to each other" [48, p. 175;49,50]. To begin with his conclusion in this chapter, he argued that this right does not protect an individual from, for example, discrimination. "It would, for example, be possible to adopt the principle and then assert that some characteristic or behavior of some human beings (that they are improvident, or atheists, or Jews, or Negroes) constitutes a moral justification for interfering with their freedom []. It is, on the other hand, clear to me that the moral justification for interference which is to constitute a *right* to interfere (as distinct from merely making it morally good or desirable to interfere) is restricted to certain special conditions and that this is inherent in the meaning of 'a right' []. Claims to interfere with another's freedom based on the general character of the activities interfered with (e.g., the folly or cruelty of 'native' practices) or the general character of the parties ('We are Germans; they are Jews') even when well-founded are not matters of moral right or obligation" [48, pp. 189–190].

Both in this essay and in his debate with Devlin, Hart thus stressed that society does not have a *right* to legislate on the basis of moral sentiments and restrict the rights of Jews, Negroes, or homosexuals. To understand this conclusion, it must be stressed that Hart, in *Are there any natural rights?*, differentiated between two types of rights: special rights, which are directed at a specific person or group of people, and general rights, which can be invoked against everyone. Special rights are typically associated with private and contract law, such as when persons A and B agree that if A fixes B's roof he will get 100 dollars. General rights are typically associated with constitutional rights, in which there exists no special relationship between the rights holder and those who are bound to respect the rights holder's rights.

With regard to the latter rights, Hart argues that they have two important characteristics, namely that to have them is to have a moral justification for determining how another shall act, namely that he shall not interfere with his right. Second, this moral justification does not arise from the character of the particular action to the performance of which the claimant has a right. What "justifies the claim is simply—there being no special relation between him and those who are threatening to interfere to justify that interference—that this is a particular exemplification of the equal right to be free" [48, p. 188]. A rights holder has a moral justification for interfering with the freedom of others, and *vice versa*, other moral agents must thus justify and provide grounds for why, for example, the right to freedom of expression or the right to privacy needs to be restricted.

With regard to the special rights, Hart suggests that the most obvious examples are those that arise out of promises. "By promising to do or not to do something, we voluntarily incur obligations and create or confer rights on those to whom we promise; we alter the existing moral independence of the parties' freedom of choice in relation to some action and create a new moral relationship between them, so that it becomes morally legitimate for the person to whom the promise is given to determine how the promisor shall act" [48, p. 183]. Hart stresses that with regard to special rights, the identity of the parties concerned is vital to the existence of rights and that the right and obligation do not arise because the promised action has itself any particular moral quality, but because of the voluntary transaction between the parties [48, p. 184].

Hart sees rights in terms of a moral justification for limiting the freedom of another person and for determining how that person should act, for example, "you should not interfere with my right to freedom of expression," or, "you should pay me 100 dollar." Having a right also means that others must provide a moral justification for interfering with it. From this perspective, it becomes clear why Hart opposes Devlin's thesis about the *right* of a society to criminalize homosexual conduct. A society might think it is morally good, efficient, or desirable to do so, and this would not conflict with the natural right of all to be free as it has given a moral justification for interfering. But it cannot itself be regarded as a *right* to interfere. Hart suggests that this would simply be a wrong term for moral statements about the desirability of the interference with other's rights [48, p. 188]. Moreover, a right to restrict the freedom of specific persons or groups in society would require a special relationship that legitimizes and justifies the interference, though in fact, there was no promise made or other private behavior conducted from which such a special right might be inferred.

Thus, Hart suggests that Devlin is mistaken in his suggestion that society has a right to criminalize homosexual conduct. There is, however, another point that follows from Hart's argument, namely that legal orders cannot deny rational choosing agents their status as rational choosing agents. It is important to note that Hart connects the possibility of rights and corresponding obligations to the capacity of human beings as a rational agent. He argues that the very idea of general rights is that, in principle, one person has the same freedom as any other person, though it may be restricted on the basis moral considerations. This not only protects the person claiming the right as a human agent, through the respect for his freedom and the guarantee that interferences may only be conducted on the basis of a moral justification, but it also means that everyone else, who needs to respect this right, is a moral agent who must (1) take into account the rights of others when making decisions and (2) make a reasoned statement for legitimate interference with the rights of others. So too, with regard to the existence of special rights, the existence is dependent on the capacity of choice of both (or all) agents. A's right to, for example, have his roof fixed or to park his car on the land of B on the basis of an agreement implies not only that B must be capable of making choice but also that *a-priori*, A does not have a right to park his car on B's land and that B is thus an agent in the possession of equal freedom.

If a legal system or a moral code of conduct wants to incorporate any rights or obligations at all, it must thus presuppose the decisional capacity of humans to pursue their preferred forms of freedom.* The point is that even general laws restricting the rights of Jews or Eskimo's on the grounds that, for example, the latter group is more prone to violence and must thus be restricted in the use of freedom presuppose that they have an equal right to freedom that can only be restricted on the basis of a moral justification. Even in this case, the dialectic relationship between human agents and rights remains; to have a right presupposes the capacity of rational choice, and to have this capacity means that a person has a natural right [51]. But now, consider a fascist government that considers only men of Aryan blood to be moral agents with rights and duties toward one another and leaves Aryans free to treat non-Aryans as if they were animals, that is, without any special moral status [52]. Such a regime would deny the claim of a group of moral agents as moral agents, which would conflict with Hart's natural right because such a moral code does not presuppose that all men have the equal right to be free.

*Hart thinks that in theory, it would be possible to create a legal system without any rights or obligations, though this suggestion has been challenged by many.

Thus, as a minimum condition in Hart's legal order, humans as moral agents (excluding those incapable of exerting choice due to mental defects) must at least be treated as moral agents, having decisional capacities to pursue forms of positive freedom they desire.

Conclusion

The current essay has argued for the close similarities between Hart's position as a positivist and as a liberal. It showed that his debate with Devlin was based not only on the question of whether governments ought to punish immoral conduct but also about the possibility of separating law and morals, about the respect for the rules of change, and the proper position of the judge in legal orders. Subsequently, it has been argued that there are minimum principles of legal orders implicit in Hart's writings, namely the respect for the *necessities of life*, the autonomy of private individuals, and their decisional capacity to pursue their preferred forms of life. Finally, these minimum principles relate to various aspects of the right to privacy, namely physical, informational, and decisional privacy.

A couple of important points follow from these findings. First, that Hart's positions as a liberal and as a positivist have influenced each other. Second, ever since his debate with Fuller, scholars have wondered what place the principles of the rule of law have in Hart's positivist account of legal orders. This essay has shown that there are at least a few minimum principles that legal orders must respect; they are more than mere principles of effective legal orders, as Hart suggested in his reply to Fuller. These principles can be regarded as *secondary rules*. Third, from the stance of privacy protection, it is important to see that not only defenders of the natural rights' doctrine or a Fullerian middle position reserve a central position in their theories for the right to privacy and the principles of the rule of law that are connected to them, but that even a seasoned positivist such as Hart must admit these as intrinsic limits on legal orders.

Wrap-up: Privacy as secondary rule

Framing privacy as an intrinsic limit of legal orders might have an additional benefit over the current privacy framework. As has been discussed in section "Privacy, Big Data and the need for intrinsic limits on legal orders" of this chapter, the current privacy paradigm is dominantly focused on the individual, his subjective rights, and the protection of his individual interests. This approach is adequate for the more conventional privacy violations, such as house searchers, telephone taps, and body cavity searches. In these instances, the privacy infringement is targeted at an individual or a small group of natural persons. The harm or the consequences of the infringement are relatively easy to define and specify, also because the infringements are usually limited in time and location. Moreover, the individual being subjected to the privacy infringement will be mostly aware of the fact that his house is searched or his body subjected to cavity searches. As the infringements are quite limited in number, it is doable for the individual to assess whether the infringement is, according to his opinion, legal, and if not, to go to court to get a rectification or financial compensation.

In the modern world, what is often called the Big Data era, these aspects have changed dramatically. Privacy infringements are not limited to specific moments or specific groups; they affect large groups or the population as a whole and continue for long periods in time. Examples are the NSA data collection, the CCTV camera's that, in cities like London, monitor everyone walking on the streets almost constantly, and the internet monitoring that takes place through cookies, device finger printing, and other means. Moreover, most people are simply unaware when, why, and to what extent they are being monitored by the NSA, through CCTV-camera's or through internet monitoring. Moreover, there are simply so many data collections affecting a specific data subject that it becomes almost impossible for the individual to assess, with respect to each of them, whether personal data are gathered, whether this is done legitimately and if not, to go to court. In addition, if he would be aware of this fact, and if he did go to court, it would be very difficult to specify individual harm. The point, for example, with CCTV-camera's is not that they film this or that person specifically, but rather that everyone is filmed constantly. It is not a specific individual's interest that is at stake here, but a common or societal interest.

Consequently, the current privacy paradigm is well suited for addressing the more traditional privacy violations, but inadequate to tackle the infringements that follow from Big Data processes. An additional problem is that in the current paradigm, the individual interests are balanced against the interests served with the privacy infringement, such as national security, and it is often outweighed because the individual interest is so vague and abstract. What seems really to be at stake in, for example, the mass surveillance cases is not a relative interests, such as an individual interest in dignity or freedom, but an absolute, minimum interest for states to respect, namely not to abuse their powers and to lay down safeguards against the abuse of power. These are preconditions for every state to respect. It seems that in the most recent case law, the European Court of Human Rights has acknowledged this fact and has finally made explicit that, in exceptional circumstances, it will allow *in abstracto* claims.

What is assessed in cases in which *in abstracto* claims regarding surveillance activities is precisely the use of power by the government as such, without a specific individual interest being at stake. This is a test of legality and legitimacy, which is well known to countries that have a constitutional court or body, such as France and Germany. These courts can assess the *constitutionality* of national laws in abstract terms. Not significantly, the term *conventionality* (or *conventionalité* in French) has been introduced in the cases discussed.* For example, in *Michaud*, the government argued that with a previous *in abstracto* decision, the court had "issued the Community human rights protection system with a 'certificate of conventionality,' in terms of both its substantive and its procedural guarantees."† Referring to the *Michaud* judgment, among other cases, in his partly concurring, partly dissenting opinion in *Vallianatos and others v. Greece*, justice Pinto De Albuquerque explained: "The abstract review of 'conventionality' is the review of the compatibility of a national law with the Convention independently of a specific case where this law has been applied."‡

He argued that the case of *Vallianatos and others*, which revolved around the fact that the civil unions introduced by a specific law were designed only for couples composed of different-sex adults, is particularly interesting in which the Grand Chamber performs an abstract review of the *conventionality* of a Greek law, while acting as a court of first instance: "The Grand Chamber not only reviews the Convention compliance of a law which has not been applied to the applicants, but furthermore does it without the benefit of prior scrutiny of that same legislation by the national courts. In other words, the Grand Chamber invests itself with the power to examine *in abstracto* the Convention compliance of laws without any prior national judicial review." When discussing *Lenev v. Bulgaria*, the court is likewise willing to pass over the domestic legal system and act as court of first instance in cases revolving around mass surveillance. Subsequent to *Michaud* and *Vallianatos*, the term *conventionality* has been used more often,§ as well as the term *convention compatibility*, for example, in the case of *Kennedy v. the UK* discussed earlier,¶ and most likely will only gain in dominance as the court opens

*See for the use of the word also: ECtHR, Py v. France, application no. 66289/01, January 11, 2005. ECtHR, Kart v. Turkey, application no. 8917/05, July 8, 2008. ECtHR, Duda v. France, application no. 37387/05, March 17, 2009. ECtHR, Kanagaratnam and others v. Belgium, application no. 15297/09, December 13, 2011. ECtHR, M.N. and F.Z. v. France and Greece, application nos. 59677/09 and 1453/10, January 8, 2013.

†Michaud, §73. See also: ECtHR, Vassis and others v. France, application no. 62736/09, June 27, 2013.

‡ECtHR, Vallianatos and others v. Greece, application nos. 29381/09 and 32684, November 7, 2013.

§See among others: ECtHR, S.A.S. v. France, application no. 43835/11, July 1, 2014. ECtHR, Avotins v. Latvia, application no. 17502/07, February 25, 2014. ECtHR, Matelly v. France, application no. 10609/10, October 2, 2014. ECtHR, Delta Pekarny A.S. v. Czech Republic, application no. 97/11, October 2, 2014.

¶See among others: ECtHR, Animal Defenders International v. the United Kingdom, application no. 48876/08, April 22, 2013. ECtHR, Emars v. Latvia, application no. 22412/08, November 18, 2014. ECtHR, Kennedy v. the United Kingdom, application no. 26839/05, May 18, 2010. ECtHR, Mikalauskas v. Malta, application no. 4458/10, July 23, 2013. ECtHR, Sorensen and Rusmussen v. Denmark, application nos. 52562/99 and 52620/99, January 11, 2006. ECtHR, Bosphorushava Yollari Turizm ve Ticaret Anonim Sirketi v. Ireland, application no. 45036/98, June 30, 2005. ECtHR, Lunch and Whelan v. Ireland, application nos. 70495/10 and 74565/10, June 18, 2013. ECtHR, Interdnestrcom v. Moldova, application no. 48814/06, March 13, 2012.

up the convention for abstract reviews of laws and policies. What is left in these types of cases is thus the abstract assessment of laws and policies as such, without a convention right necessarily being at stake. Furthermore, the court is willing to assess the *conventionality* of these laws as court of first instance.

The reason for this seems clear. For the ECtHR, what is at stake in the cases revolving around covert operations and mass surveillance is not so much the individual interests, but the minimum conditions of legal orders, related to the principles of legality, legitimacy, and the rule of law. These are principles that are not relative, they are absolute; they must always be respected by governments, even if no individual harm can be demonstrated, even if the national remedies have not been exhausted, even if the different interests cannot be balanced, even if the case transcends the mere circumstances of that particular case, and so on. This is laudable in terms of privacy protection, because the court extends its scope of protection to cases in which no individual interests have been harmed and thus moves beyond the currently dominant right-based approach. Yet it is unclear about how this approach can be theoretically grounded. Obviously, the protection of individual rights and the prevention of harm are deeply engrained in liberal discourse and liberal philosophies; but for the protection of the legitimacy and legality of the law, in connection to the principles of the rule of law, this is more difficult.

The easy road would have been to show that for natural law philosophers, there are outer limits to the legal order. If laws go beyond that or violate the minimum requirements of the rule of law, the laws cannot be seen as laws or are deemed invalid. This argument would rely on a form of extra-legal morality that the law and the legal order have to adhere to. Somewhat more challenging would have been to argue that for people taking a middle position between natural rights theorists and legal positivists, such as Lon L. Fuller, there are minimum conditions for laws and legal orders, such as those related to the right to privacy. The hardest road, but also the strongest way forward, is to suggest that even for legal positivists, who reject the contention that extra-legal morality can limit legal orders and the legality of laws, there are a number of intrinsic limits that legal orders need to respect and that these limits relate to aspects of the right to privacy.

The current chapter has developed such an argument by discussing the work of one of the most prominent legal positivists, namely H.L.A. Hart. In a number of his writing, Hart defended the respect for the private choices of people, their privacy, and the private sphere. Mostly, this work has been discussed as separated from his work as a legal positivist. This chapter has suggested that his liberal stance was, however, inspired by his thoughts on legal positivism. Many of the arguments are not about what the law should be or what the legal order should do, but about what laws can do and what legal orders are. Furthermore, this chapter has suggested that the liberal principles he put forward are not only related to his views as a legal positivist, but moreover, that they relate to the secondary rules he spelled out. These are the rules that form the minimum conditions for the legal order, which even a legal positivist as Hart felt that a legal order must respect to be called a legal order properly.* Finally, it has suggested that these minimum conditions relate to the protection of privacy. Doing so, this chapter has shown that it is possible to provide a theoretical foundation for seeing the rule of law principles related to the right to privacy as minimum conditions for legal orders, without turning to extralegal morality.

References

[1] M. Twain, My debut as a literary person. http://www.public-domain-content.com/books/Mark_Twains_Short_Stories_2/C6P7.shtml.

[2] F. Somló, *Juristische Grundlehre*, Felix Meiner, Leipzig, Germany, 1917, p. 410.

[3] J. Waldron, Positivism and legality: Hart's equivocal response to Fuller, *New York University Law Review*, 83, 1135, 2008.

[4] H. L. A. Hart, *Law, Liberty and Morality*, Stanford University Press, Stanford, CA, 1963.

[5] L. L. Fuller, Positivism and fidelity to law: A reply to professor Hart, *Harvard Law Review*, 71, 630–672, 1957.

[6] B. van der Sloot, Is the human rights framework still fit for the big data era? A discussion of the ECtHR's case law on privacy violations arising from surveillance activities, In: S. Gutwirth, R. Leenes, and P. De Hert (Eds.), *Data Protection on the Move*, Springer, Dordrecht, the Netherlands, 2016.

[7] B. van der Sloot, The individual in the big data era: Moving towards an agent-based privacy paradigm, In: B. van der Sloot, D. Broeders, and E. Schrijvers (Eds.), *Exploring the Boundaries of Big Data*, Amsterdam University Press, Amsterdam, the Netherlands, 2016, pp. 177–203.

[8] D. Spielmann, *Bringing a Case to the European Court of Human Rights: A Practical Guide on Admissibility Criteria*, Wolf Legal Publishers, Oisterwijk, the Netherlands, 2014.

---

*These are in part factual, descriptive elements, such as is the law followed by most of the people most of the time, but sometimes also normative, such as that the legal order should not be static. Moreover, the requirement that individuals should retain a form of autonomy, transcend the pure factual and descriptive approach often attributed to legal positivists.

[9] T. A. Christou and J. P. Raymon, *European Court of Human Rights: Remedies and Execution of Judgments*, BIICL, British Institute of International and Comparative Law, London, 2005.

[10] B. van der Sloot, Do privacy and data protection rules apply to legal persons and should they? A proposal for a two-tiered system, *Computer Law & Security Review*, 31(1), 26–45, 2015.

[11] B. van der Sloot, Privacy in the Post-NSA Era: Time for a fundamental revision? *Journal of Intellectual Property, Information Technology and Electronic Commerce Law*, 5, 1–11, 2014.

[12] Committee on Homosexual Offences and Prostitution, *Report of the Committee on Homosexual Offences and Prostitution*, Her Majesty's Stationery Office, London, 1957.

[13] H. L. A. Hart, Positivism and the separation of law and morals, *Harvard Law Review*, 71(4), 593–629, 1958.

[14] J. L. Coleman, Negative and positive positivism, *The Journal of Legal Studies*, 11(1), 139–164, 1982.

[15] L. Green, Positivism and the inseparability of law and morals, *New York University Law Review*, 83, 1035–1058, 2008.

[16] L. L. Fuller, *The Morality of Law*, Yale University Press, London, 1969.

[17] L. L. Fuller, Means and ends, In: L. L. Fuller, *The Principles of Social Order*, Duke University Press, Durham, NC, 1981.

[18] P. Devlin, *The Enforcement of Morals*, Liberty Fund, Indianapolis, IN, 2009.

[19] G. Dworkin, Devlin was right: Law and the enforcement of morality, *William and Mary Law Review*, 40(3), 927–946, 1999.

[20] J. F. Stephen, *Liberty, Equality, Fraternity*, Liberty Fund, Indianapolis, IN, 1993.

[21] H. L. A. Hart, *The Concept of Law*, Oxford University Press, New York, 1997.

[22] F. Schauer, A critical guide to vehicles in the park, *New York University Law Review*, 83, 1109–1134, 2008.

[23] G. Radbruch, Statutory lawlessness and supra-statutory law (1946), *Oxford Journal of Legal Studies*, 26(1), 1–11, 2006.

[24] T. Mertens, Radbruch and Hart on the grudge informer: A reconsideration, *Ratio Juris*, 15, 186–205, 2002.

[25] D. Dyzenhaus, The grudge informer case revisited, *New York University Law Review*, 83, 1000–1034, 2008.

[26] R. Dworkin, Hard cases, *Harvard Law Review*, 88(6), 1057–1109, 1975.

[27] House of Lords, Shaw Vs. Director of Public Prosecutions, 1961. http://www.legalcrystal.com/judgements/description/945161.

[28] B. Roessler, *The Value of Privacy*, Polity Press, Cambridge, 2005.

[29] Aristotle, *The Politics and The Constitution of Athens*, Cambridge University Press, Cambridge, 1996.

[30] H. Arendt, *The Human Condition*, The University of Chicago Press, Chicago, IL, 1998.

[31] D. J. Solove, *Understanding Privacy*, Harvard University Press, Cambridge, MA, 2008.

[32] S. Van der Geest, Toilets, privacy and perceptions of dirt in Kwahu-Tafo, In: S. Van der Geest and N. Obirih-Opareh (Eds.), *Toilets and Sanitation in Ghana: An Urgent Matter*, Institute of Scientific and Technological Information (INSTI), CSIR, Accra, Ghana.

[33] W. Von Humboldt, *The Limits of State Action*, Cambridge University Press, 1969, p. 16.

[34] J. S. Mill, *On Liberty and Other Writings*, Cambridge University Press, Cambridge, 2009, p. 14.

[35] E. L. Beardsley, Privacy: Autonomy and selective disclosure, In: J. R. Pennock and J. W. Chapman (Eds.), *Privacy*, Atherton Press, New York, 1971.

[36] A. F. Westin, *Privacy and Freedom*, Lowe & Brydone, London, 1967.

[37] E. Goffman, *The Presentation of Self in Everyday Life*, Penguin Books, London, 1990.

[38] H. L. A. Hart, The morality of law by Lon L. Fuller, *Harvard Law Review*, 78(6), 1281–1296, 1965.

[39] H. L. A. Hart, Social solidarity and the enforcement of morality, *The University of Chicago Law Review*, 35(1), 9–10, 1967.

[40] J. Gardner, Introduction, In: H. L. A. Hart (Ed.), *Punishment and Responsibility: Essays in the Philosophy of Law*, Oxford University Press, Oxford, 2008, p. 36.

[41] H. L. A. Hart, Legal responsibility and excuses, In: H. L. A. Hart (Ed.), *Punishment and Responsibility: Essays in the Philosophy of Law*, Oxford University Press, Oxford, 2008, p. 44.

[42] H. L. A. Hart, Problems of philosophy of law, In: P. Edwards (Ed.), *The Encyclopedia of Philosophy, Vol. 5-6 Logic to Psychologism*, Macmillan, New York, 1972, p. 274.

[43] S. D. Warren and L. D. Brandeis, The right to privacy, *Harvard Law Review*, 4(5), 193–220, 1980.

[44] S. I. Benn, Privacy, freedom, and respect for persons, In: J. R. Pennock and J. W. Chapman (Eds.), *Privacy*, Atherton Press, New York, 1971, pp. 8–9.

[45] S. I. Benn, *A Theory of Freedom*, Cambridge University Press, Cambridge, 1988.

[46] H. L. A. Hart, Between utility and rights, *Columbia Law Review*, 79(5), 828–846, 1979.

[47] H. L. A. Hart, Shell foundation lectures, 1978–1979: Utilitarianism and natural rights, *Tulane Law Review*, 53, 663–680, 1978.

[48] H. L. A. Hart, Are there any natural rights? *The Philosophical Review*, 64(2), 175–191, 1955.

[49] H. Steiner, The natural right to equal freedom, *Mind, New Series*, 83(330), 194–210, 1974.

[50] E. Mack, Hart on natural and contractual rights, *Philosophical Studies: An International Journal for Philosophy in the Analytic Tradition*, 29(4), 283–285, 1976.

[51] B. Chao, Hart on natural rights, *Civilitas*, p. 9. http://www2.cuhk.edu.hk/gpa/civilitas/Volume%203/5.%20Chao-%20Hart%20on%20natural%20rights.pdf.

[52] N. G. E. Harris, Hart on natural rights, *British Journal of Political Science*, 2(1), 125–127, 1972.

Chapter 4

Data ownership: Taking stock and mapping the issues

Florent Thouvenin

Rolf H. Weber

Alfred Früh

Introduction 112
Rationale 113
Theoretical considerations 114
Market failure in a narrow sense 115
Market failure in a wider sense 116
Practical considerations 118
Legal uncertainty 119
Consequences 120
Characteristics 120
Subject matter of protection 120
Data, information, and knowledge 120
Other taxonomies 122
Right holder 123
Potential attribution criteria 123
Collective ownership 124
Scope of protection 125
Blueprints for a data ownership right 125
Elements of a potential data ownership right 129
Publicity 134
Implementation 134
Data ownership "On Top" 134
Data ownership "Instead" 135
Contractual alternative 136
Conclusion 136
References 138

Introduction

In both legal writing and the public debate, there is a recent discussion whether there should be some type of data ownership. The objective of this chapter is to take stock and to map the relevant issues related to data ownership. This approach should lead to a solid basis for any future research needed to guide the political debate on whether or not such a right is needed and, if so, how it should be designed and implemented. Although we aim at tracing the developments in general, our analysis regarding data ownership is based on Swiss law and, wherever appropriate, on EU law.

The three main parts of this chapter cover the central aspects of a potential new property right regarding data: its *rationale*, *characteristics*, and *implementation*. These aspects are linked: Depending on the characteristics of the right, its rationale is clearer or less clear. Likewise, the implementation of the right influences its rationale. Correspondingly, the characteristics of the right, particularly its scope, affect its implementation.

Starting point of the stocktaking is the observation that, as of now, no specific property right concerning data exists in Switzerland. To our knowledge, data as such is not protected in all other European jurisdictions either (for nonpersonal data in the EU cf. [7], p. 10; for other countries see [84], p. 89).* Available legal instruments do not grant ownership with regard to data as such. In particular, data is not protected by property rights that apply to real estate or chattel. Data is also excluded from copyright protection as copyright law requires a work of art with individual character and therefore a particular expression of information. Further, even the European *sui generis* right for databases laid down in Directive 96/9/EC of March 11, 1996 on the legal protection of databases only protects the systematic gathering of information contained in the database but neither single units of data nor the database itself (cf. [31], p. 175; [91], p. 120; [40], p. 621).

Although the term *data ownership* is typically used to denote an exclusive *in rem*, *erga omnes* right regarding data, we, in the following, understand it in the widest possible sense: Our assessment includes exclusive rights, rights erga omnes, provisions prohibiting certain specific acts regarding data (i.e., torts), and even (contractual) rights *inter partes*, as we neither want to unduly limit the scope of this chapter nor to imply that the term *data ownership* in itself defines certain characteristics.

The current interest in the concept of data ownership must take into account that data ownership topics have only recently attracted more attention in both legal writing and the public debate ([106] p. 64; for wearable medical devices cf. [104]; see further [77]), but the concept of data ownership is not new. A brief review of the literature shows that it was promoted in the early 1990s in

*Only recently, the European Union has published a proposal for a so-called data producer's right as a part of its European Data Economy package dated 10 January 2017.

the United States to both strengthen privacy protection ([72], pp. 247 et seqq.) and deal with a sudden increase in data-driven unwarranted direct marketing by telephone and mailings ([71], pp. 92 et seqq.). Although at the time, the discussion did not resonate in Switzerland or other European countries, the situation is different today: Data ownership has become a hot topic. It gives hope to those wishing to unlock the potential of the data economy ([6], p. 13) and to those trying to reempower individuals that have lost control over their data (as it is doubtful whether data protection law will be of much help in this regard: [48] pp. 147 et seqq.).

The discussion about data ownership rights concerns different types of data (personal data and nonpersonal data) as well as different stakeholders (individuals and corporate entities). This leads to the question whether the subject has to be treated specifically for the different types of data and stakeholders. In fact, most scientific papers typically treat either personal data or nonpersonal data ([107], p. 19; [84], p. 102; [42], n. 6). Although the different contexts may present specific characteristics, there are good reasons to apply a holistic view to the issue of data ownership. Above all, any data based on or produced by (even the most trivial) human action are (or can become) personal data as often the data can be reattributed to that person in the context of data analysis ([107], p. 19; [51], pp. 321 et seqq.; [45,95]). The distinction between personal and nonpersonal data is therefore nebulous. As a consequence, the application of data protection law can hardly ever be ruled out, which leads to the fundamental question of the interplay of data ownership and data protection law (cf. section "Implementation"). In addition, as long as no decision is made as to who would originally be entitled to a data ownership right, the assessment cannot be limited to either individuals or corporations.

As a last introductory remark, we concede that many questions cannot be answered by law alone. Technical and economic aspects are also very important, and interdisciplinary research may be needed. Nevertheless, legal research can provide the general framework for a convincing answer. Within this general legal framework, reference should be made to other disciplines.

Rationale

When addressing the question of why some form of data ownership should be introduced, two different approaches can be applied: On the one hand, answers can be sought on a theoretical level. The introduction of a potential ownership right is reflected in academic writing, in which several arguments for a potential data ownership right can be examined (see section "Theoretical considerations"). On the other hand, looking at real-life problems in practice should give a good indication whether there is need for action (see section "Practical considerations"). In addition, we will also briefly touch on the argument of legal certainty that is relevant in both theory and practice (see section "Legal uncertainty"), before drawing conclusions (see section "Consequences").

Theoretical considerations

A thorough review of the legal literature allows grouping arguments for data ownership and assessing their power. Of course, the same could also be done for arguments *against* data ownership, but this would exceed the scope of this chapter.

First, some authors just plainly claim that there is a need for a data ownership right, without providing any justification ([56], introduction and n. 20). Such an approach does not suffice. Although introducing a data ownership right may be beneficial to potential right holders, it may clearly be detrimental for individuals that are not awarded such right and possibly even for society as a whole. As it will shift the balance of interest within society, such a new right has to be justified.

Second, other authors note that data is valuable and therefore needs to be protected by an ownership right ([34]; [59], p. 753; [61], p. 217; [43], p. 246; [40], p. 618; [68], p. 990; [31], p. 165). But this argument alone does not suffice either. The fundamental question is whether the inherent value of data may easily be misappropriated, thus causing unwanted or unjust effects.

The more refined rationales for data ownership follow a third line of thought: Scholars argue that a data ownership right should only be introduced to prevent or correct a market failure. Such kind of reasoning is in line with orthodox legal theory: Whether the introduction of a new right will remedy an existing market failure has become the main rationale for granting property rights in European legal thinking. This so-called utilitarian approach [74] has particularly been applied for the justification of intellectual property rights but arguably also extends to property rights in general ([40], p. 625; [41], pp. 373 et seqq.). In other fields such as with sui generis rights for databases or for press publishers (in Germany or Spain), this is also a key question. However, it is doubtful that in the latter cases the question was given the attention it should have received. In this paper, we propose to differentiate between market failure in a narrow (see section "Market failure in a narrow sense") and in a wider sense (see section "Market failure in a wider sense"), albeit with two caveats:

First, this chapter does not ignore that there may be nonutilitarian rationales for an ownership right: Some may argue that (personal) data is an expression of one's personality and therefore *belongs* to this person ([74] call them personality theorists), others may argue that a person (or an undertaking) should be entitled to the fruits of his, her, or its labor and therefore have a right in the data that has been produced ([74] call this the Lockean rationale). Others refer to the idea of fairness. If ever possible, this chapter tries to address these rationales within the context of market failure.

Second, we acknowledge that there is no current common notion of a market failure ([41], p. 348 et seqq. and 400 et seqq.; [53]). Even worse, the idea of market failure may be the victim of a fundamental epistemological threat: The alleged failure always requires a comparison to a purely hypothetical market condition. Nevertheless, we use the term as an analytical tool to structure the different rationales of a potential data ownership right.

Market failure in a narrow sense

A market failure in a narrow sense occurs when the subject matter of protection—data—is not being created or used, despite the fact that creation and use of data would be in the public interest. Nonrivalrous goods such as data that can be copied infinitely tend not to be overused by consumption. A data producer will therefore only have an incentive to invest in the creation of data if he or she will be able to recoup his or her investment ([99], p. 565).

Hardly any scholars support the argument that a data ownership right is needed to provide incentives for the production of data. ZECH, however, is of the opinion that data ownership would increase the incentive for the collection of data ([108], p. 144). His argument is partly based on the assumption that data as such is subject to the disclosure paradox ([108], p. 145; regarding the disclosure paradox cf. [27]; [41], p. 415). Arguably, data that is to be transferred or licensed has to be disclosed to a certain extent in order for the buyer to assess its value. It is argued that by disclosing the data it loses its value, and there is no more need to transfer the data, thus leading to a market failure. This argument, however, ignores the fact that data transferred or licensed for the purpose of Big Data analysis has little to do with a single piece of (easily understandable) know-how that is the textbook example for illustrating the disclosure paradox. Big datasets do not need to be fully disclosed before a transaction. In addition, the mere disclosure of the content of a dataset is usually of little value as processing the data to carry out analyses requires actual access to the dataset. Therefore, the argument that such data requires protection to be transferred or licensed must clearly be rejected.

Further, empirical evidence leads us to conclude that the disclosure paradox does not negatively interfere with the production and/or collection of data. Although the world generated only 130 exabytes in 2005, the figure is expected to reach 8'591 exabytes in 2015, and current estimates predict 40'026 (!) exabytes by 2020 [33]; according to another source, the Big Data market grows by roughly 25% annually and already exceeds 20 billion Euro ([87], p. 147; according to the European Commission, the growth of the Big Data market is about seven times as high as the growth of the entire information and communications technology (ICT) market [8], p. 2; see also [7], p. 2).

The widespread existence of data transfer and licensing agreements in practice also indicates that data is subject to transactions even without exclusive rights. Apparently, factual exclusivity is sufficient ([42], n. 7). The prevailing view indeed is that data production does not require additional incentives, as costs for production are minimal ([47], n. 7, with the caveat that i.e., with a worldwide rollout of sensors the situation would be different. But even then entire datasets and not individual data should be subject to protection). Some commentators also explicitly mention that people will not create more data about themselves, just because there is a property right ([89], p. 1140). Even ZECH acknowledges that the costs for data collection decline steadily and that this lessens the need to incentivize data collection by introducing property rights ([108], p. 145).

Concluding, there is a general consensus that no incentive for data production and the recoupment of investments is needed. The arguments denying a market failure in the narrow sense by far outweigh arguments for the existence of such a market failure. To be fair, however, the objection that there might be even more transactions with an ownership right cannot easily be rejected ([45], p. 1051, albeit specifically focusing on virtual property, not data in general).

Market failure in a wider sense

Market failure could also be understood in a wider sense. According to literature, data ownership could correct this market failure by (a) lowering transaction costs for contractual agreements involving data and by (b) correcting a misallocation of costs and benefits, that is, the fact that data collectors are able to externalize costs while internalizing benefits. Although only the latter is explicitly labeled as a market failure in the literature (with the exception of [41], p. 349, who observes that transaction costs may be taken into account when assessing market failure), both may lead to inefficient market allocation and therefore negatively affect the (functioning) market of transactions involving data.

Transaction costs

Market failure can be a consequence of overly high transaction costs. Some authors argue that this is the case in the current regime. Transaction costs can be divided into search costs and negotiation costs. Regarding search costs, it is argued that without standardization by a property regime, contracting parties are required to engage in expensive searches ([45], p. 1090). The same reasoning can be made in relation to negotiation costs ([45], p. 1051): Granting rights regarding data by means of contract in the current *modus operandi* is often complex. Costs related to drafting, understanding, and abiding to contractual provisions could potentially be reduced.

Standardizing data ownership as a form of property could thus in theory reduce search as well as negotiation costs. Both in United States and in Continental European jurisdictions, this standardization of property rights is achieved by the *numerus clausus* principle. This principle limits the number of types of property rights acknowledged by law. If standardization proved to save transaction costs for data-related transactions in a significant way, the *numerus clausus* principle would have to be extended. Assigning ownership rights is, in theory, also associated with increasing the marketability of data ([87], p. 149).

For a complete picture, however, the transaction costs caused by a new property right must also be taken into account. On one hand, there are doubts whether legal certainty would increase and thus transaction costs would be lowered. On the other hand, potential users of data would also face significant search and negotiation costs if they were to individually identify data owners and negotiate licensing terms with them ([89], p. 1135 and [47], n. 25, noting that this would call for a liability regime rather than a property rule).

Concluding, arguments regarding transaction costs may be valid. But they lack a solid quantitative basis. To assess whether transaction costs may be saved in comparison with the current situation, further empirical research is needed. Moreover, any change of the current regime will potentially lead to substantial new transaction costs, which would also have to be taken into account.

Misallocation of costs and benefits

A number of authors have described the fact that firms collecting data internalize gains (some scholars observe that the non-allocation of data plainly means that data can be freely collected by the information industry and then be protected by *de facto* exclusivity [84], p. 84) while externalizing losses. This has also been labeled as market failure ([96], p. 8; [71], p. 99; [40], p. 626, with further references in fn. 118; [70], p. 172; [31], pp. 165 et seqq.). Although the argument was originally made in the context of direct marketing in the 1990s (cf. [30], p. 1645; [89], p. 1125: "The market incentives for firms to collect and process personal data are very high."), it may easily be transposed to the age of Big Data and Internet platforms (cf. e.g., [70], p. 172).

Like in the 1990s, subscribers transmit personal data to companies and eventually lose control over their data. The company does not suffer losses from the disclosure of private information, but the customers do; therefore, losses are externalized ([92], p. 30). Unlike in the 1990s, today's service providers can claim that they offer valuable free services to customers in exchange for their data. But from a purely financial point of view, the service providers still internalize most of the benefit of the transactions.

Against this background, proponents of a data ownership right state that market approaches would help strengthen individual control over personal information ([71], p. 93). Clearly, nowadays the individual does barely have any bargaining power when it comes to providing companies with data. Terms of service are generally non-negotiable and impenetrable ([28], p. 494; [70], p. 173, labels this fact as market failure). The question is therefore whether anything would change if individuals were endowed with ownership rights regarding their data. Would externalities indeed be internalized? At first glance, one can be skeptical. Data ownership does not alter the fact that data subjects and data processors are not on a level playing field ([62], p. 270). Instead of tailoring contracts regarding data to their own interests (or to the detriment of data subjects), companies would just use assignment agreements that could result in an allocation of all rights to the companies, albeit with *erga omnes* effect. However, a part of the literature refuses this pessimistic view.

Some scholars are of the opinion that the *endowment effect* identified by behavioral economics could contribute to a level playing field. Orthodox economic theory predicts that "resources tend to gravitate toward their most valuable uses" as markets drive out any unexploited profit opportunities ([83], p. 12 et seq.). As long as transaction costs are zero, initial assignments of entitlements will therefore not affect the ultimate allocation of resources ([37], pp. 1 et seqq.). But this finding, known as the Coase theorem, has been challenged by behavioral economics. According to the endowment effect ([101], n. 15), individuals endowed with a property right tend to value a good higher than others and thus higher than the Coase theorem would suggest (even when transaction costs are close to zero, cf. [66]; referred to by [65], p. 1483). Accordingly, losses are weighted more heavily than gains ([65], p. 1484). This suggests that individuals would value their data higher, if they were awarded a property right in their data. Whether this would make a difference when individuals negotiate terms of service with companies such as Facebook and Google is, however, another question. Even among the proponents of a data ownership right, some are septical whether the mere existence of such a right would be sufficient to reach the desired effects ([89], p. 1136, referring to [71], p. 92, proposing an infrastructure to make the data property rights system work).

Some voices have therefore, already in the past, endorsed institutional measures. LAUDON promoted establishing a National Information Market in 1996, building on institutions such as a National Information Exchange and specific information banks ([71], p. 99 et seqq.). Recently, the idea of data cooperatives has gained some attention, particularly regarding medical data ([54], pp. 82 et seqq.; [10]). Pooling individual data to get some leverage *vis-à-vis* big firms is a model that will be market tested in the very near future. However, and for completeness, it may be noted that pooling data for concerted action does not require a data ownership right.

Practical considerations

A problem-based approach can identify current shortcomings of the law with regard to data. The question then is whether a new legal instrument, particularly in the form of a data ownership right, could remedy these shortcomings.

Among the shortcomings that we have identified so far, the most obvious seems to be the fact that under current law, data cannot be reclaimed from a bankrupt company by the person who had originally provided the data to this company. If, for example, a cloud service provider would go bankrupt under Swiss law, this would severely affect its customers. This issue was already addressed by the Federal Council in a reply to a question by a member of the

Parliament in 2014 [13]. At the time, the Federal Council treated the issue only with regard to personal data and promised to touch upon this subject when revising the Swiss Federal Act on Data Protection (FADP; [15]). Only recently, members of the parliament filed a parliamentary initiative and proposed a specific amendment of the Swiss Debt Enforcement and Bankruptcy Act ([14,21]).

If the cloud service provider did not go bankrupt but did—for whatever reasons—delete the data provided by the other party, the cloud user would generally have contractual claims against the cloud service provider to be compensated for the loss and/or further damage caused by such deletion. However, in a B2C relationship, the party providing the data to the cloud service provider may have accepted unfavorable general terms and conditions and waived his or her rights to reclaim the data or be compensated for its loss and/or further damage. The problem is thus in all likelihood more severe in B2C relationships.

Another example is the fact that the loss of data on a storage medium (such as a USB stick) can typically not be remedied if the data was erased by the person in possession of the storage medium.

Certainly, these examples are not exhaustive. But as of now, it seems that in practice only isolated problems emerge. At least, we have not yet identified basic systemic problems, such as competitors' freeriding on data of the *original* producer. Accordingly, there are good reasons to design only specific solutions to the identified specific problems. Although the current patchwork of norms may be unsatisfying and complex, introducing a data ownership right *across the board* to solve specific problems would go too far. In doing so, the legislator could cause many new problems that are yet not even foreseeable. One of these, just to give an example, is the question of taxation (cf. [76] on similar questions regarding the taxation of robots).

Legal uncertainty

Proponents of a data ownership right argue that an unambiguous legal assignment of data would be a clear starting point for contract negotiations and a default allocation of the benefits absent contracts ([108], p. 145), thus reducing legal uncertainty. Often, the user of a device and the manufacturer of that device argue who should be able and entitled to access and use the data collected by the device. Popular examples involve data produced by cars, farming trucks, and the like. But as will be shown in this chapter, an unambiguous default assignment of ownership rights may be a quite daunting task (see sections "Subject matter of protection" and "Right holder").

Quite to the contrary, other authors argue that legal uncertainty will *increase* with the introduction of a data ownership right. Introducing property rights would raise the question who, if anyone, is the owner of collected data; in addition, the ensuing data ownership litigation would be costly and inefficient ([47], n. 23).

Consequences

Analyzing the justifications put forward for a data ownership right in the light of *theoretical considerations* yields two findings: First, there is no clear evidence for a market failure in the narrow sense. Accordingly, a data ownership right cannot be justified by the argument that it would increase or incentivize data production. Second, a new data ownership right may have the potential of mitigating negative effects, that is, to correct market failures in the wider sense: A data ownership right might potentially lower transaction costs. However, a quantitative foundation for this argument is still lacking, that is, the size of these costs in the current regime is unclear. Furthermore, it is unclear whether transaction costs would actually be lowered by introducing an ownership right and whether new transaction costs would emerge. All of these questions require further economic analysis.

We make a corresponding observation regarding *practical considerations.* Some problems may exist and warrant closer attention. But to remedy the problems that are currently known to us, the introduction of a data ownership right *across the board* would most likely go too far, irrespective of its appeal to simplify the current patchwork of norms.

Characteristics

The characteristics of a potential data ownership right are determined by (See section "Subject matter of protection") its subject matter of protection, (See section "Right holder") its attribution to a right holder, (See section "Scope of protection") its scope of protection, and (See section "Publicity") its publicity.

Subject matter of protection

Clearly, data ownership rights deal with data. But the notion of data is not as straightforward as one might expect. Defining the subject matter of protection regarding data has therefore been called the *specification problem* ([102], p. 882). Along with most authors, we attribute the terms data, information, and knowledge to the syntactic, semantic, and pragmatic level, respectively, as defined in the following.

Data, information, and knowledge

Data may be protected at three distinct levels: at the syntactic, semantic, and pragmatic level ([93], p. 290; [102], p. 881). The *syntactic level* represents the structure of data, that is, a string of 0s and 1s, arranged in a particular sequence. At the same time, this data can alone or together with other data also constitute information on the *semantic level* ([11]). The semantic level consists of the meaning behind the data, that is, the information it holds ([93], p. 290; [102], p. 881; [68], p. 992; [109], pp. 51 et seq.; [108], p. 138; [57], p. 650). The transition from syntactic to semantic requires a machine to read and translate the data to extract the information ([81], p. 98). Unlike data, information carries meaning ([81], p. 98). It thus requires a recipient, that is, the cognitive capabilities of a human being ([93], p. 290). Finally, if the information is meaningful, it can alone or together with other information amount to knowledge on the *pragmatic level.* The pragmatic level thus refers to useful knowledge, understood as information causing a certain effect or serving a certain purpose ([93], p. 290; [102], p. 881). In addition to these levels, some authors mention the notion of structural information, which is defined as the physical embodiment of information ([109], pp. 51 et seqq. and pp. 251 et seqq.; [108], p. 138; [57], p. 650).

In a recent court case, these levels have illustratively been compared with a ledger containing information about the activity of a company ([112]). The letters and numbers represent the syntactic level, organized according to a particular alphabet. These letters can be read by a program, our brain, which translates them into information, into the semantic level. This information is then analyzed at the pragmatic level to produce knowledge on the activity of the company. The physical ledger itself would represent the structural information.

Although these generally accepted definitions lead us to conclude that data represents a string of 0s and 1s on the syntactic level, information on the semantic level and knowledge on the pragmatic level *also* consist of data. However, if we use the term data in the following, it only denotes data on the syntactic level.

But what should be the subject matter of protection of a potential data ownership right? The current discussion generally focuses on whether data should be protected on the syntactic or the semantic level ([68], p. 992; [56], n. 6, assumes that protection should be awarded on the semantic level). Two main positions can be identified: The majority of authors seem to accord to the—convincing—idea that the semantic level should not be protected, because this would lead to a monopoly on information ([68], pp. 992, 997). They consequently favor protection at the syntactic level, if any ([68], p. 992; [93], p. 290; [43], p. 247; [108], pp. 138 et seq.). A second line of reasoning warns that protecting the syntactic level would monopolize the very essence of data ([102], p. 883: "If you take data as the protected subject matter, you would in fact protect that part of the communication process where information is in the state of data.") and thus be harmful because at least indirectly the semantic and pragmatic level would also be affected ([102], p. 882). Variations of this view question whether the syntactic and the semantic level really can be separated at all.

Other taxonomies

The literature further mentions other taxonomies that are not directly relevant for defining the subject matter of protection but could indirectly influence the characteristics of a potential data ownership right.

Volunteered, observed, and inferred data

In 2011, the World Economic Forum (WEF) suggested a new taxonomy for data [24,25]. Instead of the common distinction between personal and non-personal data, the authors of the report differentiated between volunteered data, observed data, and inferred data. They asked the question "How is data produced?" and not "What types of data are there?"

According to this taxonomy, *volunteered data* is explicitly shared by individuals. Each individual is aware of the fact that his or her data is transferred ([25], pp. 15 et seqq.). The authors of the report note that the amount of data in this category will be the least. Individuals often have strong emotional ties to their volunteered data ([24], p. 16). If individuals share data that is not *by them* but rather *about them*, this data should be qualified as *observed data*. As described by the WEF, this type of data concerns recorded behaviors of individuals, usually without their awareness about the data collection itself or about the data's subsequent use and value. A broader definition of observed data could even encompass all types of data collected by machines or individuals and would not have to be restricted to personal data.

Finally, *inferred data* refers to different data types originating from various sources, used mostly for predictive purposes. In this situation, individuals not only lack awareness, they have also lost control over how this data is being used. This type of data, according to the WEF, has the greatest potential for innovation and economic growth.

The novel taxonomy addresses the fact that the creation of data—even by machines—requires some level of human involvement ([107], p. 19), but the individuals are rarely aware of their creation ([84], p. 102; [42], n. 6). The taxonomy is a possible starting point for recategorizing data, in particular, for those who want to challenge the common distinction between personal and non-personal data.

Data as public good, private good, or club good

Often, data is referred to as a public good ([38], p. 40; [90], p. 79 et seq.; [109], p. 117 et seqq.; [108], p. 139; [91], p. 121; [57], p. 652 et seq.), which warrants a closer assessment: By definition, public goods are both non-rivalrous and non-excludable. It is undisputed that data as such is non-rivalrous; the consumption by someone does not reduce the consumption by someone else. However, data is not *per se* non-excludable. Others may be prevented from accessing and using data by factual (i.e., secrecy or encryption) or legal means. If that is the case, data is considered a club good.

Data as unitary or commodity asset

When defining the subject matter of protection, two very different concepts can be distinguished that are pivotal for devising the scope of protection of a potential data ownership right: Data or information may either be described in unitary terms or as a commodity asset ([75], pp. 8 et seqq.). The *unitary approach* attributes rights irrespective of how others have obtained the data or the information embodied in the data. Others possessing the data or the information embodied in a particular piece of data are treated as possessing the *same* data. By contrast, the *commodity approach* defines rights with reference not only to the particular data itself but also to the person (or company) that holds the information embodied in the data. If two companies separately obtain particular information, their property rights in this information are independent of the rights of each other ([75], p. 8). Consequently, one company has no legal means to prevent the other from using independently obtained data.

When devising the normative structure, either approach can be chosen. According to literature, most modern property law regimes follow the commodity approach when dealing with information ([75], p. 8), copyright law being the most prominent case in point.

Right holder

Framing the initial attribution of a data ownership right is quite a challenge and has thus been called the *allocation problem* ([102], p. 882; [35], p. 1). First, an attribution criterion has to be defined. Then, the question must be addressed whether a data ownership right should or could have multiple owners.

Potential attribution criteria

A look at the literature shows that authors have developed a number of criteria based on which a data ownership right could be attributed to a right holder. So far, there is no consensus ([32], p. 173; [50], p. 487). The attribution criteria are (a) the scripture of the data, (b) the investment in the generation or storage of data, and (c) contractual arrangements and (d) the data subject, to which the data refers.

Scripture

Some scholars argue that the *act of writing the data*, that is, the scripture of data (so-called *Skripturakt* in German) should be decisive for identifying the right holder ([60], p. 487; [108], pp. 143 et seq.). The data would thus be attributed to the person who generates it. Resorting to the scripture allows identifying the exact moment in which data is recorded and/or stored. Consequently, if only one person is involved in the creation and/or storage, the scripture could also unambiguously define the right holder. However, in more complex situations and if several individuals are involved, defining the right holder may not be that straightforward ([57], p. 654). Two commonly used examples can illustrate this: A person driving a vehicle may have little or no means to control the scripture, despite the fact that this person is actually *causing* the scripture ([62], p. 269). Similarly, during a medical consultation, data can be recorded either by the physician, his or her assistant, an electronic device, a specialized lab, and so on, all of which would have different attribution outcomes ([57], p. 654). To mitigate these problems, some authors have argued that emphasis should lie on a given person's influence on the scripture ([60], p. 488 et seq.). But with this criterion, attribution tends to become even more difficult.

Investment

Some authors suggest that the deciding criterion should be who caused the generation or storage of the data from an organizational or economic point of view ([109], p. 431; [108], p. 144). But even then, an unambiguous attribution of the right may not be possible: Both the owner and the manufacturer of a car have invested in generating data. Similarly, the physician, the medical device manufacturer, and the medical lab as potential owners have all made significant investments. It is thus doubtful whether this criterion would bring about the expected clarity.

Contract

Parts of the literature suggest that although the originator should generally be the owner of the data, contractual arrangements such as employment or agency contracts may lead to an *original* ownership arising in another person (data made for hire; [59], p. 753 et seq.). But these special rules do not provide a default attribution for all cases.

Data subject

Authors who understand data ownership rights as a means to help individuals to regain control over their personal information attribute data ownership rights to the data subject ([84], p. 83 et seq.). But this line of reasoning is limited to personal data. It generally also disregards the interests of persons or companies that have stored the data or invested in the production of the personal data.

Collective ownership

As the foregoing examples show, it is unlikely that one of the proposed criteria will lead to an unambiguous attribution of data ownership rights in all potential constellations. The presence of personal data causes further complications.

This leads us to assume that specific rules on collective ownership would have to be formulated for a new data ownership right—a thought that is hardly ever addressed in literature. However, these rules on collective ownership vary, depending on the characteristics of the right: If the data ownership right would, for example, resemble a property right in physical objects, one could draw on the concepts of co-ownership (e.g., in the sense of Art. 646 of the Swiss Civil Code [CC]) or joint ownership (e.g., in the sense of Art. 652 CC ([56], n. 43)). But if the data ownership right was merely based on provisions targeting and prohibiting certain specific acts, such as tort law, and not on rights in rem, collective ownership would be neither possible nor necessary (cf. section "Blueprints for the scope of a data ownership right" regarding the different blueprints for a data ownership right).

Scope of protection

To assess the scope of protection of a potential data ownership right, the approach of this chapter is twofold: (See section "Blueprints for the scope of a data ownership right") On the one hand, we examine existing concepts regarding the attribution of rights to a right holder in order to assess whether they can serve as blueprints. (See section "Elements of a potential data ownership right") On the other hand, we specifically focus on the powers conferred by the right and its possible limitations, both of which shape the scope of protection of a potential data ownership right.

Blueprints for a data ownership right

As other *civil law* jurisdictions, Swiss law can resort to a broad range of legal instruments when faced with the task of designing a data ownership right. Some of these instruments, such as physical property and intellectual property rights as well as neighboring rights, confer exclusive in rem, *erga omnes* rights. Although not providing rights in rem, data can also be *attributed* by tort law provisions, and, finally, by contracts that only have *inter partes* effects.

Property rights

Property rights in physical objects (such as land and chattel) give the owner full control over an object. He or she may enforce that control against all other persons (*erga omnes*; e.g., [19], Arts. 641 et seqq. of the CC; [52], ZGB 641 N 4; [103], ZGB 641 N 3; [39], ZGB 641 N 5; [82], N 220; [94], N 1002). This includes that the owner can dispose of the object as he or she pleases—including possessing it, using it, consuming it, subjecting it to rights in rem, or transferring it to a third party—, within the limits of the law (power of disposition, Art. 641 para. 1 CC; [52], ZGB 641 N 6 et seq.; [98], §97 N 3 et seqq.; [26], ZGB 641 N 28; [39], ZGB 641 N 8; [82], N 222 et seq.).

If someone is withholding the object, the owner has also the right to reclaim it (*rei vindicatio,* Art. 641 para. 2 CC). Furthermore, the owner can protect the property from any undue interference (*actio negatoria*, Art. 641 para. 2 CC). Although the respective provisions of the Civil Code do not explicitly define the subject matter of protection, there is a general consensus that property rights apply to physical objects only ([52], Einleitung ZGB 641–729 N 20 et seq.; [103], ZGB 641 N 29; [98], §87 N 2 and §97 N 1; [39], Vor Art. 641–654a N 4; [26], ZGB 641 N 6).

The paramount argument against designing a data ownership right based on the blueprint of property rights is the fact that data lacks the properties of physical objects (i.e., data is non-rivalrous and generally non-exclusive; [47], n. 31; [57], p. 656; [64], p. 92, arguing that the non-rivalrous quality of data speaks against a protection that is not limited in time). Nevertheless, some authors favor using property rights as a blueprint for a data ownership right ([60], p. 488; [56], n. 39 and 42).

Intellectual property rights

Intellectual property rights—especially those conferred by copyright and patent laws—provide the right holder with exclusive rights that have an *erga omnes* effect (cf. Arts. 9 et seqq. Swiss Copyright Act [CopA, cf. 16] and Arts. 8 et seqq. Swiss Patent Act [PatA, cf. 17]; e.g., for copyright, see [86], URG 9 N 4; [63], URG 9 N 1; [80], LDA 9 N 5 and 8; [29], URG 9 N 9). There is a *numerus clausus* of intellectual property rights. In essence, all of these rights protect the right holder against the use of the intangible good in question (cf. e.g., Art. 10 CopA). The right holder can decide to transfer his or her right or to grant a license (see [79], URG 10 N 1; [36], LDA 10 N 8 et seq.; [29], URG 10 N 6).

The intangible good has to meet specific requirements to qualify for protection (e.g., an invention must be novel and non-obvious [e.g., Art. 1 PatA] and a literary or artistic work will only be copyright protected if it is considered a creation of the mind with an individual character [e.g., Art. 2 para. 1 CopA]). As the subject matter of protection is intangible (e.g., a literary or artistic work or an invention), there needs to be a balance between the right holder's and the general public's interests. Intellectual property regimes therefore contain limitations that allow particular uses of the protected intangible good (e.g., the private use of copyright protected work in Art. 19 para. 1 lit. a CopA and the use of patented inventions for research and experimental purposes in Art. 9 lit. b PatA, either for free or by paying a fee). In addition, the protection expires after a certain period of time. Patent protection lasts for 20 years from the registration (e.g., Art. 14 para. 1 PatA), whereas copyright protection expires 50 years after the death of the author of a computer program and 70 years after the death of the author for all other works of literature or art (e.g., Art. 29 para. 2 CopA).

Some authors in favor of a data ownership right refer to copyright law and its numerous exceptions and limitations as a potential model to deal with club goods and public goods ([91], p. 122; [110], pp. 1159 et seq.; [108], p. 146;

see however [102], p. 882; regarding a possible use of data for research and experimental purposes see [108], p. 146; [102], p. 882). Some also point out that, in any case, a data ownership right should be limited in time ([102], p. 882). However, it must be noted that a potential data ownership right would most likely not require the data to fulfill specific requirements regarding its quality (unlike non-obviousness in patent law or individual character in copyright law).

Neighboring rights

Neighboring rights confer exclusive rights with *erga omnes* effects to the right holder ([29], URG 33 N 14 et seqq.). Most jurisdictions provide for neighboring rights or the so-called ancillary copyrights for: performers (e.g., Arts. 33 et seqq. CopA), producers of phonograms and videograms (e.g., Art. 35 CopA), and broadcasting organizations (e.g., Art. 36 CopA). Unlike copyright-protected works, the protected subject matter, that is, the actual performance, recording or broadcast, does not need to fulfill qualitative requirements (however, some authors still argue that performers' rights require a certain degree of individuality or originality to be worthy of protection [73], pp. 912 et seq.; cf. [29], URG 33 N 10; [105], p. 151).

The neighboring rights were mainly created as a reaction to technical advances that made copying of protected works easier and much cheaper. Accordingly, these rights (also—and more fittingly—termed *Leistungsschutzrechte* in German language) allow the right holder to take action against free riders and thus protect specific investments. Although these rights are formally incorporated into copyright law, they have a much closer relation to unfair competition law with regard to their substance ([58], *passim*). In addition, limitations provided by copyright law apply to these rights *mutatis mutandis* (e.g., Art. 38 CopA), many of which replace the right to claim injunctive relief with a liability rule. The protection of neighboring rights expires after 50 years (e.g., Art. 39 para. 1 CopA).

Similarly, the *sui generis* protection for databases provided by European law also protects investments ([1]). But more precisely, and unlike the neighboring rights, the European Directive granting these rights was enacted to ensure protection of investment in obtaining, verifying or presenting the contents of databases, not in the production of data itself ([1], recital 40; [111], n. 24 et seqq.). Under Swiss law, there is no such *sui generis* protection for databases.

Some proponents of a data ownership right argue that neighboring rights would prevent third parties from freeriding. They would treat data as a commodity asset (not a unitary asset, cf. above C.I.2.c) and therefore, the scope of protection provided by the right would not extend to the independent creation, extraction, or gathering of the same or similar data by third parties ([108], p. 146; [110], pp. 1159 et seq.; [102], pp. 881 et seq.).

Torts

Quite a few provisions target and prohibit certain specific acts, without conferring any rights in rem. These provisions have *erga omnes* effects; anyone who does not abide to them will face tort claims or criminal as well as administrative sanctions ([42], n. 18; see in particular Arts. 137 et seqq. of the Swiss Criminal Code [SCC, cf. 18] and the provisions on unfair competition in Arts. 2 to 8 of the Swiss Federal Act on Unfair Competition [UCA, cf. 22]).

Typical provisions may be found in the context of the protection of trade secrets (Art. 162 SCC and Art. 6 UCA). In combination with technical measures to restrict the access to and the use of data by third parties, these provisions provide an effective control of data. Similarly, in Switzerland, the unique provision of Art. 5 lit. c UCA prohibits the use of the result of someone else's labor. Although the current interpretation of this provision by courts is rather narrow [115], a broader interpretation could amount to a level of protection resembling an ownership right in data. Some authors suggest that a data ownership right should be based on these legal grounds ([42], n. 28; [108], p. 140).

Adding to this, basic tort provisions (e.g., Arts. 41 et seqq. of the Swiss Code of Obligations) could provide the claimant with a claim for injunctive relief and restitution of the data (and not merely financial compensation). This has been argued regarding personal data ([88], DSG 15 n. 41; [69], OR 43 N 4). However, for non-personal data, the question has not been discussed.

Lastly, it is noteworthy that the EU has recently enacted a new Directive on the protection of trade secrets that has to be implemented by member states by June 9, 2018 [2]. At present, it is unclear whether data will be treated as trade secret under this Directive. Some authors therefore argue that the implementation of the Directive should be awaited before drafting a potential new legal instrument granting ownership in data ([42], n. 28).

Contractual rights

Today, a large and increasing number of contracts cover the transfer and use of data. Although there is no *erga omnes* right in rem in data, these agreements generally treat data as if there was one (for details on the advantages and disadvantages of this *status quo*, see [108], p. 140). Typical wordings state that *ownership of data* is *transferred* from one party to the other or that data ownership *remains with the seller*. Even if these terms are legally incorrect, they do not alter the validity of the agreement (Art. 18 para. 1 Code of Obligations [CO, cf. 20]; see also [102], p. 878) and provide quite clear information as to the intention of the parties with regard to the residual use of the data that is not regulated in the contract.

Contracts are a powerful tool and much can be achieved by contractual means. For this reason, some authors argue in favor of preserving the status quo and deem these contractual solutions with *inter partes* effects regarding data to be sufficient ([40], p. 628; [102], p. 884, regarding B2B contracts). However, the question remains whether this is also true for B2C-relationships.

If the contracting parties are not on a level playing field, the less powerful party—usually the customer—may be worse off, typically by accepting general terms and conditions that affect control over the data. Against this background, some voices request that the legal provisions related to general terms and conditions be reviewed and, if necessary, amended ([6], pp. 78 et seqq.).

Elements of a potential data ownership right

The scope of a potential data ownership right may not only be defined by drawing from existing legal concepts as shown previously. It is also the sum of all powers conferred to the right holder, minus the limitations of the right. Both powers and limitations warrant a closer look.

Core powers and limitations

Control over access to data

With regard to access, the concerned types of data must be distinguished; in particular, a different treatment of personal data and non-personal data appears to be necessary: In the case of personal data, the issue of access depends on the design of the applicable data protection laws. To various degrees and scopes, these laws grant the individuals concerned a right to be informed about the processing (including the mcre storage) of his or her personal data. At least in theory, the individuals therefore already enjoy control over access to personal data based on data protection laws.

The legal framework is less clear for non-personal data or datasets derived from depersonalized data through Big Data analytics. Such data mostly has an increased value making it more attractive for market players to ask for access. The controller of the data being the *original* producer is often inclined to retain the data and analyze it in proprietary silos. An increasing amount of machine-generated data is created without direct intervention of an individual by computer processes, applications, or services, or by sensors processing information received from equipment, software, or machinery, whether virtual or real ([7], p. 9). Regardless of such data being stored in-house or in a cloud, third parties are usually denied access. Therefore, a reuse of the data may not occur. As far as trade secrets are concerned, the denial of sharing can be justified. With regard to other data, access might improve its commercialization. Until now, data market places are indeed only slowly emerging ([7], p. 10) evidencing that data exchange is still limited.

According to the European Commission, the issues of access to raw data (i.e., data that has not been processed or altered since its collection; [7], p. 8) as well as access to machine-generated data are pivotal to the emergence of a data economy and require careful assessment. The Commission apparently takes the view that the *original* producer's control over access should be limited, meaning that third parties may have to be granted access. In its publications, the Commission identified specific sectors in which the rights in data and access to data are of particular relevance ([9], p. 25 et seqq.) and emphasized the importance of the objectives of improving access to anonymous machine-generated data, facilitating and incentivizing the sharing of such data and minimizing lock-in effects ([7], p. 11 et seq.). To this end, the Commission also wants to discuss a potential data producer's right and access against remuneration ([7], p. 12 et seq.).

Concluding, control over access to data would be a cornerstone of a data ownership right. However, anecdotal evidence shows that for both personal and non-personal data, exercising this control is already possible to a large extent, namely by keeping the data secret and denying access to it, and by trade secret law as well as criminal law provisions against data theft. This leads us to doubt whether the introduction of a new ownership right for data is necessary in view of the data access issue. The access rights envisaged by the European Commission that intend to facilitate the data market could indeed to a far extent be implemented by changes in the existing regulations. If a data ownership right were introduced, these access rights would have to take shape in the form of limitations to such right.

Control over copying of data

Similarly to the power of controlling data access, the control over copying the protected data would be a cornerstone of a data ownership right. On the basis of a new data ownership right, this power would be attributed to the original right holder. He or she could prohibit others from copying his or her data. The right holder could then grant specific permissions allowing others to copy the data. These permissions could factually amount to a transfer of the data.

But at the same time, others may also have valid interests in a right to copy. This can be illustrated by two ongoing debates that are both related to copying: The right to copy and the right to data portability.

Right to copy: The Swiss Federal Council was recently invited by a motion of a member of the Swiss Parliament to assess the desirability of introducing a right to copy in the federal constitution. The right should particularly allow copying of personal data for reuse ([12]). According to this motion, the individual should be vested with a right enabling him or her to commercialize his or her personal data. The background of this political request concerns the value potential of personal data that the individual could realize in case of reuse. The incentive stems from the healthcare sector. If an individual can copy his or her data, a commercialization of such data could become an option. So far, the reaction of the Swiss Federal Council has not been enthusiastic ([5], p. 38).

The scope of such a new right to copy is not intended to cover all data; the focus of the request lies on personal data. But particularly for personal data, the merit of a new constitutional provision appears to be unclear for the time being. Even if copied, the data will remain with the data controller. In addition, already under current data protection law, an information request can be filed with the data controller, having by and large the same effects as a specific right to copy.

It is thus difficult to see how the right to copy could attain the objective that the data subject can participate in the commercialization of his or her data in the data value chain. The value of the data of a specific individual is regularly relatively low ([97], p. 25) and only increases if a large amount of data is combined without regard to individual data being possibly protected. Consequently, the objective of participating in the commercialization of data should rather be realized through cooperative benefit models than by introducing a new right to copy.

Data portability: The term *data portability* means that individuals and businesses have a right to transfer their data from one system to another ([7], p. 15). Economically, data portability is realized if the switching costs are low and anticompetitive barriers do virtually not exist. In principle, these two conditions can be more easily met in the data economy than in the physical economy.

The right to data portability is based on the idea that each individual should have control over his or her data ([100], p. 66). If this is the case and switching costs are low, individuals can benefit from the value of their data. Originally, portability is a competition law issue. Portability is widely known in connection with lock-in effects in the case of installed software. However, competition law can only be applied if the *controller* of the data has a market dominant position (Art. 102 TFEU [3]; Art. 7 Swiss Federal Act on Cartels and other Restraints of Competition [23]). Therefore, notwithstanding some strengths of the antitrust rules, some weaknesses exist if data portability must be enforced via competition law ([42], n. 32; [100], pp. 67 et seqq.).

To overcome the competition law tensions and unlike the preceding Directive [4], the General Data Protection Regulation (GDPR) now contains a specific provision introducing a *right to data portability* (Art. 20). After a long history with many ups and downs, the final wording reads that the controller has to transfer the personal data "in a structured and commonly used machine-readable format" to the provider designated by the data *owner*; such transfer should take place without hindrance from the controller and without costs imposed on the data *owner*.

The new right to data portability contained in Art. 20 GDPR has been subject to many critical assessments ([55], p. 648; [78], DSGVO 20 N 3; for further details see [100], pp. 69 et seq.). In the currently ongoing revision of the Swiss FADP, the federal council's draft of the new law does not foresee a right to portability, arguing that experiences in the European Union should be awaited ([5], p. 22).

Data portability depends on the power to copy data but does not necessarily depend on the acknowledgment of a data ownership right. With the exception of a bankruptcy situation, a data ownership right would hardly be stronger and more efficient than an appropriate regulatory regime stating the conditions and the consequences of a transfer of data from one system to another.

Indeed, such a regime is not yet available for nonpersonal data, not even for widely used online services such as cloud hosting providers. In the context of such data, similar regulation as in the GDPR seems to be worthwhile for consideration. A corresponding data governance concept would have to encompass transparency for users, managed access and interoperability to link different platforms together in ways that stimulate innovation ([7], p. 15).

Control over use and integrity

The ability to use the data for one's own specific purposes could be another fundamental power of a potential data ownership right ([75], p. 10). Although controlling access to certain specific data generally also includes controlling its use, a data ownership right may also grant access to data without allowing specific uses. Often and for efficiency purposes, Big Data analyses are performed in a decentralized manner, without copying data to a central silo before processing it. Consequently, the person controlling the data must have the power to permit the data's use within his or her sphere.

Further, control over integrity, that is, the assurance that the data will not be altered or destroyed without consent of the *owner* could also be considered a fundamental power of a new data ownership right ([75], p. 10). Regarding personal data, data protection law already covers an aspect of this power by requiring data processors to take reasonable measures to ensure and maintain the correctness of the data (Art. 5 FADP). Further, criminal law also protects integrity of data in Art. 144bis SCC, albeit with no means to restore the original state of the data.

Additional powers

Authors who are in favor of tailoring data ownership rights in analogy to property rights in physical goods claim that the data owner should enjoy (i) the power to reclaim data from anyone withholding it from him or her and (ii) to protect it against any unwarranted interference (both in Art. 641 para. 2 CC; [56], n. 42). But even if applied by way of analogy, these powers seem ill-suited to ubiquitous and nonrivalrous data and it is unclear why they should be necessary if access to, copying of, use of, and integrity of the data can be controlled.

Additional limitations

Clearly, the limitations depend on the scope of the right as defined by the individual powers. As seen earlier, the rights to control access to, copying of, and use of data possibly need to be limited. The literature also discusses additional limitations.

General interest access

Related to the general claim for access to data to increase the *free flow of data*, the European Commission has suggested that public authorities should be granted access to data where this would be in the "general public interest" and where it would "considerably improve the functioning of the public sector" ([7], p. 12). Examples are access for statistical offices to business data or the optimization of traffic management systems on the basis of real-time data from private vehicles. The Commission points out that these exceptions and limitations would have to be clearly specified ([7], p. 12).

Private use

Some authors argue that a data ownership right should not allow to limit the use of data for private purposes ([108], p. 146; [110], pp. 1159 et seq.). But it is noteworthy that separating private activities from business activities has become more difficult for two reasons: On the one hand, individuals create and share data with purely private intentions, whereas the platforms that store and make available these data are driven by business intentions. On the other hand, the business models of the sharing economy blur the boundaries of private and business activities more than ever ([102], p. 882).

Scientific use

Some authors propose that a data ownership right should not allow to prohibit the use of data for the purpose of scientific research ([108], p. 146; [102], p. 882). Concurring with this view, the European Commission emphasizes that access to data and the ability to combine data from different sources for scientific research in fields such as medical, social, and environmental sciences should not be hindered ([7], p. 12 et seq.).

Time limitation

Many authors propose to limit the duration of a data ownership right ([67], p. 646, without going into detail). For some, this is simply the consequence of the fact that only rivalrous goods merit limitless protection ([64], p. 92). Protection could either have a fixed term or could be renewed in analogy to trademark law ([102], p. 882, proposing a five-year term).

Publicity

Most of the existing concepts that attribute *erga omnes* rights to a right holder provide a means to identify the right holder, be it the land register, IP registers, or factual possession of a physical good. Copyright law is the exception to this rule. Some of the problems related to the enforcement of copyright in the digital age are certainly related to the missing publicity. This may be illustrated by the fact that particular solutions for orphan works had to be found within copyright law. Publicity is thus an issue that a data ownership right would have to address. Not knowing the right holder of specific data could result in costly searches and raise transaction costs to prohibitive levels. Although authors have argued for an electronic registration of the right ([102], p. 882), the publicity question has not yet been examined in depth.

Implementation

If the need for a property right in data is affirmed, this subsequently triggers the question of how such a right should be implemented. Besides the more formal aspects that are very country specific and would go beyond the scope of this chapter, any perspective that includes personal data has to deal with the question how a potential data ownership right would integrate with existing data protection law. Generally, two positions can be distinguished. Either the data ownership right provides an additional layer of protection to existing data protection law (See section "Data ownership 'On Top"') or the latter would be—at least to some extent—replaced by the new data ownership right (See section Data ownership "Instead"). In addition, we examine a contractual solution (see section "Contractual alternative").

Data ownership "On Top"

The consequences of implementing data ownership rights without repealing existing data protection law have not yet been addressed in depth. The prevailing view among authors seems to assume that data protection and data ownership laws would coexist despite some possible amendments to data protection law ([31], pp. 166 et seq., calling data protection right the "necessary boundary of a future data ownership right"; [110], p. 1160, talking about the coexistence of these regimes). Some even argue that a data ownership right would not replace the legal foundations of privacy protection, but strengthen it ([71], p. 93).

Other scholars prefer limiting data ownership to a *syntactical* level ([43]; [44], p. 273; [110], p. 1159). In this implementation, the data owner would bear no rights with regard to the semantics of the data. Ownership would extend merely to rights in the actual determination of the data, that is, the string of 0s and 1s, and data would be protected as a commodity asset (cf. p. 127, where "commodity asset" is a defined term).

We argue that the consequences of implementing a data ownership right without repealing existing data protection law will vary depending on the scope of such an ownership right. Regarding *personal* data, the powers granted by an ownership right would overlap with the protection granted by data protection law on the *semantic* level. As data owner and data subject could mutually prohibit the use of the data ([97], p. 30), this potential stalemate is a shortcoming of this implementation. The complicated entitlement situation could be detrimental to the property right's intended rationale of antagonizing market failure by providing clear allocations. Overcoming this problem by limiting an ownership right to the syntactical level sounds appealing in theory, but will face similar problems, as the syntactic and semantic level of data often are inseparable.

As far as *non-personal* data is concerned, however, a data ownership right would not overlap with existing data protection law. But as the line between personal and non-personal data is blurry, conclusive allocations are again not easy to make.

Data ownership "Instead"

As shown, adding property rights on top would encompass tricky conflict-of-rights issues. Hence, property rights in data could also be implemented by partly replacing current data protection law. One benefit of replacing parts of data protection law with a data ownership right would be the reduction of compliance costs ([89], p. 1136) and the increased transferability of personal data. Nevertheless, one should bear in mind that data protection law encompasses more than the attribution of legal positions. No property right can guarantee, for example, transparency with regard to data processing, data quality, or security standards. Accordingly, these provisions would still be justified.

As an implementation of an ownership right in data that does not have to be balanced against data protection law would grant a strong position toward other stakeholders, the question of who should be the right holder (cf. section "Right holder") becomes even more essential. Furthermore, it seems evident that property rights in data cannot simply trump *ordinary* ownership of the physical ledger. Thus, a difficult balancing of conflicting rights needs to be made. As there are two in rem entitlements in question, turning to established law and practice of property law is deemed a passable route by some ([60], p. 487).

Contractual alternative

Some authors deem contractual solutions to be a viable alternative in fostering economic transactions with data ([97], p. 31 et seq.). However, obligations concerning personal data are somewhat imperfect, as according to current data protection law standards, a data subject's consent to such transactions is always revocable. This notion stems from data protection's foundation in the right to personality. Accordingly, a data subject's obligations are non-binding and afflicted with uncertainties. However, this dogma has been contested in a recent Swiss Federal Court decision [114]. The case concerned an erotic model/escort agent that, in exchange for a free photoshoot, had agreed to publicize her pictures as long as her face is almost not recognizable. The model had irrevocably transferred the respective rights to the agency. Although the right to repurchase the pictures was contractually reserved, the model argued that she had an imperative right to withdraw her consent to publication, meaning she could forbid publication without having to pay the agreed sum of money. The Swiss Federal Court reasoned that indeed there are certain aspects of one's personality right in which no contractual obligation is possible, that is, the *core* of one's personality. However, if the economic interest in commercializing an aspect of his or her personality was crucial for the person concerned, a binding covenant with regard to *other aspects* of personality is possible. The Swiss Federal Court deemed erotic pictures do not affect the core of personality but rather be within the scope of these *other aspects of personality* ([114], consid. 5.2). Similarly, it is held that consent to processing data is not revocable in all instances ([85], DSG 13 N 14) and a certain balancing of interests needs to take place ([113], consid. 44). On the contrary, Art. 7 para. 3 GDPR grants the right to withdraw consent without mentioning a balance of conflicting interests and thus is seen as an imperative right ([46], DSGVO 7 N 16).

In sum, transactions in personal data would require overcoming the dogma of consent being withdrawable at all times. With regard to data protection law in general and the GDPR in particular, this does not seem possible without further ado.

Conclusion

In this chapter, we take stock of the ongoing debate regarding data ownership and try to map the relevant issues by addressing the rationale, characteristics, and implementation regarding a potential data ownership right.

With regard to the *rationale* of a potential data ownership right, we conclude that there is no clear evidence for a market failure in the narrow sense;

there is thus no need to incentivize data production or collection by introducing a property right. But we acknowledge that there are voices arguing that a data ownership right might potentially lower transaction costs. However, this argument lacks an empirical foundation and transaction costs might also increase with the introduction of a new right. Moreover, solving existing problems by introducing a data ownership right *across the board* would most likely go too far. As we have only encountered few and specific problems so far, there is reason to believe that this would be the case and that introducing a data ownership right across the board would cause a number of (yet) unforeseeable new problems. Accordingly, the identified problems should rather be solved by specific regulation.

When looking at the *characteristics* of a potential data ownership right, most parameters are still very unclear. Academics have only just begun to think about the possible subject matter of protection (be it data on the syntactic level or information on the semantic level) and whether data or information should be protected as unitary asset (attributing rights irrespective of how others have obtained the subject matter of protection) or as a commodity asset (allowing others to use independently obtained data or information). Similarly, there is no consensus about the criteria on how to originally attribute the right to a right holder. It is even unlikely that one of the proposed criteria will lead to an unambiguous attribution of a data ownership right. This leads us to assume that specific rules on collective ownership would have to be formulated.

We further observe that a potential data ownership right does not neatly fit into existing categories of property rights and liability provisions. When looking at the powers and limitations of a potential data ownership right, controlling *access to the data* and *copying of the data* have been identified as the core powers a right holder should be granted, which may be illustrated by ongoing discussions regarding a right to copy and a right to data portability. Furthermore, control over the use and integrity of the data would also play an important role when designing such a right. In addition, many authors ask for general and specific limitations of the right.

One of the central issues regarding the *implementation* of a potential data ownership right is its integration with existing data protection law. The data ownership right could either replace the existing data protection law or could be implemented on top. We have observed that the means to implement any ownership right in data depends on the characteristics of such right. Accordingly, the literature is divided on how to advance. A third option would be to overcome the dogma of consent to processing of personal data being irrevocable at all times.

Taking stock has shown that a lot of research has been done already. But mapping the data ownership issues paints a picture that is both complex and unfinished; almost all aspects require further research.

References

Sources

[1] Directive 96/9/EC of 11 March 1996 on the legal protection of databases, *Official Journal* L 77, 1996, 20–28.

[2] Directive 2016/943/EU of June 8 2016 on the protection of undisclosed know-how and business information (trade secrets) against their unlawful acquisition, use and disclosure, *Official Journal* L 157, 2016, 1–18.

[3] Consolidated versions of the Treaty on European Union and the Treaty on the Functioning of the European, *Official Journal* C-326, 2012, 47–390.

[4] Regulation (EU) 2016/679 of 27 April 2016 on the protection of natural persons with regard to the processing of personal data and on the free movement of such data, and repealing Directive 95/46/EC (General Data Protection Regulation), *Official Journal* L 119, 2016, 1–88.

[5] Eidgenössisches Justiz- und Polizeidepartement. Erläuternder Bericht zum Vorentwurf für das Bundesgesetz über die Totalrevision des Datenschutzgesetzes und die Änderung weiterer Erlasse zum Datenschutz of 21 December 2016.

[6] Bundesministerium für Wirtschaft und Energie (BMWi). Weissbuch Digitale Plattformen, Digitale Ordnungspolitik für Wachstum, Innovation, Wettbewerb und Teilhabe, March 2017.

[7] European Commission. Communication on building a European data economy. January 10, 2017, COM (2017), 9 final.

[8] European Commission. Communication, towards a thriving data-driven economy. July 2, 2014, COM (2014), 442 final.

[9] Commission staff working document on the free flow of data and emerging issues of the European data economy, Communication, January 10, 2017, SWD (2017) 2 final.

[10] Mydata2016.org, accessed April 4, 2017.

[11] International Information Technology Standard ISO/IEC 2382:2015.

[12] Postulat 15.4045 Fathi Derder: Recht auf Nutzung der persönlichen Daten. Recht auf Kopie.

[13] Anfrage 14.1064 Jean Christophe Schwaab: Muss das Konkursrecht in Bezug auf Computerdaten ergänzt werden?

[14] Parlamentarische Initiative 17.410 Marcel Dobler: Daten sind das höchste Gut privater Unternehmen. Datenherausgabe beim Konkurs von Providern regeln.

[15] Swiss Federal Act on Data Protection (FADP), SR/RS 235.1.

[16] Swiss Federal Act on Copyright and Related Rights (Copyright Act, CopA), SR/RS 231.1.

[17] Swiss Federal Act on Patents for Inventions (Patents Act, PatA), SR/RS 232.14.

[18] Swiss Criminal Code (SCC), SR/RS 311.0.

[19] Swiss Civil Code (CC), SR/RS 210.

[20] Swiss Code of Obligation (CO), SR/RS 220.

[21] Swiss Debt Enforcement Act (DEBA), SR/RS 281.1.

[22] Swiss Federal Act on Unfair Competition (UCA), SR/RS 241.

[23] Swiss Federal Act on Cartels and other Restraints of Competition (Cartel Act, CartA), SR/RS 251.

[24] World Economic Forum. Personal data: The emergence of a new asset class, January 2011.

[25] World Economic Forum. Rethinking personal data: A new lens for strengthening trust, May 2014.

Literature

[26] R. Arnet. ZGB 641, in *Handkommentar zum Schweizer Privatrecht, Sachenrecht, Art. 641–977 ZGB*, 3rd ed., edited by P. Breitschmid and A. Rumo-Jungo. Zurich, Switzerland: Schulthess, 2016.

[27] K. J. Arrow. Economic welfare and the allocation of resources for invention, in *The Rate and Direction of Inventive Activity: Economic and Social Factors*, edited by Universities-National Bureau Committee for Economic Research, Committee on Economic Growth of the Social Science Research Council National Bureau of Economic Research. Princeton, NJ: Princeton University Press, 1962, pp. 609–626.

[28] S. Baker. The privacy problem: What's wrong with privacy? in *The Next Digital Decade: Essays on the Future of the Internet*, edited by B. Szokaa and A. Marcus. Washington, DC: TechFreedom, 2010, pp. 483–508.

[29] D. Barrelet and W. Egloff. *Le nouveau droit d'auteur, Commentaire de la loi fédérale sur le droit d'auteur et les droits voisins*, 3rd ed. Bern: Stämpfli, 2008.

[30] R. Bartlett. Developments in the law—The law of cyberspace, *Harvard Law Review* 112, 1999, 1574–1704.

[31] M. Berberich and S. Golla. Zur Konstruktion eines «Dateneigentums»—Herleitung, Schutzrichtung, Abgrenzung, in *PinG*, 2015, pp. 165–176.

[32] C. Berger. Verkehrsfähigkeit „Digitaler Güter", *ZGE*, 2016, pp. 169–194.

[33] P. Bräutigam and T. Klindt, Eds. *Digitalisierte Wirtschaft/Industrie 4.0, Gutachten im Auftrag des BDI zur rechtlichen Situation, zum Handlungsbedarf und zu ersten Lösungsansätzen.* Berlin, Germany: BDI.

[34] R. G. Briner. Big data und Sachenrecht, *Jusletter IT*, May 21, 2015.

[35] J. Caspar. Drei Fragen zum „Dateneigentum" Interview, *PinG*, 2016, pp. 1–2.

[36] I. Cherpillod. LDA 8–10, in *Commentaire romand, Propriété intellectuelle*, edited by J. de Werra and P. Gilliéron. Basel, Switzerland: Helbing Lichtenhahn Verlag, 2013.

[37] R. H. Coase. The problem of social cost, *Journal of Law & Economics* 3, 1960, 1–44.

[38] R. Cooter and T. Ulen. *Law and Economics*, 6th ed. Boston, Berkeley Law Books, 2016.

[39] T. Domej. ZGB 641, in *Kurzkommentar, Schweizerisches Zivilgesetzbuch*, edited by A. Büchler and D. Jakob. Basel, 2011.

[40] M. Dorner. Big Data und «Dateneigentum», Grundfragen des modernen Daten- und Informationshandels, *CR*, 2014, pp. 617–628.

[41] M. Dorner. *Know-how-Schutz im Umbruch.* Cologne, Carl Heymanns Verlag, 2013.

[42] J. Drexl, R. Hilty, L. Desaunettes, F. Greiner, D. Kim, H. Richter, G. Surblyte, and K. Wiedemann. Position statement "data ownership and access to data." *Position Statement of the Max Planck Institute for Innovation and Competition of 16 August 2016 on the Current European Debate*, August 16, 2016.

[43] M. Eckert. Digitale Daten als Wirtschaftsgut: digitale Daten als Sache, *SJZ*, 2016, pp. 245–249.

[44] M. Eckert. Digitale Daten als Wirtschaftsgut: Besitz und Eigentum an digitalen Daten, *SJZ*, 2016, pp. 265–274.

[45] J. A. T. Fairfield. Virtual property, *Boston University Law Review* 85, 2005, 1047–1102.

[46] E. M. Frenzel. DSGVO 7, in *Datenschutz-Grundverordnung, Beck'sche Kompakt Kommentare*, edited by B. P. Paal and D. A. Pauly. Munich, C.H. Beck, 2017.

[47] G. Fröhlich-Bleuler. Eigentum an Daten? *Jusletter*, March 6, 2017.

[48] A. Früh. Roboter und Privacy, Informationsrechtliche Herausforderungen datenbasierter Systeme, *AJP*, 2017, pp. 141–151.

[49] P. Golle. Revisiting the uniqueness of simple demographics in the US population, *Proceedings of the 5th ACM Workshop on Privacy in Electronic Society*, 2006, pp. 77–80.

[50] M. Grützmacher. Dateneigentum—Ein Flickenteppich, *CR*, 2016, pp. 485–495.

[51] M. Gymrek, A. L. McGuire, D. Golan, E. Halperin, and Y. Erlich. Identifying personal genomes by surname inference, *Science* 339, 2013, 321–324.

[52] R. Haab, A. Simonius, W. Scherrer, and D. Zobl. ZGB 641, in *Zürcher Kommentar, Kommentar zum Schweizerischen Zivilgesetzbuch, Band IV: Das Sachenrecht, 1 Abteilung: Das Eigentum, Art. 641–729 ZGB*, 2nd ed., Zurich, Switzerland: Schulthess Polygraphischer Verlag, 1977.

[53] P. Hacker. The ambivalence of algorithms. Gauging the legitimacy of personalized law, in *Personal Data in competition, Consumer Protection and IP Law—Towards a Holistic Approach?* edited by M. Bakhoum, B. C. Gallego, M.-O. Mackenrodt, and G. Surblyte, forthcoming.

[54] E. Hafen, D. Kossmann, and A. Brand. Health data cooperatives—Citizen empowerment, *Methods of Information in Medicine* 53, 2014, 82–86.

[55] N. Härting. „Dateneigentum"—Schutz durch Immaterialgüterrecht? *CR*, 2016, pp. 646–649.

[56] U. Hess-Odoni. Die Herrschaftsrechte an Daten, *Jusletter*, May 17, 2004.

[57] T. Heymann. Rechte an Daten, Warum Daten keiner eigentumsrechtlichen Logik folgen, *CR*, 2016, pp. 650–657.

[58] R. M. Hilty. Die Leistungsschutzrechte im schweizerischen Urheberrechtsgesetz, *UFITA* 124, 1994, 85–140.

[59] T. Hoeren. Big data and the ownership in data: Recent developments in Europe, *E.I.P.R* 36(12), 2014, 751–754.

[60] T. Hoeren. Dateneigentum, Versuch einer Anwendung von §303a StGB im Zivilrecht, *MMR*, 2013, pp. 486–491.

[61] T. Hoeren. Sieben Beobachtungen und eine Katastrophe, *sic!*, 2014, pp. 212–217.

[62] G. Hornung and T. Goeble. Data ownership im vernetzten Automobil, *CR*, 2015, pp. 265–273.

[63] G. Hug. URG 9, in *Stämpflis Handkommentar, Urheberrechtsgesetz (URG)*, 2nd ed., edited by B. K. Müller and R. Oertli. Bern, Stämpfli Verlag, 2012.

[64] D. Hürlimann and H. Zech. Rechte an Daten, *sui-generis*, 2016, pp. 89–95.

[65] C. Jolls, C. R. Sunstein, and R. Thaler. A behavioral approach to law and economics, *Stanford Law Review* 50, 1998, 1471–1550.

[66] D. Kahneman, J. L. Knetsch, and R. H. Thaler. Experimental tests of the endowment effect and the Coase theorem, *Journal of Political Economy* 98, 1990, 1325–1348.

[67] A. Kerber. Digital markets, data and privacy: Competition law, consumer law and data protection, *GRUR Int.*, 2016, pp. 639–647.

[68] W. Kerber. A new (intellectual) property right for non-personal data? An economic analysis, *GRUR Int.*, 2016, pp. 989–998.

[69] M. A. Kessler. OR 43, in *Basler Kommentar OR-I*, 6th ed., edited by H. Honsell et al. Basel, Helbing Lichtenhahn Verlag, 2015.

[70] W. Kilian. Personal data: The impact of emerging trends, *CRi*, 2012, pp. 169–175.

[71] K. C. Laudon. Markets and privacy, *Communications of the ACM* 39, 1996, 92–104.

[72] L. Lessig. Privacy as property, *Social Research* 69, 2002, 247–269.

[73] C. M. Kauthen. La qualité d'artiste interprète: de la théorie à la pratique!, *sic!*, 2006, 912–914.

[74] A. D. Moore and K. E. Himma. Intellectual property, in *Stanford Encyclopedia of Philosophy*, edited by E. N. Zalta. Stanford, Center for the Study of Language and Information, 2011, substantive revision dating of 22 September 2014.

[75] R. T. Nimmer and P. A. Krauthaus. Information as property: Databases and commercial property, *International Journal of Law and Information Technology* 1, 1993, 1–34.

[76] X. Oberson. Taxer les robots? L'émergence d'une capacité contributive électronique, *AJP*, 2017, pp. 232–239.

[77] G. Oettinger. Speech at a fair in Hannover in April 2015: "Wir brauchen ein virtuelles und digitalen Sachenrecht, das auch für Daten gilt", cf. EU-Kommission versus Google, Günther Oettinger erwartet baldige Entscheidung, www.spiegel.de, accessed April 14, 2015.

[78] B. P. Paal. DSGVO 20, in *Datenschutz-Grundverordnung, Beck'sche Kompakt-Kommentare*, edited by B. P. Paal and D. A. Pauly. Munich, C.H.Beck, 2017.

[79] H. Pfortmüller. URG 10, in *Stämpflis Handkommentar, Urheberrechtsgesetz (URG)*, 2nd ed., edited by B. K. Müller and R. Oertli. Bern, Stämpfli Verlag, 2012.

[80] E. Philippin. LDA 9, in *Commentaire romand, Propriété intellectuelle*, edited by J. de Werra and P. Gilliéron. Basel, Helbing Lichtenhahn Verlag, 2013.

[81] D. Pombriant. Data, information and knowledge—Transformation of data is key, *CRi*, 2013, pp. 97–102.

[82] W. Portmann. *Wesen und System der subjektiven Privatrechte*. Zurich, Switzerland: Schulthess, 1995.

[83] R. A. Posner. *Economic Analysis of Law*, 9th ed. New York: Aspen, 2014.

[84] N. Purtova. The illusion of personal data as no one's property, *Law, Innovation and Technology* 7, 2015, 83–111.

[85] C. Rampini. DSG 13, in *Datenschutzgesetz, Öffentlichkeitsgesetz*, 3rd ed., edited by U. Maurer-Lambrou and G. P. Blechta. Basel, Helbing Lichtenhahn Verlag, 2014.

[86] M. Rehbinder and A. Viganò. URG 10, in *Orell Füssli Kommentar, URG Kommentar*, 3rd ed. Zurich, Switzerland: Orell Füssli, 2008.

[87] J. C. Sahl. Gesetz oder kein Gesetz, das ist hier die Frage, *PinG*, 2016, pp. 146–151.

[88] D. Rosenthal. DSG 15, in *Handkommentar DSG*, edited by D. Rosenthal and Y. Jhöri. Zurich, Schulthess Verlag, 2008.

[89] P. Samuelson. Privacy as intellectual property? *Stanford Law Review* 52, 2000, 1125–1173.

[90] H.-B. Schäfer and C. Ott. *Lehrbuch der ökonomischen Analyse des Zivilrechts*, 5th ed. Berlin, Germany: Springer, 2012.

[91] R. Schwartmann and C.-H. Hentsch. Parallelen aus dem Urheberrecht für ein neues Patenverwertungsrecht, *PinG*, 2016, pp. 117–126.

[92] C. Shapiro and H. R. Varian. *US Government Information Policy.* Berkeley, CA: University of California, 1997, pp. 1–50.

[93] L. Specht. Ausschliesslichkeitsrechte an Daten—Notwendigkeit, Schutzumfang, Alternativen, *CR*, 2016, pp. 288–296.

[94] P.-H. Steinauer. *Les droits réels*, Tome I, 5th ed., Bern, Stämpfli Verlag, 2012.

[95] L. Sweeney. Simple demographics often identify people uniquely, data privacy (Working Paper with publicly available data), Pittsburgh, Carnegie Mellon University, Data Privacy Working Paper 3, 2000.

[96] P. P. Swire and R. E. Litan. *None of Your Business: World of Data Flows, Electronic Commerce, and the European Privacy Directive.* Washington, DC: Brookings Institution Press, 1998.

[97] F. Thouvenin. Wem gehören meine Daten? *SJZ*, 2017, 21–32.

[98] P. Tuor, B. Schnyder, J. Schmid, and A. Jungo. *Das Schweizerische Zivilgesetzbuch*, 14th ed. Zurich, Switzerland: Schulthess Verlag, 2015.

[99] H. Ullrich. Lizenzkartellrecht auf dem Weg zur Mitte, *GRUR Int.*, 1996, pp. 555–568.

[100] R. H. Weber. Data portability and big data analytics. New competition policy challenges, *Concorrenza e Mercato* 23, 2016, 59–72.

[101] R. H. Weber and L. Chrobak. Rechtsinterdisziplinarität in der digitalen Datenwelt, *Jusletter*, April 4, 2016.

[102] A. Wiebe. Protection of industrial data—A new property right for the digital economy? *GRUR Int.*, 2016, pp. 877–884.

[103] W. Wiegand. ZGB 641, in *Basler Kommentar, Zivilgesetzbuch II*, 5th ed., edited by H. Honsell et al. Basel, Helbing Lichtenhahn Verlag, 2015.

[104] J. T. Wilbanks and E. J. Topol. Comment: Stop the privatization of health data, *Nature* 535, 2016, 345–348.

[105] G. Wild. *Die künstlerische Darbietung und ihre Abgrenzung zum urheberrechtlichen Werkschaffen.* Freiburg, Schulthess Verlag, 2001.

[106] M. Winterkorn, with respect to user-generated data in cars: „The data belong to us!“, cf. Der Spiegel, March 7, 2015.

[107] K. Żdanowiecki. Recht an Daten, in *Digitalisiert Wirtschaft/Industrie 4.0*, edited by P. Bräutigam and T. Klindt. Munich, Germany: Noerr LLP, 2015, pp. 19–29.

[108] H. Zech. Daten als Wirtschaftsgut—Überlegung zu einem „Recht des Datenerzeugers“, *CR* 2015, 137–146.

[109] H. Zech. *Information als Schutzgegenstand.* Tübingen, Germany: Mohr Siebeck, 2012.

[110] H. Zech. "Industrie 4.0"—Rechtsrahmen für eine Datenwirtschaft im digitalen Binnenmarkt, *GRUR* 117, 2015, 1151–1160.

Case Law

[111] ECJ, C-338/02—Fixtures Marketing Ltd v. Svenska Spel AB, November 9, 2004.

[112] Your Response Ltd v Datateam Business Media Ltd [2014], EWCA Civ 281.

[113] BAG, Urteil vom 11. Dezember 2014, Az. 8, AZR 1010/13.

[114] BGE, 136 III 401, May 27, 2010.

[115] Commerical Court of the Canton of Berne, 17 June 2015, "Theorieprüfung für Motorfahrzeugfahrer", *sic!* 2016, pp. 56–60.

Chapter 5

Philosophical and methodological foundations of text data analytics

Beth-Anne Schuelke-Leech

Betsy Barry

Introduction 147
Text data mining and words as data 151
Language context and content coupled 153
Example of text data analytics using linguistics 156
Sustainable transportation 157
Methodology 158
Discussions and conclusions 164
References 165

Introduction

With the rise of electronically produced and stored information, there has been a substantial and sustained increase in the quantity of publicly available information in the past 20 years. Much of this information is available for perusal and investigation and can provide significant insight into everything from regulatory practices to the roles and actions of elected officials, public administrators to public discourse. However, this information is underutilized, and insights remain unrealized, without reliable methodologies for collecting, organizing, and analyzing these vast stores of data. The contribution of this chapter is to look at the philosophical and methodological issues of unstructured text data.

Traditionally, there have been three dominant methodologies for social science research: statistics (e.g., econometrics, descriptive statistics), qualitative research (e.g., observations, case studies, and interviews), and experiments (Cresswell, 2014; Weathington et al., 2010). These methodologies have recently been joined by Big Data Analytics. Although Big Data Analytics would seem to be just an extended form of statistics, it is actually more of a combination of modeling, evaluation, quantitative, and qualitative techniques on datasets so sufficiently large that is impossible to manage them with simple data management tools. There have been many such datasets in science, engineering, medical, and mathematics fields; however, dealing with the sheer scale and scope of Big Data has been far less common in the social sciences.

It is only in the past several years that Big Data has become part of the mainstream conversations of research methodologies in social science. In contrast, managing, storing, and mining Big Data has been an industry staple since before the nomenclature pervaded the lexicon. Private corporations, such as Google, Amazon, Netflix, Microsoft, and those in the Pharmaceutical and Healthcare industries, have been processing and mining Big Data for sales and marketing, as well as research and development-related enterprises. Government intelligence agencies such as the National Security Administration (NSA) have also become experts at gathering, managing, and analyzing vast amounts of data.

Generally speaking, data can be classified into three types: numeric, audiovisual, and text (Schuelke-Leech et al., 2015). Numeric data comprise numbers, quantities, and binary code. Audiovisual is made up of images, recordings, and videos. Text is made up of natural language data.

Another useful distinction between data types is structured versus unstructured data. Structured data resides in fixed fields (columns and rows) in a file or a record. Numeric data are considered structured data. It has the advantage of being easily entered, organized, queried, and analyzed. Conversely, unstructured data are not easily organized neatly into predetermined fields or data models. Text and multimedia content is unstructured data. It is estimated that unstructured data, the bulk of which is text-based data, make up 80%–90% of all of the data produced by all organizations (Holzinger et al., 2013). Despite the fact that unstructured data, specifically, unstructured text-based data, constitute a large percentage of what we refer to as *Big Data*, much of the focus of data analytics has been on structured numeric data (Chen et al., 2012). This is in part due to the nature of the data itself. Relatively speaking, mining and exploiting structured numeric data are a more straightforward task. On the other hand, unstructured text data are considered more complex and therefore more difficult to manage, process, and analyze (Schuelke-Leech and Barry, 2016).

The focus of this chapter is unstructured text data. Before this can be discussed in detail, it is necessary to address the idea of *complexity* with respect to the nature of the data itself (see Schuelke-Leech and Barry [2016] for a fuller discussion). First, unstructured text data originate from a wide variety of sources, such as e-mail, reports, press releases, social media, newspapers, essays, books, web pages, or any place where written language is used to express ideas or communicate information. Moreover, unstructured text may exist in a variety of file structures (pdf, txt, html, doc, rtf, etc.). Thus, transforming unstructured text into an analyzable dataset requires technical expertise.*

* *Technical expertise* refers to the range of natural language processing and computational linguistic techniques used in data preparation methods, as well as general computational requirements for processing and storage.

Simply put, it is not as easy as importing numbers into a database and then querying the database. The technical *complexity* of unstructured text data is significant and poses a challenge for text analysis, especially in the era of Big Data in which datasets originate from disparate sources, across a variety of technology-mediated environments.

The second aspect to the complexity of unstructured text is because of the fact that text-based data are natural language data (Schuelke-Leech and Barry, 2016). Linguistic complexity is because of the fact that language is innovative, infinitely varied, and changes over time (Siemund, 2011). Every linguistic style has particular characteristics and specialized lexicons, as does every genre. For example, an informal, personal Instant Message conveys information very differently than a formal business memorandum. Likewise, every industry has specific linguistic characteristics and specialized lexicons that form the linguistic habits of the industry, habits extant in their business communications and documentation (Stubbs, 1996).

Context is important in linguistics. Meaning is dependent on context. If you have a collection of unstructured text from the automotive industry, the presence of the form *crash* is not likely to refer to the stock market crash. Likewise, if you have a dynamic, varied collection of unstructured text from disparate data sources, conveying varied content covering a spectrum of different themes, styles, and genres, the form *crash* may take on a range of different meanings, depending on the linguistic context in which it is used. Crash may mean a physical collision, a metaphorical plummet, a loud noise, or to enter a gathering without an invitation. Crash in the presence of *vehicles* will constrain the range of possible interpretations, just as crash in the presence *stock market* or *computer*. Thus, it is the relationship between linguistic forms and context that inform interpretation and meaning. When dealing with natural language text, one cannot assume a one-to-one correspondence between form and function without understanding and accommodating linguistic context (Stubbs, 2001b). Unlike numbers in which the symbol "1" can be taken always to represent the quantity of "1," words can represent multiple things depending on the context.

The technical and linguistic complexity of unstructured text is magnified exponentially when dealing with the sheer volume or quantity in today's era of Big Data. The quality and the quantity of data make it extremely difficult for a person (or even a team of people) to collect, process, and analyze them effectively. Large collections of data are only useful if there is some ability to extract useful information, discover interesting trends, patterns, and correlations that can inform the decision-making process. *Text Data Analytics* is the term for analysis of large datasets of unstructured text and is used to generally describe processing and analyzing text-based natural language data.

Text Data Analytics is really a collection of various techniques, tools, and methodologies that have been developed in different fields with the aim of analyzing text for some specific purpose. Some of these tools and techniques developed from disciplines that focus on the rich content of text, with text being anything from a small passage of a speech, to a collection of speeches spanning decades. The text itself is the object of study. Researchers in these fields evaluate meaning and context in great detail, often manually with little or no technological intervention. Other researchers in different fields have developed computer technologies and algorithms that allow for the processing and analysis of large, disparate language corpora. The spectrum of Text Data Analytics is considerable.

Different tools and techniques have different intellectual origins and applications. Figure 5.1 presents the different areas of text data analytics, divided according to whether the methodology requires computer assistance for analysis, and depending on whether the methodology considers the smallest unit of analysis (linguistic forms or *words*) as discrete entities regardless of linguistic context, or whether content and context (linguistic form and function) are

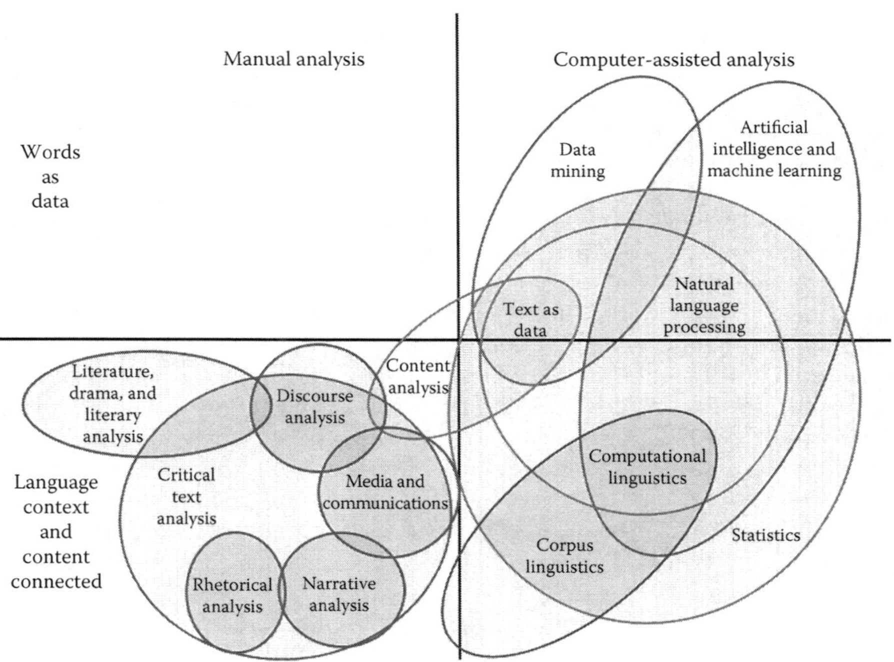

FIGURE 5.1: Disciplinary foundations for text data analytics. Miner et al. (2008) has a Venn diagram of six foundational fields of text mining (p. 31): Data Mining; AI and Machine Learning; Statistics; Computational Linguistics; Databases; and Library and Information Sciences. Their Venn diagram was helpful as the seed for thinking about the disciplines that have formed the numerous foundations of text data analytics.

studied *in toto*, considering the relationship a central aspect in conveying and interpreting meaning.

The upper left-hand quadrant represents the space in which words are considered discrete datum, but the analysis is done manually, without computer assistance. There are no commonly used techniques in this space. The upper right-hand quadrant is for the techniques in which computer assistance is used to analyze the text using techniques that consider words as data. The majority of techniques in this quadrant come from computer science and mathematics, such as natural language processing (NLP) and data mining. The lower left-hand quadrant contains more traditional methods of manual analysis of texts, such as literary analysis and discourse analysis. The lower right-hand quadrant also assumes the coupling of content and context, but it uses computer assistance for analysis.

Not all of the methodologies in the typology are used in policy, public administration, or political science research. We will now discuss the more commonly used ones, including looking at their strengths and weaknesses.

Text data mining and words as data

One of the challenges in analyzing and evaluating text is that everyone has an intuitive sense of language, which often means that researchers will impose meaning and value unconsciously on familiar words and grammatical structures based on their own particular domain expertise. As users of language, analysts often run the risk of taking for granted that words have a consistent meaning throughout text or across text types.

Data mining techniques developed with the intention of classifying, clustering, and analyzing large repositories of information and data to find patterns and trends that are not necessarily obvious with a manual analysis (Fayyad, 1997; Fayyad and Uthurusamy, 1999). Text data mining allows for a much faster organization and analysis of text data than what could be done manually as it uses semiautomated data mining techniques. Information and data retrieval is heavily dependent on similarity of content, identified by computer algorithms that match content to specified search terms (Hand et al., 2001) or linguistic forms. Typically, the text is tokenized* and reduced to an algebraic vector with a magnitude and direction, essentially imposing a mathematical structure on unstructured data. Similarity is based on the relative proximity

*Tokenizing a document means that the text is broken down into individual tokens. This typically means using the punctuation and white spaces in a text to delineate the tokens (Miner et al., 2012). In linguistic terms, a token is approximately the length of a word. According to Baeza-Yates and Riberio-Neto (1999), the average length of a book is 64,000 words.

of the data to a reference one (Hand et al., 2001). This conversion of text into numeric data is common. Typically, electronic *documents*[*] are reduced[†] and converted into a binary format that a computer can then decipher and transmit.

Text data mining originated primarily in the fields of library and computer science (Hand et al., 2001). These fields were generally interested in data management and the classification, retrieval, and summarization of information (Feldman and Sanger, 2007). One of the primary goals of text data mining is the discovery of patterns, especially the distribution, proportion, and frequency of words, as well as the associations and colocations of words (ibid). Text data mining uses tools from computer science, information systems, and mathematics, particularly machine learning, data mining, information retrieval, NLP, knowledge management (ibid), and case-based reasoning and statistics (Spinakis and Peristera, 2004). These tools provide a means for developing computer algorithms to divide the text into meaningful components, tag the parts of speech, and syntactically parse the words, sentences, and phrases (Feldman and Sanger, 2007). This allows for categorizing text and extracting information automatically once the computer has been *trained.*

NLP is a foundational field of text data mining. NLP processes texts to understand human language usage, and in turn, program computers to model language use, to impart and interpret meaning, in the same way people impart and interpret meaning. One goal of NLP is to create "domain-independent linguistic features" (Feldman and Sanger, 2007, p. 58) to develop software that can analyze unstructured text-based natural language regardless of context, style, or genre. To do this, NLP techniques analyze content and context independent of one another, as well as the interdependency of content and context. NLP is a subset of the larger field of artificial intelligence and machine learning. The goals of these fields are broader and investigate ways in which computers and machines can simulate and demonstrate intelligence (Grishman, 2010), a significant aspect of that is natural language usage.

Grimmer and Stewart (2013) present an excellent overview of the application of text data analytics to political science in their paper *Text as Data: The Promise and Pitfalls of Automatic Content Analysis Methods for Political Texts*. Grimmer and Stewart place themselves into the realm of text as data within the content analysis sphere. They focus on the automation of text analysis at the document level employing a *bag-of-words* technique, in which the root word is used in the analysis (called stemming). The noise or stop words (e.g., the, to, from, and, for, etc.)[‡] and punctuation are discarded, as

[*] *Document* is a term that refers to any individual file that contains unstructured text, not simply a word processing document.

[†] Reduced because the entire document is truncated to the first 100–500 tokens.

[‡] Stop words are grammatical words that occur at high frequencies and make up large percentages of the total number of words in text. They are called "function" words in linguistics as they provide grammatical function, as opposed to content words, which impart ideas or actions, and so on.

are very uncommon words (i.e., those that occur at a raw frequency of one in each documents). A small set of documents is hand-coded or a coding dictionary created, and then this is used to train a computer to classify the rest of the documents.

Content analysis is one of the few areas that cross between manual and computer-assisted analysis and between the coupling and decoupling of content and context. The borders of content analysis are somewhat porous. Originally, content analysis focused on a quantitative analysis of the text, such as the frequency of words, but it quickly expanded to include syntactic, semantic, and pragmatic functions.* Thus, content analysis incorporated statistical analysis relatively early. Content analysis now includes automated content analysis.

This technique has been the most commonly used one in policy and political science research. It has been employed in analyzing political agendas (Laver et al., 2003), legislative agendas (Grimmer, 2010), committee hearings (Jones et al., 2009), treaties (Spirling and McLean, 2007), political manifestos (Gabel and Huber, 2000; Hansen, 2008; Volkens et al., 2009), comparative politics (Lucas et al., 2015), political speeches (Laver and Benoit, 2002), and other discernible genres within the policy realm. As computer programs and information technologies make it increasingly easier to gather text, the applications will grow.

Language context and content coupled

The *words as data* techniques are only used with computer-assisted analysis. In their paper, looking at the analysis of political agendas, Laver et al. (2003) contrast this method of words as data with some of the other types of text analysis. They note that their technique deviates from the manual text analysis methods in which texts are carefully read for meaning and the content and context are coupled. Similarly, Grimmer and Stewart (2013) acknowledge that the automated analysis of texts cannot completely replace the manual analysis of texts.

In contrast, much of the work in Critical Text Analysis requires a careful, close reading of texts. Thus, many techniques remain in the realm of manual analysis and have long-standing scholarly tradition. Texts have been analyzed

*Content analysis originated in the field psychology [referred to as statement analysis as well] to study individuals through their language usage, not necessarily to generally study language usage in and of itself, and extract meaning from language decoupled from what it tells us about an individual. Its applications include psychiatry, psychology, history, anthropology, education, philosophy, literary analysis, political science, and linguistics (Krippendorff, 1980).

to understand the author's intent and message (e.g., literary, literature, drama analysis, and rhetorical analysis), how the writer creates meaning (e.g., narrative analysis) (Riessman, 1993), the cultural and social context in which the text was written (e.g., content and discourse analysis) (Neuendorf, 2002), and the structure of language (e.g., linguistics) (Biber et al., 1998; Coulthard, 1985; Hunston, 2002; McEnery and Hardie, 2012). Texts have also been analyzed in light of different critical frameworks, such as feminist critique, gender identity, or racial identity.

These different techniques come from different academic fields. Discourse analysis and Critical Discourse Analysis, for instance, originated in sociology, psychology, philosophy, and linguistics. Discourse analysis views language as a form of social interaction. It explicitly links language and social structure (Fairclough, 1989; Schiffrin, 1994; Stubbs, 2001a; van Dijk, 1992; Wodak, 1989). Discourse analysis is concerned with texts as objects of analysis in the context of culture, social structures, and historic dialogues. Instead of looking at the linguistic structure of language, discourse analysis is interested in the texts' cultural meaning and the power relationships that exist there, in line with the work of Foucault and Bourdieu (Jorgensen and Phillips, 2002). For discourse analysts, language and society are intertwined, in other words, language is a social construct and cannot be divorced from the social context in which it is used (Gee, 1999). Language shapes society and culture, which in turn shapes the way that language is used (known as linguistic relativity or the Sapir-Whorf hypothesis, Brown and Lenneberg [1954]). Analyzing texts provides some insight into society, power, relationships, ideology, and psychology. For researchers in this area, individual texts are always interposed within an ongoing historical dialog and discourse and a larger sociocultural framework.

The close reading and analysis of texts is necessarily a human undertaking and computer assistance has generally been insignificant. However, computer assistance does not necessarily require a decoupling of content and context, the way that *text as data* or *bag-of-words* does. Bag-of-words is named thus because the words are treated as independent of the original order. The punctuation, *noise* words, and *infrequently* used words are removed. This technique is extremely useful when the goal is classification, frequency counts, and clustering of the words. However, the context of words also holds clues as to the meaning of the word (Sinclair, 1967). Removing the noise words and punctuation removes information that contextualized natural language, creating linguistic nuance and affecting meaning. A worthwhile analogy is to consider the effect on numerical data if individual points are removed because the analyst decides that they are unnecessary, inconvenient for the research, or a methodological nuisance. These decisions result in the loss of information.

There are methodologies that allow for a much more nuanced and complete understanding of the data. Linguistic methods, for instance, are developed with an understanding of the importance of the relationship between content and context, form and function, within the structure of language (Biber et al., 1998). Linguistic methodologies are the foundation of many of the analytical tools used in text data mining (Kuechler, 2007). These methodologies look for patterns and trends in the text corpus.* Again, they rely on the context, as well as the content, to understand meaning. Instead of limiting the analysis to classifications, clusters, and frequency, corpus-based and computational linguistics allow for both a quantitatively rigorous analysis and a principled, qualitative investigation of the context and patterns in language (Biber et al., 1998; Chattamvelli, 2009; Feldman and Sanger, 2007; Hand et al., 2001; McEnery and Hardie, 2012). In essence, qualitative, data-driven linguistic methodologies can validate quantitative methodologies, in which qualitatively investigative frameworks inform what forms or patterns will be measured, or quantified, in analyzing text-based natural language data. When dealing with large quantities of data, the analytical techniques and algorithms used must scale to incorporate computer-assisted processing and management (Barry, 2008; Barry et al., 2015; Darwin, 2008).

Corpus linguistics is the computer-mediated study of language structure and use text-based corpora representing natural language in *real world* contexts. Computational linguistics explicitly integrate computer systems for the purpose of understanding the nature of language as a phenomenon (Grishman, 2010). Both fields incorporate technology to extract and understand meaning and patterns of linguistic behavior in a large text datasets. Using a linguistic framework, it is possible to investigate the systematic associations of words, historical trends, meanings of words, and sentiment analysis, in addition to the frequency, clusters, and classifications that are used in the *words as data* analysis (Biber et al., 1998). Furthermore, consulting linguistics makes it possible to address linguistic complexity in valid and reliable ways, rather than relying on *reducing* or *simplifying* natural language data to facilitate analytical endeavors. Rather than simply being a frequency count of the words, both corpus-based and computational linguistic analysis facilitate an investigation of the context and content of the data. Indeed, a pervasive linguistic axiom is "words are known by the company they keep" (Firth, 1957).

In all researches, the methodology employed is determined by the research question of interest and the data. This overview demonstrates that there are many tools and techniques, not simply one methodology, and that the researcher must determine the methodology, based on the data and specific research question. At the same time, the tools and techniques available will determine what research questions can reasonably be asked as well as the outcome of all research endeavors.

---

*Corpus refers to a collection of text-based natural language data.

Example of text data analytics using linguistics

A rudimentary demonstration of Text Data Analytics using corpus and computational linguistics is presented here. The data comes from the official record of the U.S. Congress from 1981 through 2014. The Congressional corpus is comprised of speech, debate, and Hearing transcripts, and Congressional reports and documents. The transcripts are a particularly robust source of data as they provide a record of the give-and-take conversations in both chambers, and in the committee hearings and meetings. Though the transcripts are edited for grammar, spelling, and clarity, they are not edited for political correctness or ideology. They represent the ongoing context and quality of the conversation between various stakeholders in the policy process. Every topic that has been taken up by Congress over the last three and a half decades is extant in this corpus. Thus, the content is highly variable.

As discussed previously, the methodology employed is determined by the research question of interest and the data. For example, when dealing with technically complex, variable dataset of unstructured text such as the Congressional data, one that is variable in file type, file size, and file quality, it requires an additional methodological layer in transforming the original data into a dynamic, analyzable corpus.* In addition, a linguistically complex dataset such as this that is comprised of a wide variety of content, styles, and genres, requires comprehensive qualitative investigation and assessment as the foundation of any quantitative endeavors. The reason is due to the linguistic complexity characteristic of large, variable collections of text. It is not enough to rely on one's own intuition about how different concepts are concretely expressed in the face of such linguistic variability. It is necessary to investigate and validate the language used to express concepts and themes under investigation, *before* one can measure these concepts and themes. Furthermore, it is not enough to simply verify the existence of concepts qua natural language usage, but it is also important to validate the extent of variation that comprise the concepts or themes of interest. To put it succinctly, you cannot measure what you do not know. Thus, it is both the technical and linguistic complexity of large, varied corpora that informs not only what kinds of research questions you can ask of your data, but also what sorts of processing and analytical methodologies are appropriate to work with, rather than work around, these complexities to address your research questions in the most valid and reliable way possible.

*The corpus for the 97th through the 113th Congress consists of 89,528 files with a total of 5.516 billion tokens. The size of the corpus makes computer assistance in the analysis imperative. Most of the files were originally pdfs, though there were also html and text files. The files were first converted to text files, then converted to utf-8. They were then tokenized and organized according to Congressional terms to preserve the original organization of the archive from which the data was collected.

Sustainable transportation

The example in this chapter considers how the concept of sustainable transportation is discussed in the U.S. Congress. As the purpose of this example is to demonstrate the methodology, the literature, theory, and implications of the results are necessarily brief. Instead, the focus is on how the methodology can be used to investigate a topic of interest.

Sustainability has become an important topic of conversation in many areas of research and society. It is now coupled with our food system, transportation, natural resource development, energy, economic development, urban planning, and so on. Creating a sustainable and resilient system requires addressing some of the unsustainable aspects of that system. In the United States, there are 253.6 million registered vehicles for highway usage (U.S. Department of Transportation, 2012). Transportation-related uses account for 28% of all energy consumed in the United States (approximately 27 Quadrillion BTUs of energy) (U.S. Energy Information Administration, 2012b) and 71% of all petroleum used in the country (U.S. Energy Information Administration, 2012a).

Much of the sustainability debate started in the 1970s and 1980s with scholars and activists grappling with the constraints and limitations of the natural environment. In 1987, the United Nations issued their report on the Environment and Development, more commonly called the Brundtland Report (United Nations, 1987). The Brundtland Report defined sustainable development broadly as human activities that meet current needs without comprising society's abilities to meet future needs. Since that report was issued, scholars and practitioners have struggled with what "sustainability" really means and how to redesign and change existing systems to achieve sustainability and resilience.

For transportation, sustainability is tied to addressing three problems that make the current system unsustainable: (1) the use of fossil fuels as the primary fuel source and the associated pollution; (2) traffic congestion; and (3) safety. Thus, a sustainable transportation system requires developing and adopting new technologies, as well as changing human behavior, public policies, and economic factors (Richardson, 1999).

Public policies, regulations, and government directives are important components of greater sustainability. However, it is not always clear whether federal policymakers are committed to sustainability, or even believe that sustainability is a significant issue to Congress. The U.S. Congress fulfills important functions in determining the priorities and allocation in the budget of the U.S. government. Thus, the conversation in the U.S. Congress about sustainable transportation is an important indicator of whether federal policies will support the goal of a transition to a more sustainable transportation system.

Methodology

We follow the methodology outlined in Schuelke-Leech et al. (2015) and Schuelke-Leech and Barry (2016). This methodology accounts for the complexity and volume of large unstructured datasets, rather than simplifying the dataset by removing noise words and order.

The first stage of any text data analytic investigation involves exploring and understanding the corpus under investigation. This includes understanding the documents that comprise the corpus, investigating how language is used in the corpus, and determining the statistically salient language in the overall corpus. Once this general investigation is completed, a more specific investigation of the concept of interest can be done. In practice, this requires the development of linguistic marker sets that represent the concept under investigation. This is an iterative process that makes this methodology a data-driven investigation, in which the use and application of language for the concept in the specific corpus is determined. That is, rather than simply doing key word searches and assuming that this will result in a complete set of results for the concept of interest, research in the corpus itself is done to ensure that the search returns are actually representative of this concept. This research also generates the statistical association of language that co-occurs with the linguistic markers. This shows related words and linguistic variation. Each marker and marker set is independently validated through this process.

Table 5.1 presents results of searches with marker sets in which transportation is narrowly defined and in which it is more broadly defined. The narrowly defined marker set is: automo*; car; cars; motor coach; motorcycle; motor vehicle; motor vehicles; passenger vehicle; passenger vehicles; sport utility; suv; suvs; tractor trailer; truck; trucks. For the more broadly defined marker set, the following words were added: bus; buses; transport; transportation; vehicle; vehicles.

The results for Transportation-related returns are presented in Table 5.1. The average number of files for each session is 5,333 files with 334.5 million tokens. The broader definition of transportation returns approximately twice as many results as the narrower definition. Transportation returns using a broader definition is an average of 0.4% of the total tokens, whereas a narrower definition returns about 0.2% of the total tokens. An important measure of the intensity of discourse is the hits per million tokens. This measure standardizes the returns. The results of returns per million tokens do show that the level of transportation-related discussions have remained fairly consistent in the past three decades. These returns are essentially frequency counts. Using the absolute returns numbers, it is difficult to know whether transportation is an important topic to Congress as there are so many discussions and topics. The relative discussions are often more revealing. This requires investigating

TABLE 5.1: Transportation returns

Session	Year 1	Year 2	Number of files	Number of tokens	Files with transportation returns	Number of returns	% of Files that contain transportation return	Returns per million tokens
113	2013	2014	4208	164,306,646	1,683	20,760	40.00	126.3
112	2011	2012	4561	164,236,662	1,740	23,907	38.15	145.6
111	2009	2010	6110	247,243,388	2,610	41,630	42.72	168.4
110	2007	2008	6940	263,816,803	2,825	47,821	40.71	181.3
109	2005	2006	4517	232,074,372	2,244	42,766	49.68	184.3
108	2003	2004	7104	319,856,928	2,801	53,784	39.43	168.2
107	2001	2002	6026	301,627,593	2,393	56,838	39.71	188.4
106	1999	2000	6039	275,512,343	2,042	44,536	33.81	161.6
105	1997	1998	5071	252,394,411	1,550	41,866	30.57	165.9
104	1995	1996	4858	417,460,481	3,012	67,171	62.00	160.9
103	1993	1994	4117	375,886,264	2,590	70,544	62.91	187.7
102	1991	1992	4153	335,393,629	2,377	84,272	57.24	251.3
101	1989	1990	5134	422,590,786	3,169	94,910	61.73	224.6
100	1987	1988	5622	460,083,483	3,446	90,371	61.29	196.4
99	1985	1986	3332	328,261,343	2,107	57,311	63.24	174.6
98	1983	1984	6506	530,712,147	3,804	123,033	58.47	231.8
97	1981	1982	5230	424,917,856	3,155	109,254	60.32	257.1
Average			5332.50	334,504,281	2,617	65,626	50.12	190.5
Stdev			1072.14	97,449,853	615	27,683		33
total			89528.00	5,516,375,135	43,548	1,070,775		3174

the specific topics of transportation more carefully using associations and proximity of concepts. In this case, we will use sustainable transportation as the concept of interest.*

Once a marker set is defined, queries can be conducted either on an individual marker set, or in combination to look at the overlap. This overlap looks at the proximity of the words, or the *linguistic context*, and allows for the investigation of the relationship between the markers as it impacts both form and meaning. Thus, it is possible to investigate how tightly coupled, or associated, concept such as sustainability is with transportation. To assess the overlap of the conversations, the marker sets are layered by specifying the proximity (i.e., constraining the linguistic context) of the results from the one marker set relative to the other. The closer the proximity between marker sets, the closer the lexical-semantic relationship. For example, specifying proximity of 5 tokens between marker sets means that you are looking for a very tight coupling of categories, or a close lexical-semantic relationship, as the words of each respective set are often collocated, or in the same phrase or sentence, modifying one another. Proximity of 15 or 25 tokens obviously means that there is less direct coupling of the categories, and a looser lexical-semantic relationship, even though the linguistic markers are still relatively close (often within the same paragraph or excerpt of discourse). Proximity of 50 or 100 tokens is wider, and although the categories are on the same document page or contained within the same file, they may actually be part of completely separate and distinct discussions, in which no lexical–semantic relationship exists between them.

Thus, the proximity range has a substantial effect on the returns, as demonstrated in Tables 5.2 and 5.3.

One of the important aspects of investigating is to validate the returns to see whether they are truly indicative of the desired research topic. When the proximity is small and the association is close, then a broader definition can be used, as the returns have few false positives. That is, the vast majority of the returns are directly related to the concept of sustainable transportation. On the other hand, once the proximity is specified to be large (starting at 25 tokens), many more false positives are included in the returns. So, returns like the following are included, which are not part of the target discussion:

- Cars without seatbelts or airbags; Or maybe we recall times when we travel throughout our community and we notice not only a heavy fog but polluted (113th Congressional Session, Congressional Record, February 26, 2014).

*The sustainability marker set includes: conservation; eco-friendly; environmental; non-renewable; renewable; sustainable; and sustainability. When the associations are investigated, additional sustainability terms that are specifically related to transportation were included: alternative fuel; green; hybrid.

TABLE 5.2: Sustainable transportation returns with a narrower definition of transportation

Session	Transportation tokens	Sustainable markers and transportation markers within 5 tokens of each other	Sustainable markers and transportation markers within 10 tokens of each other	Sustainable markers and transportation markers within 15 tokens of each other	Sustainable markers and transportation markers within 25 tokens of each other	Sustainable markers and transportation markers within 50 tokens of each other
113	126.3	3.4	6.6	9.6	15.7	30.7
112	145.6	3.8	7.1	10.0	16.5	31.5
111	168.4	3.1	6.8	10.4	17.1	33.7
110	181.3	5.5	10.6	15.5	25.4	49.7
109	184.3	3.3	6.2	9.1	15.4	30.6
108	168.2	3.3	6.4	9.4	15.5	30.5
107	188.4	3.3	6.6	10.0	16.7	33.1
106	161.6	3.7	7.2	10.8	17.9	35.4
105	165.9	1.8	3.2	4.7	8.1	15.9
104	160.9	1.9	3.5	5.1	8.2	15.4
103	187.7	2.0	3.9	5.8	9.3	17.7
102	251.3	3.0	5.9	9.3	15.6	31.4
101	224.6	4.5	8.8	12.9	20.7	40.0
100	196.4	2.1	3.9	5.7	9.3	17.6
99	174.6	1.3	2.5	3.6	6.0	11.6
98	231.8	1.5	2.8	4.0	6.4	11.7
97	257.1	4.5	7.8	10.9	17.1	32.0
Average	190.5	2.8	5.4	8.0	13.0	25.4

TABLE 5.3: Sustainable transportation returns with a broader definition of transportation

Session	Transportation tokens	Sustainable markers and transportation markers within 5 tokens of each other	Sustainable markers and transportation markers within 10 tokens of each other	Sustainable markers and transportation markers within 15 tokens of each other	Sustainable markers and transportation markers within 25 tokens of each other	Sustainable markers and transportation markers within 50 tokens of each other
113	260.6	9.8	19.2	29.2	48.3	94.3
112	361.4	9.3	17.4	25.6	41.0	79.0
111	380.1	12.0	22.9	34.5	55.9	107.9
110	412.3	15.9	29.6	43.3	70.9	137.0
109	416.2	14.2	25.2	36.2	59.0	114.5
108	461.3	15.3	26.2	37.2	59.7	114.9
107	457.0	13.4	24.3	35.4	57.9	111.0
106	359.7	11.5	21.3	31.5	52.5	102.8
105	438.2	7.6	14.0	19.5	33.0	64.9
104	321.3	6.1	11.6	16.9	27.5	52.3
103	354.0	7.8	14.2	20.5	32.9	63.2
102	399.3	10.3	19.7	29.6	49.3	98.6
101	441.8	15.9	29.2	42.6	69.4	134.3
100	335.5	4.4	8.9	13.6	23.2	46.1
99	329.7	2.7	5.7	8.9	15.5	29.9
98	397.8	2.7	5.8	8.9	14.8	28.7
97	433.7	6.3	12.5	18.6	30.5	60.5
Average	393.7	9.7	18.0	26.4	43.3	84.1

- Liquid natural gas (LNG) bulk tank cars, LNG locomotive tenders, and technologies suitable to retrofit tank cars (discussing railroad cars, which was not the target conversation) (113th Congressional Session, Congressional Record, December 11, 2014, Book 2).
- Environmental Response, Compensation, and Liability Act of 1980 included lead oxide in the list of chemicals subject to the tax. The typical automobile (98th Congressional Session, WAM Hearing 1984).
- Clean Air Act. As citizens we are concerned that clean air be maintained; as players in the automotive aftermarket industry we are concerned that government rules not arbitrarily upset the competitive structure in the marketplace (98th Congressional Session, Hearing before the Subcommittee on Commerce, Transportation, and Tourism, of the Committee of Energy and Commerce, House of Representatives, February 22, 1984).
- Our legal system thus says the following: Thou shalt not paint thy truck green while, at the same time, permitting trucks painted with an equal mixture of blue and yellow paints. Unfortunately, liability today hinges in no small measure on whether one applies a *green* (98th Congressional Session, HEC Hearing February 2, 1984).

The other challenge in investigating language is that the meaning of words and phrases changes over time. So, for instance, in the early 1980s, discussions of *green* coupled with *trucks* are about military vehicles, not sustainability:

- Military-green pickup trucks of a new type. They bear official Air Force markings, hut they are Volkswagens (97th Congressional Session, Congressional Record, May 14, 1981).
- A row of green-and-black camouflaged trucks and jeeps are lined up outside the training center (97th Congressional Session, Congressional Record, August 10, 1982).

Thus, a qualitative assessment of the associations and context must be part of the empirical research, as well as a quantitative analysis of the relative frequency, norms, and* subcorpus statistics. The proximity and layering are not clustering or associating document topics. It is investigating the actual usage of the language and concepts of interest. It is possible through this method of investigation to identify topics associated with the main research question and to look at the saliency and sentiment of discussions.

Fewer results are returned with a smaller proximity than a larger one, just as fewer results are returned when relying on narrowly defined marker sets. The more tightly constrained the linguistic context, and the more narrowly defined categories, the smaller the query returns. This means that the research protocol must consider how closely associated the categories should

*Demonstrating these techniques would require more space than is available here and, thus, this will be left for other papers.

be and why. Again, it is not simply enough to establish the existence of co-occurrence or overlapping categories according to some randomly assigned proximity. It is important to investigate the relationship of the co-occurrence of the overlapping categories to make sure that the language content and context contribute to the overall research objectives.

The results show that there is a consistent increase in the conversations about sustainability in automotive transportation from the early 1980s to the 2010s, though there is quite a bit of volatility. The interpretation of the connections of the conversations of sustainability with transportation in the U.S. Congress is heavily dependent on the marker sets and the specified proximity. When a narrow definition of transportation is used and the proximity is small (i.e., when the concepts are very tightly couple) at five tokens, there appears to be a very small overlap of between sustainability and transportation with an average of 2.8 returns per million tokens (compared with 190.5 for transportation) or approximately 1.6% of the transportation returns. On the other hand, when transportation is broadly defined and the proximity is specified to be much larger (within 50 tokens), the concepts of sustainability and transportation appear to be more frequently linked with an average of 84.1 returns per million tokens, or 21.0% of the transportation returns. That is, how much of the overall conversation about transportation appears to be related to sustainability depends on how broadly transportation is defined, how broadly sustainability is defined, and how closely the association between the two is specified. Using a narrow definition of sustainable transportation, the proportion of the transportation conversation connected to sustainability does not exceed 15% of the transportation returns. This is also true if a broader definition is used, but the proximity is specified at 25 or fewer tokens. The broader definition of sustainable transportation, coupled with the larger proximity of 50 tokens, generally has too many results that are not directly related to sustainable transportation. Thus, these larger proximities would not be acceptable. Sustainability is certainly a part of the conversations of transportation, but definitely not dominant.

Given the importance of public policies in addressing the issues of sustainable transportation, the relatively low portion of the transportation conversation related to sustainability (less than 15%) indicates that Congress may not be discussing and implementing substantive policies that will address these issues.

Discussions and conclusions

Text data analytics is an important emerging methodology in policy and social science research. It allows for empirical investigations of all sorts of new research questions using rigorous, principled methodologies. As this paper has outlined, there are different methods and techniques that are appropriate for different research questions and data. There is not one single way of doing text data analytics because there is not one type of text data or one type of research question. In our case, the complexity of the data and research question necessarily translate into using a methodology that can account for this complexity, rather than trying to reduce or eliminate it. Corpus and computational linguistics are predicated on the complexity of language, and thus, have developed suitable tools and techniques.

The example of sustainable transportation highlights some of the issues associated with the methodology to potential researchers and reviewers. It is possible to investigate complex concepts. However, how the linguistic marker set is constructed and the proximity used in any association investigations will influence the results, and therefore, the implications and conclusions coming from those results. This is one of the reasons that validation is absolutely crucial. As it can be difficult to replicate the dataset and computer algorithm, research assumptions must be explicitly stated so as to allow reviewers to assess the methodology and conclusions.

References

Baeza-Yates, R., and B. Riberio-Neto, (1999), *Modern Information Retrieval*, New York: Addison-Wesley.

Barry, B., (2008). *Transcription as Speech-to-Text Data Transformation.* PhD Dissertation, The University of Georgia, Athens, GA.

Barry, B., S. Smith, B.-A. Schuelke-Leech, and C. Darwin, (2015), From big data to better data: Issues in text-based analytics, *I/S: A Journal of Law and Policy for the Information Society*, 10 (3), 45–57.

Biber, D., S. Conrad, and R. Reppen, (1998), *Corpus Linguistics: Investigating Language Structure and Use*, New York: Cambridge University Press.

Brown, R. W., and E. H. Lenneberg, (1954), A study in language and cognition, *The Journal of Abnormal and Social Psychology*, 49 (3), 454–462.

Chattamvelli, R., (2009), *Data Mining Methods*, Oxford, UK: Alpha Science International Ltd.

Chen, H., R. H. L. Chiang, and V. C. Storey, (2012), Business intelligence and analytics: From big data to big impact, *MIS Quarterly*, 36 (4), 1165–1188.

Coulthard, M., (1985), *An Introduction to Discourse Analysis*, New York: Longman Group Limited.

Cresswell, J. W., (2014), *Research Design: Qualitative, Quantitative, and Mixed Methods Approaches*, 4th ed., Thousand Oaks, CA: Sage Publications.

Darwin, C. M., (2008), *Construction and Analysis of the University of Georgia Tobacco Documents Corpus.* PhD Dissertation, The University of Georgia, Athens, GA.

Fairclough, N., (1989), Discourse and power, in *Language and Power*. London: Longman.

Fayyad, U., (1997), Editorial, *Data Mining and Knowledge Discovery*, Vol: 1, No. 1.

Fayyad, U., and R. Uthurusamy, (1999), Data mining and knowledge discovery in databases: Introduction to the special issue, *Communications of the ACM*, 39 (11).

Feldman, R., and J. Sanger, (2007), *The Text Mining Handbook: Advanced Approaches in Analyzing Unstructured Data*, New York: Cambridge University Press.

Firth, J. R., (1957), A synopsis of linguistic theory, 1930–1955, in J. R. Firth (Ed.), *Studies in Linguistic Analysis, with an Introduction by J.R. Firth, Special Volume of the Philological Society*, Oxford, UK: Basil Blackwell, pp. 1–32.

Gabel, M. J., and J. D. Huber, (2000), Putting parties in their place: Inferring party left-right ideological positions from party manifestos data, *American Journal of Political Science*, 44 (1), 94–103.

Gee, J. P., (1999), *An Introduction to Discourse Analysis: Theory and Method*, New York: Routledge.

Grimmer, J., (2010), A Bayesian hierarchical topic model for political texts: Measuring expressed agendas in senate press releases, *Political Analysis*, 18 (1), 1–35.

Grimmer, J., and B. M. Stewart, (2013), Text as data: The promise and pitfalls of automatic content analysis methods for political texts, *Political Analysis*, 21, 267–297.

Grishman, R., (2010), Information extraction, in A. Clark, C. Fox, and S. Lappin (Eds.), *The Handbook of Computational Linguistics and Natural Language Processing*, Malden, MA: Wiley-Blackwell Publishing, pp. 517–530.

Hand, D., H. Mannila, and P. Smyth, (2001), *Principles of Data Mining*, Cambridge, MA: The MIT Press.

Hansen, M. E., (2008), Back to the archives? A critique of the Danish part of the manifesto dataset, *Scandinavian Political Studies*, 31 (2), 201–216.

Holzinger, A., C. Stocker, B. Ofner, G. Prohaska, A. Brabenetz, and R. Hofmann-Wellenhof, (2013), Combining HCI, natural language processing, and knowledge discovery—Potential of IBM content analytics as an assistive technology in the biomedical field, in A. Holzinger and G. Pasi (Eds.), *Human-Computer Interaction and Knowledge Discovery in Complex, Unstructured, Big Data*, Berlin, Germany: Springer, pp. 13–24.

Hunston, S., (2002), *Corpora in Applied Linguistics*, New York: Cambridge University Press.

Jones, B. D., J. Wilkerson, and F. R. Baumgartner, (2009), The policy agenda project. Retrieved April 5, 2015, from http://www.policyagendas.org/page/about-project.

Jorgensen, M., and L. J. Phillips, (2002), *Discourse Analysis as Theory and Method*, Thousand Oaks, CA: Sage Publications.

Krippendorff, K., (1980), *Content Analysis: An Introduction to Its Methodology*, Newbury Park, CA: Sage Publications.

Kuechler, W. L., (2007), Business applications of unstructured text, *Communications of the ACM*, 50 (10), 86–93.

Laver, M., and K. Benoit, (2002), Locating TDs in policy spaces: The computational text analysis of Dáil speeches, *Irish Political Studies*, 17 (1), 59–73.

Laver, M., K. Benoit, and J. Garry, (2003), Extracting policy positions from political texts using words as data, *The American Political Science Review*, 97 (2), 311–331.

Lucas, C., R. Nielsen, M. Roberts, B. Stewart, A. Storer, and D. Tingley, (2015), Computer assisted text analysis for comparative politics, *Political Analysis*, 23, 254–277.

McEnery, T., and A. Hardie, (2012), *Corpus Linguistics: Method, Theory, and Practice*, New York: Cambridge University Press.

Miner, G., J. Elder IV, T. Hill, R. Nisbet, D. Delen, and A. Fast, (2012), *Practical Text Mining and Statistical Analysis for Non-structured Text Data Applications*, Waltham, MA: Academic Press.

Neuendorf, K. A., (2002), *The Content Analysis Guidebook*, Thousand Oaks, CA: Sage Publications.

Richardson, B., (1999), Toward a policy on a sustainable transportation system, *Transportation Research Record: Journal of the Transportation Research Board*, 1670 (1), 27–34.

Riessman, C. K., (1993), *Narrative Analysis* (Vol. 30), Newbury Park, CA: Sage.

Schiffrin, D., (1994), *Approaches to Discourse* (Vol. 8), Oxford, UK: Blackwell.

Schuelke-Leech, B.-A., and B. Barry, (2016), Complexity of textual data in entrepreneurship and innovation research, in A. Kurckertz and E. Berger (Eds.), *Complexity in Entrepreneurship, Innovation and Technology Research—Applications of Emergent and Neglected Methods*, New York: Springer, pp. 459–480.

Schuelke-Leech, B.-A., B. Barry, M. Muratori, and B. J. Yurkovich, (2015), Big data issues and opportunities for electric utilities, *Renewable and Sustainable Energy Reviews*, 52, 937–947.

Siemund, P., (2011), Universals and variation: An introduction, in P. Siemund (Ed.), *Linguistic Universals and Language Variation* (*Trends in Linguistics. Studies and Monographs*), Berlin, Germany: De Gruyter Mouton, pp. 1–22.

Sinclair, H., (1967). *Acquisition du langage et développement de la pensée: sous-systèmes linguistiques et opérations concrètes*. PhD Dissertation, Dunod, Paris, France.

Spinakis, A., and P. Peristera, (2004), Text mining tools: Evaluation methods and criteria, in S. Sirmakessis (Ed.), *Text Mining and Its Applications: Results of the NEMIS Launch Conference*, Berlin, Germany: Springer-Verlag, pp. 131–150.

Spirling, A., and I. McLean, (2007), UK OC OK? Interpreting optimal classification scores for the U.K. house of commons, *Political Analysis*, 15 (1), 85–96.

Stubbs, M., (1996), *Text and Corpus Analysis: Computer-Assisted Study of Language and Culture*, Oxford, UK: Blackwell Publishers.

Stubbs, M., (2001a), *Discourse Analysis: The Sociolinguistic Analysis of Natural Language*, Oxford, UK: Blackwell Publishers.

Stubbs, M., (2001b), *Words and Phrases: Corpus Studies of Lexical Semantics*, Oxford, UK: Blackwell Publishers.

U.S. Department of Transportation, (2012), Number of U.S. aircraft, vehicles, vessels, and other conveyances. Retrieved May 11, 2015, from http://www.rita.dot.gov/bts/sites/rita.dot.gov.bts/files/publications/national_transportation_statistics/html/table_01_11.html.

U.S. Energy Information Administration, (2012a), Annual energy review. Retrieved May 11, 2015, from http://www.eia.gov/totalenergy/data/annual/pecss_diagram.cfm.

U.S. Energy Information Administration, (2012b), International energy statistics. Retrieved May 11, 2015, from http://www.eia.gov/cfapps/ipdbproject/IEDIndex3.cfm?tid=44&pid=44&aid=2.

United Nations, (1987), *Our Common Future: Report of the World Commission on Environment and Development*, UN World Commission on Environment and Development, Switzerland.

van Dijk, T. A., (1992), Discourse and the denial of racism, *Discourse & Society*, 3 (1), 87–118.

Volkens, A., J. Bara, and I. Budge, (2009), Data quality in content analysis. The case of the comparative manifestos project, *Historical Social Research/Historische Sozialforschung*, 34 (1), 234–251.

Weathington, B. L., C. J. L. Cunningham, and D. J. Pittenger, (2010), *Research Methods for the Behavioral and Social Sciences*, Hoboken, NJ: John Wiley & Sons.

Wodak, R., (1989), *Language, Power, and Ideology*, Amsterdam, the Netherlands: Benjamins.

Chapter 6

Mobile commerce and the consumer information paradox: A review of practice, theory, and a research agenda

Matthew S. Eastin

Nancy H. Brinson

Introduction ... 171
Data monitoring ... 172
Personalized advertising ... 173
Privacy paradox and the AdChoices icon ... 174
Privacy management and trust ... 175
Theoretical approach: Communication privacy management theory ... 176
Motivational models of use ... 177
  Convenient information seeking ... 178
  Personal and social status ... 179
  Monetary benefits ... 179
Research agenda ... 180
  Grounding the agenda ... 180
  Generational differences ... 181
  Personality traits ... 182
Conclusion ... 182
References ... 184

Introduction

As consumers increasingly integrate mobile technologies into their lives, the information they collect not only offers an array of conveniences and benefits but also presents opportunities for third parties to access users' personal data for their own purposes. Moreover, the volume and depth of personal information being collected is staggering. According to the 2014 Global Information Technology Report, over two and a half quintillion bytes of data are created each day, and 90% of the world's total stored data have been created since 2012 [1]. Further, it is projected that all digital data created, replicated, or consumed—known as the *digital universe*—will double in size annually through the year 2020 [2]. Mobile technology and the targeted, specific, and constant access to consumers that it permits will be a fundamental contributor to the Big Data universe. The accelerated growth of *Big Data* is attributed in part to the proliferation of smartphones and other mobile devices, which track up to 100 data points about individual users, including their precise location, online behavior, past purchase history, e-mail and SMS communications, social contacts, and even biometrics [1]. As a result, it is likely that data gleaned from personal mobile devices will be a central focus of marketers and corporate organizations as they seek to identify effective tactics for their communication campaigns, as well as government agencies and regulators as they recognize the problematic privacy issues these practices represent. To this end, this chapter examines the context of Big Data within data collection methods and data utilization. Theoretical, managerial, and policy perspectives are overviewed, critiqued, and then applied within potential research agendas aimed at furthering the social scientific perspective of the influence of Big Data on society.

Data monitoring

Since the earliest days of the information age, scholars noted the increasing capability of information systems to monitor the communications and activities of individuals. The term *dataveillance*, coined by Roger Clarke [3], describes a new type of surveillance made possible by growing quantities of data collected by governments in partnership with large corporations and data brokers. Prior to the digital age, datasets were limited to record integration, file analysis, and elementary computer matching. As Web 2.0 emerged, offering richer user experiences and unprecedented levels of data sharing, the potential threat to individuals' information privacy escalated. Proliferating social network sites allow many aspects of social life to be quantified, including friendships, interests, conversations, and information searches. Mayer-Schoenberger and Cukier [4] noted this transformation of social action into online quantified data resulted in the commodification of human activity (including for real-time tracking and predictive analysis), which they termed *datafication*.

Modern consumers' information privacy concerns are largely rooted in this rapidly expanding Big Data ecosystem. Conceptualized as the rights of individuals whose information is communicated to others [5], information privacy and the protection of personal data have long been viewed as fundamental human rights [6]. Currently, human recognition (or *personally identifiable information*) is portrayed as the legal threshold condition for the loss of anonymity or privacy. However, the nature of digital communication suggests a need to rethink this definition for the modern age. An individual's digital identity encompasses a wide range of traceable offline characteristics (e.g., age, residence, income) in addition to a variety of online profiles, passwords, pin numbers, access codes, and behaviors—all of which establish concrete links between social and technological understandings of identity [7]. Today's digital consumer is no longer entirely anonymous as virtually every form of communication and behavior generates data that can be collected, aggregated, and analyzed [7–9]. Information gathered for one purpose can be readily retrieved for another, and the possible linkage between mass amounts of aggregated data about an individual conceivably makes almost every point of collected data personally identifiable. Indeed, in its 2010 report, the Federal Trade Commission (FTC) [10] recognized and addressed the "diminishing distinction between personally identifiable information ... and supposedly anonymous or de-identified information" (p. 93).

As a result, today's electronic *marketspace* (represented by a vast network of consumer and product databases fueled by Big Data) is dramatically different from the traditional physical marketplace [11]. Marketers now have the ability to aggregate an astounding number of information sources to profile consumers, which can be used to narrowly target them with various forms of personalized marketing communications [12]. According to the FTC (2010), more than 90% of websites and 100% of search engines gather visitors' data, either covertly (by storing digital *cookies* on users' devices) or overtly (by requiring users to submit personal information to gain access to the site). These databases are often bolstered by cross-platform information sharing between various sites and applications [13], and later sold to data brokers, who incorporate them into their comprehensive databases [14]. Once these enormous datasets are collected and aggregated, they are then resold for three primary purposes—to verify an individual's identity, for marketing of products or services, and for detecting fraud [15]. This aggregated information may be in the form of actual data collected about consumers in addition to modeled or *derived data*, which results from drawing inferences about consumer characteristics designed to predict future behavior [16].

Personalized advertising

Today's consumers are increasingly barraged with advertising messages targeted to them based on their personal data. The 2015 Internet Advertising Revenue Report reveals that targeted online advertising revenues hit an historic high of $27.5 billion for the second half of 2015, representing a 19% increase over the same period in 2014 [17]. Although there is some debate over the definition, most contemporary scholars agree that personalized advertising involves tailoring a message and/or delivery channel to individual consumers while retaining principles of mass message dissemination [18]. A key difference between modern advertising personalization and what was possible a decade ago is the development of hyper-targeted message delivery based on real-time location as well as recent online and offline behavior powered by Big Data [19]. Although asserting that personalized advertising provides benefits to both consumers and marketers, researchers acknowledge evidence that some forms of personalized messaging are not well received. Baek and Morimoto's research on ad avoidance identified two key triggers for consumers' negative attitudes toward personalized advertising: (1) when the message is not well targeted to their needs and interests, and (2) when the message raises issues of privacy concern [20]. Other researchers [21,22] have noted the effectiveness of personalized advertising is often contingent upon the context as well as the type of information necessary for personalization to occur. That is, when highly sensitive personal information is required, it appears the net value of the exchange decreases, along with the individual's willingness to disclose personal information.

Privacy paradox and the AdChoices icon

The purported advantage of data-driven marketing for consumers is that they receive highly relevant messages according to their individual behaviors, needs, and preferences, often at the precise point of need. However, a recent Pew study found that many consumers are anxious about the collection of their personal information (particularly within sensitive contexts), via search engines, websites, mobile devices, and data aggregators, with 68% reporting an unfavorable view of this practice based on privacy concerns [23]. This reaction is well supported by industry research showing that consumers are increasingly turning to technologies that allow them to elude tracking, block online ads, and register on do-not-track lists [24].

These divergent attitudes about sharing personal data (often referred to as the *Privacy Paradox*) reflect the complex nature of concern about information privacy management in the modern age [25,26]. Incentives such as giveaways, lower prices, convenience, and better selection, combined with consumers' reported feelings of powerlessness to protect their personal data that have all been advanced as explanations for this phenomenon [21]. Others argue that users' openness to sharing their personal data online reflects a lack of awareness about this practice or inaccurate perceptions of vulnerability [27]. Indeed, national surveys consistently suggest that although most adults are aware that companies are using their personal data for a variety of purposes and have concerns about this practice, their understanding of exactly how the data are being collected and used is severely lacking [28,29].

In response to criticism from consumers looking for oversight of personal data use by advertisers, the FTC instructed industry groups to develop a method to notify consumers regarding the collection and use of their online behavioral data. As a result, the AdChoices Icon notification program was developed by the Digital Advertising Alliance and launched in March 2011. The AdChoices Icon is displayed in or near personalized online advertising messages to inform recipients of personalized data tracking practices as well as offer them the ability to conveniently opt out of the online behavioral ads [30].

Prior to the launch of the AdChoices Icon program, Hastak and Culnan confirmed the majority of consumers were not comfortable in receiving targeted advertising based on their personal data [31]. However, they also indicated that although transparency and control did make consumers more comfortable with the practice, consumer education was needed to improve awareness. Since its launch in 2011, groups such as the Electronic Information Privacy Center and the National Information Infrastructure Task Force have criticized the AdChoices Icon campaign as ineffective and misunderstood by consumers [32,33].

In response to this criticism, along with a general dearth of literature evaluating AdChoices Icon effectiveness, Brinson and Eastin found that the inclusion of the AdChoices Icon in a personalized advertising message increased attitudes toward the ad as long as the recipient is knowledgeable of the Icon's meaning [34]. These findings were consistent with the persuasion knowledge model, suggesting when a consumer "perceives the topic to be relevant (i.e., personally targeted to them), and the agent to be trustworthy (by declaring use of the target's personal data via the AdChoices Icon), consumers are more likely to overlook their persuasion knowledge schema and be receptive to an advertisers' personalized message" [34, p. 11]. Although this research did further current understanding of the impact of the AdChoices Icon, additional research is needed to address effective ways to educate the public about this program, as the authors found the majority of respondents were not aware of it nor its meaning.

Privacy management and trust

Although numerous studies provide useful insight into individuals' perceptions about information privacy [35,36], they shed limited light on the determinants of information disclosure to particular recipients in online settings. Trust and perceived risk are considered two principal components individuals weigh when attempting to balance the costs and benefits involved in privacy disclosure in interpersonal relationships. Historically, trust works in tandem with perceived risk to predict behaviors, and together the trust-risk equation is considered the most influential variable in driving behavior in interpersonal relationships [37]. Rotter defines trust as a generalized expectance held by an individual that the word, promise, oral or written statement of another individual or group can be relied upon [38]. Trust represents a "willingness to make oneself vulnerable to another in the presence of risk" [39, p. 104] and involves a cognitive element as well as a behavioral element [40]. Recent literature related to mass communication conceptually groups trust into three dimensions: ability, benevolence, and integrity. *Ability*, as defined by Pavlou, reflects consumers' perception that an advertiser has the resources and capabilities to perform the necessary job, *benevolence* reflects the confidence consumers have that an advertiser is positively oriented toward their interests, and *integrity* expresses the belief that an advertiser abides by a moral or professional code (p. 101). Though they may be viewed separately, these elements are most often combined as a measure for consumers' trusting beliefs. Studies related to the adoption, acceptance, and attitudes toward data collection and personalized advertising in a variety of contexts [41,42] suggest that trust plays a key role in determining consumers' attitudes and behaviors toward these practices.

Theoretical approach: Communication privacy management theory

Advancing technology has generated new forms of communication that span the structural and functional characteristics of mass and interpersonal communication. As a result, some scholars look to mass communication theories such as uses and gratifications (U&G) to explain computer-mediated communication (CMC)-related behaviors [43–45], whereas others argue that interpersonal communication paradigms such as expectancy violations theory [46] and social identity theory [47] offer more useful insights due to the seemingly interpersonal nature of CMC. An alternative approach is to consider communication privacy management (CPM) theory in conjunction with concepts related to expectancy outcomes rooted in U&G approach to generate new insights. This approach offers to enhance understanding of the benefits sought by today's mobile media consumers in their interactions with personalized advertising, as well as account for perceived risks that influence users' information sharing and processing behaviors in mobile contexts.

CPM theory purports that individuals experience a dialectical tension between privacy and disclosure when deciding whether or not to share private information with others in face-to-face settings [48,49]. The key driver behind these decisions is the individual's value judgment of the risks versus the benefits of disclosure in a given context, moderated by their motivations, culture, and gender. Petronio [48,49] classifies these risks and benefits within the interpersonal relational context (such as self-expression, relationship development, loss of face, and loss of control), overlooking critical factors that may be introduced due to the nature of CMC.

According to CPM theory, people believe their personal information is protected by private and public boundaries, which are maintained by rules rooted in social norms. The permeability of these boundaries is ever changing and requires negotiation and coordination between the coowners of the shared information [48,49]. Once an individual decides to reveal personal information to another person, their coownership of this information is characterized by knowledge of the rules for a particular disclosure as well as shared responsibility for protecting the other's privacy. When these rules are not mutually understood or maintained between coowners, boundary turbulence can occur, which threatens the level of trust between them. In addition to trust, Petronio asserts that personal control is also central to an individual's privacy boundary management (an issue that has become infinitely more complicated in the age of computer-mediated communication) [48,49]. In today's highly networked world, the opportunity to disclose private information to one or many (whether intentional or not) has increased exponentially—via smartphones and other mobile devices, search engines, e-mail, social media, and e-commerce sites. Each of these platforms threatens to expose various levels of an individual's private information—from identity and location, to hobbies and interests, to health and lifestyle, to financial history, and personal relationship status—all with or without their consent.

Although CPM theory provides a workable framework for understanding how personalized advertising might be perceived as violating an individual's privacy boundaries, it does not fully account for all of the potential motivations for disclosure in a computer-mediated environment. For example, social networks and community forums typically require members to register and create an online identity to secure the benefits associated with these communities. Further, e-commerce sites, at minimum, require consumers to provide their name, address, and credit card data to complete transactions (in addition to collecting their purchase history). The cost to consumers who choose not to disclose their personal information to these various online and mobile platforms can be substantial, if not inescapable. They risk being denied critical information, convenience, social support, and/or selection depending on the context. In its current form, CPM theory falls short of addressing all of the dynamics related to online information disclosure in today's computer-mediated environment. Therefore, examining consumers' perceptions about the risks and benefits of sharing their personal data to participate in mobile commerce activities through the lens of CPM integrated with concepts of expectancy outcomes rooted in U&G yields important insights for scholars and practitioners.

Motivational models of use

Although there are many predictive models of media use, historically, U&G has been widely applied within media consumption. The U&G approach helps researchers understand the connection between media gratification sought and obtained [50]. The U&G paradigm was introduced in the 1940s as researchers began to question why audiences engaged in media behaviors such as listening to the radio or reading the newspaper [51,52]. Simply, U&G examines why and how people actively use specific media to satisfy specific needs. Early U&G research suggested five basic assumptions. First, users consume media based on their goals and purposes. Second, media users select content actively. Third, media behaviors are affected by social and psychological variables. Fourth, there are functional alternatives to media use, in that other communication can also satisfy wants and needs. Finally, media selection is considered a conscious choice.

U&G suggests social and psychological motives direct audiences to select a particular media to satisfy needs [50,53,54]. Thus, studies [54–56] have applied this approach to better understand why people choose a particular medium to fulfill their needs. Relaxation, entertainment, social interaction, information, arousal, escape, and parasocial interaction are among the reasons recognized by researchers for users' consumption of media [53,57]. That said, information, entertainment, and social gratifications are considered primary reasons that individuals select a particular media to use.

Building on more than 60 years of research, researchers such as Robert LaRose and Matthew Eastin (as well as others) have taken a social-cognitive approach to U&G, purporting that media consumption behavior is determined by the expected outcomes that result from previous consumption [58]. Similar to U&G, social cognitive theory (SCT) frames media exposure in terms of behavioral incentives (needs) and expected outcomes (gratifications); with the expected outcomes organized around six broad incentives for human behavior: novel sensory, social, status, monetary, enjoyable activity, and self-reactive incentives [59,60]. From the SCT perspective, expectancy outcomes are rooted within an expectancy value framework [61], in which past experiences drive future behavior. Within the context of this chapter, this means that positive and negative experiences are cognitively weighed and then positioned within an expectancy outcome framework, which drives consumer behavior and potential attitudes.

Convenient information seeking

According to U&G, the benefit of information seeking is that it satisfies the user's curiosity, contributes to learning through self-education, and provides a sense of security through knowledge [50]. Mobile devices in particular afford entry into an interactive network that allows individuals to stay in constant contact with one another, as well as with commercial entities interested in tracking their behavioral data and location [29]. A further benefit offered to mobile device users is that they are able to access the information they desire with relative ease and connect with applications that extend the benefits offered by these devices in a myriad of useful ways.

Personal and social status

At their core, all relationships are purposive and in that they add structure and meaning to an individual's life; and they have the power to significantly alter or reinforce perceived self-identity [62]. According to U&G, individuals regularly look to various forms of media to reinforce their personal status [50], both by gaining insight into themselves as well as identifying with valued others. Recent conceptualizations of personal status gratification associated with mobile media include self-expression [63], as well as coolness and novelty [57]; which have been associated with mobile devices by popular media sources [64].

Monetary benefits

Another important motivator for mobile technology users suggested by SCT and U&G is access to a host of monetary benefits offered by tracking and sharing their data with appropriate parties [50,65]. As demonstrated by previous studies, a variety of monetary incentives including discounts, rewards, and special offers [66], as well as free content, priority service, or status awards [67], are consistently shown to be predictors of positive consumer attitudes and behavior in a variety of media contexts.

When considering CPM and U&G within the context of privacy and mobile commerce, the following model is proposed as a merger of the interpersonal and mass media frameworks (Figure 6.1). Understanding the delicate balance

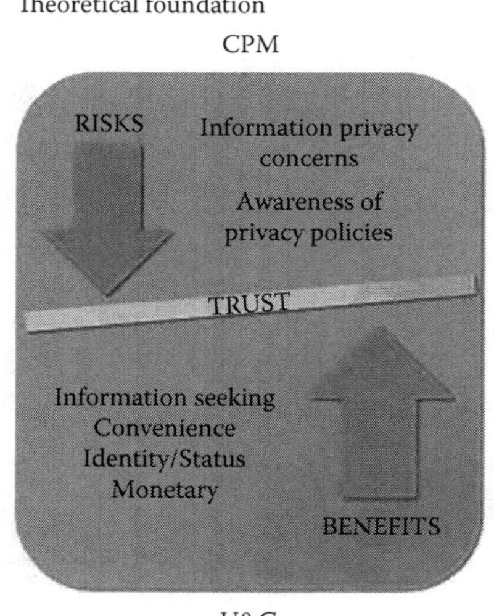

FIGURE 6.1: Theoretical Foundation Integrating CPM and Uses and Gratifications.

between perceived risks and benefits will enable research to better understand how, why, and with what effect mobile consumers engage in m-commerce behavior.

Research agenda

Grounding the agenda

As new media and new media behavior emerge, old frameworks such as U&G and expectancy outcomes are being applied. In addition, although this is a seamless transition at times, sometimes this is not the case. For instance, during the transition from radio to television, Bradley Greenberg's research agenda recognized the potential for new gratifications and, thus, conducted some of the first and now considered grounding breaking focus groups on children [68]. These focus groups identified new and existing gratifications that would guide the literature for years to come.

As consumer attention turned to the Internet, researchers including Andrew Flanagin and Miriam Metzger [56] took a similar exploratory approach to understanding the different dimensions driving Internet use. Robert LaRose and Matthew Eastin [44] theoretically approached the U&G framework through an expectancy outcome lens. In doing so, they built on Bandura's SCT framework [59,60], which defined six expectancy values (*as previously mentioned*). These expectancies, in combination with self-efficacy, provided strong predictive power of Internet use. With the emergence of smartphones, technological convergence, and perhaps most importantly a data-driven society, it is time to reconsider what consumers expect from mobile media experiences. For example, concepts such as the Privacy Paradox suggest that consumers are willing to accept some level of privacy violation in exchange for tailored, valuable content [12]. Meaning, what would have been considered a negative expectancy driving subsequent decreased device use, could in fact be commingling with positive expectancies of monetary rewards and relevant content, ultimately increasing device use. As such, rather than looking to past research to understand motivations, researchers should take a methodological step back and explore how content is currently being perceived and thus, motivating use.

U&G has never been considered a strong predictive framework, with research pointing to poor self-report measures and gratification sought versus obtained error. We suggest, in its current form, the possibility that U&G is no longer a viable framework in the current media environment. The technological convergence may be too intermingled for consumers to separate motivations or gratifications sought. For example, on many social networks, it is difficult if not impossible to separate social, entertainment, and information expectancies. If consumers are unable to separate these motivations on a use-by-use case (*use as a function of time may also be an irrelevant measurement*), it is hard to imagine a micro approach such as that used by U&G researchers gaining predictive strength. If anything, the error in recall or expected outcome from use will increase, subsequently attenuating predictive power in the future. To this end, using broader motivational constructs—measures that afford integrated inclusion (i.e., infotainment, socialtainment), or going back to a more qualitative approach in which consumers can express motivations through methods including focus groups or think-aloud sessions—could shed needed light on this area of research as it relates to general use, privacy, and mobile commerce engagement.

Generational differences

Another area in need of deeper examination is the purported generational differences in attitudes and behavior related to mobile privacy and e-commerce. A review of the comparative literature on generational groups and information privacy suggests that youth privacy perceptions and media usage patterns tend to differ widely from their adult counterparts [69]. As purported by 25 years of socialization research, youth generally lack the cognitive skills and life experiences necessary to understand the motives of those interested in collecting their personal data [70]. Moreover, adolescents are driven by a different set of motivations when interacting with various forms of online and mobile media, with boys primarily seeking achievement, whereas girls are more focused on social rewards [71]. Further, the fragmentation of traditional media along with the emergence of new technologies and 24/7 digital platforms have significantly increased the amount of time younger generations spend consuming various forms of media. A recent Nielsen report revealed that 99% of youth in the United States (aged 2–17) are exposed to live or streamed television content on a daily basis. This translates to an average of 7 hours and 38 minutes of media consumption on a typical day [72], exposing young audiences to approximately 16,000 television commercials per year. The heaviest reported viewing levels are among youths aged 8–17, who manage to pack in a total of 10 hours and 45 minutes of media consumption across multiple platforms [72].

Eastin examined Internet use among teens (aged 14–17) to determine what needs were driving their use of this increasingly influential medium, as well as what social influences and self-regulatory behaviors might be mediating their usage [73]. Findings from this study indicate that although parental influence increases positive outcomes and counters negative effects from media consumption, teens' increasingly strong ties with their peers combined with parents' comparatively deficient skills with Internet technologies make it less clear how parental and peer influences affect teen Internet media consumption [73]. Similarly, Nathanson found that although parental oversight was found to be a factor, the dominant influence for teen Internet use and self-regulation was the participants' peers [74].

Personality traits

In addition to examining motivational states and generational differences, our research agenda also suggests the need to better understand the role of personality traits in determining consumers' attitudes and behaviors related to personalized mobile advertising and e-commerce. A large body of psychological research employs a trait approach to describe relatively enduring characteristics of individual human behavior across a wide range of situations [75,76]. Further, communication scholars have demonstrated that individual personality traits such as extraversion, conscientiousness, and neuroticism have a direct relationship to their attitudes and behaviors related to various forms of online [77] and mobile media [78] usage. Through factor analysis, Eysenck [75] reduced the multitude of human traits into what is commonly referred to as the *Big Five* personality factors—extraversion, conscientiousness, agreeableness, openness, and neuroticism. Amiel and Sargent noted distinctive patterns of Internet use and usage motives for those of different personality types [79]. For example, those scoring high in neuroticism reported using the Internet to feel a sense of *belonging*, whereas extraverts made more instrumental and goal-oriented use of Internet services and were more likely to reject its communal aspects. Further, Landers and Lounsbury found that extraversion and conscientiousness were the most significant personality factors determining a broad range of Internet use motivations [77]. To this end, we propose a deeper exploration of the relationships between Eysenck's Big Five personality dimensions commonly associated with information sharing—extroversion (*measuring energy, assertiveness, and need for solitude*), conscientiousness (*measuring self-discipline, competence, and desire for order*), and neuroticism (*measuring the ability to trust, tendency to worry, and self-consciousness*)—and individuals' attitudes and behaviors related to personalized mobile advertising and e-commerce. Previous research in this area is promising, yet a deeper examination of these complex relationships offers potential insights that would be useful to scholars as well as advertisers and privacy policymakers.

Conclusion

Researchers recognize that significant gaps exist in the ability of scholars and practitioners to consistently predict why some consumers are receptive to personalized mobile advertising, whereas others are not. Exploring these relationships offers to advance research and practice, as well as inform developing policy standards. From a theoretical perspective, contrasting and extending frameworks typically associated with mass-mediated communication (expectancy values rooted in U&G) and interpersonal communication (CPM theory) challenges scholars to consider an interdisciplinary framework that more accurately reflects the dynamics associated with personalized forms of communication in mobile contexts. The U&G paradigm [50] suggests a host of consumer benefits potentially driving receptivity to personalized communication (e.g., convenient information gathering, personal status maintenance, and monetary benefits) that are not validated in all contexts. Although CPM theory [48,49] suggests valuable insights into consumer perceptions related to privacy and online information sharing, it does not consistently predict attitudes about personalized communication in all contexts. Further, this chapter suggests the possibility that media complexity has blurred the constructs of usage and motivation unreliable. Thus, a number of noted scholars in this arena [47,80,81] posit that the emergence of digital and mobile technologies has destabilized the traditional dichotomy between mass communication and interpersonal communication, calling for a fresh theoretical approach.

A more comprehensive understanding of consumers' perceptions about the risks and benefits associated with personalized advertising will also enable marketers to improve their personalized advertising outcomes. Consumers choosing to ignore or avoid messages intended to inform or persuade them could have potentially negative implications not only for advertisers, but also for public policymakers, educators, healthcare providers, and public safety advocates. Adding further complexity to this situation is a growing sentiment that online advertising has become progressively annoying and intrusive, prompting a significant number of consumers (approximately 198 million worldwide as of December 2015) to install various forms of ad-blocking software on their computers and mobile devices [82]. U.S. publishers and advertising industry leaders estimate that ad blocking by consumers cost them in excess of $22 billion in revenue in 2015, representing a serious threat to the economic viability of the current media economy [83].

Given increased efforts by lawmakers and privacy advocates to initiate *Do Not Track* standards, along with advertising industry efforts to outlaw ad-blocking software [83], the collection and use of consumers' personal data becomes of mounting concern to government regulators and lawmakers as well. A review of the existing U.S. regulations, policies, and laws addressing information privacy and security in the context of personalized advertising indicates a lack of clear, well-defined rules and practices. By recognizing the urgency of this situation, the White House, FTC, and the U.S. Department of Commerce have each produced separate reports to address various aspects of consumer privacy rights in the modern information era [10]. All parties involved agree that existing laws and policies do not adequately protect the collection and aggregation of personal data in all contexts.

The current chapter seeks to contribute to the important theoretical, managerial, and policy research discussions related to personalized advertising in a variety of contexts. Emerging mobile technologies suggest a whole new set of concerns related to data privacy; particularly as 73% of 13–17 year olds currently own a smartphone, and this number is only expected to grow [84]. Moreover, recent news about the proliferation of mobile devices and apps targeting children, including Pokémon Go [85], suggest the need for a deeper examination and analysis of mobile data collection practices and consumer attitudes toward messages targeted to them based on these data.

References

[1] IBM. (2015). *Big Data.* Available at http://ibm.com/big-data/us/en.

[2] Cisco. (2016). *VNI Global IP Traffic Forecast, 2015–2020.* Available at http://www.cisco.com/c/en/us/solutions/collateral/service-provider/visual-networking-index-vni/mobile-white-paper-c11-520862.shtml.

[3] Clarke, R. (1988). Information technology and dataveillance. *Communications of the Association for Computer Machinery,* 31(5), 198–512.

[4] Mayer-Schonberger, V., and Cukier, K. (2013). *Big Data: A Revolution that Will Transform how We Live, Work, and Think.* New York: Houghton Mifflin Harcourt.

[5] Westin, A.F. (1967). *Privacy and Freedom.* New York: Athenäum.

[6] Schwartz, P., and Solove, S. (2011). The PII problem: Privacy and a new concept of personally identifiable information. *NYU Law Review,* 86, 1814.

[7] Wessels, B. (2012). Identification and the practices of identity and privacy in everyday digital communication. *New Media & Society,* 14(8), 1251–1268.

[8] Buckingham, D. (2008). Introducing identity. In D. Buckingham (Ed.)., *Youth, Identity, and Digital Media,* pp. 1–24. Cambridge, MA: The MIT Press.

[9] Zwick, D., and Dholakia, N. (2004). Whose identity is it anyway? Consumer representation in the age of database marketing. *Journal of Macromarketing,* 24(1), 31–43.

[10] Federal Trade Commission. (2010). *Protecting Consumer Privacy in an Era of Rapid Change: A Proposed Framework for Businesses and Policymakers,* December 2010, 72–119.

[11] Rayport, J.F., and Sviokla, J.J. (1994). Managing in the marketspace. *Harvard Business Review,* 72(6), 141–150.

[12] Eastin, M.S., Brinson, N.H., Doorey, A., and Wilcox, G. (2016). Living in a big data world: Predicting mobile commerce activity through privacy concerns. *Computers in Human Behavior*, 58, 214–220.

[13] Finley, K. (2015). Facebook and IBM team up to supercharge personalized ads. *Wired*, May 6, 2015. Available at http://www.wired.com/2015/05/facebook-ibm-team-supercharge-personalized-ads/.

[14] Federal Trade Commission. (2014). *Data Brokers: A Call for Transparency and Accountability*. Available at https://www.ftc.gov/system/files/documents/reports/data-brokers-call-transparency-accountability-report-federal-trade-commission-may-2014/140527databrokerreport.pdf.

[15] Privacy Rights Clearinghouse. (2015). *Data Brokers and Your Privacy*. Available at https://www.privacyrights.org/print/content/data-brokers-and-your-privacy.

[16] United States Senate. (2013). *A Review of the Data Broker Industry: Collection, Use, and Sale of Consumer Data for Marketing Purposes.* Last modified December 2013. Available at http://www.commerce.senate.gov/public/_cache/files/bd5dad8b-a9e8-4fe9-a2a7-b17f4798ee5a/D5E458CDB663175E9D73231DF42EC040.12.18.13-senate-commerce-committee-report-on-data-broker-industry.pdf.

[17] Internet Advertising Bureau. (2015). *Internet Advertising Revenue Report.* Available at http://www.iab.net/media/file/IAB_Internet_Advertising_Revenue_Report_HY_2015.pdf.

[18] Vesanen, J. (2007). What is personalization? A conceptual framework. *European Journal of Marketing*, 41, 409–418.

[19] Teradata. (2015). *Global Data-Driven Marketing Survey: Progressing Toward True Individualization.* Available at http://applications.teradata.com/DDMSurvey/welcome/.ashx.

[20] Baek, T., and Morimoto, M. (2012). Stay away from me: Examining the determinants of avoidance of personalized advertising. *Journal of Advertising*, 41, 59–76.

[21] Metzger, M.J. (2007). Communication privacy management in electronic commerce. *Journal of Computer-Mediated Communication*, 12, 335–361.

[22] White, T. (2004). Consumer disclosure and disclosure avoidance: A motivational framework. *Journal of Consumer Psychology*, 14(1&2), 41–51.

[23] Purcell, K., Brenner, J., and Rainie, L. (2012). Search engine use 2012. *Pew Internet & American Life.* Available at http://pewinternet.org/Reports/2012/Search-Engine-Use-2012.aspx.

[24] Lerman, K. (2014). *Beyond the Bulls-eye: Building Meaningful Relationships in the Age of Big Data.* Available at https://www.communispace.com/uploadedfiles/researchinsights/best_practices/best practices_beyondthebullseye_buildingrelationshipsintheageofbigdata.pdf.

[25] IPG Media Lab. (2015). *Going Deeper: What Consumers Really Want from Personalized Ads.* Available at http://www.ipglab.com/2015/04/03/ipg-lab-yahoo-giving-consumers-the-personalization-they-want/.

[26] Zhang, J., and Wedel, M. (2009). The effectiveness of customized promotions in online and offline stores. *Journal of Marketing Research*, 46, 190–206.

[27] Jensen, C., Potts, C., and Jensen, C. (2005). Privacy practices of Internet users: Self report versus observed behavior. *International Journal of Human-Computer Studies*, 63, 203–227.

[28] Pew Research Center. (2014). *Half of Online Americans Don't Know What a Privacy Policy is.* Available at http://www.pewresearch.org/fact-tank/2014/12/04/half-of-americans-dont-know-what-a-privacy-policy-is/.

[29] Turow, J. (2011). *The Daily You: How the New Advertising Industry is Defining Your Identity and Your Worth.* New Haven, CT: Yale University Press.

[30] IAB. (2011). *Self Regulatory Program for Online Behavioral Advertising Factsheet.* Available at https://www.iab.com/wp-content/uploads/2015/06/OBA_OneSheet_Final.pdf.

[31] Hastak, M., and Culnan, C. (2010). *Future of Privacy Forum Online Behavioral Advertising "Icon" Study.* Available at https://fpf.org/final_report.pdf.

[32] Way, H. (2014). *Harnessing the Power of Big Data: New Media and Advertising.* Available at https://www.parksassociates.com/report/advertising-big-data.

[33] eMarketer. (2015). *AdChoices: Do Consumers Know They Can Control the Creepiness*? Available at http://www.emarketer.com/Article/AdChoices-Do-Consumers-Know-They-Control-Creepiness/1012623.

[34] Brinson, N.H., and Eastin, M.S. (2016). Juxtaposing the persuasion knowledge model and privacy paradox: An experimental look at ad personalization, public policy and public understanding. *Cyberpsychology: Journal of Psychosocial Research on Cyberspace*, 10(1), article 7.

[35] Cleff, E. (2007). Privacy issues in mobile advertising. *International Review of Law Computers and Technology*, 21(3), 225–236.

[36] Dutta, S., and Bilbao-Osorio, B. (2014). *The Global Information Technology Report 2014—Rewards and Risks of Big Data.* INSEAD and World Economic Forum, Geneva, pp. 35–93.

[37] Golembiewski, R.T., and McConkie, M. (1975). The centrality of interpersonal trust in group processes. *Theories of Group Processes*, 131, 185.

[38] Rotter, J. (1980). Interpersonal trust, trustworthiness, and gullibility. *American Psychologist*, 35(1), 1.

[39] Kim, P., Ferrin, D., Cooper, C., and Dirks, K. (2004). Removing the shadow of suspicion: The effects of apology versus denial for repairing competence-versus integrity-based trust violations. *Journal of Applied Psychology*, 89(1), 104.

[40] Pavlou, P.A. (2003). Consumer acceptance of electronic commerce: Integrating trust and risk with the technology acceptance model. *International Journal of Electronic Commerce*, 7(3), 101–134.

[41] Karjaluoto, H., and Alatalo, T. (2007). Consumers' attitudes towards and intention to participate in mobile marketing. *International Journal of Services Technology and Management*, 8(2), 155–173.

[42] Mir, I. (2011). Consumer attitude towards m-advertising acceptance: A cross-sectional study. *Journal of Internet Banking & Commerce*, 16(1), 1–22.

[43] Jun, J.W., and Lee, S. (2007). Mobile media use and its impact on consumer attitudes toward mobile advertising. *International Journal of Mobile Marketing*, 2(1), 50–58.

[44] LaRose, R., and Eastin, M.S. (2004). A social cognitive theory of Internet uses and gratifications: Toward a new model of media attendance. *Journal of Broadcasting & Electronic Media*, 48, 358–377.

[45] Papacharissi, Z., and Rubin, A. (2000). Predictors of Internet usage. *Journal of Broadcasting & Electronic Media*, 44, 175–196.

[46] Dolnicar, S., and Jordaan, Y. (2007). A market-oriented approach to responsibly managing information privacy concerns in direct marketing. *Journal of Advertising*, 36, 123–149.

[47] Luders, M. (2008). Conceptualizing personal media. *New Media Society*, 10, 683–702.

[48] Petronio, S. (1991). Communication boundary management: A theoretical model of managing disclosure of private information between married couples. *Communication Theory*, 1, 311–335.

[49] Petronio, S. (2002). *Boundaries of Privacy: Dialectics of disclosure.* New York: State University of New York Press.

[50] Katz, E., Blumler, J., and Gurevitch, M. (1974). Uses and gratifications research. *The Public Opinion Quarterly*, 37, 509–523.

[51] Dozier, D., and Rice, R. (1984). Rival theories of electronic newsreading. In R. Rice (Ed.), *The New Media*, pp. 103–128. London: Sage Publications.

[52] Ruggiero, T. (2000). Uses and gratifications theory in the 21st century. *Mass Communication & Society*, 3, 3–37.

[53] Rubin, A.M. (2009). The uses-and-gratifications perspective on media effects. In J. Bryant and M.B. Oliver (Eds.), *Media Effects: Advances in Theory and Research*, 3rd ed., pp. 165–184. New York: Routledge.

[54] Eastin, M.S., Cicchirillo, V., and Mabry, A. (2015). Extending the digital divide conversation: Examining the knowledge gap through media expectancies. *Journal of Broadcasting & Electronic Media*, 59(3), 416–437.

[55] Charney, T., and Greenberg, B. (2001). Uses and gratifications of the Internet. In C. Lin and D. Atkin (Eds.), *Communication, Technology and Society: New Media Adoption and Uses*, pp. 379–407. Cresskill, NJ: Hampton Press.

[56] Flanagin, A.J., and Metzger, M.J. (2001). Internet use in the contemporary media environment. *Human Communication Research*, 27, 153–181.

[57] Sundar, S.S., and Limperos, A.M. (2013). Uses and grats 2.0: New gratifications for new media. *Journal of Broadcasting & Electronic Media*, 57(4), 504–525.

[58] Wei, R. (2008). Motivations for using the mobile phone for mass communications and entertainment. *Telematics and Informatics*, 25, 36–46.

[59] Bandura, A. (1986). *Social Foundations of Thought and Action: A Social Cognitive Theory.* Englewood Cliffs, NJ: Prentice Hall.

[60] Bandura, A. (2001). Social cognitive theory of mass communication. *Media Psychology*, 3, 265–299.

[61] Rayburn, J.D., and Palmgreen, P. (1984). Merging uses and gratifications and expectancy-value theory. *Communication Research*, 11(4), 537–562.

[62] Fournier, S. (1998). Consumers and their brands: Developing relationship theory in consumer research. *Journal of Consumer Research*, 24(4), 343–373.

[63] Ko, H., Cho, C.H., and Roberts, M.S. (2005). Internet uses and gratifications: A structural equation model of interactive advertising. *Journal of Advertising*, 34(2), 57–70.

[64] Ockerman, E. (2013). 'Quantified self' craze helps people track their health. *USA Today*. Available at http://www.usatoday.com/story/news/nation/2013/08/06/data-tracking-puts-people-in-touch-with-their-health/2626533/.

[65] Bandura, A. (1997). *Self-efficacy: The Exercise of Control*. New York: Freeman.

[66] Ducoffe, R. (1996). Advertising value and advertising on the web. *Journal of Advertising Research*, 17(1), 21–35.

[67] Varnali, K., Yilmaz, C., and Toker, A. (2012). Predictors of attitudinal and behavioral outcomes in mobile advertising: A field experiment. *Electronic Commerce Research and Applications*, 11(6), 570–581.

[68] Greenberg, B.S. (1974). Gratifications of television viewing and their correlates for British children. *The Uses of Mass Communications: Current Perspectives on Gratifications Research*, 3, 71–92.

[69] Barnes, S.B. (2006). A privacy paradox: Social networking in the United States. *First Monday*, 11(9). Available at http://firstmonday.org/ojs/index.php/fm/article/viewArticle/1394.

[70] John, D. (1999). Consumer socialization of children: A retrospective look at twenty five years of research. *Journal of Consumer Research*, 26, 183–212.

[71] Baranowski, R., Buday, R., Thompson, D.I., and Baranowski, J. (2008). Playing for real: Video games and stories for health-related change. *American Journal of Preventative Medicine*, 34(1), 74–82.

[72] Nielsen. (2015). *Kids' Audience Behavior Across Platforms*. Available at http://www.nielsen.com/content/dam/corporate/us/en/reports-downloads/2015-reports/kids-audience-behavior-across-platforms-aug-2015.pdf.

[73] Eastin, M.S. (2005). Teen Internet use: Relating social perceptions and cognitive models to behavior. *Cyberpsychology & Behavior*, 8(1), 62–75.

[74] Nathanson, A.I. (2001). Parent and child perspectives on the presence and meaning of parental television mediation. *Journal of Broadcasting & Electronic Media*, 45(2), 201–220.

[75] Eysenck, H. (1991). Dimensions of personality: The biosocial approach to personality. In *Explorations in Temperament*, J. Strelau and A. Angleitner (Eds.), pp. 87–103. New York: Guilford.

[76] Pervin, L., and John, O. (1997). *Personality: Theory and Research*, 7th ed. Oxford, UK: John Wiley & Sons.

[77] Landers, R., and Lounsbury, J. (2006). An investigation of big five and narrow personality traits in relation to Internet usage. *Computers in Human Behavior*, 22, 283–293.

[78] Tosun, L., and Lajunen, T. (2009). Does Internet use reflect your personality? Relationship between Eysenck's personality dimensions and Internet use. *Computers in Human Behavior*, 26, 162–167.

[79] Amiel, T., and Sargent, S. (2004). Individual differences in Internet usage motives. *Computers in Human Behavior*, 20, 711–726.

[80] Child, J., Haridakis, P., and Petronio, S. (2012). Blogging privacy rule orientations, privacy management, and content deletion practices: The variability of online privacy management activity at different stages of social media use. *Computers in Human Behavior*, 28, 1859–1872.

[81] Walther, J. (1996). Computer-mediated communication: Impersonal, interpersonal, and hyperpersonal interaction. *Communication Research*, 23(1), 3–43.

[82] PageFair. (2015). *The 2015 Ad Blocking Report.* Available at https://blog.pagefair.com/2015/ad-blocking-report/.

[83] Morrison, M., and Peterson, T. (2015). Yes, there is a war on advertising. Now what? *Advertising Age*, September 14, 2015. Available at http://adage.com/article/print-edition/a-war-advertising/300336/.

[84] Pew Research Center. (2015). *Teens, Social Media and Technology Overview 2015.* Available at http://www.pewinternet.org/2015/04/09/teens-social-media-technology-2015/.

[85] Singer-Vine, J., and Troianovski, A. (2013). How kid apps are data magnets. *The Wall Street Journal*, June 27, 2013. Available at http://www.wsj.com/articles/SB10001424127887324520904578553662943430052.

Chapter 7

The impact of Big Data on making evidence-based decisions

Rodica Neamtu

Caitlin Kuhlman

Ramoza Ahsan

Elke Rundensteiner

Introduction 192
The decision-making process 194
Deriving value from Big Data 195
  Data extraction, integration, cleaning, and storage 195
    Data extraction 195
    Data transformation 198
    Data loading 199
  Efficient data exploration 200
  Using visualization to better incorporate data in the decision-making process 204
Real world case studies on using Big Data to make decisions 207
  Case study in heart arrhythmia 207
  Case study in Big Data integration for economic competitiveness analytics 210
  Big Data in various application domains 212
    Big Data for business decisions: Netflix 212
    Big Data fighting crime 212
    Big Data to predict weather 212
    Using Big Data to make data-driven medical decisions 213
    Using Big Data to predict stock market fluctuations 214
What does the future hold? 215
Glossary 217
References 218

Introduction

The main contribution of this chapter is to give an overview of core concepts related to Big Data in the context of decision making. After describing the general decision-making process, Chapter 1 offers a theoretical view of the journey of data from source to becoming intrinsic part of decisions. This part addresses issues and tools having to do with data extraction, cleaning, integration, and storage, as necessary steps to prepare the much needed data for assisting with decision making. The next crucial step in deriving value from Big Data is the exploration of these vast amounts of information. We describe tools for efficient data exploration as well as visualization tools that allow analysts better interpretation of the results. The second part of our chapter brings some "story-telling with Big Data," describing real-world use cases showing how Big Data is embedded in the process of decision making. Finally, the chapter offers a glimpse in the future of our new *data-driven* culture.

The concept of Big Data has diverse definitions and interpretations in different application domains. The Oxford English Dictionary defines it as "data of a very large size, typically to the extent that its manipulation and management present significant logistical challenges." Attempts to rigorously define Big Data led to many definitions featuring the underlying theme of its large size and the challenges associated with the process of leveraging it. In the computing world, data scientists break Big Data into four dimensions, known as the four Vs: volume, variety, veracity, and velocity,* as displayed in Figure 7.1.

- *Volume*: Big Data implies enormous volumes of data. A very large contributor to the ever expanding digital universe is the Internet of Things with sensors all over the world in all devices creating data every second. Data nowadays are generated by machines, networks, and human interaction on systems such as social media due to which the volume of data to be analyzed is massive.

- *Variety*: Big Data refers to the many sources and types of data both structured and unstructured from sources such as spreadsheets and databases to data in the form of e-mails, photos, videos, monitoring devices, PDFs, audio, and so on [1]. The wide variety of data require different techniques to manage the data from collection, storage, manipulation to interpretation of all raw data.

- *Veracity*: Big Data refers to the biases, noise, abnormality, and quality of data collected. Low quality and/or unreliable data can cause a lot of problems for organizations loosing trust in the insights drawn from it

*http://www.ibmbigdatahub.com/infographic/four-vs-big-data, http://insidebigdata.com/2013/09/12/beyond-volume-variety-velocity-issue-big-data-veracity/

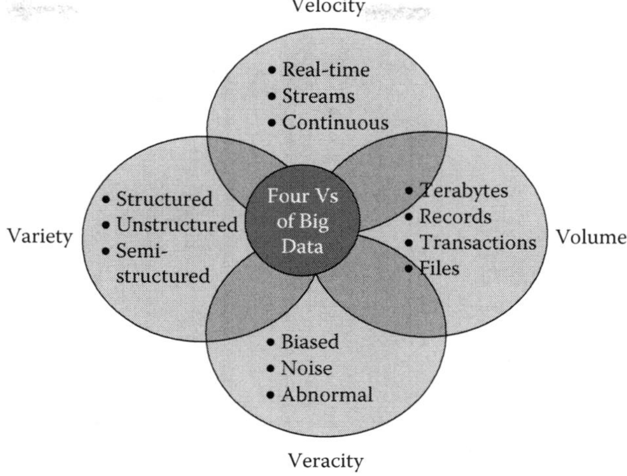

FIGURE 7.1: The four Vs of Big Data.

by consumers. Therefore, organizations need to ensure that the data are correct and derived from a trusted source, in addition to insuring that analyses performed on the data are correct.

- *Velocity*: Big Data deals with the pace at which real-time data with ever increasing speed are processed, stored, and analyzed. This continuous flow of massive data incurs tremendous challenges. These challenges are compounded by organizations increasingly needing to render decisions based on such data streams in situations in near real time.

With the unprecedented rising increase of each of the "four Vs of Big Data" in most application domains, there is a crucial need for transforming the quantity of data into quality insights. Many organizations focus on identifying opportunities and challenges presented by Big Data because it has been well recognized that leveraging its power to gain a competitive advantage is the key to yielding significant economic and societal benefits. Understanding the role that data can play in becoming a strategic differentiator is shared by governments, organizations, and individuals alike. In an era when data-driven decisions are on every organization's agenda, much work has to be done to seamlessly integrate data into the decision-making process. Research and business communities are coming together to create the necessary tools for taming Big Data and capitalizing on its power.

In the current chapter, we analyze the journey of data from its sources to becoming an asset in the decision-making progress, while briefly describing the challenges of *wrangling it* into the most suitable forms for exploration.

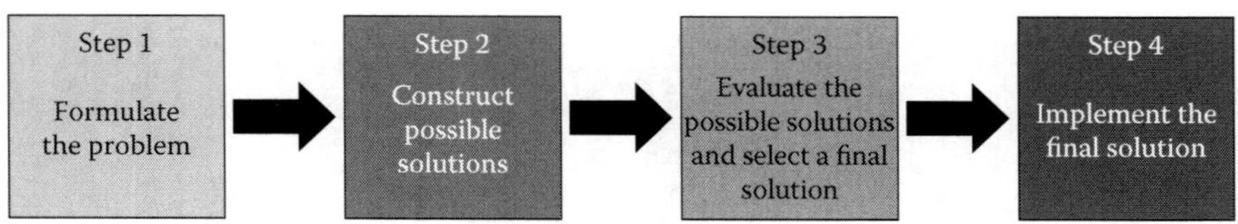

FIGURE 7.2: Steps of the decision-making process.

The decision-making process

In our quest to investigate the impact of Big Data on making decisions, we first characterize the general process of making decisions. As shown in Figure 7.2, there are typically four stages in the classical decision-making model. This assumes that people make logical decisions that are the optimum in furthering the organization's best interests.*

Each step of this process relies on having access to data and analyzing it before moving to the next step. This is a rational prescriptive model, describing how people *should* make decisions, and not necessarily how people actually make decisions. The rational model is based on the assumption that people have complete information and are able to make the best decision, one that is not based on emotion, but rather on information that is given to them. In summary, these assumptions include the following:

- Having complete and error-free information
- Using logical, unemotional analysis
- Having the intention to make the best decision

Generally, data can be used to assist people in making a decision or it can be incorporated into an automated decision-making process. Either way, data are one of the key ingredients in making decisions. To make it accessible to organizations and individuals, data have to be stored in data warehouses and/or data marts. A data warehouse is a large store of data accumulated from a wide range of sources and used to guide management decisions [2–4]. A data mart is a subset of a data warehouse usually oriented to a specific business line or team [2,3]. After the data are stored in the warehouse, it is *delivered* to analysts in the most suitable form that allows them to interpret it and incorporate it into the decision-making process.

Big Data is turning the process of decision-making inside out. Instead of starting with a question or hypothesis, people "data mine" to see what patterns they can find. If the

* *highered.mheducation.com/sites/dl/free/0078029546/.../kin29546*$_c$*h07*

patterns reveal a business opportunity or a threat, then a decision is made about how to act on the information.*

Professor Alex Pentland
Director of the Human Dynamics Laboratory at MIT

As the quote hints, such dramatic changes in the decision-making process are due to the existence of vast amounts of data, and the sophisticated exploratory tools to mine it.

Deriving value from Big Data

The first step in deriving value from data is the ability to quickly find and extract data from multiple sources and integrate them [5]. Although sometimes considered a menial task, data preprocessing and integration is a crucial step in data analysis. According to data scientists, bulk of their time may be spent on preparatory tasks to ensure that valid analysis of data is possible. Accurate and meaningful results depend on this process, which typically requires manual effort, technical expertise, and domain knowledge.

The challenges posed by this initial step are a ubiquitous barrier to progress in working with large datasets across domains. However, many tools have been developed to perform this task using smart technologies. The automation of data integration tasks has the potential to empower nonexperts to leverage the huge amounts of data available and to facilitate faster and more accurate data science.

Usually, data integration is approached in a modular fashion. Starting with the extraction of data from sources and ending with the delivery of clean, accurate information to be used in decision-making, this journey, involving several challenging steps, is known as *ETL: Extract, Transform, and Load* [6]. We explain each of these steps in the Figure 7.3.

Data extraction, integration, cleaning, and storage

Data extraction

Data scientists typically break the deluge of Big Data into two categories: *structured* and *unstructured* data. Structured data are generally stored in traditional relational databases [7], in which information is organized according to some *schema*. In this scenario, a table with rows representing data

*http://www.bdvc.nl/images/Rapporten/Capgemini-Big-Data-Decision-Making.pdf

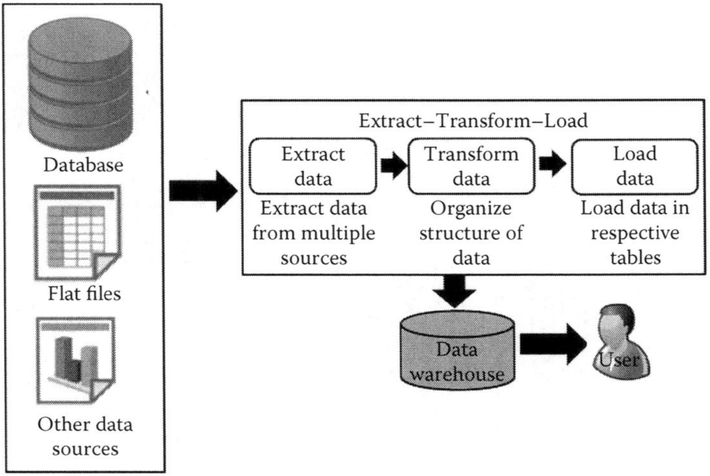

FIGURE 7.3: Extract, transform, and load processes.

points and columns corresponding to various data attributes is an example of structured data. A more intuitive example of structured data includes tables and spreadsheets of Census containing income, employment, dates, and place of birth, and so on of individuals. When faced with multiple types of structured data, schema must be resolved into some *unified data model.* In contrast, unstructured data are not organized in any particular way [8]. Examples are corpora of text such as social media content, news articles, or medical records. The data extraction task is to identify meaningful information contained therein. Many tools and techniques for parsing text and extracting meaning have been developed in the Computer Science field of *Natural Language Processing* [9], with extremely sophisticated processing now available for both the data extraction and transformation steps for unstructured data.

He who integrates data badly is lost.*

Theodor Adorno
Philosopher, Sociologist

Data extraction is the process of acquiring raw data points from these diverse types of sources and relies on access to the data-storage systems. Proprietary and open-source software options are available for information

*https://www.linkedin.com/pulse/worlds-best-data-quotes-martyn-jones

integration solutions that take autonomy, heterogeneity, and dynamics of data sources into account. These include services offered by large companies such as IBM, Microsoft, and Oracle to data integration and management tools such as Talend,* KNIME,† and Pentaho.‡ Other tools are tailored to specific fields, such as the Ingenuity platform for genomics.§ From these data integration systems to web-based mash-ups pulling data from multiple online providers [10], the extraction of the rich variety of data required to answer today's increasingly complex questions poses a variety of technical challenges, which go right to the heart of the Vs of Big Data.

Challenges related to data extraction:

- *Complexity of the process of extracting a "Variety" of data*: Extraction may require access to proprietary sources. State-of-the-art Big Data integration solutions exist that target enterprise data-management systems [11], in which data may be stored across in-house data repositories. Data may also be provided by other companies in the "Data as a Service" model, or from other alternate sources. In these cases, application programming interfaces (APIs) provide access. An API is a specification that allows developers to request data directly. However, in many cases, APIs are not available, and data are published in other ways, meant for human consumption, not programmatic access. Structured content may be provided in various types of files: text, spreadsheets, PDFs, and in machine readable formats such as XML and JSON. Semistructured data may be embedded within web pages in HTML tables, or data may be unstructured text or images. Identifying such sources of information can be automated using *web-crawling*, which is the process that search engines use to retrieve results relevant to a user query [12]. Then, the process of extracting data from these sources is known as *web-scraping*, in which automated tools parse websites and retrieve the relevant information and convert it into a structured format.

- *Difficulty in dealing with the "Velocity" of data*: Data extraction systems must accommodate data produced at ever increasing paces. Some data are reported on fixed schedules, such as government reporting, whereas other sources such as social media or sensor data are produced in a continuous stream. Many techniques have been developed to handle streaming data [13], and dedicated systems known as stream processing engines are used to specifically handle time-sensitive continuous data streams [14]. For data delivered periodically or continuously, data sources can be volatile, and changes at the source or noise in the stream must be handled to ensure robust data acquisition without disruption.

*https://www.talend.com/

†https://www.knime.org/

‡http://www.pentaho.com/

§http://www.ingenuity.com/

Data transformation

To ensure that high-quality data are used for decision-making, data need to be cleaned, aggregated, and properly formatted. This step unifies the data and its terminology across varied datasets and transforms it into an integrated data product, huge power of which can be harnessed. *Data cleaning* is critical to handle noisy, missing, or irrelevant information [15]. This includes correcting misspellings, deduplicating redundant entries, and resolving semantic differences in the way entities are represented and maintained as knowledge. While challenging, data-cleaning modules specific to the target can be learned to resolve differences in a process commonly referred to as entity resolution [16].

Further transformation may also be required to effectively represent entries from source files in the integrated data warehouse. Data are reported with varying levels of granularity and may need to be aggregated or filtered. For example, quarterly earnings may need to be summed to compute an annual income figure. Data encoded in different units must be scaled or converted. Data integration systems leverage knowledge regarding these encodings to avoid erroneous results.

Challenges related to data transformation:

- *Difficulty in dealing with the "Variety" of data*: Data collected from diverse sources tends to feature both semantic and structural discrepancies even when representing the same entities. These differences must be resolved either by manual inspection, or automatically using intelligent technologies by extracting information and mapping it to the correct entities. However, semantic ambiguity poses a great challenge. For example, some words like "China" must be correctly classified as the country or as fine dishes, based on semantic context. Other words such as "New York" need to be correctly classified in context to avoid confusion between the city or the newspaper *New York Times*. Failure to correctly deal with semantic ambiguity can lead to misinterpretation and inaccuracy of data. Much research has been done in Natural Language Processing to address these tasks [17].

- *Complexity of dealing with the "Veracity" of data*: With so much data available, trustworthiness of data is an important concern. Decision makers do not trust results that just come out of a black box, but rather they require transparency of systems. Therefore, maintenance of *data provenance* is critical. This term has been adopted from the field of Art History and refers to tracking the origin and history of data [1]. Information such as source URLs, file names, and date of extraction must be preserved as metadata and transformations applied to the data from the initial extraction to its final capture must be tracked. This provides the capability to trace back to and verify against the source and to maintain the confidence of users in the quality of the derived data product [18].

Data loading

Finally, the integrated data product must be stored and maintained for use and analysis. From an architectural perspective, two approaches to data integration are prevalent [19]. "Mediator-based integration" performs data integration on-the-fly. In this scenario, data are pulled from the original sources to answer a particular user's questions upon demand. This approach avoids data replication and directly leverages the storage and maintenance of the source.

Alternatively, "warehousing-based integration" extracts and integrates relevant data *a priori* into a Big Data store, the data warehouse. Analytics tasks thereafter are directly conducted on this curated data product. Often, to enable an interactive data exploration experience, continuous visual feedback is imperative and requires performance difficult to achieve on demand. Adopting warehousing assures that the resource-intensive tasks of data cleaning, unification, and transformation—which at times require human domain expertise—are accomplished offline. However, the consolidated data store must be continuously updated as new data become available, as opposed to pulling the most recent data each time as in the mediator-based approach. Therefore, the best approach depends on the types of data and the final application.

The data warehouse solution involves the selection of a storage model and must address the challenge of the first V of Big Data—*volume*. Traditional data warehousing uses a *relational database management system* [2–4], which are designed and managed using *Structured Query Language* (*SQL*). In such systems, data are organized in *relations*, or tables, according to a logical model such as a star schema structure [20], which is composed of one central fact table and numerous dimension tables that radiate out from it [21]. Primary values are recorded in the fact table, and descriptive metadata are stored in separate dimension tables. This design is a tried-and-true solution for traditional databases. However, it relies on one centralized storage solution managed in-house and is somewhat rigid in the organizational structure it allows.

> In pioneer days, they used oxen for heavy pulling, and when one ox couldn't budge a log, they didn't try to grow a larger ox. We shouldn't be trying for bigger computers, but for more systems of computers.*
>
> Grace Hopper
> Computer scientist

---

*The Wit and Wisdom of Grace Hopper http://cs-www.cs.yale.edu/homes/tap/Files/hopper-wit.html

Today's data *volume* often exceeds the resources available on a single machine, and data *variety* requires storage of many different kinds of information. Therefore, traditional approaches are no longer sufficient. This has led to the development and popularization of new data storage systems, and distributed solutions for data storage. Many different types of databases exist now. These alternative data storage options offer data models other than the tabular structure of relational databases. Such *NoSQL* models [22] include document-based, key-value, graph, and columnar data models. Examples of NoSQL databases include Mongodb* and Cassandra.†

The Big Data era has also seen increased use of distributed computing through clusters of many networked machines, in particular, due to strategies developed at Google [23] and Yahoo! [24] to manage their huge amounts of data. This has led to the wide adoption of technologies like Hadoop [24] and Spark,‡ open-source distributed computing architectures. These storage solutions distribute data across many machines, providing a scalable solution for data storage. They require new data access layers to facilitate warehousing and use for decision-making. For example, Apache Hive [25] allows for the use of SQL commands to access and manage data stored on the Hadoop distributed file system. Many companies now choose to outsource the storage of their data to the cloud, using platforms such as Amazon Web Services,§ Microsoft Azure,¶ and Google Cloud Platform.** They provide access to distributed data storage platforms, and often additional high-value management and analytics services. Such approaches can be used to analyze massive sets of complex networks [26].

Efficient data exploration

The second step in deriving value from Big Data is to effectively *explore* these large collections of data. This process requires tools that allow analysts to sift through huge amounts of information in their quest to find answers to complex questions. It is vital to understand that organizations are both producers and consumers of data. Thus, as producers of data, they have to make the right decisions in terms of selecting specific categories of data and the form in which they will archive over time these data for meaningful future exploration. As consumers of data, they have to decide what categories of data and what exploration methods are most appropriate.

Big Data analytics involve analyzing large sets of data to discover useful information such as hidden patterns, unknown correlations, trends, similarities, and differences. Extracting value from Big Data is accomplished using a wide

---

*https://www.mongodb.com/

†https://cassandra.apache.org/

‡http://spark.apache.org/

§https://aws.amazon.com/

¶https://azure.microsoft.com/

**https://cloud.google.com/

variety of methods, from traditional statistical analysis to techniques from the field of artificial intelligence. Machine learning approaches are designed to learn from input and identify patterns automatically, without a particular hypothesis being explicitly programed. Tasks that can be accomplished using such methods include forecasting/predictive analytics, causal modeling, descriptive analytics, visualization, and data mining.

Harnessing the power of Big Data is a key success factor for organizations in today's world, leading to faster and better decisions. In exchange, better decisions translate in the ability to reduce costs, offer new products and services, and overall improvements in business activities.

For instance, in applications ranging from finance, business, and medicine to meteorology [27,28], vast amounts of data are presented as stock fluctuations, electrocardiogram (ECG), rainfall amounts, and so on. In these applications, the latent value of data is unlocked by detecting similarities and differences between data records and *transforming* the raw data into quality insights. This is a time-consuming process, as research reports [29] indicate that employees spend roughly 25%–35% of their time searching for the information they need to do their jobs.

The process of sifting through vast amounts of information to find hidden relationships is at the core of data analytics. To capitalize on the power of Big Data, many exploration tools provide services via modeling, analysis, and reporting. Here, we list a few of the many available tools to illustrate the data exploration capabilities of such systems.

- *Rapid Miner* is a software platform that provides an integrated environment for machine learning, data mining, text mining, predictive analytics, and business analytics. It supports several data mining tasks such as data preparation, visualization, and validation.[*] It is used for business and commercial applications as well as for research, education, training, rapid prototyping, and application development.

- Waikato Environment for Knowledge Analysis (Weka) is a popular open-source machine-learning software developed in JAVA.[†] It contains a collection of algorithms for data analysis and predictive modeling, together with graphical user interfaces for easy access to these functions. Weka supports several standard data mining tasks such as data preprocessing, clustering, classification, and regression.

- *KNIME* is an open-source data analytics, reporting, and integration platform written in JAVA. It integrates various components of machine learning and data mining using modular data pipelines similar to Rapid Miner. It also provides graphical interface for ETL tasks.[‡]

---

[*] https://rapidminer.com

[†] http://www.cs.waikato.ac.nz/ml/weka/

[‡] https://www.knime.org/knime-analytics-platform

- *R Studio* is a free software environment for statistical computing and graphics. The R language is widely used among data miners for developing statistical software and data analysis. Besides, many data mining algorithms, it provides statistical and graphical techniques, including linear and nonlinear modeling, time-series analysis, classification, and clustering.*

- *SPSS Modeler* is a data mining and text analytics software application from IBM. It provides a range of advanced algorithms and techniques, including text analytics, entity analytics, decision management, and optimization to deliver actionable insights in near real time.†

Many challenges impede the process of data exploration. We enumerate here a few:

- *Scalability*: Exploring huge collections of data is clearly challenging, with data sizes increasingly becoming unwieldy.‡ Issues related to data *volume* and *velocity* often arise. High data cardinality leads to decreased responsiveness, and the power of Big Data for decision-making can be hindered by time constraints in fast-moving environments. Systems for analyzing data whether financial records, sensor readings, or customer feedback require real-time turn-around. The scale of Big Data can also be a double-edged sword. When data are large, it is challenging to process and store; however, today's advanced machine-learning methods may only yield meaningful results when applied to very large data. For instance, *deep learning* is a hot area of artificial intelligence used extensively for image and voice recognition tasks [30], which typically require huge sets of data and times ranging from days to weeks to train the models for effective use.

- *Analyst's expertise*: Applying advanced analytics to Big Data requires a high level of expertise and talent. Experts in the Computer Science and Data Science fields can prove costly and hard to come by for many organizations. Reports from the McKinsey Institute [31] and Gartner Research [32] project shortages of experts in this field, with over 100,000 jobs predicted to be unfilled in the United States by 2018. Sophisticated understanding of data is required at all levels management, in order for businesses to make effective use of insights pulled from the data using advanced methods.

- *Data trustworthiness*: With so much data and many advanced techniques available, it is essential that decision makers feel that they can trust the output produced by data exploration systems. Often, when choosing

*https://www.rstudio.com/

†http://www-03.ibm.com/software/products/en/spss-modeler

‡https://followthedata.wordpress.com/2014/06/24/data-size-estimates/

data models, there is a tradeoff between accuracy and interpretability. Accepting lower accuracy may be preferable to gain understanding of relationships among the data. For instance, using rule-based predictive models that allow analysts to examine the factors driving predictions has been shown to be preferable in the healthcare field [33]. In one example, a complex model was using a preexisting condition as an indicator of good outcomes after emergency room admission. The simpler model revealed this factor, allowing analysts to uncover the real reason this correlation existed—because patients with this condition carried a higher risk and received more aggressive care immediately when admitted. If leaders do not understand the mechanisms of underlying patterns exposed by advanced data analysis, then potential insights can be missed, or worse yet, dangerous policies put into place.

- *Danger of bias*: Big Data holds the key to data-driven advances in many fields, but by the same token, it carries the potential for harm. Experts warn against the scenarios in which bias can sneak into the predictions made by opaque automatic systems and negatively impact certain groups of people [34]. Even if not used explicitly as input, factors such as race or gender may unduly influence models used for social applications such as criminal justice and policy making. Privacy concerns are also a key consideration for businesses that collect personal information about their customers, as demonstrated by high-profile data breaches.* In this new information age, we must all be vigilant in ensuring that data are used to promote prosperity and drive innovation through equitable and ethical use.

> Organizational judgment is in the midst of a fundamental change from a reliance on a leader's "gut instinct" to increasingly data-based analytics. [35]
>
> Erik Bryjolfsson
> Director, MIT Sloan Center for Digital Business

Companies must now develop a data-driven culture in which executives, analysts, and strategic partners are active participants in managing a meaningful data *lifecycle.* Tomorrow's successful companies will be equipped to harness new sources of information and take responsibility over accurate data creation, maintenance, and sharing. This will enable organizations to *tame* data and turn it into powerful, informative insights.

*https://www.privacyrights.org/data-breaches

Using visualization to better incorporate data in the decision-making process

Having access to the utmost-of-to-date data is only part of successfully incorporating data into the processes of enterprises and organizations. Despite having access to such data and sophisticated tools for mining it, analysts are overwhelmed by the richness of insights provided by artificial intelligent and machine-learning tools and crave more intuitive, visual tools that enable them to give better interpretation to the results.

> When you come across visualizations of the data its almost a relief like coming across a clearing in the jungle.*
>
> David McCandless
> Author, Information Is Beautiful

It is important to have good visualization tools that enable analysts to interpret data from different, heterogeneous sources, to compare side-by-side results from multiple sources and manipulate data to get better insights. Every part of data incorporates a story and these data-visualization tools are the gateway to figuring out this story. The research community and industry offer a large array of visualization tools to support data analytics, including the following:

- *Data-driven documents or D3*† uses HTML, cascading style sheets (CSS), and scalable vector graphics (SVG) to render intuitive charts and diagrams. D3 emphasis on web standards gives analysts the full capabilities of modern browsers without tying them to any type of framework. It combines powerful visualization components with a data-driven approach. For example, Figure 7.4‡ shows a sample D3 visualization of tech employment in multiple states.
- *Datawrapper* is an open-source tool that allows analysts to create customized charts and maps in much reduced time.
- *Dygraphs* is a fast, flexible, and highly interactive open-source JavaScript charting library that allows users to explore and interpret huge datasets. For example, Figure 7.5§ shows a sample chart drawn using Dygraph showing comparison of temperatures in New York City versus San Francisco.

---

*http://www.energycollection.us/Energy-Information-Technology/Whats-Big-Deal.pdf
†https://d3js.org/
‡http://matters.mhtc.org/
§http://dygraphs.com

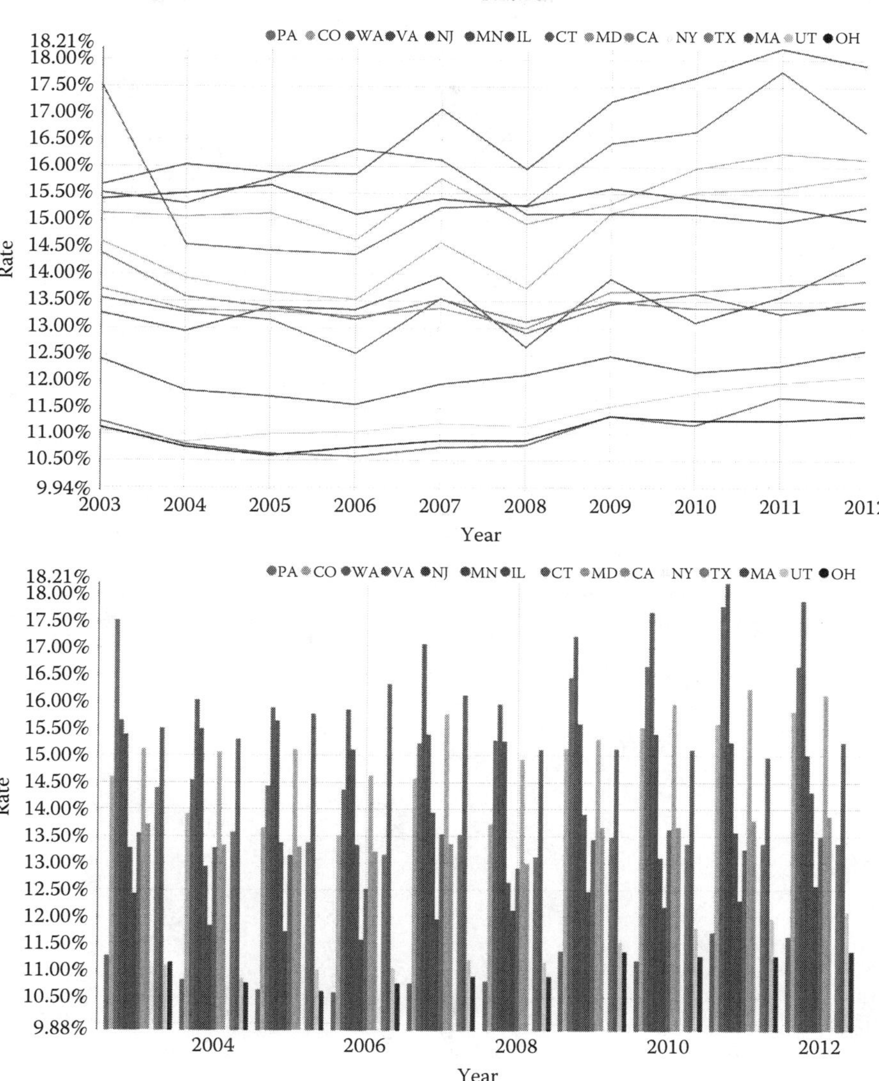

FIGURE 7.4: D3 visualization showing tech employment in multiple states.

- *Fusion charts suite XT* provides the ability to create charts with animation and rich interactivity.
- *Google charts* offer a perfect way to visualize data on websites. From simple line charts to complex hierarchical tree maps, the chart gallery offers a large array of chart types. Charts are exposed as JavaScript

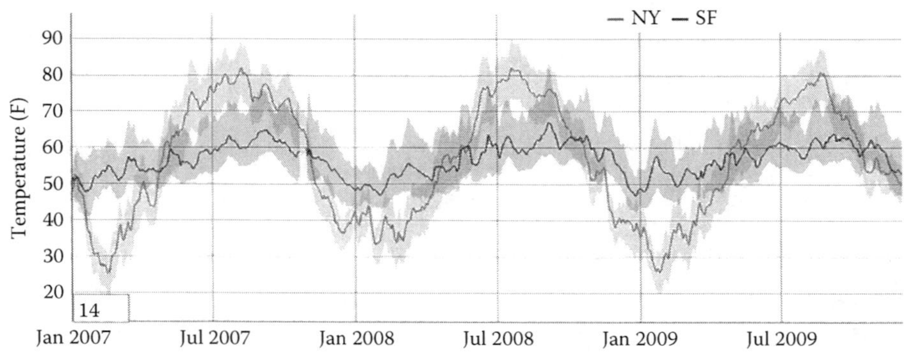

FIGURE 7.5: Dygraphs chart showing comparison of temperatures in New York City versus San Francisco.

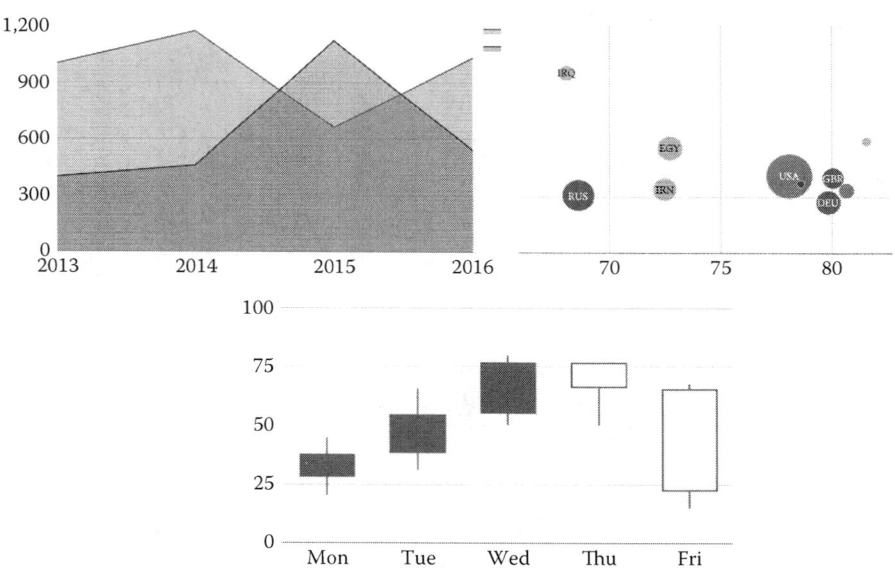

FIGURE 7.6: Google charts sample visualizations.

classes that can be customized according to the analyst's needs. For example, Figure 7.6* shows a sample visualization drawn using Google Charts.

- *Tableau* is a data-visualization tool for manipulating Big Data, and it has two variants "Tableau Server" and cloud-based "Tableau Online"

*https://developers.google.com/chart/interactive/docs/

specifically designed for Big Data related organizations. It facilitates powerful calculations from existing data, drag-and-drop reference lines and forecasts, and review statistical summaries.

Such tools have the ability to summarize, aggregate, and *pack* far more information into a visualization display than traditional raw data representations. Furthermore, visualization technologies like those described earlier enable nontechnical users and analysts to easily compare data across categories, silos, data types, and other traditional data representations. Such distribution and sharing of insights leads to more dynamic and inclusive decision-making strategies.

In summary, according to McKinsey Global Institute, there are many broad ways in which using Big Data can create value*

First, as organizations create and store more transactional data in digital form, they can collect more accurate and detailed performance information on everything from product inventories to sick days and therefore expose variability and boost performance. Leading companies are using data collection and analysis to conduct controlled experiments to make better management decisions; others are using data for basic low-frequency forecasting to high-frequency *nowcasting* to adjust their business levers just in time.

Second, sophisticated analytics can substantially improve decision making.

Third, Big Data can be used to improve the development of the next generation of products and services. For instance, manufacturers are using data obtained from sensors embedded in products to create innovative after-sales service offerings such as proactive maintenance (preventive measures that take place before a failure occurs or is even noticed).

Real world case studies on using Big Data to make decisions

Case study in heart arrhythmia

Many medical and research institutions become partners in the quest to tame Big Data. For example, Beth Israel Deaconess Medical Center and MIT support research into arrhythmia analysis and related subjects. Together they created the MIT-BIH Arrhythmia database that offers a set of standard test material for evaluation of arrhythmia detectors.

*http://www.mckinsey.com/business-functions/digital-mckinsey/our-insights/big-data-the-next-frontier-for-innovation

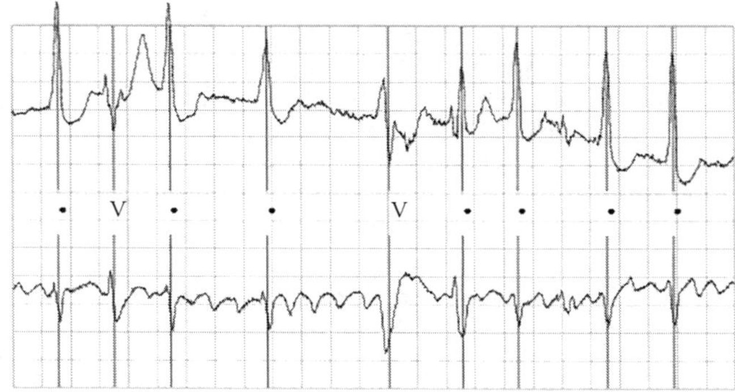

FIGURE 7.7: Arrhythmia shape from MIT-BIH arrhythmia database.

The MIT-BIH Arrhythmia database [36,37] contains 48 half-hour excerpts of two-channel ambulatory ECG recordings, obtained from 47 subjects studied by the BIH Arrhythmia Laboratory between 1975 and 1979. Twenty-three recordings were chosen at random from a set of 4000 24-hour ambulatory ECG recordings collected from a mixed population of inpatients (about 60%) and outpatients (about 40%) at Boston's Beth Israel Hospital; the remaining 25 recordings were selected from the same set to include less common but clinically significant arrhythmias that would not be well represented in a small random sample.

The recordings were digitized at 360 samples per second per channel with 11-bit resolution over a 10-mV range. Two or more cardiologists independently annotated each record, and disagreements were resolved to obtain the computer-readable reference annotations for each beat (approximately 110,000 annotations in all) included with the database (Figure 7.7).

Exploring similarity of ECG sequences is crucial for diagnosing arrhythmia that refers to any change from the normal sequence of electrical impulses. The electrical impulses may happen too fast, too slowly, or erratically causing the heart to beat too fast, too slowly, or erratically. When the heart does not beat properly, it cannot pump blood effectively. When the heart does not pump blood effectively, the lungs, brain, and all other organs cannot work properly and may shut down or be damaged.

Clinical diagnoses and basic investigations are dependent on the ability to record and analyze physiological signals. Examples of such signals include ECG and heart-rate recordings from patients at a high risk of sudden death and healthy control subjects as seen in Figure 7.8, fluctuations of hormone and other molecular biological signal messengers and transducers in neuroendocrine dynamics, and multiparameter recordings in sleep apnea and epilepsy.

Cardiologists need to have the ability to explore massive amounts of such data to find similar trends and patterns. For example, it is very helpful for

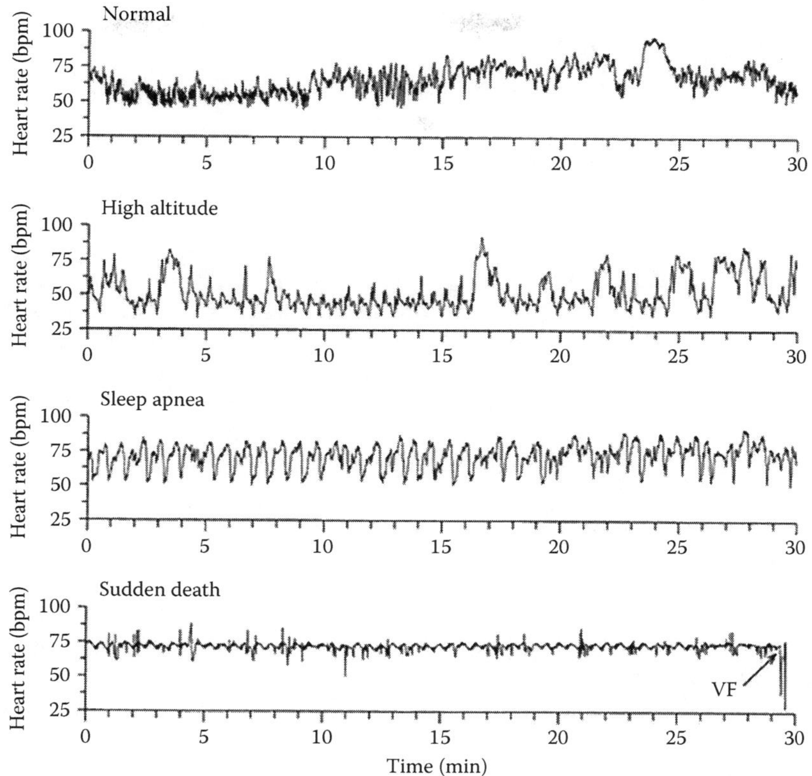

FIGURE 7.8: Heart rate time series from MIT-BIH database.

cardiologists to be able to retrieve similar ECG shapes from a database. This way, they can find shapes characteristic to specific heart conditions that belong to different patients. The retrieval of such shapes enables doctors to make meaningful, evidence-based observations and assists them in properly diagnosing patients.

Another example of using the power of vast amounts of such information is to *learn* the patterns in an ECG immediately preceding a heart attack. A doctor has to be able to detect these patterns, not just by direct observation, but by using a system that can automatically detect and identify them, alerting the cardiologist about the imminence of cardiac failure. These are just some examples of the many ways to use Big Data to better diagnose cardiac conditions and decide on the most appropriate treatment for each individual patient.

Case study in Big Data integration for economic competitiveness analytics

Civic data are made available today at an increasingly fast pace across many websites and are of tremendous value to businesses, nonprofits, and other community organizations. As stated in a 2014 report from President Obama's office, its use has the potential "to grow our economy, improve health and education, and make our nation safer and more energy efficient" [38]. Toward this end, The Massachusetts Talent, Technology, and Reporting System (MATTERS)* is an online platform designed to find data-driven solutions to answer the complex social, environmental, and economic questions around building the technology economy in the United States by harnessing the power of diverse online public data. Developed by a council† comprising senior executives from high-tech industries, research organizations, and academic institutions in Massachusetts, this dynamic system integrates a wide array of *key national economic competitiveness measures* to monitor and compare the economic climate in U.S. states.

Providing a single access point to this unique collection of data, MATTERS enables users to compare diverse metrics across states and over time. The datasets have been carefully curated by experts and partners of the Massachusetts High Technology Council. Insights gained from this rich collection of data can inform the public and policy makers of factors influencing the economy in their state.

The MATTERS framework employs a custom data integration platform that extracts information from a number of high-value public websites. These datasets are then integrated in a data warehouse to facilitate interactive analysis. Data extraction components including custom wrappers for specific high value websites are used in conjunction with an open-source ETL tool to map the source data to the unified MATTERS data model. Cleaning components specific to this data domain are plugged in, and cleaned source data are stored in the MATTERS warehouse along with its provenance and semantic metadata.

An online administration panel provides a suite of easy-to-use integration services. Pipelines can be constructed by a nontechnical administrator for new web sources using the ETL tool offline. These pipelines then are uploaded to the system and scheduled to run automatically. In addition, a manual upload service provides rapid yet safe upload of time-sensitive data. Automatic data pipelines are manually uploaded. These pipelines are tracked by a logger with robust error reporting.

Easy-to-use descriptive analytics tools help users derive value from the rich data source at their fingertips. Any combination of states and years can be selected and compared using a set of custom visualizations. These views can be

---

*http://matters.mhtc.org/

†Massachusetts High Tech Council, http://mhtc.org/

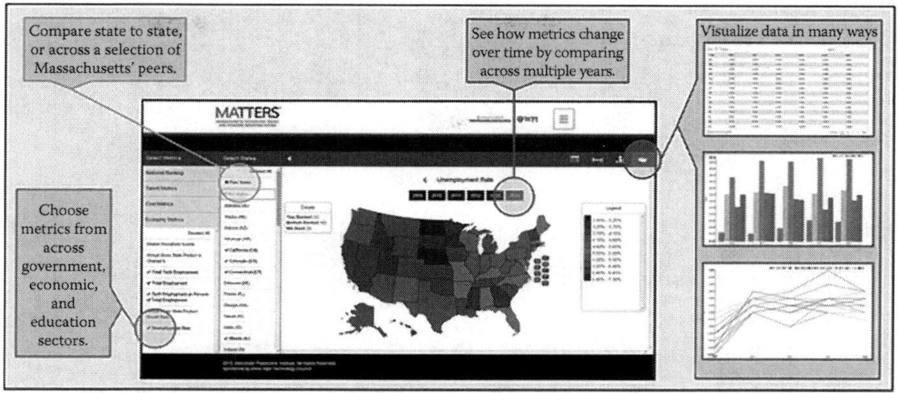

FIGURE 7.9: MATTERS online analytics dashboard.

exported as reports, or shared online. MATTERS also provides a public-facing API to facilitate data sharing and use by other developers (Figure 7.9).

Since its initial release, the site has served as an invaluable tool for the council, its partners, and the state of Massachusetts. Massachusetts Governor Charlie Baker praised the project saying "Our administration is committed to using data to identify and advance pro-growth economic policies and we are excited about using MATTERS as a primary tool in those efforts."* Leveraging this dynamic data now housed in the MATTERS system, a team of domain experts from industry, academia, and the research community in Massachusetts has developed a comprehensive set of national rankings, using weighted averages of key metrics for each state.

Four MATTERS Rankings have been published for the key categories of talent, tax/financial climate, cost of doing business, and quality of life. These rankings are used to create an individual profile for each state gauging its economic competitiveness. Links back to the original data sources ensure data transparency and validation. These rankings can be compared and contrasted with all other metrics in the system for a comprehensive look at factors impacting each state.

MATTERS not only integrates heterogeneous data but also has provided a platform for a new value-added data service. The council's inaugural Executive Competitiveness Insight Survey was published in MATTERS in October 2016, to be repeated biannually. The survey is intended to gather perspectives of CEOs and senior executives regarding the business climate in Massachusetts and to find trend data in those perspectives over time.†

*http://www.mhtc.org/news/high-tech-agenda/the-high-tech-agenda-march-2015

†http://matters.mhtc.org/resources/MATTERS_Executive_Competitiveness_Insight_Survey_Fall_2016.pdf

Addressing issues of data integration, usability, visualization, and analytics, MATTERS exemplifies the way Big Data can inform important issues in an open and transparent way. With this single repository consolidating cost, economic and talent metrics, executives, policymakers, and researchers can make better informed, data-driven decisions.

Big Data in various application domains

Big Data for business decisions: Netflix*

Based on its extensive analysis of customers' viewing habits and preferences, Netflix decided in 2011 to outbid a few established TV networks and invest 100 million dollars in the series House of Cards. This decision led to an increase of 7% or 2 million new U.S. subscribers in the first quarter of 2013, compared with the previous quarter, in addition to 1 million new subscribers from outside the United States. These 3 million new subscribers almost paid the entire cost of House of Cards within a single quarter.

Big Data fighting crime†

Predictive crime mapping pilot projects have been developed in Britain and the United States in collaboration with IBM, a major predictive analytics developer. At a conference in Winchester, UK, IBM suggested that over the past seven years, its technology had helped reduce crime in Memphis, Tennessee, by more than 30%. Another company working on predictive analytics, PredPol, based in Los Angeles, California, has assisted Los Angeles Police Department (LAPD) with crime-fighting software since 2011. The LAPD, with assistance from researchers at the University of California, analyzed 13 million crimes recorded over 80 years, so it can predict where a crime will occur in the future. The results of the analysis, focused on one LAPD precinct, led to a 12% decrease in property crime and a 26% decrease in burglary.‡

Big Data to predict weather§

It is a well-known fact that the weather has a big impact on businesses. Routine weather cost U.S. businesses over 500 billion dollars in 2014. Outside of political turmoil, weather is the most powerful force that can interfere with business. Predictable weather information using the three billion global forecast reference points and its effects on business in the near or distant

*https://blog.kissmetrics.com/how-netflix-uses-analytics/
http://www.business2community.com/big-data/predictive-analytics-changing-ecommerce-conversion-rate-optimization

†http://www.bbc.com/news/technology-20068722

‡https://datafloq.com/read/los-angeles-police-department-predicts-fights-crim/279

§http://www.ibmbigdatahub.com/blog/business-value-weather-data

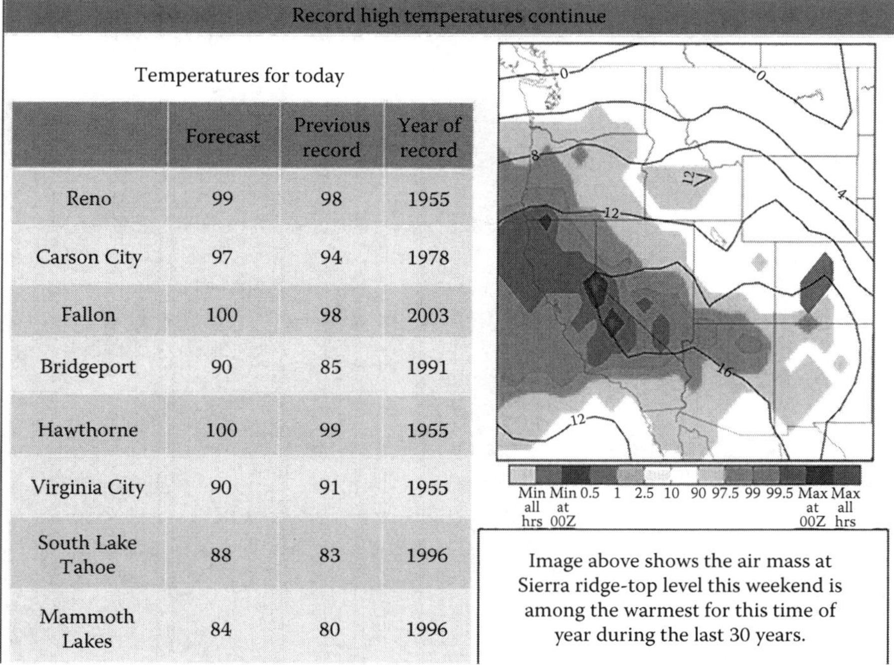

Record high temperatures continue

Temperatures for today

	Forecast	Previous record	Year of record
Reno	99	98	1955
Carson City	97	94	1978
Fallon	100	98	2003
Bridgeport	90	85	1991
Hawthorne	100	99	1955
Virginia City	90	91	1955
South Lake Tahoe	88	83	1996
Mammoth Lakes	84	80	1996

FIGURE 7.10: Big Data to predict weather.

future could be worth more to companies than just a weather forecast. In this light, IBM started a fundamental shift of transforming itself from a big IT and mainframe provider to a digital data and insight company by acquiring the Weather Company.* According to the CEO of IBM, the main focus has shifted toward cognitive computing, analytics, Internet of Things, APIs, hybrid cloud, and digital platforms that support big corporations to reinvent themselves and engage in the digital economy. For instance, Figure 7.10† shows how data are used to predict weather temperatures.

Using Big Data to make data-driven medical decisions‡

At Beth Israel Deaconess Medical Center in Boston, Massachusetts, Big Data is used in the context of real-world applications that lead to data-driven clinical decisions for patients. Among these, new mobile apps for patients (which measure and manage health outcomes) could yield clinical and financial benefits. For example, "screening sheets" are used to support continuous

*http://www.wsj.com/articles/ibm-nearing-acquisition-of-weather-co-s-digital-and-data-assets-1445984616

†Image taken from National Weather Service, Reno, Nevada

‡https://hbr.org/2015/12/using-big-data-to-make-wiser-medical-decisions

data analysis. Experts determine what data elements and what questions are important for common diseases, then this information is built into the screening-sheets tool. As patients receive new medications, lab results, and diagnoses, the electronic health record alerts clinicians when to take action. For example, a patient with newly diagnosed diabetes is automatically enrolled in a protocol that includes eye exams, foot exams, and pneumonia vaccines. Any gaps in care for the patient are recognized, flagged, and then automatically coupled with information about best practices. The clinician is proactively informed about both so that he or she can make a wise clinical choice. In the near future, data from the genome will be incorporated into screening sheets. These analytics do not overwhelm clinicians with data rather reduce their burden by staying one step ahead of what they need at their fingertips to be able to make wise clinical decisions.

Using Big Data to predict stock market fluctuations*

Tobias Preis of Warwick Business School in the United Kingdom, Helen Susannah Moat of University College London, and H. Eugene Stanley of Boston University revealed results [39] indicating that Google Trends data were useful in predicting daily price moves in the Dow Jones Industrial Average, which consists of 30 stocks. Their research result showed that "an uptick in Google searches on finance terms reliably predicted a fall in stock prices." *Debt* was the most reliable term for predicting market ups and downs, the researchers found. By going long when debt searches dropped and shorting

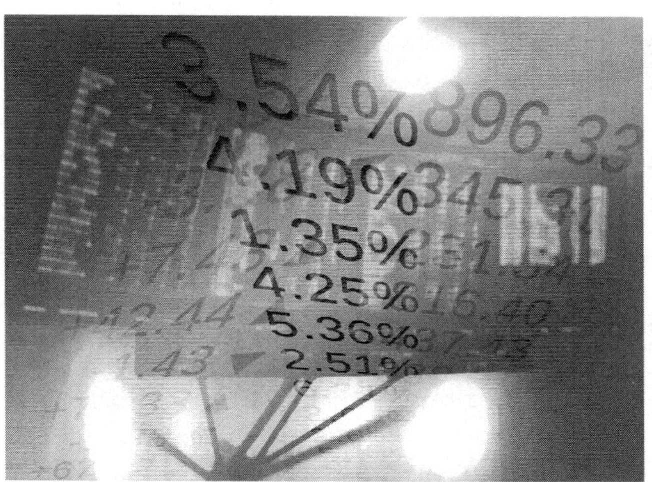

FIGURE 7.11: Big Data to predict stock prices.

*http://www.forbes.com/sites/davidleinweber/2013/04/26/big-data-gets-bigger-now-google-trends-can-predict-the-market/#3f340af1613a

the market when debt searches rose, the researchers were able to increase their hypothetical portfolio by 326%. In comparison, a constant buy-and-hold strategy yielded just a 16% return during that same time period.

The findings are scientifically "truly exciting," Preis said, because they have implications far beyond the stock market. Online chatter could help predict disease spread, civil unrest, and political elections, he said. And Google is only the beginning, he added. Wikipedia, for example, provides open-source information on how many people view specific articles hour-by-hour, making the online encyclopedia another potential predictor of stock markets and other real-life behavior and phenomena (Figure 7.11).

What does the future hold?

Building a *data-driven* culture and a foundation of analytics are the cornerstones of successful organizations in the future. New technologies, with their ease of adoption, point toward the next horizon of data analytics. Adapting and transforming organizations to deeply incorporate data into everything they do is becoming the target of many existing organizations, big and small. Such transformations demand new actions beyond the tools: more focus, more job redefinition, and more cultural change.

The shortage of experts in data analytics is so acute that it may be years before a sufficient supply can be trained. The McKinsey Global Institute estimates that up to 190,000 are needed now in the United States, along with 1.5 million managers capable of using their work. The shortage appears to be growing along with the potential for competitive advantage associated with data analytics. All these raise many questions. Will the age of Big Data eliminate most or all uncertainty from business decisions for those most able to make effective use of "all the facts in the world?" Will it fuel the next *gold rush* for talent in a quest for competitive advantage? How, if at all, will this affect education for management?*

> Where is the wisdom we have lost in knowledge? Where is the knowledge we have lost in information?
>
> T.S. Elliot

---

*http://hbswk.hbs.edu/item/how-will-the-age-of-big-data-affect-management

We end by briefly discussing some areas in which we expect future advances that will further change the utilization of Big Data for decision-making.

1. Although current utilization of Big Data tools from data extraction, integration to storage requires dedicated, skilled computer professional staff, there is research underway to improve the autotuning and self-management capabilities of such systems to reduce the amount of hand-holding required to run such systems.

2. Similarly, the application of analytics to derive insights out of big datasets, including data mining and machine-learning methods, is currently still a craft requiring extensive data science expertise. This expertise starts with determining which particular machine-learning methods to apply to solve one's application question. In the future, advanced support systems will provide a natural language interface, in which upon entry of your dataset and your inquiry, the system will offer recommendations about machine techniques to apply to answer one's analytic task in question.

3. Although Data-as-a-Service has emerged supported by many vendors, data-science-as-a-service is now increasingly on the horizon. This offers a manager the capability to work with sophisticated techniques without requiring the staffing of in-house systems for their development and utilization.

4. Currently, once an analytics task has been conducted, it remains challenging to interpret the returned results. This ranges from the number of results produced sometimes being large than the initial data itself, such as in the case of association rule mining, other times the results produced being directly based and possibly biased by the model constructed to begin with, such as in the case of Bayesian networks, or the results simply not being statistically significant enough to be trustworthy. This requires advances in techniques to detect and then warn of possible issues with the conducted analysis, pointing out data skew, or biases to be rectified for an effective analysis.

5. Future research will also produce innovations in so-called explanation services, in which the system will not simply return results, be they clusters or outliers, but will augment such data products with associated explanations—extracted and then fused from the domain itself in a terminology that makes sense externally; even if internally, the system may exclusively operate with numerical compact data representations. Visual environments that support this process of interpretation and user interaction will skillfully facilitate the engagements of managers with their data products; letting them ask what-if questions of complex nature with ease.

Glossary

Analytics: The systematic computational analysis of data or statistics.

Big Data: Extremely large datasets that may be analyzed computationally to reveal patterns, trends, and associations, especially relating to human behavior and interactions.

Causal Model: Is an abstract model that describes the causal mechanisms of a system. The model must express more than correlation because correlation does not imply causation.

Data Extraction: The act or process of retrieving data out of (usually unstructured or poorly structured) data sources for further data processing or data storage.

Data Integration: The combination of technical and business processes used to combine data from disparate sources into meaningful and valuable information.

Data Mining: The practice of examining large databases to generate new information.

Data Warehouse: A large store of data accumulated from a wide range of sources within a company and used to guide management decisions.

Cloud Computing: The practice of using a network of remote servers hosted on the Internet to store, manage, and process data, rather than a local server or a personal computer.

Entity Resolution: The process of identifying and resolving different representations of entities across different data sources.

Extract, Transform, and Load (ETL): A process in database usage and especially in data warehousing that performs the following: Data extraction extracts data from homogeneous or heterogeneous data sources.

Natural Language Processing (NLP): A field of computer science, artificial intelligence, and computational linguistics concerned with the interactions between computers and human (natural) languages.

Relational Database Management System (RDBMS): Traditional, widely used, database system in which data are organized according to the relational model. Data are represented as tuples, which are organized in relations (or tables).

Structured Data: Kinds of data with a high level of organization, such as information in a relational database.

Structure Query Language (SQL): Is used to communicate with a database. It is the standard language for relational database management systems.

Supervised Learning: Is the machine-learning task of inferring a function from labeled training data. The training data consist of a set of training examples. In supervised learning, each example is a pair consisting of an input object (typically a vector) and a desired output value (also called the supervisory signal).

NoSQL Database: A database that offers a different model for data organization than a relational database. Data may be represented in different ways including documents, graphs, and key-value pairs.

Unstructured Data: Information that either does not have a predefined data model or is not organized in a predefined manner.

Unsupervised Learning: Is the machine-learning task of inferring a function to describe hidden structure from unlabeled data.

Web-Crawling: A program or automated script that browses the World Wide Web in a methodical, automated manner.

Web-Scraping: A technique employed to extract large amounts of data from websites whereby the data are extracted and saved to a local file in your computer or to a database in table (spreadsheet) format.

References

[1] P. Buneman, S. Khanna, and W.-C. Tan. Data provenance: Some basic issues. In *International Conference on Foundations of Software Technology and Theoretical Computer Science*, pp. 87–93. London: Springer, 2000.

[2] S. Chaudhuri and U. Dayal. An overview of data warehousing and OLAP technology. *ACM Sigmod record*, 26(1): 65–74, 1997.

[3] W. H. Inmon. The data warehouse and data mining. *Communications of the ACM*, 39(11): 49–51, 1996.

[4] A. Vaisman and E. Zimányi. *Data Warehouse Systems*. Heidelberg, Germany: Springer, 2014.

[5] X. L. Dong and D. Srivastava. Big data integration. In *2013 IEEE 29th International Conference on Data Engineering (ICDE)*, pp. 1245–1248. IEEE, 2013.

[6] P. Vassiliadis. A survey of extract–transform–load technology. *International Journal of Data Warehousing and Mining (IJDWM)*, 5(3): 1–27, 2009.

[7] B. C. Desai. *An Introduction to Database Systems*. St. Paul, MN: West Publishing, 1990.

[8] S. Soderland. Learning information extraction rules for semi-structured and free text. *Machine learning*, 34(1–3): 233–272, 1999.

[9] N. F. Noy. Semantic integration: a survey of ontology-based approaches. *ACM Sigmod Record*, 33(4): 65–70, 2004.

[10] G. Di Lorenzo, H. Hacid, H.-Y. Paik, and B. Benatallah. Data integration in mashups. *ACM Sigmod Record*, 38(1): 59–66, 2009.

[11] U. Dayal, M. Castellanos, A. Simitsis, and K. Wilkinson. Data integration flows for business intelligence. In *Proceedings of the 12th International Conference on Extending Database Technology: Advances in Database Technology*, pp. 1–11. New York: ACM, 2009.

[12] A. N. Langville and C. D. Meyer. *Google's PageRank and Beyond: The Science of Search Engine Rankings*. Princeton, NJ: Princeton University Press, 2011.

[13] P. Zikopoulos and C. Eaton. *Understanding Big Data: Analytics for Enterprise Class Hadoop and Streaming Data*. McGraw-Hill Osborne Media, 2011.

[14] N. Tatbul. Streaming data integration: Challenges and opportunities. In *2010 IEEE 26th International Conference on Data Engineering Workshops (ICDEW)*, pp. 155–158. IEEE, 2010.

[15] E. Rahm and H. H. Do. Data cleaning: Problems and current approaches. *IEEE Data Engineering Bulletin*, 23(4): 3–13, 2000.

[16] J. Kubica and A. W. Moore. Probabilistic noise identification and data cleaning. In *ICDM*, pp. 131–138, 2003.

[17] R. Navigli. Word sense disambiguation: A survey. *ACM Computing Surveys (CSUR)*, 41(2): 10, 2009.

[18] Y. Cui and J. Widom. Lineage tracing for general data warehouse transformations. *The VLDB Journal—The International Journal on Very Large Data Bases*, 12(1): 41–58, 2003.

[19] P. Ziegler and K. R. Dittrich. Data integration—Problems, approaches, and perspectives. In *Conceptual Modelling in Information Systems Engineering*, pp. 39–58. Berlin, Germany: Springer, 2007.

[20] N. Tryfona, F. Busborg, and J. G. B. Christiansen. Starer: A conceptual model for data warehouse design. In *Proceedings of the 2nd ACM International Workshop on Data Warehousing and OLAP*, pp. 3–8. New York: ACM, 1999.

[21] R. Kimball and M. Ross. *The Data Warehouse Toolkit: The Complete Guide to Dimensional Modeling.* New York: John Wiley & Sons, 2011.

[22] R. Cattell. Scalable SQL and NoSQL data stores. *ACM Sigmod Record*, 39(4): 12–27, 2011.

[23] J. Dean and S. Ghemawat. Mapreduce: Simplified data processing on large clusters. *Communications of the ACM*, 51(1): 107–113, 2008.

[24] K. Shvachko, H. Kuang, S. Radia, and R. Chansler. The Hadoop distributed file system. In *2010 IEEE 26th Symposium on Mass Storage Systems and Technologies (MSST)*, pp. 1–10. IEEE, 2010.

[25] A. Thusoo, J. S. Sarma, N. Jain, Z. Shao, P. Chakka, S. Anthony, H. Liu, P. Wyckoff, and R. Murthy. Hive: A warehousing solution over a map-reduce framework. *Proceedings of the VLDB Endowment*, 2(2): 1626–1629, 2009.

[26] M. Dehmer, F. Emmert-Streib, S. Pickl, and A. Holzinger. *Big Data of Complex Networks.* Boca Raton, FL: Chapman and Hall/CRC, 2016.

[27] S. Hirano and S. Tsumoto. Cluster analysis of time-series medical data based on the trajectory representation and multiscale comparison techniques. In *Sixth International Conference on Data Mining (ICDM'06)*, pp. 896–901. IEEE, 2006.

[28] E. J. Ruiz, V. Hristidis, C. Castillo, A. Gionis, and A. Jaimes. Correlating financial time series with micro-blogging activity. In *Proceedings of the Fifth ACM International Conference on Web Search and Data Mining*, pp. 513–522. New York: ACM, 2012.

[29] P. Zezula, G. Amato, V. Dohnal, and M. Batko. *Similarity Search: The Metric Space Approach.* New York: Springer Science & Business Media, 2006.

[30] Y. LeCun, Y. Bengio, and G. Hinton. Deep learning. *Nature*, 521(7553): 436–444, 2015.

[31] J. Manyika, M. Chui, B. Brown, J. Bughin, R. Dobbs, C. Roxburgh, and A. H. Byers. *Big Data: The Next Frontier for Innovation, Competition, and Productivity.* McKinsey, 2011.

[32] D. Laney and L. Kart. Emerging role of the data scientist and the art of data science. Gartner Group. White paper, 2012.

[33] R. Caruana, Y. Lou, J. Gehrke, P. Koch, M. Sturm, and N. Elhadad. Intelligible models for healthcare: Predicting pneumonia risk and hospital 30-day readmission. In *Proceedings of the 21th ACM SIGKDD International Conference on Knowledge Discovery and Data Mining*, pp. 1721–1730. New York: ACM, 2015.

[34] C. O'Neil. *Weapons of Math Destruction: How Big Data Increases Inequality and Threatens Democracy.* New York: Crown Publishing Group, 2016.

[35] E. Brynjolfsson, L. M. Hitt, and H. H. Kim. Strength in numbers: How does data-driven decision making affect firm performance? *Available at SSRN 1819486*, 2011.

[36] G. B. Moody and R. G. Mark. The impact of the MIT-BIH arrhythmia database. *IEEE Engineering in Medicine and Biology Magazine*, 20(3): 45–50, 2001.

[37] A. L. Goldberger, L. A. N. Amaral, L. Glass, J. M. Hausdorff, P. C. Ivanov, R. G. Mark, J. E. Mietus, G. B. Moody, C.-K. Peng, and H. E. Stanley. Physiobank, physiotoolkit, and physionet components of a new research resource for complex physiologic signals. *Circulation*, 101(23): e215–e220, 2000.

[38] J. Podesta, P. Pritzker, E. Moniz, J. Holdren, and J. Zients. *Big Data: Seizing Opportunities, Preserving Values.* Executive Office of the President. Washington, DC: The White House, 2014.

[39] T. Preis, H. S. Moat, and H. E. Stanley. Quantifying trading behavior in financial markets using Google trends. *Scientific Reports*, 3, 2013.

Chapter 8

Automated business analytics for artificial intelligence in Big Data@X 4.0 era

Yi-Ting Chen

Edward W. Sun

Introduction ... 223
The X 4.0 era: Evolutionary aspect ... 225
Industry 4.0 ... 225
Web 4.0 ... 226
Business intelligence and analytics 4.0 ... 228
Machine learning for artificial intelligence ... 229
Deep learning ... 229
Reinforcement learning ... 230
Ensemble learning ... 230
The methodological framework ... 231
Reinforcement learning ... 231
Wavelet transform ... 234
Thresholding ... 235
Reinforcement learning with generalized optimal wavelet decomposing algorithm ... 236
Simulation study ... 239
The data ... 239
The methodology ... 240
Simulation results ... 242
Future work ... 248
References ... 249

Introduction

Big Data and its analytical capabilities have made a leap forward in recent years. The available data volume that can be normally dealt with has grown exponentially; more sophisticated platforms, softwares, and algorithms have been developed, and computational power and storage have been steadily improved. The convergence of these trends is fueling rapid technology advances and business disruptions, see McKinsey Global Institute 2016 report.

Reference 1 characterizes Big Data as the datasets (1) whose source is heterogeneous and autonomous; (2) whose dimension is diverse;* (3) whose size and/or format does not conform to the conventional processes or tools to effectively and affordably capture, store, manage, analyze, and exploit; and (4) whose relationship is complex, dynamic, and evolving. Reference 1 points out that enterprises are increasingly facing increasing challenges of Big Data, and a wide variety of techniques should be developed and adapted to aggregate, manipulate, organize, analyze, and visualize them. The techniques currently applied on Big Data usually draw from several fields, including statistics, applied mathematics, and computer science are not sufficient, and enterprises that intend to derive value from Big Data must employ more flexible, reliable, and multidisciplinary methods.

MGI 2016 report [2] states that "most companies are capturing only a fraction of the potential value from data and analytics. The biggest barriers companies face in extracting value from data and analytics are organizational; many struggle to incorporate data-driven insights into day-to-day business processes. Another challenge is attracting and retaining the right talent—not only data scientists but business translators who combine data savvy with industry and functional expertise."

Big Data is being transformed to a critical enterprises' asset. It comes from diversified resources such as the Internet, sensors, mobile phones, payment systems, cameras, telematics, and wearable devices. Its value is being realized with its ultimate use ubiquitously. Reference 2 points out that "while data itself will become increasingly commoditized, value is likely to accrue to the owners of scarce data, to players that aggregate data in unique ways, and especially to providers of valuable analytics. Data and analytics are changing the basis of competition. Leading companies are using their capabilities not only to improve their core operations but to launch entirely new business models. The network effects of digital platforms are creating a winner-take-most dynamic in some markets."

Big Data and analytics underpin several disruptive models. Introducing new types of data view such as orthogonality can disrupt industries, and massive data integration capabilities can break through institutional and technological silos, enabling new insights and analytical tools. Hyperscale E-commerce platforms, such as Electronic Communication Networks, can match buyers and sellers in real time, transforming inefficient markets. Granular data can be used to personalize products and services (e.g., Industry 4.0)—and, most intriguingly, healthcare. New analytical techniques can

*An information system is heterogeneous if the software that creates and manipulates data is different at all sites and such data follow different structure and format that do not adhere to all sites. Autonomy refers to databases being under separate and independent control. Diverse dimensionality refers to the existence of different representations based on the feature of perspective, and the features involved to represent each single perspective are varied. See Reference 1 and references therein.

fuel discovery and innovation. Above all, data and analytics can enable faster and more intelligent decision-making [2,3].

Recent advances in machine learning can be used to solve a tremendous variety of problem—and deep learning is pushing the boundaries even further. Systems enabled by machine learning can provide customer service, manage logistics, analyze medical records, or even write news stories. The value potential is everywhere, even in industries that have been slow to digitize. These technologies could generate productivity gains and an improved quality of life—along with job losses and other disruptions. Reference 2 highlights, "previous MGI research found that 45% of work activities could potentially be automated by currently demonstrated technologies; machine learning can be an enabling technology for the automation of 80% of those activities. Breakthroughs in natural language processing could expand that impact even further."

Big Data and analytics are already shaking up multiple industries, and bigger wave of change is looming on the horizon as automated learning reaches maturity, giving machines unprecedented capabilities to think, decision-making, and communication. In this chapter, we propose a framework of reinforcement learning (RL) with generalized optimal wavelet decomposing algorithm (GOWDA) system that can decompose noise intelligently from signals with wavelet transformation and preserve information automatically.

We organized the chapter as follows. We briefly introduce the X 4.0 era with an evolutionary review on Industry 4.0, Web 4.0, and business intelligence and analytics (BI&A) 4.0 in section "The X 4.0 era: Evolutionary aspect." In section "Machine learning for artificial intelligence," we briefly discuss machine learning for artificial intelligence. We propose a methodological framework of RL with GOWDA system. In section "Simulation study," we execute a simulation study by applying our method to analyze two stylized data and illustrate both in-sample modeling and out-of-sample forecasting results. We summarize with future works in section "Future work."

The X 4.0 era: Evolutionary aspect

Industry 4.0

Industry 4.0 marks a new era of automation and data exchange that integrates cyber-physical systems (such as Internet of Things), information and communication technology, and cloud computing in manufacturing. The term Industry 4.0 refers to the fourth industrial revolution* and is often understood

*The first industrial revolution (i.e., mechanization) was the introduction of mechanical production facilities starting in the second half of the eighteenth century and being intensified throughout the entire nineteenth century. The second industrial revolution (i.e., electrification) led by electrification and the division of labor started from the 1870s. The third industrial revolution (i.e., digitalization) was set out in the 1970s, when advanced electronics and information technology developed widely.

as the application of the generic concept of cyber-physical systems to industrial production with introduction of Internet technologies [4]. Similar ideas have been brought up under the name Industrial Internet by General Electric in United States of America and Made in China 2025 by State Council in China.

Three hypotheses have been highlighted by Drath and Horch [4] to well understand the concept of cyber-physical systems: "(1) Communication infrastructure in production systems will become more affordable and, hence, be introduced everywhere. It is useful for various purposes such as engineering, configuration, service, diagnostics, operation and service of products, field devices, machines, or plants. It will become a self-evident part of future production systems. (2) Field devices, machines, plants, and factories (even individual products) will increasingly be connected to a network (e.g., the Internet or a private factory network). They will be available as data objects in the network and may store real-time data. Therefore, they become searchable, explorable, and analyzable in the network. This will lead to an explosion of available objects and data, accessible from anywhere. (3) Field devices, machines, plants, and factories (even individual products) will become able to store documents and knowledge about themselves outside their physical body in the network. By doing so, they obtain a virtual living representation in the net, with individual identifiers. They will store documents, three-dimensional (3D) models, simulation models, requirements, and so on. This information, stored outside the body of the physical objects, is updatable and, hence, represents the latest available version. In addition to those data, different functionalities will act for the physical objects: negotiation functions, exploration functions, and so on. These data objects augment the corresponding real device and form a second identity in the network, where these data objects form a knowledge base for various applications."

Reference 4 points out, "the novelty in such a scenario is not in a new technology, but in that it combines the available technology in a new way. The availability of bulk data allows various new business models. In combination with third-party services such as weather, calendar, payment services, geolocation, or historical data, new levels of organization and scheduling are possible." Like all members of the *as a service* family, Data as a Service (DaaS) builds on the concept that the product (data in this case) can be provided on demand to the user regardless of geographic or organizational separation of provider and consumer. In addition, the emergence of service-oriented architecture has also rendered the actual platform on which the data reside irrelevant. This development has enabled the emergence of the relatively new concept of DaaS.

Web 4.0

Web is the largest transformable-information construct that its idea was first introduced in 1989 by Tim Burners-Lee, the inventor of the World

Wide Web and one of Time Magazine's "100 Most Important People of the 20th Century." Much progress has been made about the web and related technologies in the past two decades. Web 1.0 as a web of cognition, Web 2.0 as a web of communication, Web 3.0 as a web of cooperation, and Web 4.0 as a web of integration are introduced such as four generation of the web since the advent of the web [5]. Web 4.0 is about *the ultra-intelligent electronic agent.*

According to Berners-Lee, Web 1.0 is the first generation of the web and could be considered the read-only web and also as a system of cognition. Web 1.0 began as an information place for people and organizations to share information broadcasted. The early web provided limited user interactions or content contributions and only allowed to search the information and read it. Some of the technologies developed during this stage include: file and web servers, content and enterprise portals, search engines (such as Yahoo!), personal information managers, E-mail, P2P file sharing, and publish and subscribe technologies.

Web 2.0 was defined by Dale Dougherty, the founder and CEO of Maker Media, Inc., in 2004 as a read–write web. The technologies of Web 2.0 in this stage are: blogs, wikis (e.g., Wikipedia), social bookmarking, social networks (e.g., Facebook, MySpace), instant messaging, mash-ups, auction web sites (e.g., eBay), and professional networking (e.g., LinkedIn). These technologies enable individuals from all around the world to participate in content creation and sharing and allow assembling and managing large global crowds with common interests in social interactions. People can leverage and utilize communities to create and share content (such as Facebook) in communities.

Focusing on connecting content and allowing people to interact and collaborate, technologies did not provide the knowledge about relationships among the information that they were connecting. Therefore, Web 3.0 endeavors to connect the information of the web together in new ways that utilize semantic technologies to describe what an item is, not just how it should look. This semantic information will allow computers to look up other matches based on similar properties. Web 3.0 or semantic web desires to decrease human's tasks and decisions and leave them to machines by providing machine-readable contents on the web [5]. In general, Web 3.0 contains two major platforms: semantic technologies and social computing environment. The former represents open standards that can be applied on the top of the web, and the latter allows human–machine cooperations. Some of the key technologies that are being developed during this stage include the following: ontologies (e.g., YAGO, DBPedia), semantic searching, thesauri and taxonomies, personal intelligent digital assistants, and knowledge bases.

Once Web 3.0 technologies are firmly entrenched in the World Wide Web such as better natural language processing, developing intelligent systems to enable ability of thinking (such as learning and reasoning) turns to be emergent. Web 4.0 is also known as symbiotic web [5] that enables interaction between humans and machines in symbiosis. It will be possible to build more powerful interfaces with intelligence using Web 4.0 in which machines would extract information and react in the form of executing and deciding what to execute first and then build more commanding interfaces.

Business intelligence and analytics 4.0

BI&A has emerged as an important area reflecting the magnitude and impact of data-related problems to be solved in contemporary business organizations. BI&A 1.0, BI&A 2.0, and BI&A 3.0 are defined and described by Chen et al. [6] in terms of their key characteristics and capabilities.

Reference 6 points out that as a data-centric approach, BI&A has its roots in the long-standing database-management field and relies heavily on various data collection, extraction, and analysis technologies [7]. The BI&A technologies and applications adopted in industry can be considered as BI&A 1.0 if the data are mostly structured, collected by companies through various legacy systems, and often stored in commercial relational database management systems. The analytical techniques commonly used in these systems, popularized in the 1990s, are grounded mainly in statistical methods developed in the 1970s and data-mining techniques developed in the 1980s.

BI&A 2.0, in the 2000s, centered on text and web analytics for unstructured web content with development of web intelligence, web analytics, and the user-generated content collected through Web 2.0-based social and crowdsourcing systems. The many Web 2.0 applications developed after 2004 have also created an abundance of user-generated content from various online social media such as forums, online groups, web blogs, social networking sites, social multimedia sites (for photos and videos), and even virtual worlds and social games. BI&A 2.0 systems require the integration of mature and scalable techniques in text mining (e.g., information extraction, topic identification, opinion mining, and question-answering), web mining, social network analysis, and spatial-temporal analysis, see Reference 6 and references therein.

The October 2011 article in *The Economist* reports that the number of mobile phones and tablets (about 480 million units) surpassed the number of laptops and PCs (about 380 million units) for the first time in 2011. The ability of mobile and Internet-enabled devices to support highly mobile, location-aware, person-centered, and context-relevant operations and transactions will continue to offer unique challenges and opportunities throughout the 2010s. Mobile interface, visualization, and human–computer interaction design have ushered the Web 3.0 (mobile and sensor-based) era. The underlying mobile analytics and location and context-aware techniques (e.g., Internet of Things) for collecting, processing, analyzing, and visualizing such large-scale and fluid mobile and sensor data are comprising the BI&A 3.0, see Reference 6 and references therein. Big Data analytics have been well established in this stage; see Reference 1 and references therein.

Proliferated by artificial intelligence and interaction between humans and computers, BI&A 4.0 is ultraintelligent and enabled to make optimal decisions automatically. BI&A 4.0 can be achieved with different Big Data systems and evaluated by sophisticated quality measures (see Reference 8, and references therein). Reference 9 points out that advances in BI&A 4.0 have combined physical and virtual environments, giving rise to the omnichannel strategies in which online, offline, and online-to-offline (i.e., the O-cubed: O^3) channels converge to deliver a seamless shopping experience. Tighter integration between online and offline communication channels raises concerns about analytical efficiency. A strategic matrix has been proposed by Sun [9] in which the row is for the *O-cubed* attribution (i.e., online, offline, and O2O) and column for the *O-biquadrate* attribution (i.e., object, opportunity, organization, and operation). Advanced tools have been applied to deal with course of dimensionality [10]; for example, Alpha Go and its upgraded version Master Go have been annihilating some of the world's best Go players online lately. Similar smart learning processes can be applied for automated decision making, and we are going to briefly introduce them in section "Machine learning for artificial intelligence."

Machine learning for artificial intelligence

McKinsey Global Institute 2016 report points out that the increasing availability of data has fueled advances in analytical techniques and technologies, with machine learning at the forefront. A standard software program is hard-coded with strict rules for the tasks it needs to execute. But it cannot adapt to new variables or requirements unless a programer updates it with specific new rules. Although this works well in some contexts, it is easy to see why this approach is not scalable to handle all the complexities of the real world. Machine learning, meanwhile, uses an inductive approach to form a representation of the world based on the data it sees. It is able to tweak and improve its representation as new data arrive. In that sense, the algorithm *learns* from new data inputs and gets better over time. The key requirement for machine learning is vast quantities of data, which are necessary to train algorithms.

Vastly, larger quantities of rich data have enabled remarkable improvements in machine-learning algorithms [10–12], including deep learning. Among the most important advances in machine-learning techniques over the past few years are the following [2].

Deep learning

This branch of machine learning uses deep neural networks with many hidden layers. Two of the most common types of deep neural networks are feedforward and recursive (see Reference 13, and references therein). Convolutional neural networks are often used for recognizing images by processing a hierarchy of features—for instance, making the connection between a nose, a face, and eventually a full cat. This image recognition capability has important applications in the development of autonomous vehicles, which need to recognize their surroundings instantly. In contrast, recursive neural networks are used when the overall sequence and context are important, as in speech recognition or natural language processing. Deep learning systems are the clearest example of the utilization of abundant data, processing power, and increasingly sophisticated algorithms. Neural networks were developed decades ago, but they lacked the massive quantities of data and processing power needed to reach their full capabilities. Now that those barriers have been overcome, data scientists are making rapid advances in deep learning techniques [2].

Reinforcement learning

RL takes actions toward a specified goal, that is, the value functions are formalized (see Reference 14, and references therein). The algorithms explore a broad range of possible actions while gradually learning which ones are most effective, thereby incorporating an element of creativity. The most popular algorithm will allow the agent to select an action that will maximize the value function (i.e., reward) in the long term (i.e., have infinite horizon) and not only in the immediate future. In practice, this is done by learning to estimate the value of a particular state. This estimate is adjusted over time by propagating part of the next state's reward. If all the states and all the actions are tried a sufficient amount of times, this will allow an optimal policy to be defined; the action that maximizes the value of the next state is picked (see Reference 14, and references therein).

Ensemble learning

This set of techniques uses multiple machine-learning methods to obtain better predictions than any one method could achieve on its own, which initiates the ensemble methods, such that multiple learning algorithms to obtain better predictive performance than could be obtained from any of the constituent learning algorithms alone. One classification technique is the Bayes optimal classifier that ensembles all the hypotheses in the hypothesis space. Bayesian parameter averaging is an ensemble technique that seeks to approximate the Bayes optimal classifier by sampling hypotheses from the hypothesis space, and combining them using Bayes' law. The accuracy of Bayesian parameter averaging in variable selection and estimation in high-dimensional settings performs well (see Reference 15, references therein).

When dealing with Big Data or large-scale systems with dynamic programing, there are up to three curses of dimensionality: the state space, the outcome space, and the action space. Approximate dynamic programing has emerged as a powerful tool for tackling a diverse collection of stochastic optimization problems. Passive learning strategies will collect information and update beliefs about functions, without making any explicit attempt at collecting information in a way that would accelerate the learning strategy.

Active learning refers to strategies in which we are willing to make suboptimal actions explicitly because the information gained will add value later in the process [10]. Reference 11 points out that most of the literature has focused on simple heuristics, but in some cases, these heuristics have provable suboptimality bounds. Therefore, the approximate dynamic programing approach will focus primarily on the knowledge gradient policy, which maximizes the rate of learning, and offers both theoretical and practical features in a Bayesian setting that focuses on minimizing expected opportunity cost [10,11,13].

The methodological framework

In the current section, we describe the automated data-driven analytical framework based on RL for the GOWDA proposed by Sun et al. [1]. Following a typical signal-processing format, a signal (e.g., the intrinsic value of dynamics) is sampled in the presence of noise (e.g., deviating data or behavior), and we are going to reconstruct the underlying process with few coefficients to reveal the signal dynamics. Assume the observational equation of X can be expressed as follows:

$$X_t = S(t) + N_t, \quad t \in T = \{1, \ldots, n(= 2^J)\}$$

where:

n is the total number of regularly sampled time points

$S(t)$ is the unknown function at time t that represents the signal

N_t is the additive noise variables that are independently and identically distributed and sampled at time t [16]

Reinforcement learning

Markov decision process is a framework to model a Markovian dynamic system, which is composed of a tuple $\langle \mathcal{S}, \mathcal{A}, T, C \rangle$, where $\mathcal{S}$ is a set of states, $\mathcal{A}$ is a set of actions, T is a transition function, and C is a cost function. A state $s \in \mathcal{S}$ can be continuous or discrete, and it describes intrinsic features of the system. An action $a \in \mathcal{A}$ controls the state of the system. A transition $T(s_t, a, s_{t+1})$ describes the transition of the state at the time t by applying an action a from s_t to s_{t+1}. The cost function C evaluates how good the state s is for the system. Given $\langle \mathcal{S}, \mathcal{A}, T, C \rangle$, the agent can evaluate every possible policy. For example, when an agent is under the state s_t and apply a policy π that suggests an action $a_t = \pi(s_t)$, it will receive the cost $c_t = C(s_t, a_t, s_{t+1})$, and its state will change to s_{t+1}.

The goal of the RL is to make an agent be able to make a best policy π^* and behave in the environment, and the best policy π^* is the policy with the minimum cost. Value function $V^{\pi}(s)$ evaluates how good the policy π is, that is, how much the expected cost is, when an agent is in the state s. It can be also expressed in a recursive manner as Equation 8.2 and further expressed in terms of Bellman equation as Equation 8.3 that indicates that the value of π equals the immediate cost from the states transfer and the values of the possible next state weighted by the transition probability and a discount factor γ.

$$V^{\pi}(s) = \mathbb{E}\left\{\sum_{i=0}^{\infty} \gamma^i c_{t+i}\right\} \tag{8.1}$$

$$= \mathbb{E}\{c_t + \gamma V^{\pi}(s_{t+1})|s = s_t\} \tag{8.2}$$

$$= \sum_{s'} T(s, \pi(s), s')(C(s, a, s') + \gamma V^{\pi}(s_{t+1})) \tag{8.3}$$

The best policy π^* with the minimum cost V^{π^*}, satisfies $V^{\pi^*}(s) \leq V^{\pi}(s)$, $\forall s \in \mathcal{S}$ and $\forall a \in \mathcal{A}$.

$$V^*(s) = \arg\min_{a'} \sum_{s'} T(s, \pi(s), s')(C(s, a, s') + \gamma V^{\pi}(s_{t+1}))$$

In state s under the best policy π^*, the corresponding action can be derived as follows:

$$\pi^*(s) = \arg\min_{a'} \sum_{s'} T(s, \pi(s), s')(C(s, a, s') + \gamma V^{\pi}(s_{t+1}))$$

Value function also can be expressed by the state-action function Q [14] that evaluates the expected cost when an agent takes a certain action a in the state s_t. Compared with V-function, Q-function does not take the forward state into consideration, and it will be appropriate for those problems with unclear transition function T. Similar to V-function, Q-function also can be expressed in terms of Bellman equation as Equation 8.5.

$$Q(s, a) = \mathbb{E}\left\{\sum_{i=1}^{\infty} \gamma^i c_{t+i}\right\} \tag{8.4}$$

$$= \sum_{s'} T(s, \pi(s), s')(C(s, a, s') + \gamma \max_{a'} Q(s, a')) \tag{8.5}$$

The value of state s under the best policy $V^*(s)$ can be expressed as

$$V^*(s) = \arg\min_{a'} Q(s, a)$$

In addition, the corresponding action taken in the state s under π^* can be derived from

$$\pi^*(s) = \arg\min_{a'} Q(s, a)$$

RL can be classified into two categorical methods [14]. The first is model-free and the other is model-based method. In the model-free methods, the agent will directly extract the optimal policy through sequences of explorations and modifications. Model-based methods will construct a model based on the collected data and use this model to extract the optimal policy.

Bayesian RL (BRL) inherits the idea of Bayesian learning that the uncertainty can be expressed by prior distribution, and the learning is achieved through sequences of Bayesian inference. Compared with traditional RL, BRL enables us to encode the domain knowledge into the prior distribution and uses the collected data to reduce the uncertainty. BRL also can be separated into model-free and model-based methods. Similar to RL, the model-free BRL methods use Bayesian technique to model the distribution over the parameters of the value function or the policy. The model-based BRL methods adopt the Bayesian technique to model the distribution of the parameters over the transition, or reward functions. Taking Bayesian Q-learning as an example, it models the distribution of the Q-function of each state-action (s, a) pair and helps one to select more appropriate actions. In the classical Q-function, $Q(s, a)$ denotes the value when taking an action a in the state a. In BRL, let $q(s, a)$ be a random variable of $Q(s, a)$ and $\mathbb{E}[q(s, a)] = Q(s, a)$. BRL maintains different distributions for each (s, a) pair. BRL makes some assumptions: (1) Each $q(s, a)$ follows a normal distribution with the mean $\mu(s, a)$ and standard deviation $\sigma(s, a)$. (2) Prior of $q(s, a)$ is independent and follows the Gamma distribution. Compared with the classical Q-function, Bayesian Q-learning does not focus on the Q-value of each (s, a) pair, but keep updating the hyperparameters $\mu(s, a)$ and $\sigma(s, a)$ of the distribution of each (s, a) pair.

Reference 17 proposes Gaussian Process Temporal Difference to extend Q-function learning. Let $\mathbf{z}$ be a state-action pair $\mathbf{z} = (s, a)$ and a state-action sequence $\mathbf{z}_0, \mathbf{z}_1, \cdots, \mathbf{z}_t$. In GPTD, Gaussian process is defined as the distribution over Q-function such that the set of value of $Q(\mathbf{z})$ evaluated at the given data $\mathbf{z}_0, \mathbf{z}_1, \cdots, \mathbf{z}_t$ follows the Gaussian distribution with the mean function $\mu(\mathbf{z}) = \mathbb{E}[Q(\mathbf{z})]$ and the covariance function $k(\mathbf{z}, \mathbf{z}') = \mathbb{E}[(\mu(\mathbf{z}) - Q(\mathbf{z}))(\mu(\mathbf{z}') - Q(\mathbf{z}'))]$. Let $q(\mathbf{z})$ denote the random variable of $Q(\mathbf{z})$ and $\mathbb{E}[q(\mathbf{z})] = Q(\mathbf{z})$ and follow the definition of $Q(\mathbf{z})$, and we derive

$$q(\mathbf{z}) = c(\mathbf{z}) + \gamma q(\mathbf{z}'), \text{where} \quad \mathbf{z}' \sim P^{\pi}(\mathbf{z}'|\mathbf{z})$$

If we replace $c(\mathbf{z})$ with $Q(\mathbf{z}) + \Delta Q(\mathbf{z})$, we further obtain

$$c(\mathbf{z}) = Q(\mathbf{z}) + \gamma Q(\mathbf{z}') + N(\mathbf{z}, \mathbf{z}'), \text{where} \quad \mathbf{z}' \sim P^{\pi}(\mathbf{z}'|\mathbf{z}) \tag{8.6}$$

which links the observable cost function c-function and the unobservable Q-function.

Then, we are interested in the joint distribution of the function value $Q(\mathbf{z}_0), \cdots, Q(\mathbf{z}_t)$. We denote $\mathbf{Q}_t = (Q(\mathbf{z}_0), \cdots, Q(\mathbf{z}_t))^T$, $\mathbf{c}_t = (c(\mathbf{z}_0), \cdots, c(\mathbf{z}_t))^T$, and $\mathbf{N}_t = (N(\mathbf{z}_0, \mathbf{z}_1), \cdots, N(\mathbf{z}_{t-1}, \mathbf{z}_t))^T$. Equation 8.6 can be expressed in a matrix form

$$\mathbf{c}_t = \mathbf{H}_t \mathbf{Q}_t + \mathbf{N}_t$$

where:

$$\mathbf{H}_t = \begin{bmatrix} 1-\gamma & 0 & \cdots & 0 \\ 0 & 1-\gamma & \cdots & 0 \\ \cdots & \cdots & \cdots & \cdots \\ 0 & 0 & 1 & 1-\gamma \end{bmatrix}$$

If we make an assumption that c-function is a noise-free observation, $\Delta Q(\mathbf{z}_0), \cdots, \Delta Q(\mathbf{z}_t)$ satisfies zero-mean Gaussian distribution. As more data are collected, the posterior covariance decreases, which reflects the confidence of estimate $\hat{Q}$.

There are two approaches to search the best policy. The first is value function-based methods that search in the space of the value function for the optimal value and then to extract the best policy, such as Q-Learning, state-action-reward-state-action (SARSA) methods. The other approach searches directly from the policy space. The Markov decision process evaluates policies.

In the current chapter, we focus on the model-free and value function approach when applying the GOWDA framework introduced in the following sections.

Wavelet transform

The continuous wavelet transform is a function of two variables $\psi_{a,b}(t)$ and is obtained by simply projecting $S(t)$ onto a particular wavelet function ψ via

$$\mathcal{W}(a,b) = \int_{-\infty}^{\infty} S(t)\psi_{a,b}(t)dt$$

where

$$\psi_{a,b}(t) = \frac{1}{\sqrt{b}}\psi\left(\frac{t-a}{b}\right)$$

is the translated (by a) and dilated (by b) version of the original wavelet function. The resulting wavelet coefficients are a function of two parameters that identify the location and scale of μ and σ. When the admissibility condition is satisfied such that

$$\mathcal{W}_{\Psi} = \int_0^{\infty} \frac{\Psi(f)}{f} df < \infty$$

where $\Psi(f)$ is the Fourier transform of the frequency f of $\psi(t)$, an inverse operation $\mathcal{W}^{-1}$ is performed to produce $\tilde{S}(t)$ from its wavelet coefficients:

$$\tilde{S}(t) = \frac{1}{\mathcal{W}_{\psi}} \int_0^{\infty} \int_{-\infty}^{\infty} \mathcal{W}(a,b)\psi_{a,b}(t)da\frac{db}{b^2}$$

References 18 and 19 provide more details, and further literature can be found in Reference 20 and references therein.

Thresholding

As we are going to reconstruct the process in a sparse way in which few coefficients reveal the information that we are looking for, we need to remove the redundant coefficients with the thresholding—to remove the coefficients when they are beyond a predetermined thresholding γ. Then Equation 8.7 can then be expressed as follows:

$$\tilde{f}(x) = \sum_{k=1}^{2^{j_0}} \xi_{j_0 k} \psi_{j_0 k}(x) + \sum_{j=j_0}^{J-1} \sum_{k=1}^{2^j} \theta_{j,k} \mathbb{1}_{(\theta_{j,k} > \gamma)} \psi_{j,k}(x)$$

where:

$\xi_{j_0,k}$ are the whole structure terms at the coarsest resolution level

$\theta_{j,k}(j = 1, ..., J-1, k = 1, ..., 2^j)$ are the empirical wavelet coefficients at level j, which represent the detailed structure at scale 2^j

Several threshold rules have been adopted by Sun et al. [1] to decide which redundant coefficients after wavelet decomposition should be removed.

Reference 21 proposes the universal threshold by setting $\gamma = (2 \log n)^{1/2} \hat{\sigma}$, where $\hat{\sigma}$ stands for the estimated noise level, and Reference 22 suggests the SURE thresholding that minimizes the Stein's unbiased estimator of risk:

$$\mathrm{SURE}\,(\gamma, \theta_j) = N_j - 2 \sum_{k=1}^{N_j} \mathbb{1}_{(\theta_k \leq \gamma)} + \sum_{k=1}^{N_j} \left(\min\{|\theta_k|, \gamma\}\right)^2$$

where:

$\mathbb{1}$ is an indicator function

N_j is the number of wavelet coefficients at the j-th level of decomposition

Furthermore, Reference 23 suggests a heuristic approach (i.e., the heuristic SURE) by applying SURE thresholding to some levels of decomposition and universal thresholding to others. In addition, Reference 24 proposed another thresholding named minimax that minimizes the following expression:

$$\inf_{\gamma} \sup_{\mu} \frac{R_\gamma(\mu)}{n^{-1} + \min\{\mu^2, 1\}}$$

where $R_\gamma(\mu) = \mathrm{E}(\theta_j - \mu)^2$, $\theta_j \sim N(\mu, 1)$.

The Birgé–Massart thresholding is a level-dependent threshold method developed by Birgé and Massart [25]. Let j^* be the maximal decomposition level and m be the length of the coarsest approximation coefficients. The numbers j^*, m, and α define the following rule: for each level, j from 1 to j^*, the coefficients of each level larger than θ_j are kept; otherwise, they are discarded. In the denoising case, we choose $\alpha = 3$

$$\theta_j = \frac{m}{(j^* + 2 - j)^\alpha}$$

Reference 26 proposes a block thresholding that thresholds wavelet coefficients in groups instead of individually. At each level j, the wavelet coefficients are divided into nonoverlapping blocks of length L. Let jb be the indices of the coefficients in the b-th block at j-level, that is, $(jb) = \{(j,k) : (b-1)\mathrm{L} + 1 \leq k \leq b\mathrm{L}\}$. Let $S_{jb}^2 = \sum_{k\in jb} \theta_{j,k}^2$ denote the sum of squares of the wavelet coefficients in the block. A block (jb) is deemed important if S_{jb}^2 is larger than a threshold $\gamma = \lambda \mathrm{L} n^{-1}\sigma^2$, and all the coefficients in the block are retained; otherwise, all the coefficients in the block are discarded. Block thresholding depends on the choice of the block size L and thresholding constant λ. Reference 27 suggests to choose $\mathrm{L} = (\log n)^2$ and $\lambda \geq 48$, and we thus have

$$\tilde{f}(x) = \sum_{k=1}^{2^{j_0}} \xi_{j_0 k}\psi_{j_0 k}(x) + \sum_{j=j_0}^{J-1}\sum_{b}\sum_{k\in jb} \theta_{j,k}\mathbb{1}_{(\theta_{j,k}^2>\gamma)}\psi_{j,k}(x)$$

Reinforcement learning with generalized optimal wavelet decomposing algorithm

Reference 1 defines two metrics (smoothness and synchronicity) to gage the goodness of noise decomposition, that is, to see how close $\tilde{S}_t$ is toward S_t as follows: Let x_t be a sequence and $x_t = |S_t - \tilde{S}_t|$. If there exist constants c and ε, then the smoothness is when $\forall \varepsilon > 0$,

$$\lim_{t\to\infty} \Pr\left(|x_t - c| > \varepsilon\right) = 0$$

As is shown, the sequence x_t of the difference between $\tilde{S}_t$ and S_t must approach a controllable constant c. The resulting difference sequence between $\tilde{S}_t$ and S_t indeed converges in probability to c. Reference 20 points out that error convergence requires that (i) the structural change (e.g., jumps) between $\tilde{S}_t$ and S_t is synchronous, (ii) there is no outliers in x_t, and (iii) the local extremum in x_t is bounded and leads to the following measures.

Let $(Y_1, Y_2)^T$ be a vector of continuous random variables with marginal distribution functions F_1, F_2, and then the coefficient η_H is

$$\eta_H(u) = \lim_{u\to 1} P\left(Y_2 > F_2^{-1}(u) | Y_1 > F_1^{-1}(u)\right)$$

and the coefficient η_L is

$$\eta_L(u) = \lim_{u\to 0} P\left(Y_2 < F_2^{-1}(u) | Y_1 < F_1^{-1}(u)\right)$$

When $\forall\ \varepsilon > 0$, $\exists\ u_0$, $\forall\ u_0 > u$, obtain

$$\left|\frac{\eta_H(u)}{\eta_L(u)} - 1\right| < \varepsilon$$

then Y_1 and Y_2 are synchronous—that is, $\eta_H(u) \sim \eta_L(u)$.

When $\eta_H > 0$, there exists upper tail synchronousness, and the positive extreme values in Y_1 and Y_2 can be observed simultaneously; when $\eta_L > 0$, there exists lower tail synchronousness, and the negative extreme values can be observed simultaneously. Furthermore, we require the smoothness measure to be able to detect artifacts and jumps. Reference 1 suggests two different measures: One considers artifacts (τ_1, based on an outliers test) and the other considers jumps (τ_2, based on local extrema) such that τ_1 is to detect the global extrema and τ_2 for the local extrema. Both of them have the ability to detect boundary problems—an inefficient approximation at the beginning and end of the signal.

Following Reference 20, the Grubbs test for identifying artifacts, which is an iterative test for outliers based on an approximately normal distributed sample, has been employed as follows:

Let T be the sample size (i.e., the length of the sequence x_t), $\mu = \frac{1}{T}\sum_1^T x_t$ is the sample mean, and $s^2 = \frac{1}{T-1}\sum_1^T (x_t - \mu)^2$ is the sample variance. The test statistic is then given by

$$G = \frac{\max|x_t - \mu|}{s}$$

Here, G can be assumed to be t-distributed, and a test for outliers with significant level α (e.g., $\alpha = 0.05$) can easily be performed by rejecting the null hypothesis of no outliers if

$$G > z_\alpha = \frac{T-1}{\sqrt{T}} \times \sqrt{\frac{t^2_{\frac{\alpha}{2\times T},T-2}}{T-2+t^2_{\frac{\alpha}{2\times T},T-2}}}$$

When a deviating observation (i.e., the global extremum) is detected, it is removed from the data, and the test will proceed. As a measure of the amount of artifacts (or jumps of high magnitude), we can identify the number of iterations to run the test until it confirms that there is no outlier. Reference 1 applies this test until $g(x) = 0$ and count the number of deviating observation as a measure of structure with definition 3: Let $\mathcal{C}(x)$ be a function determining whether there is one outlier in vector X:

$$\mathcal{C}(x) = \begin{cases} 1, & if \quad G > z_\alpha \\ 0, & if \quad \text{otherwise} \end{cases}$$

define τ_1 as

$$\tau_1 = \sum_{i=1}^{T} 1 \times \mathbb{1}_{\mathcal{C}(x)=1}$$

where T is the sample size.

To control all structural changes to be bounded, Reference 1 investigates the local extrema (maxima or minima, respectively) at a certain magnitude. To avoid redundant computation (as τ_1 controls the outlier detection), one can only run the test procedure for the output data after the wavelet transform. The local extrema here are the largest and smallest values that a function takes at a point within a given neighborhood. If there exists a $\Lambda \in \mathbb{R}$, for any subsequence x_{t_n} of x_t, $\forall n$, we have

$$\limsup_{t_n \subset T} x_{t_n} \leq \Lambda$$

and then Λ is the local maxima. If there exists a $\lambda \in \mathbb{R}$, such that

$$\liminf_{t_n \subset T} x_{t_n} \geq \lambda$$

then λ is the local minima.

Let $\mathcal{D}(x)$ be a function that detects local maxima:

$$\mathcal{D}(x) = \begin{cases} 1, & if \quad x_t \geq \Lambda \\ 0, & if \quad \text{otherwise} \end{cases}$$

and $\mathcal{D}^*(x)$ detects local minima

$$\mathcal{D}^*(x) = \begin{cases} 1, & if \quad x_t \leq \lambda \\ 0, & if \quad \text{otherwise} \end{cases}$$

We define τ_2 as

$$\tau_2 = \sum_{i=1}^{T} 1 \times \mathbb{1}_{\mathcal{D}(x)=1} + \sum_{i=1}^{T} 1 \times \mathbb{1}_{\mathcal{D}^*(x)=1}$$

where T is the sample size.

In definition 1, Reference 1 defines $x = |S - \tilde{S}|$ as the observed error, and the traditional root mean square error (RMSE) is then

$$\tau_3 = \sqrt{\frac{\sum\limits_{t=1}^{T} (S_t - \tilde{S}_t)^2}{T}}$$

where T is the sample size.

The Akaike Information Criterion and the Bayesian Information Criterion are defined as follows:

$$\tau_4 = \ln \left(\frac{\sum\limits_{t=1}^{T} (S_t - \tilde{S}_t)^2}{T} \right) + \frac{2p}{T}$$

$$\tau_5 = \ln \left(\frac{\sum\limits_{t=1}^{T} (S_t - \tilde{S}_t)^2}{T} \right) + \frac{p \ln T}{T}$$

where p is the number of parameters and T is the sample size.

Let $\mathcal{M}(x)$ be a function that detects the error of signs:

$$\mathcal{M}(x) = \begin{cases} 1, & if \quad S_{t+1}\tilde{S}_{t+1} \leq 0 \\ 0, & if \quad \text{otherwise} \end{cases}$$

we define τ_6 as

$$\tau_6 = \sum_{t=1}^{T} 1 \times \mathbb{1}_{\mathcal{M}(x)=1}$$

where T is the sample size.

The RL framework of GOWDA proposed in this chapter is to obtain the sequential decisions by minimizing the multivariate linear cost function $\mathcal{T}(\cdot)$—that is,

$$\mathcal{T}(\tau_\mathrm{i}) = \sum_{i=1}^{6} \tau_i$$

The linear cost function $\mathcal{T}(\cdot)$ evaluates the approximation error of sequential denoising decision. It eventually investigates the similarity of the original data and its sparse representation (i.e., the denoised data) based on the monotonic synchronicity; τ_1 investigates the goodness to deal with big jumps and τ_2 for moderate fluctuations; τ_3, τ_4, and τ_5 measure the asynchronism with respect to its average amplitude and adjusted amplitudes based on the size of observations and the number of parameters involved for analysis; and τ_6 indicates the total size of asynchronism. At the same smoothness level, the higher the synchronization, the lower the approximation error [that is measured by $\mathcal{T}(\cdot)$], and the better the performance of underlying system.

Simulation study

We conduct a simulation study to investigate the performance of the proposed algorithm. The purpose of this simulation study is twofold. First, we show for any arbitrary signal, the proposed method will result in a better performance than the nonoptimized method (i.e., arbitrarily determining the union of wavelet, level of decomposition, and threshold rule). Second, we are going to illustrate the properties of our algorithm by particularly showing the consistency of our algorithm—the error generated by our method is bounded and less than those of nonoptimized methods.

The data

In the current study, we perform the Monte Carlo simulations in which errors (jumps) are generated from two different patterns to describe

(1) excessive volatility (Pattern I) and (2) excessive volatility with Markov-switching multifractals (Pattern II). We create a time series data of length 2^{13} with a total of 2^9 samples for each pattern being investigated. The trend is based on a sine function, whose amplitude and frequency are drawn from a uniform distribution. For generating the Pattern I signals, following the simulation employed by Sun et al. [1], we add jumps to this trend. Jump occurrences are uniformly distributed (with a Poisson arrival rate), and the jump size follows a normal distribution with zero mean unit variance. The signal is constant between the jumps. The skewed contaminated normal noise, which has heavy tails to capture the excessive volatility (see Reference 28, and references therein), is added to the signal afterwards. For the Pattern II signals, we repeat the method used for the Pattern I signals but shift the trend up and down once to generate a signal characterized as excessive volatility with Markov-switching multifractals. The amplitude of the shift is four times the previous trend. Figure 8.1 illustrates the Q–Q plots of these two different signals.

The methodology

In this simulation study, we choose Haar, Daubechies (DB), Symlet (LA), and Coiflets (Coif) as wavelet functions [19]. We apply the GOWDA suggested by Sun et al. [1], and the candidates of the denoising factors of GOWDA in our simulation are

- $\mathcal{F} \in$ { Haar, DB(4), DB(8), LA(8), Coif(4), Coif(6)}
- $\mathcal{L} \in \{i : i = 1, 2, 3\}$
- $\mathbb{S} \in$ {Birgé–Massart, heuristic SURE, Minimax, SURE, Universal}

In this simulation, the alternative methods we compare with GOWDA under our learning process are five single wavelet functions, that is, Haar, DB(4), DB(8), LA(8), and Coif(6), working with both the discrete wavelet transform (DWT) and the maximal overlap discrete wavelet transform (MODWT), and Fourier transform as we did in Reference 1.

We run the simulation for the two different data patterns described earlier. We use our algorithm to identify the best denoising method that optimally combines wavelet function, level of decomposition, and thresholding rule. For each pattern, we conduct the simulation based on a moving window design following [1]. We investigate our algorithm for both in-sample approximation and out-of-sample forecasting. For the out-of-sample forecasting, we work for both one-step and two-step forecasting. As the true trend (for both in-sample and out-of-sample) of the simulated stylized data is known, we then use RL-GOWDA and alternative methods to denoise the simulated data and compare the approximated trend and forecasted trend with their true counterparts. Obviously, the smaller the difference is compared with the true trend, the better the goodness-of-fit will be for the underlying algorithm.

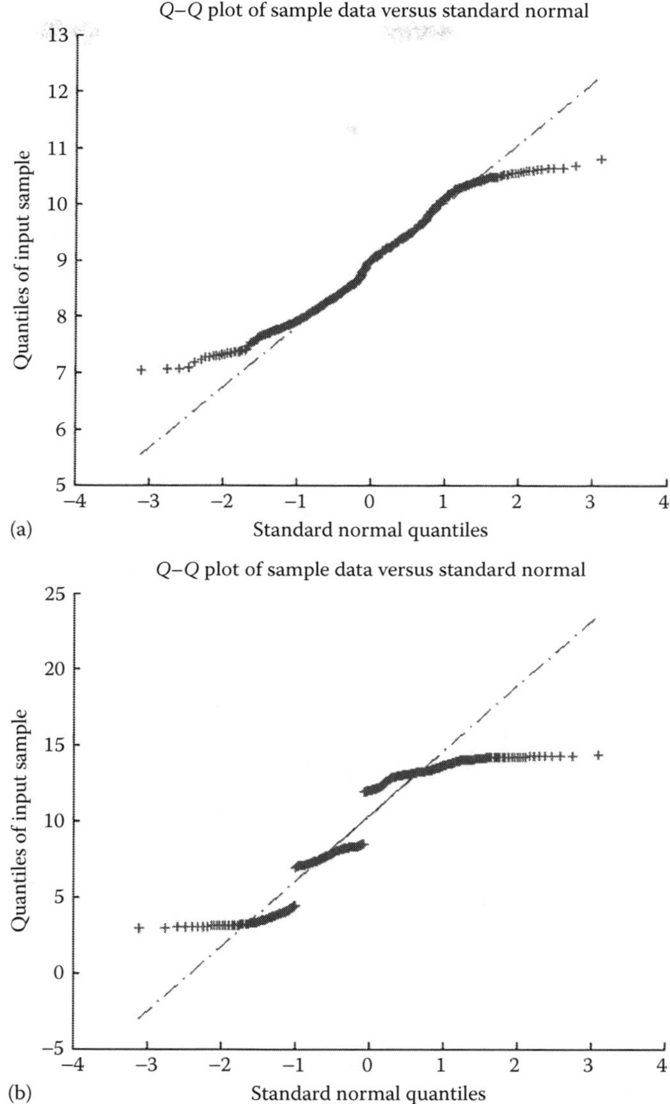

FIGURE 8.1: Normal Q–Q plot for two different simulated data patterns. Panel (a) illustrates excessive volatility, and panel (b) illustrates excessive volatility with Markov-switching multifractals.

Three criteria for goodness-of-fit tests are employed: RMSE, see Equation 8.7, Anderson–Darling (AD) distance, Kolmogorov–Smirnov (KS) distance, and Cramér–von Mises (CVM) distance, which are defined as follows:

$$\mathrm{AD} := \sup_{x \in \mathbb{R}} \frac{|F_n(S) - F(\tilde{S})|}{\sqrt{F(\tilde{S})(1 - F(\tilde{S}))}}$$

$$\mathrm{KS} := \sup_{x \in \mathbb{R}} |F_n(S) - F(\tilde{S})|$$

$$\mathrm{CVM} := \int_{-\infty}^{\infty} (F_n(S) - F(\tilde{S}))^2 \, \mathrm{d}F(\tilde{S})$$

where:

$F_n(S)$ denotes the empirical sample distribution of S

$F(\tilde{S})$ is the distribution function of the approximation (i.e., the output of GOWDA)

We conclude that the smaller these distances are, the better the approximation will be on scale J of the wavelet to preserve the distribution of S. More details can be found in Reference 1 and references therein.

Simulation results

The data length is 8,192 (2^{13}) for each pattern. For the moving window design, we set the in-sample size as 200 and the out-of-sample size as 10 for both one-step ahead and two-step ahead forecasting. The number of window moves is then 800, and we generate 512 (2^9) series data for each pattern. Therefore, for each pattern, we test RL-GOWDA 4,096,000 times for in-sample approximation, one-step forecasting (validation), and two-step forecasting. In our simulation, we have 8,192,000 runs in total.

For each run, we compute the RMSE, KS distance, AD distance, and CVM distance. RMSE presents the distance between the true signal and its approximation. KS focuses on deviations around the median of the distance between the true signal and its approximation, and CVM measures the sensitivity of dispersion between the true signal and its approximation in respect to the change in the true signal. We report the mean value of three distances and their corresponding variances (in parenthesis) for each method in Tables 8.1 and 8.2. The smaller the distance is, the better the performance will be, and then we can identify the following facts.

For both DWT (Table 8.1) and MODWT (Table 8.2), GOWDA with RL shows the smallest values of RMSE, KS, AD, and CVM for these two different data patterns in both in-sample and out-of-sample analyses.

TABLE 8.1: Comparison of goodness-of-fit of RL-GOWDA$_{\text{DWT}}$ with other alternative methods for the in-sample approximation, one-step ahead (validation), and two-step ahead forecasting measured by mean and standard deviation (in parenthesis) of RMSE, Anderson–Darling (AD) distance, Kolmogorov–Smirnov (KS) distance, and Cramér–von Mises (CVM) distance for two different stylized data patterns

		Pattern 1				Pattern 2			
		RMSE $\times 10^{-1}$	AD	KS $\times 10^{-1}$	CVM	RMSE $\times 10^{-1}$	AD	KS $\times 10^{-1}$	CVM
In-Sample	GOWDA	1.1881	0.5828	0.8969	0.0586	1.1852	0.5702	0.8873	0.0567
	std	(0.4131)	(0.2279)	(0.2623)	(0.0577)	(0.3979)	(0.1959)	(0.2403)	(0.0509)
	Haar	1.9204	0.5965	1.2340	0.1420	1.9296	0.5807	1.2245	0.1403
	std	(0.6274)	(0.2066)	(0.2198)	(0.0623)	(0.6485)	(0.1741)	(0.1995)	(0.0565)
	DB(4)	1.4361	0.5951	0.9595	0.0700	1.4235	0.5773	0.9421	0.0658
		(0.5438)	(0.2168)	(0.2733)	(0.0747)	(0.5483)	(0.1816)	(0.2478)	(0.0590)
	DB(8)	1.4292	0.6047	0.9648	0.0705	1.4143	0.5887	0.9408	0.0660
		(0.5373)	(0.2195)	(0.2720)	(0.0740)	(0.5498)	(0.1880)	(0.2456)	(0.0597)
	Coif(6)	1.4215	0.5989	0.9588	0.0687	1.4235	0.5803	0.9445	0.0653
		(0.5439)	(0.2133)	(0.2655)	(0.0701)	(0.5483)	(0.1786)	(0.2414)	(0.0558)
	LA(8)	1.4396	0.5923	0.9568	0.0683	1.4394	0.5742	0.9425	0.0651
		(0.5518)	(0.2145)	(0.2660)	(0.0678)	(0.5615)	(0.1790)	(0.2396)	(0.0550)
One-Step	GOWDA	4.1376	2.7503	9.3518	1.8617	4.1321	2.7416	9.3318	1.8491
		(2.1148)	(0.1360)	(0.2937)	(0.1636)	(1.9272)	(0.1425)	(0.3175)	(0.1696)
	Haar	4.7384	2.7851	9.4391	1.8957	4.7821	2.7894	9.4411	1.8888
		(2.0810)	(0.1143)	(0.2402)	(0.1437)	(1.9929)	(0.1128)	(0.2481)	(0.1438)
	DB(4)	4.0552	2.7721	9.4114	1.8818	4.1142	2.7663	9.3990	1.8758
		(1.8347)	(0.1236)	(0.2693)	(0.1610)	(1.7938)	(0.1246)	(0.2752)	(0.1577)
	DB(8)	4.0468	2.7725	9.4122	1.8854	4.1134	2.7724	9.4111	1.8825
		(1.8029)	(0.1214)	(0.2667)	(0.1617)	(1.7839)	(0.1239)	(0.2723)	(0.1582)

(*Continued*)

TABLE 8.1: ***(Continued)*** Comparison of goodness-of-fit of RL-GOWDA$_{\mathrm{DWT}}$ with other alternative methods for the in-sample approximation, one-step ahead (validation), and two-step ahead forecasting measured by mean and standard deviation (in parenthesis) of RMSE, Anderson–Darling (AD) distance, Kolmogorov–Smirnov (KS) distance, and Cramér–von Mises (CVM) distance for two different stylized data patterns

		Pattern 1				Pattern 2			
		RMSE $\times 10^{-1}$	AD	KS $\times 10^{-1}$	CVM	RMSE $\times 10^{-1}$	AD	KS $\times 10^{-1}$	CVM
	Coif(6)	4.0940	2.7778	9.4163	1.8821	4.1437	2.7726	9.4077	1.8825
		(1.8854)	(0.1279)	(0.2847)	(0.1625)	(1.7913)	(0.1260)	(0.2785)	(0.1621)
	LA(8)	4.1003	2.7750	9.4192	1.8879	4.1544	2.7677	9.4011	1.8805
		(1.8792)	(0.1296)	(0.2854)	(0.1554)	(1.7929)	(0.1271)	(0.2768)	(0.1579)
Two-Step	GOWDA	3.9483	2.4216	8.8659	1.5966	3.9403	2.4273	8.8782	1.6098
		(1.8438)	(0.1280)	(0.2609)	(0.1453)	(1.9091)	(0.1331)	(0.2769)	(0.1470)
	Haar	4.2641	2.6739	9.3608	1.7771	4.2284	2.6715	9.3606	1.7763
		(2.1927)	(0.1241)	(0.2717)	(0.1586)	(2.1272)	(0.1314)	(0.2984)	(0.1688)
	DB(4)	4.0531	2.6807	9.3983	1.7931	4.0877	2.6849	9.4084	1.7946
		(1.8561)	(0.1227)	(0.2747)	(0.1534)	(1.8886)	(0.1270)	(0.2841)	(0.1559)
	DB(8)	4.0838	2.6754	9.3744	1.7865	4.1093	2.6815	9.3916	1.7864
		(1.8486)	(0.1209)	(0.2802)	(0.1550)	(1.8912)	(0.1246)	(0.2829)	(0.1660)
	Coif(6)	4.1132	2.6879	9.4219	1.7980	4.0987	2.6797	9.4033	1.7890
		(1.8436)	(0.1196)	(0.2730)	(0.1503)	(1.8621)	(0.1246)	(0.2780)	(0.1669)
	LA(8)	4.0956	2.6884	9.4228	1.7968	4.0761	2.6821	9.4081	1.7880
		(1.8358)	(0.1219)	(0.2700)	(0.1497)	(1.8611)	(0.1247)	(0.2781)	(0.1609)

TABLE 8.2: Comparison of goodness-of-fit of RL-GOWDA$_{\text{MODWT}}$ with other alternative methods for the in-sample approximation, one-step ahead (validation), and two-step ahead forecasting measured by mean and standard deviation (in parenthesis) of RMSE, Anderson–Darling (AD) distance, Kolmogorov–Smirnov (KS) distance, and Cramér–von Mises (CVM) distance for two different stylized data patterns

		Pattern 1				Pattern 2			
		RMSE $\times 10^{-1}$	AD	KS $\times 10^{-1}$	CVM	RMSE $\times 10^{-1}$	AD	KS $\times 10^{-1}$	CVM
In-Sample	GOWDA	0.9966	0.4646	0.8795	0.0562	1.0045	0.4451	0.8651	0.0540
		(0.3661)	(0.2067)	(0.2574)	(0.0643)	(0.3528)	(0.1638)	(0.2417)	(0.0529)
	Haar	1.3805	0.5643	1.0150	0.0779	1.3733	0.5482	1.0028	0.0748
		(0.5236)	(0.2136)	(0.2280)	(0.0702)	(0.5358)	(0.1870)	(0.2011)	0.0548)
	DB(4)	1.3379	0.5591	0.9332	0.0651	1.3316	0.5405	0.9128	0.0607
		(0.5058)	(0.2119)	(0.2689)	(0.0721)	(0.5178)	(0.1738)	(0.2424)	(0.0562
	DB(8)	1.3449	0.5785	0.9420	0.0657	1.3394	0.5604	0.9201	0.0616
		(0.5049)	(0.2101)	(0.2667)	(0.0712)	(0.5169)	(0.1738)	(0.2433)	(0.0562)
	Coif(6)	1.3378	0.5602	0.9333	0.0651	1.3316	0.5417	0.9127	0.0607
		(0.5056)	(0.2123)	(0.2695)	(0.0720)	(0.5175)	(0.1743)	(0.2429)	(0.0562)
	LA(8)	1.3449	0.5785	0.9420	0.0657	1.3394	0.5604	0.9201	0.0616
		(0.5049)	(0.2101)	(0.2667)	(0.0712)	(0.5169)	(0.1738)	(0.2433)	(0.0562)
One-Step	GOWDA	3.9033	2.7577	9.3640	1.8686	3.9564	2.7452	9.3375	1.8540
		(1.7476)	(0.1133)	(0.2437)	(0.1631)	(1.6905)	(0.1264)	(0.2788)	(0.1474)
	Haar	4.1762	2.7603	9.3769	1.8662	4.1594	2.7639	9.3796	1.8690
		(2.1254)	(0.1306)	(0.2905)	(0.1375)	(1.9650)	(0.1366)	(0.2980)	(0.1587)
	DB(4)	3.9804	2.7798	9.4257	1.8881	4.0405	2.7775	9.4224	1.8869
		(1.8057)	(0.1201)	(0.2680)	(0.1539)	(1.7521)	(0.1244)	(0.2754)	(0.1537)

(Continued)

TABLE 8.2: ***(Continued)*** Comparison of goodness-of-fit of RL-GOWDA$_{\text{MODWT}}$ with other alternative methods for the in-sample approximation, one-step ahead (validation), and two-step ahead forecasting measured by mean and standard deviation (in parenthesis) of RMSE, Anderson–Darling (AD) distance, Kolmogorov–Smirnov (KS) distance, and Cramér–von Mises (CVM) distance for two different stylized data patterns

		Pattern 1				Pattern 2			
		RMSE $\times 10^{-1}$	AD	KS $\times 10^{-1}$	CVM	RMSE $\times 10^{-1}$	AD	KS $\times 10^{-1}$	CVM
	DB(8)	4.0163	2.7760	9.4200	1.8849	4.0797	2.7756	9.4194	1.8882
		(1.8261)	(0.1204)	(0.2711)	(0.1564)	(1.7748)	(0.1248)	(0.2760)	(0.1597)
	Coif(6)	3.9827	2.7804	9.4270	1.8884	4.0429	2.7774	9.4221	1.8871
		(1.8071)	(0.1198)	(0.2681)	(0.1542)	(1.7536)	(0.1243)	(0.2754)	(0.1534)
	LA(8)	4.0163	2.7760	9.4200	1.8849	4.0797	2.7756	9.4194	1.8882
		(1.8261)	(0.1204)	(0.2711)	(0.1564)	(1.7748)	(0.1248)	(0.2760)	(0.1597)
Two-Step	GOWDA	3.9483	2.6707	9.3748	1.7786	3.9517	2.6690	9.3735	1.7791
		(1.7579)	(0.1190)	(0.2579)	(0.1384)	(1.7785)	(0.1159)	(0.2598)	(0.1532)
	Haar	4.2030	2.6870	9.3996	1.7910	4.1655	2.6844	9.3916	1.7845
		(2.1601)	(0.1237)	(0.2750)	(0.1477)	(2.0931)	(0.1251)	(0.2813)	(0.1630)
	DB(4)	4.0221	2.6884	9.4258	1.7990	4.0283	2.6927	9.4311	1.8004
		(1.8113)	(0.1189)	(0.2673)	(0.1469)	(1.8410)	(0.1204)	(0.2745)	(0.1540)
	DB(8)	4.0554	2.6907	9.4181	1.7986	4.0629	2.6883	9.4214	1.7960
		(1.8297)	(0.1152)	(0.2619)	(0.1484)	(1.8632)	(0.1216)	(0.2763)	(0.1555)
	Coif(6)	4.0242	2.6886	9.4249	1.7994	4.0304	2.6922	9.4304	1.7998
		(1.8126)	(0.1189)	(0.2683)	(0.1471)	(1.8426)	(0.1205)	(0.2744)	(0.1539)
	LA(8)	4.0554	2.6907	9.4181	1.7986	4.0629	2.6883	9.4214	1.7960
		(1.8297)	(0.1152)	(0.2619)	(0.1484)	(1.8632)	(0.1216)	(0.2763)	(0.1555)

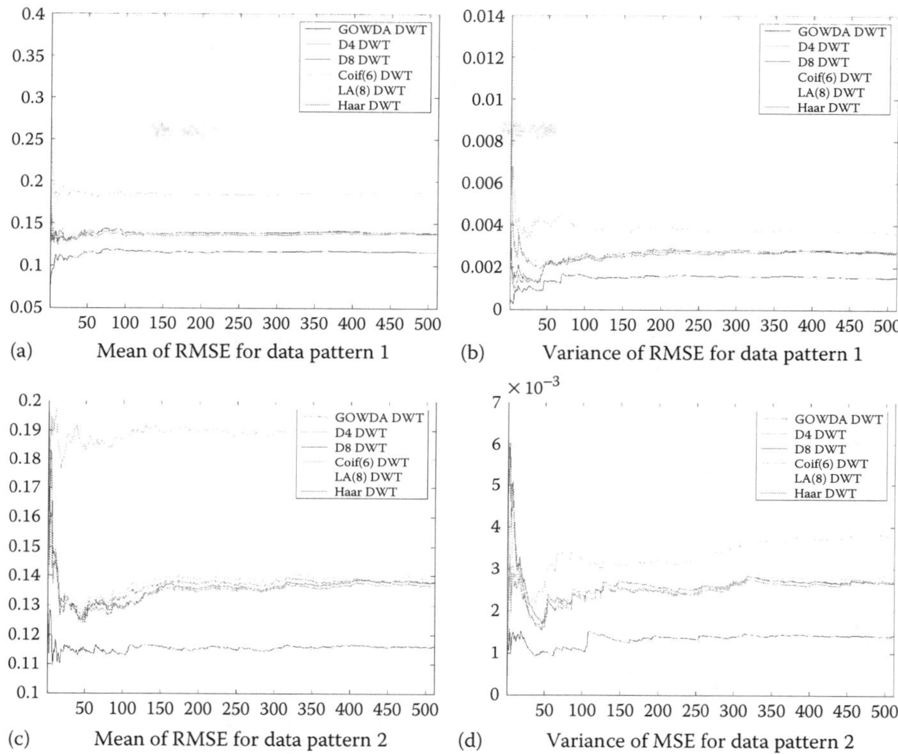

FIGURE 8.2: Comparison of denoising performances of RL-GOWDA with other alternative methods under DWT measured by mean and variance of RMSE for two different stylized data patterns.

We therefore can conclude that the proposed GOWDA RL procedure performs better than the classic wavelet methods and the Fourier transform for the two data patterns we investigated. We summarize the results with Figures 8.2 and 8.3. We easily see that the mean value of RMSE of GOWDA RL is smaller than that of alternative methods, and the standard deviations of RMSE for GOWDA are smaller than that obtained by using alternative wavelet methods. In addition, we identify that when increasing the number of simulation runs, the standard deviation of RMSE decreases. The speed of the decrease in variance (i.e., the speed of error convergence to its limit) of GOWDA RL is relatively faster than that of alternative methods. The results we obtain in this simulation coincide with some analytical properties shown by [1] and we conclude that GOWDA RL algorithm has better performance than alternative methods.

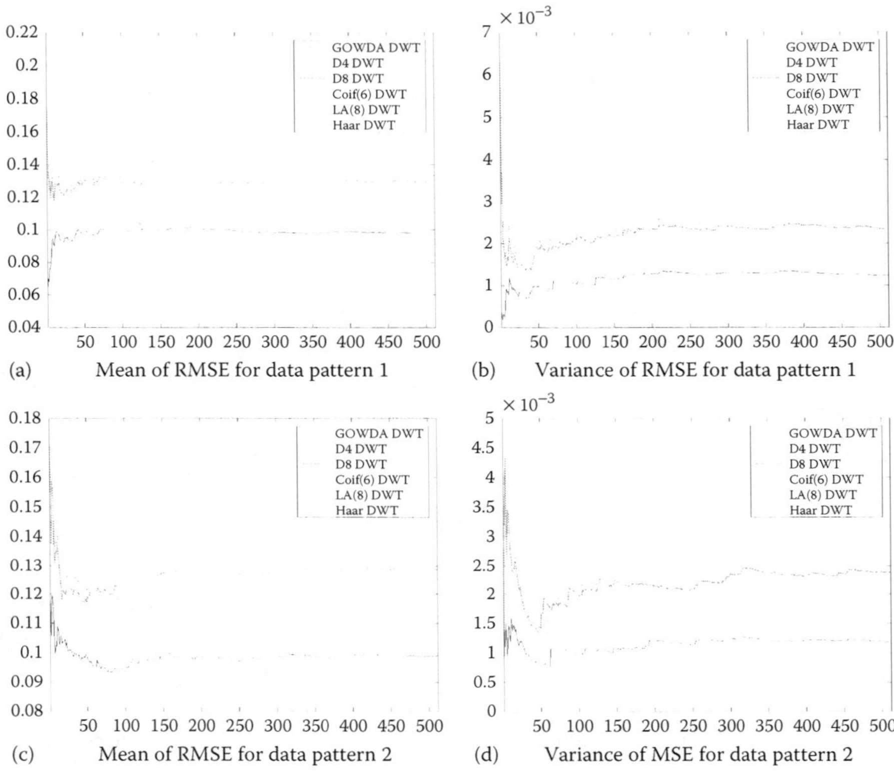

FIGURE 8.3: Comparison of denoising performances of RL-GOWDA with other alternative methods under MODWT measured by mean and variance of RMSE for two different stylized data patterns.

Future work

The significant performance of GOWDA RL algorithm will lead to automated analytics and help end users to increase the efficiency of their decision-making based on Big Data. The Pattern I data illustrate a typical stylized fact of data, that is, heavy-tails or excessive fluctuation (caused by unexpected changes occasionally with large amplitude), and the Pattern II data show excessive fluctuation with Markov-switching multifractals, that is, several large persistent changes occur (see Reference 28, and references therein). Many decision-making models are very sensitive to these stylized facts. Failing to deal with these stylized facts will lead to (1) underestimating the uncertainty and

(2) an inappropriate response (e.g., trading too passively or too aggressively) in their decision-making. Therefore, the proposed GOWDA RL framework can improve the decision-making process by representing the appropriate information.

Financial technology, also known as FinTech, is an industry composed of companies that use new technology and innovation to leverage available resources to compete in the marketplace of traditional financial institutions and intermediaries in the delivery of financial services. FinTech refers to new applications, processes, products, or business models in the financial services industry [29–31]. The proposed framework can be applied for FinTech in terms of goal-based automated decision-making, for example, for robo-adivsors.

References

[1] E. Sun, Y.-T. Chen, and M.-T. Yu. Generalized optimal wavelet decomposing algorithm for big financial data. *International Journal of Production Economics*, 165:194–214, 2015.

[2] N. Henke, J. Bughin, M. Chui, J. Manyika, T. Saleh, B. Wiseman, and G. Sethupathy. The age of analytics: Competing in a data-driven world. *McKinsey Global Institute Report*, December:1–136, 2016.

[3] E. Sun, T. Kruse, and M.-T. Yu. High frequency trading, liquidity, and execution cost. *Annals of Operations Research*, 223:403–432, 2014.

[4] R. Drath and A. Horch. Industrie 4.0: Hit or hype? *IEEE Industrial Electronics Magazine*, 8(2):56–58, 2014.

[5] S. Aghaei, M.A. Nematbakhsh, and H.K. Farsani. Evolution of the world wide web: From web 1.0 to web 4.0. *International Journal of Web & Semantic Technology*, 3(1):1–10, 2012.

[6] H. Chen, R. Chiang, and V. Storey. Business intelligence and analytics: From big data to big impact. *MIS Quarterly*, 36(4):1165–1181, 2012.

[7] S. Chaudhuri, U. Dayal, and V. Narasayya. An overview of business intelligence technology. *Communications of the ACM*, 54(8):88–98, 2012.

[8] Y.-T. Chen, E. Sun, and Y.-B. Lin. Coherent quality management for big data systems: A dynamic approach for stochastic time consistence. *Working Paper*, NCTU, Hsinchu City, Taiwan, pp. 201–208, 2016.

[9] E. Sun. Lecture Note of Bank Marketing. *KEDGE Business School France*, 2017.

[10] W.B. Powell and I.O. Ryzhov. *Optimal Learning.* John Wiley & Sons, Hoboken, NJ, 2012.

[11] W.B. Powell. *Approximate Dynamic Programming: Solving the Curses of Dimensionality*, 2nd ed. John Wiley & Sons, Hoboken, NJ, 2011.

[12] Y.-T. Chen and E.W. Sun. Axiomatic framework for optimal quality management of big data systems. *NCTU Working Paper*, NCTU, Hsinchu City, Taiwan, pp. 1–40, 2016.

[13] Y.-T. Chen and E.W. Sun. Artificial intelligence with parallel neural networks for Internet of Energy: A system for big data analytics. *KEDGE Working Paper*, KEDGE, Bordeaux, France, pp. 1–36, 2016.

[14] M. Wiering and M. van Otterlo, editors. *Reinforcement Learning: State-of-the-Art.* New York: Springer, 2012.

[15] M.-H. Lin, E. W. Sun, and M.-Teh Yu. Efficient risk measures for portfolios of high-dimensional dependent assets: A Bayesian approach. *NCTU Working Paper*, NCTU, Hsinchu City, Taiwan, pp. 1–29, 2016.

[16] Y.-T. Chen, E. Sun, and M.-T. Yu. Improving model performance with integrated wavelet denoising method. *Studies in Nonlinear Dynamics & Econometrics*, 19(4):445–467, 2015.

[17] Y. Engel, S. Mannor, and R. Meir. Reinforcement learning with Gaussian processes. *Proceedings of the 22 International Conference on Machine Learning*, Bonn, Germany, pp. 201–208, 2015.

[18] R. Gençay, F. Selçuk, and B. Whitcher. *An Introduction to Wavelets and Other Filtering Methods in Finance and Economics.* Academic Press, San Diego, CA, 2002.

[19] D.B. Percival and A.T. Walden. *Wavelet Methods for Time Series Analysis.* Cambridge University Press, Cambridge, 2006.

[20] E.W. Sun and T. Meinl. A new wavelet-based denoising algorithm for high-frequency financial data mining. *European Journal of Operational Research*, 217:589–599, 2012.

[21] D.L. Donoho and I.M. Johnstone. Ideal spatial adaptation by wavelet shrinkage. *Biometrika*, 81:425–455, 1994.

[22] D.L. Donoho and I.M. Johnstone. Adapting to unknown smoothness via wavelet shrinkage. *Journal of the American Statistical Association*, 90(432):1200–1224, 1995.

[23] D.L. Donoho, I.M. Johnstone, G. Kerkyacharian, and D. Picard. Wavelet shrinkage: asymptotia. *Journal of the Royal Statistical Society: Series B*, 57(2):301–369, 1995.

[24] D.L. Donoho and I.M. Johnstone. Minimax estimation via wavelet shrinkage. *Annals of Statistics*, 26:879–921, 1998.

[25] L. Birgé and P. Massart. Minimum contrast estimators on sieves: Exponential bounds and rates of convergence. *Bernoulli*, 4(3):329–375, 1998.

[26] T. Cai and B. Silverman. Incorporating information on neighboring coefficients into wavelet estimation. *Sankhya: The Indian Journal of Statistics*, 63:127–148, 2001.

[27] P. Hall, G. Kerkyacharian, and D. PicardSheth. Block threshold rules for curve estimation using kernel and wavelet methods. *Annals of Statistics*, 26(3):922–942, 1998.

[28] W. Sun, S. Rachev, and F. Fabozzi. Fractals or I.I.D.: Evidence of long-range dependence and heavy tailedness from modeling German equity market returns. *Journal of Economics and Business*, 59:575–595, 2007.

[29] R. Hayen, *FinTech: The Impact and Influence of Financial Technology on Banking and the Finance Industry.* CreateSpace Independent Publishing, 2016.

[30] J. Reed, editor. *FinTech: Financial Technology and Modern Finance in the 21st Century.* CreateSpace Independent Publishing, 2016.

[31] P. Sironi, editor. *FinTech Innovation: From Robo-Advisors to Goal Based Investing and Gamification.* Wiley, West Sussex, UK, 2016.

Chapter 9

The evolution of recommender systems: From the beginning to the Big Data era

Beatrice Paoli

Monika Laner

Beat Tödtli

Jouri Semenov

The rise of recommender systems 254
The advent of Big Data 255
Data storage 259
Data preprocessing 259
Recommender systems in the era of Big Data 260
Latent factor models and matrix factorization 261
The alternating least-squares algorithm for matrix factorization 262
Big Data frameworks and machine-learning toolkits for recommender systems 263
Introduction 263
The MapReduce paradigm and Apache Hadoop 264
Apache Mahout 266
Spark 266
Spark machine-learning library 267
Flink 267
Flink-ML 267
Dato GraphLab 268
Declarative large-scale machine learning 268
Evaluation of recommendation systems 268
The future of recommender systems 269
Emotion recognition 270
Deep learning 270
User experience 271
Streaming recommender systems 272
From context-aware to context-driven recommendation 272

Conclusions 273
References 274

The rise of recommender systems

Recommender systems help people to select the most suitable product from a huge amount of available options, based on their preferences, history of purchase, demographic information, and so on. The field of recommender systems emerged as an independent research area in the mid-1990s with first papers on collaborative filtering [1–3] opening new opportunities to retrieve personalized information on the Internet. There are different ways to reach the goal of recommending items to people; therefore, researchers developed many recommender systems for almost every domain such as entertainment, social networking, e-commerce, tourism, and so on.

In the early stage of recommender systems research, much attention was devoted to the development of new algorithms and their performance. Among the most popular techniques of recommender systems are collaborative filtering techniques [4,5], which have already been used in the earliest recommendation engines. They use ratings of other users stored in the system to predict the rating of an object for a particular user. These algorithms produce personal recommendations by computing the similarity [6] between the preference of one user and the preferences of other users. Collaborative filtering techniques can be further classified into model-based and memory-based algorithms [7]. Memory-based algorithms use the entire dataset to make predictions, whereas model-based algorithms use a part of the data as a training set to create a model and then calculate the predictions using that model.

Another class of recommender systems is content-based recommender systems [8]. The basic idea behind this approach is to recommend items that are similar to those that the user liked in the past. The similarity between two or more items can be calculated on the basis of their features. The content-based approach has its roots in the information retrieval [9] and information-filtering [10] communities. Patterns that can serve as the basis to make an appropriate recommendation are found by additional analysis of user profiles (tastes, preferences, and needs) and the usage of various algorithms (Bayesian classifiers, clustering, decision trees, artificial neural networks, etc.) to analyze the content of text documents.

Although collaborative filtering and content-based systems are the most known and most widely used approaches, other techniques exist as well. Hybrid approaches combine the two aforementioned approaches to overcome the shortcomings of one by the other. Physics or network-based systems can be employed on data with unary ratings. These algorithms represent the input data with a so-called bipartite user-item network in which users are connected with the items they share. Standard processes used in physics such as random walks [11,12] and heat diffusion [13] can then be employed on the network to obtain recommendations for individual users. Other techniques include spectral analysis [14], latent semantic models, and matrix factorization [15,16]. One of the reasons why matrix factorization algorithms became very popular is that they decisively contributed to the winning solution [17] in the well-known Netflix prize contest [18].

Although the field of recommender systems has undergone a significant development, certain problems are still challenging. Great concern must be given to aspects such as the quality of the recommendations, the sparsity of the data, scalability, and how to cope with the so-called cold start problem [19,20] that deals with users and items with limited or no previous information. The recommendations need to attract the user's interest and be useful. The items that a user has already purchased should not be recommended again, as well as the items that are not matching the user's taste. By providing high-quality recommendations, the user's trust to the recommender system is augmented, and he or she is likely to continue using it.

Upon the advancement of Big Data, the research focus shifted from building new and more accurate algorithms toward the development of a computing infrastructure able to deal with the continuously increasing amount of data. The advent of Big Data together with the challenges it poses and the effect on recommendation systems are the main topics of the present chapter.

The remainder of this chapter is organized as follows. Section "The advent of Big Data" gives an overview on the advent of Big Data and the challenges it poses. Section "Recommender systems in the era of Big Data" describes the need for scalable recommender systems due to the advent of Big Data. Section "Big Data frameworks and machine-learning toolkits for recommender systems" gives an overview of major Big Data tools together with their machine-learning libraries that implement recommender systems. Section "The future of recommender systems" attempts to the future of recommender systems.

The advent of Big Data

The first decade of the twenty-first century has seen the massive increase in data collection. The technological revolution has made information acquisition easy and cheap through automated data-collection processes. Now huge amounts of high-dimensional and unstructured data are continuously produced and stored at cheaper costs than ever before. The data sources vary and pose challenges in different fields from biomedical sciences to engineering and social sciences. This development calls for efficient and innovative ways of processing for enhanced insight and decision making. Therefore, Big Data is one of the current and future research frontiers. In 2012, it was listed in the Gardner's "Top 10 Critical Tech Trends For the Next Five Years" [21].

To define the concept of Big Data, several attempts have been made [22–25], resulting in a general agreement on three characteristics: *Volume*, *Variety*, and *Velocity*.

- *Volume* refers to the large amount of data, the management of data storage, and processing paradigms to develop the tools needed to properly analyze data.
- *Variety* refers to the heterogeneity of data, its diverse and incompatible data formats, and to the need of grouping them from different, seemingly unrelated data sources.
- *Velocity* refers to the rate at which data are generated, processed, and analyzed.

In the following years, additions to this list have been proposed [26]:

- *Veracity* refers to the unreliability inherent in some source of data such as customer sentiments in social media, which are uncertain but can contain valuable information.
- *Variability* refers to the variation in the data-flow rates and to the fact that Big Data is generated from diverse sources.
- *Value* refers to the analysis performed on Big Data and how it is turned into information and eventually into value.
- *Visualization* refers to the ability of making the vast amount of data comprehensible. Visualizations are often complex representations that include many variables of data while ideally remaining readable and understandable.

Big Data is characterized by a large sample size and high dimensionality. With diversified data sources, such as sensors, telescopes, scientific experiments, and high-throughput instruments, the datasets increase at exponential rate [27,28] as shown in Figure 9.1.

In 2012, a report from McKinsey [30] claimed that especially in the areas of healthcare, public-sector administration, retail, global manufacturing, and personal location data, Big Data can generate value [30]. An overview of industries that are using Big Data to improve their business model is given in Figure 9.2. This additional value can be generated in different ways, thus contributing to the growth of the world economy by enhancing the productivity and competitiveness of enterprises:

- By making information transparent and usable at much higher frequency
- By enabling the collection of transactional data in digital form, providing a more accurate and detailed performance information to improve management decisions, forecasting, or boost performance

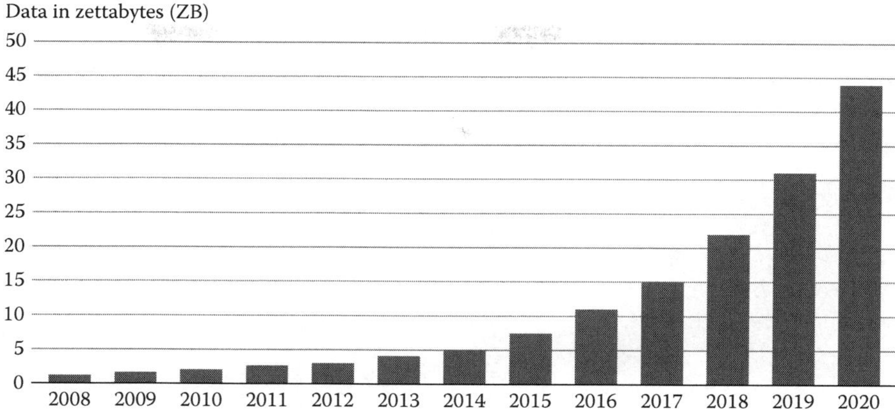

FIGURE 9.1: Data are growing at a 40% annual rate, reaching nearly 45 ZB by 2020. (From Hagen, C. et al., Big data and the creative destruction of today's business models, *A.T. Kearney Report*, 2013.)

Retail	Manufacturing
• Customer relationship management • Store location and layout • Fraud detection and prevention • Supply chain optimization • Dynamic pricing	• Product research • Engineering analytics • Predictive maintenance • Process and quality analysis • Distribution optimization
Financial services	**Media and telecommunications**
• Algorithmic trading • Risk analysis • Fraud detection • Portfolio analysis	• Network optimization • Customer scoring • Churn prevention • Fraud prevention
Advertising and public relations	**Energy**
• Demand signaling • Targeted advertising • Sentiment analysis • Customer acquisition	• Smart grid • Exploration • Operational modeling • Power-line sensors
Government	**Healthcare and life sciences**
• Market governance • Weapon systems and counterterrorism • Econometrics • Health informatics	• Pharmacogenomics • Bioinformatics • Pharmaceutical research • Clinical outcomes research

FIGURE 9.2: Industries that are using Big Data to transform their business models and improve performance in many areas. (From Hagen, C. et al., Big data and the creative destruction of today's business models, *A.T. Kearney Report*, 2013.)

- By allowing a narrow segmentation of customers and therefore personalized products or services
- By improving decision making by sophisticated analytics
- By improving the development of the next generation of products and services

Besides the potential offered by Big Data, new challenges such as data inconsistence and incompleteness, scalability, timeliness, and data security [31,32] arise. These challenges are posed from the main features (volume, variety, and velocity) of Big Data themselves. Large volumes of data have to be processed in a time-effective manner, unstructured or semistructured data need to be represented, accessed, and analyzed from multiple, heterogeneous sources, and high-speed query processing is needed. Another branch of research is the study of structured data (such as complex networks) [33]. In addition, policies related to privacy, security, and intellectual property are other issues to be addressed. A brief overview of the challenges of recommender systems used in combination with Big Data is given in the following.

Scale and complexity: Managing and analyzing large and rapidly increasing volumes of data are challenging issues. Data analysis, organization, retrieval, and modeling are also difficult due to scalability issues and the complexity of data. Such challenges are mitigated by enhancing processor speed. However, data volume increases at a faster rate than computing resources and CPU speed. Big Data analysis necessitates time-consuming navigation through a vast search space to provide guidelines and obtain feedback from users.

Heterogeneity: One source of the difficulties of Big Data analysis is the presence of heterogeneous data, consisting of e-mail attachments, images, pdf documents, medical records, X rays, voice mails, graphics, video, audio, and so on and, thus, cannot be stored in row/column format as structured data. So most part of the data are unstructured, highly dynamic and do not have a particular format. Therefore, new technologies have to be adopted for dealing with such data or transforming them into a structured format.

Incompleteness: It refers to the missing of data-field values for some samples, creating uncertainties in the analysis. Most modern data-mining algorithms have in-built solutions to handle missing values, for example, ignoring data fields with missing values.

Timeliness: As the size of the datasets to be processed increases, it takes more time to analyze them. In some situations, results for a subsection of the data are required immediately or frequently. Analyzing the entire dataset to get partial results is impractical due to the amount of data. Therefore, partial results are needed in advance so that a small amount of incremental computation with new data can be used to reach the desired results. But a full analysis of a user's purchase history is not feasible in real time.

Privacy: Traditionally, various methods of deidentification such as anonymization, pseudonymization, encryption, key-coding, or data sharing were sufficient to distance data from identities [34]. As more data become available, the risk of data leaks and correlation of potentially sensitive datasets also increases leading to problems such as lack of control and transparency [35–39] and profiling [40].

Data storage

Big Data has changed the way by which data are captured and stored [41]. The existing database management tools are unable to process the large amount of data generated nowadays. Big-Data storage is concerned with storing of a virtually unlimited amount of data, coping with high rates of random read and write access, flexibly and efficiently dealing with a range of different data models, and working with encrypted data for privacy issues.

For Big Data storage, Not only SQL (NoSQL) database [42] technologies have become the first alternative to relational databases, with scalability, availability, and fault tolerance being key deciding factors. Characteristics of those databases are a flexible and schema-less data model, horizontal scalability, distributed architectures, and the use of multiple languages and interfaces. NoSQL systems may support structured query language (SQL)-like query languages. Big Data is one of the key forces driving the growth and popularity of NoSQL databases.

Data preprocessing

Due to the diversity of sources, the collected dataset quality may vary in terms of noise, redundancy, consistency, and so on. Prior to data analysis, data must be prepared. Therefore, data-preprocessing techniques including data cleaning, data integration, data reduction, and data transformation should be applied to remove noise and inconsistencies. Each subprocess faces a different challenge with respect to data-driven applications. The most relevant types of data preprocessing are as follows:

- *Data cleaning*: Data cleaning identifies and corrects errors and removes noise. The key issue is to maintain relevant data while discarding unimportant data. Data cleaning identifies inaccurate or incomplete data and repairs or deletes data to improve quality [43,44]. Common techniques of data cleaning are filling in missing values, smoothing noisy data, identifying or removing outliers, and resolving inconsistencies. Methods used in data cleaning are statistical, clustering, pattern-based, and parsing methods, association rules and outliers identification [45,46].

- *Data integration*: Data integration techniques merge data from different sources, provide a unified view of the data and a coherent storage, and detect and resolve data value conflicts.

- *Data reduction*: Data reduction reduces the data volume by aggregating and eliminating redundancies and generates a representative and much smaller dataset that produces (nearly) the same analytical results as the original raw dataset. Commonly used techniques are data compression, clustering, sampling, dimension reduction, heuristic methods, regression, feature selection, and feature discretization [47].

- *Data transformation*: Data transformation can construct or aggregate new attributes and new features. Typical data transformation techniques are smoothing for removing noise from data, aggregation to summarize data, normalization techniques such as min–max normalization, and z-score [47].

Recommender systems in the era of Big Data

Recommendation engines can be used anywhere users are looking for products/services or people without expressing an explicit wish. Thus, they have become a standard feature for most of the large online players ranging from retailers to online travel websites.

In the Big Data era, there is a mutual exchange between Big Data and recommender systems, in which each side helps one to further the development of the other. On one hand, recommender systems work as information filter to allow the user to find relevant information. On the other hand, the amount of data available enable recommender systems to improve their recommendations, techniques, and implementations bringing them to a new scale [48–50]. New parallel computing frameworks were developed, on which large-scale computations could be run efficiently. This makes distributed computing an important part of Big Data applications, with systems such as Hadoop [51] and Spark [52] allowing the use of cheap hardware to build applications that scale to Big Data.

As pointed out in section "The rise of recommender systems," a widely used approach for computing recommendations is collaborative filtering. Matrix factorization proved to be a better model than traditional nearest-neighbor approaches in the Netflix Prize competition [18], and since then there has been a great deal of work dedicated to the design of fast and scalable methods for large-scale matrix factorization problems [16,53,54].

In recent recommender system competitions, alternating least squares (ALS) and stochastic gradient descent (SGD) appear to be the two most widely used methods for matrix factorization. ALS switches between updating the latent factors of users and those of items while fixing the other. As mentioned in Reference 16, SGD has become one of the most popular methods for matrix factorization in recommender systems due to its efficiency and simple implementation. The time complexity per iteration of SGD is lower than ALS. However, compared with ALS, SGD usually needs more iterations to obtain a good enough model, and the performance is sensitive to the choice of the learning rate.

Sections "Latent factor models and matrix factorization" and "The alternating least-squares algorithm for matrix factorization" give an overview on matrix factorization models with particular attention to ALS, the only parallel matrix factorization implementation for collaborative filtering used by Apache Mahout [55], one of the most used Big Data frameworks.

Latent factor models and matrix factorization

A latent factor based model characterizes both users and items by a low number of factors inferred from the ratings pattern. For example, for movies the factors could consist of comedy versus drama, amount of action, or orientation to children. For users, each factor measures how much the user likes movies that score high on each factor.

Matrix factorization takes an $m \times n$ matrix R of ratings given by m users to n items. R is factorized into two matrices, the $k \times m$ user latent factor matrix P and the $k \times n$ item latent factor matrix Q, such that $R \approx \hat{R} = P^T Q$, where k is the number of latent factors. The dimensions of the user and item latent factor matrices are smaller than the original $m \times n$ rating matrix, rendering the factorization process time- and cost-efficient. Their matrix product $\hat{R}$ approximates R in a least-squares fashion.

Matrix factorization can be seen as an optimization task. Given the original matrix R and the two unknown matrices P and Q, the task is to minimize the cost function with respect to all entries in P and Q:

$$J(P,Q) = ||R - P^T Q||_F^2 + \lambda \left(||P||_F^2 + ||Q||_F^2\right) \tag{9.1}$$

with $||.||_F$ being the Frobenius norm. The term $||P||_F^2$ is given by the sum of squares of all matrix entries in P. This cost function contains two hyperparameters: k and the regularization parameter λ. Although P and Q are optimized whenever the recommender system learns, λ and k are fixed during a training run, but their values must be chosen carefully.

For Big Data applications, most entries in the matrix R have no value as users only rate a tiny fraction of the available items. A rating value of zero could be assigned to unrated items at the cost of memory space. The cost function in Equation 9.1 can be rewritten in component notation

$$J(P,Q) = \sum_{\substack{u,i: \\ r_{ui} \neq \varnothing}} (r_{ui} - \hat{r}_{ui})^2 + \lambda \left(\sum_{u,k} p_{uk}^2 + \sum_{i,k} q_{ik}^2 \right) \tag{9.2}$$

with the components of $\hat{R}$ being $\hat{r}_{ui} = \sum_k p_{uk} q_{ik}$. The matrices R, P, and Q are written in terms of their components r_{ui}, p_{uk}, and q_{ik}, and the sums now only run over the elements for which data are actually available.

The first term in the cost function J (Equation 9.2) is the Mean Square Error distance measure between the original rating matrix R and its approximation $\hat{R} = P^T Q$.

Minimizing the cost function J is nontrivial because as a function of P and Q, $J(P, Q)$ is not convex and therefore optimization strategies might reach only a local minimum. For realistic data, using those local minima usually gives good recommendations. In the following section, we describe the ALS algorithm, an efficient and parallelized algorithm to find such minima.

The alternating least-squares algorithm for matrix factorization

There are several algorithms to compute matrix factorizations. Among the most known are ALS and SGD, alongside a variety of algorithms combining the two models and improving on efficiency, stability, and scalability such as CCD++ [56].

ALS updates user and item variables alternatingly, while keeping the other constant. By fixing either P or Q, the nonconvex optimization problem is turned into an *easy* quadratic one [57].

The procedure of ALS can be summarized as follows:

- Fix the item latent vectors Q
- Minimize J with respect to P
- Fix the updated user latent factors P and minimize J with respect to Q
- Repeat this two-step optimization until convergence

In this way, one derives the following update rules:

$$p_u = \left(\sum_{i' : r_{ui'} \neq \varnothing} q_{i'} \; q_{i'}^T + \lambda 1_{k \times k} \right)^{-1} \sum_{i : r_{ui} \neq \varnothing} r_{ui} q_i \qquad \text{user update} \qquad (9.3)$$

$$q_i = \left(\sum_{u' : r_{u'i} \neq \varnothing} p_{u'} p_{u'}^T + \lambda 1_{k \times k} \right)^{-1} \sum_{u : r_{ui} \neq \varnothing} r_{ui} p_u \qquad \text{item update} \qquad (9.4)$$

Here, $\sum_{i' : r_{ui'} \neq \varnothing}$ denotes the sum over all items that have been rated by the current user u and $\sum_{u' : r_{u'i} \neq \varnothing}$ the sum over all users who have rated the current item i. The two update steps are completely analogous due to $J(P, Q) = J(Q, P)$, and therefore the user and item update step can be calculated with the same update routine.

In this update procedure, several aspects contribute to an efficient calculation of the recommendations. The term $\lambda 1_{k \times k}$ can be stored in memory on a single node, and the inversion of the whole sum is a computation requiring only $\mathcal{O}\left(k^3\right)$ operations. In the case of the user update, this inverted matrix is then multiplied with a sum of rated item latent factors scaled by the user's ratings ($\sum_{i:r_{ui}\neq\varnothing} r_{ui}q_i$), which requires only $\mathcal{O}\left(k^2\right)$ operations. For a user update, only those item latent factors the user rated are needed. The data for these latent factors can be distributed over many nodes in a cluster. Sending the updated latent factors of all items, a user rated to a single node requires some network traffic. However, as long as R is sparse, only a few latent factors will be required per user. Further optimization potential lies in grouping onto the same nodes users with similar activities or the precomputation of $q_i q_i^T$.

A crucial contribution to ALS-parallelization strategies is the fact that the update of a user latent factor vector p_u does not depend on any user latent factor. Regarding the required item latent factors, any estimate for an item's latent factors can be used. This means that ALS can be run asynchronously, that is, keeping a predetermined execution order of item versus user latent factor updates is not necessary. This opens room for parallel computing frameworks to optimize node workloads while keeping the convergence rate and quality of results high.

Big Data frameworks and machine-learning toolkits for recommender systems

Introduction

The fundamental idea to approach a Big Data problem is to partition a large data problem into independent, affordable subproblems. Each subproblem is then tackled in parallel by different processing units. Although on a small scale such an approach can be implemented either by multicore computing or grid computing, in large-scale problems the design of a highly adaptive and fault-tolerant computing system is very challenging. These demands motivated the development of new computer infrastructures that can support massively parallel data storage and processing.

Recommender systems dealing with a massive amount of data have been implemented long time ago by several internet giants such as Amazon, Facebook, and Google. These systems suggest new items that might be of interest to the user by analyzing the user's profile, their activities on the websites, and their purchase history. However, Big Data sharpens the information overload problem, posing more challenges on recommender systems as it should provide recommendations to a large number of users by analyzing vast amounts data of customers and products. In other words, high quality, scalability, and performance become the concerns.

Earlier systems, technologies, and tools show their limitation in processing and managing the increasing amount of data leading to the development of new technologies to meet Big Data needs by using newly invented tools and technologies. In addition, it encourages more research work on recommendation algorithms and the use of new tools and frameworks such as Apache Hadoop [51], Spark [52], and Flink [58] in the development of scalable systems. Another important consideration is preventing the computational cost from going up while processing a vast amount of data [59].

The processing models used for many computer infrastructures can be categorized as either batch or streaming [60]. In batch processing, data are first stored and then analyzed. Data are collected, entered, and processed, and then the batch results are produced. Examples of systems relying on batch data processing are payroll and billing systems. MapReduce [61] is one example of a batch-processing tool and has become the dominant batch-processing model.

In contrast, real-time data processing (or streaming) involves a continuous input, process, and output of data. Data must be processed in a small time period (or near real-time). Examples of systems relying on real-time data processing are radar systems, customer services, and bank ATMs. Real-time streaming analytics have the potential to accelerate *time to insight* from the massive amounts of data originating from market data, sensors, mobile phones, the Internet of Things, Web clickstreams, and transactions.

Both batch and real-time data processing have advantages and disadvantages. The decision to select the best data processing system for the specific job at hand depends on the types and sources of data and processing time needed to get the job done and create the ability to take immediate action if needed.

As the aim of the current chapter is to discuss the evolution of recommender systems in the era of Big Data, we restrict our attention to those Big Data frameworks that implement recommender system algorithms. The latter are usually included in machine-learning toolkits.

A variety of machine-learning toolkits have been developed. Distributed learning algorithms are not easy to implement; therefore, copies or extensions of existing implementations are often used.

The Big Data frameworks along with their MLlibs that will be discussed in the following sections are as follows: Apache Hadoop [51] (based on MapReduce [61]) and the MLlib Apache Mahout [55], Spark [52] with MLlib [62], Flink [58] with Flink-ML [63], and Dato GraphLab [64], the latter being the only tool outside the Hadoop ecosystem. For a comprehensive review of these as well as other frameworks see Reference 65.

All of the presented libraries have a wide range of methods implemented, both for recommender systems and general machine-learning tasks. In addition, they implement ALS matrix factorization.

The MapReduce paradigm and Apache Hadoop

MapReduce was introduced in 2004 by Google [61] and paved the road for Hadoop (from the Apache Software Foundation [51]), which has played

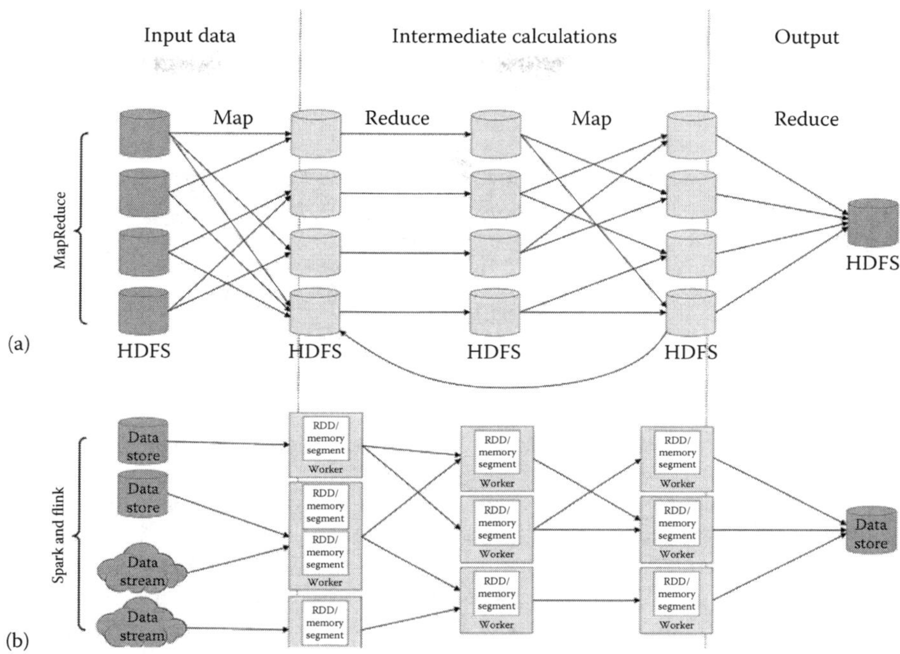

FIGURE 9.3: Comparison of processing models for various processing engines: (a) MapReduce and (b) Spark and Flink. (Adapted from Landset, S. et al., *J. Big Data*, 2, 24, 2015.)

a significant role in the Big Data era. It contains two key functions, the *Map* function that locally transforms the data and the *Reduce* function that aggregates them (Figure 9.3). MapReduce can work with raw data stored in file disks, relational databases, or both. The data may be structured or unstructured.

The MapReduce approach to machine learning performs batch learning, in which the training dataset is read in its entirety to build a learning model. The biggest drawback of this batch model is a lack of efficiency in terms of speed and computational resources due to the frequent disk I/O operations (*Map/Reduce*). Although this approach may be suitable for certain projects such as analyzing past events, it becomes problematic when data evolve, as the full process must be repeated each time a model requires updating. The fault tolerance mechanism employed by MapReduce is achieved through data replication, which can affect scalability by increasing the size of data even further. The need for data replication has been found to be responsible for 90% of the running time of machine-learning tasks in MapReduce [50] and is perhaps the biggest impediment to fast data processing. In the last years, MapReduce has begun to fall out of favor, particularly in the machine-learning community, due to its lack of speed, and to the fact that many machine-learning tasks do not easily fit into the MapReduce paradigm. This led to the development of tools such as Spark [52] and flink [58].

Hadoop [51] is a Java-based software framework introduced in 2007 for distributed data management and processing. It contains a set of open-source libraries for distributed computing based on the MapReduce programming model and its own distributed file system Hadoop Distributed File Systems. Hadoop automatically facilitates scalability and takes care of detecting and handling failures. Using the MapReduce model, Hadoop distributes in a fault-tolerant way the computation to the data nodes alleviating the problem of Big Data.

Apache Mahout

Mahout [55] is one of the more well-known tools for machine learning using the MapReduce paradigm. It is known for having a wide selection of robust algorithms, but with inefficient runtime due to the slow MapReduce engine. The algorithms included in Mahout focus primarily on classification, clustering, and collaborative filtering and have been shown to scale well as the size of the data increases [98]. One of Mahout's most commonly cited assets is its extensibility, and many have achieved good results by building off of the baseline algorithms [66–68]. However, to take advantage of this flexibility, strong proficiency in Java programming is required [66,69,70]. The current focus is on a mathematical environment called Samsara [55], which includes linear algebra, statistical operations, and data structures. The goal of the Mahout-Samsara project is to help users build their own distributed algorithms, rather than simply a library of already-written implementations (see also section "Declarative large-scale machine learning").

Among the more commonly cited complaints about Mahout is the difficulty to set it up on an existing Hadoop cluster [93–95] along with the lack of updated documentation. However, this is a common problem of many machine-learning tools, partially alleviated by an active user community willing and able to help [71,72]. Some researchers have also cited difficulty with configuration or with integrating it into an existing environment [69,73–75].

Spark

Spark [52] was initially developed at the University of California, Berkeley [76] and is now an Apache top-level project. It is a general-purpose and fault-tolerant cluster computing engine designed to optimize general execution graphs. Unlike MapReduce, an execution graph optimization engine is used to improve the parallelization efficiency. It supports iterative computation and improves on speed and resource issues by utilizing in-memory computation (Figure 9.3), significantly cutting down on the number of read and write operations necessary. The main abstraction structures of Spark are called Resilient Distributed Datasets (RDD), which store data in-memory and provide fault tolerance without replication [77]. RDDs are read-only distributed shared memory [78]. The RDD application programming interface (API) was extended in 2015 to include DataFrames, which allows users to group a distributed collection of data by column, similar to a table in a relational database. Spark can not only be installed on the top of Hadoop but can also run in standalone mode.

Although the iterative batch approach to data processing improves on many of the deficiencies of MapReduce, it still does not offer the ability to process data in real time.

For streaming applications, Spark offers Spark Streaming, a library that uses micro-batching, a technique simulating real-time processing. In this approach, an incoming stream is packed into sequences of small chunks of data, which can then be processed by a batch system [60]. Although this may be adequate for many projects, it is not a true real-time system.

Spark machine-learning library

The MLlib [62] covers the same range of learning categories as Mahout and adds regression models. It also has algorithms for topic modeling and frequent pattern mining. Additional tools include dimensionality reduction, feature extraction and transformation, optimization, and basic statistics. MLlib has an ALS implementation of matrix factorization, offering both explicit feedback and implicit feedback matrix factorization. In general, MLlib's reliance on Spark's iterative batch and streaming approaches, as well as its use of in-memory computation, enable jobs to run significantly faster than those using Mahout [79]. However, the fact that it is tied to Spark may present a problem for performing machine learning on multiple platforms [80]. The research that has been published indicates it is considered to be a relatively easy library to set up and run [81]. The documentation is thorough, but the user community is not nearly as active as the development community.

Flink

Flink [58] was developed at the Technical University of Berlin under the name Stratosphere [82]. It graduated the Apache incubation stage in January 2015 and is now a top-level project. It offers capability for both batch and stream processing and has its own runtime, rather than being built on top of MapReduce. As such, it can be integrated or run completely independent from the Hadoop ecosystem. Flink's processing model applies transformations to parallel data collections [83,84] (Figure 9.3).

Flink-ML

Flink-ML [63] is a MLlib currently in development for the Flink platform. It supports implementations of Logistic Regression, k-Means Clustering, and ALS for recommendation. It also supports Mahout's Domain Specific Language for linear algebra that can be used for optimization of learning algorithms, and plans are underway to implement pre- and postprocessing tools. For graph processing, the Gelly API provides methods for vertex-centric iterations. Also included is a cost-based optimizer that automatically selects the best execution strategy for each job. Similar to Spark, Flink also offers iterative batch as well as streaming options, though their streaming API is based on individual events, rather than the micro-batch approach that Spark uses.

Dato GraphLab

Dato, formerly GraphLab, is a standalone product that can be connected with Hadoop for graph analysis and machine-learning tasks. It was fully open source, but in late 2014, they transitioned into a commercial product. Their C++ processing engine Dato Core [64] has been released to the community on Github along with their interprocess communication library (for translating between C++ and Python) and graph analytics implementations. Their MLlibs are unavailable outside their enterprise packages. Dato GraphLab comprises a scalable machine-learning toolkit that includes implementation, for example, Deep learning, factor machines, topic modeling, clustering, and nearest neighbors. Distributed processing on Hadoop enables large-scale learning.

Declarative large-scale machine learning

A new type of tools called declarative large-scale machine-learning systems is taking the development of distributed machine learning applications to a new level [83]. Their main goal is to provide developers of recommender systems and other machine-learning applications with a high-level language to specify machine-learning tasks and algorithms, in particular linear algebra operations such as matrix multiplications. They simplify the development of machine-learning algorithms by translating these domain-specific languages into an optimized scaling application. By using such tools, new application prototypes can be implemented quickly and without time-consuming concerns for the particularities of the distributed computing system. Optimizations of scalability may be tackled once the application proves viable. Examples of a domain-specific languages are SystemML for Apache Spark [84] and Samsara for Mahout [55].

Evaluation of recommendation systems

Following the Netflix Prize competition, accuracy metrics [such as root mean square error (RMSE)]) became a de facto standard in the community to evaluate and compare performance of recommendation algorithms. Initially most recommender systems were evaluated on the basis of their prediction power, that is, their ability to predict items accurately.

The traditional evaluation approach to recommender systems is based on offline tests in which a portion of existing data is withheld from the recommendation algorithm during the training phase [85]. These withheld data, the so-called test set, is then used to measure the predictive accuracy of the algorithm, either in a top-n or rating prediction scenario. In this offline framework precision, recall and root mean square error are often used to evaluate the recommender. The lower the rating prediction error, or the higher the precision, the better the recommendation algorithm [85] deemed to be.

However, accuracy is not always the best way to quantify the quality of recommendations, especially in the context of predicting online performance from offline evaluations [85–87]. A recommender system can produce highly accurate recommendations, have a reasonable good coverage, and still does not satisfy a user [88,89]. Popularity bias, as well as aspects such as novelty, diversity, serendipity, and others, could potentially affect the evaluation negatively. Thus, it makes sense to look at those metrics, and in particular the trade-off between them [90].

Subjective metrics, as their name suggests, measure the subjective opinion of the users. Diversity generally applies to a set of items and is related to how different the items are with respect to each other. Novelty and serendipity are two properties that are correlated one to the other. Novel recommendations are the ones for items that the user did not know about. Serendipity is the experience of discovering an unexpected and fortuitous item that otherwise would not have been discovered. Thus, the introduction of serendipity should help one to reveal unexpressed users' wishes.

To overcome the drawbacks of offline testing only, online evaluation attempts to capture the quality of the recommendation as perceived by the users by analyzing their interaction patterns with the system as well as explicitly asking questions.

Online evaluation commonly involves a user study. Users can be made aware of or encouraged to participate, or participate unknowingly. In studies of real-life systems, users are usually not made aware of their participation in tests [91]. The concepts of A/B testing are used to estimate different algorithms' qualities [91]. A/B testing involves assigning a subset of a system's users to the algorithm under evaluation. The interactions of the users are then analyzed, and the performance of the systems is compared.

The future of recommender systems

Recommender systems are applications that provide personalized advice to users about products or services they might be interested in. These systems play a major role in the Digital and Social Networking Revolution and are becoming a part of everyday life. They help people to manage content overload efficiently and dive into the long tail of content discovery. Currently, big trends as Big Data and more advanced techniques from Artificial Intelligence such as Deep learning are becoming available and will eventually be applied to recommender systems. The idea is to provide a new perspective to support users in developing, exploring, and understanding their unique personal preferences, thus improving their experience.

Intelligent recommendation systems were developed to suggest items that match browsing history, user preferences and help them make better choices and decisions. However, it is reached a point in which personalized solution providers need to look beyond algorithms and focus on user interactions, decision-making processes, and overall experiences. Taking into consideration this change, recommendation platforms should focus on understanding how people make choices and how the process of making choices can be supported by intelligent product recommendations.

In the next sections, the future directions of recommender systems' research are briefly discussed.

Emotion recognition

Emotions play a cardinal role in the decision-making task [92], and their influences should be taken into account during the recommendation process to propose solutions that could improve the positive emotional state of the user. Traditional recommender systems do not include emotions in the computational process, and although measurement of emotions in a controlled laboratory environment has been studied extensively [93], emotion recognition in real-world environments is still a challenge [93,94].

Deep learning

The past few years have seen the tremendous success of deep neural networks in a number of complex tasks such as computer vision, natural language processing, and speech recognition. Deep learning techniques have been successfully implemented in various domains, for example, in music recommendation applications such as Spotify and YouTube [95] and were discussed as one of the next trends in recommendation systems technology int the 10th ACM Conference on recommender systems [96].

Deep learning algorithms are one promising research topic dealing with the automated extraction of complex data representations (features) at high levels of abstraction. Such algorithms develop a layered, hierarchical architecture of learning and representing data, in which higher-level (more abstract) features are defined in terms of lower-level (less abstract) features. The hierarchical learning architecture of Deep learning algorithms is motivated by artificial intelligence emulating the learning process of the human brain [97,98]. Although there exist already seminal works on Deep learning for recommender systems [95,99–102], Deep learning techniques applied to recommender systems have not yet been fully exploited. Traditional recommender systems tend to recommend items based on ratings, but due to the data sparsity, this information is not sufficient and additional information such as review texts, images, or user profiles are needed to learn user preferences and item properties. Deep learning techniques enable models to automatically learn features for users and items from different types of data sources thus enabling a better understanding of what users need. This further improves the recommendation quality. They range from very simple models relying on artificial neural networks to Restricted Boltzmann Machines and Autoencoders [100] to convolutional neural networks [103]. If more information can be gathered about intrinsic details of the user, patterns, while using a particular software application, or the user's behavior, and if all this information can be processed and used by Deep learning techniques, then the use of Deep learning techniques in recommender systems will offer a unique opportunity in the future.

User experience

In the period after the emergence of recommender systems, a majority of research focused on objective accuracy criteria, and less attention has been paid to user experience—the delivery of the recommendations to the user and the interaction of the user with those recommendations. Most current recommender system interfaces are static, that is, they do not tailor the interface to these user characteristics. Therefore, there is a need to adapt recommender systems, and their user interfaces from a one-size-fits all approach to a personalized environment in which user-specific circumstances are taken into account. The way users interact with the system and the efficacy of interface designs from users' perspectives plays a pivotal role in the optimization, design, and adaptation of the contents of a website. To provide personalized information, it is necessary to monitor the users' behavior and make generalizations and predictions based on these observations.

This requires a deep understanding of human decision processes. This goal can be achieved by analyzing existing psychological theories of human decision making and their impact on the construction of recommender systems [104]. New recommendation technologies will take into account the context of the current user [7]. Information, such as the users' short- and long-term preferences, geographical position, movement data, calendar information, information from social networks, and so on, can be exploited for detecting the current context of the person. This information enhances intelligent recommendations [105]. Measuring user experience is challenging for recommender systems research. It requires developing a system, including both algorithms and user interface, and carrying out field studies with long-term users of the system.

Streaming recommender systems

The increasing popularity of real-world recommender systems produces data continuously and rapidly, and it becomes more realistic to study recommender systems under streaming scenarios.

Such data are temporally ordered, continuous, of high-velocity, and time varying, which determine the streaming nature of data in recommender systems. In recent years, there is a large literature exploiting temporal information [17,36,106,107], and it is evident that explicitly modeling temporal dynamics greatly improves the recommendation performance [17,108].

As pointed out by Chang et al. [109], recommendation under streaming settings needs to tackle three challenges simultaneously.

- *Real-time updating*: One inherent characteristic of data streams is their high velocity; the recommender system needs to update and response instantaneously to catch users' instant intention and demands.
- *Unknown size*: New users or fresh posted items arrive continuously in data streams. The number of users and the size of recommendation lists are unknown in advance.
- *Concept shift*: Data stream evolution leads to concept shifts, for example, a new product launch reduces the popularity of previous versions. Likewise, user preferences drift over time. The recommender system should have the ability to capture such signals and timely adapt its recommendations accordingly.

Chang et al. [109] proposed a streaming recommender system with real-time update for a shifting concept pool of unknown size. The input streams are modeled as three types of events: user feedback activities, new users, and new items. The system continuously updates its model to capture dynamics and pursue real-time recommendations. In particular, they tackle all three challenges simultaneously by a novel streaming recommender system framework, which is not only able to track the dynamic changes of user/item topics, but also provides real-time recommendations in a prospective way.

From context-aware to context-driven recommendation

A critical change has occurred in the status of context in recommender systems [110]. In the past, context has been considered additional information. However, any present application domains face continuous cold start conditions and must exploit session rather than user information. In many applications, such as recommending a vacation package, personalized content on a website, or a movie, it may not be sufficient to consider only users and items, but it is also important to incorporate the contextual information into the recommendation process to recommend items to users in certain circumstances. In recent years, the recommender system community has discovered the benefits of context. A common characterization of context-aware recommender systems is that they "try to incorporate or utilize additional evidence (beyond information about users and items) to estimate user preferences on unseen items" [111]. As described by Pagano et al. [110], it is time for a *Contextual Turn*, which acknowledges that being aware of context is not always enough: We are moving from context-aware recommendations toward context-driven recommendations. In contrast to context-aware recommendation, in context-driven recommendation users and items take a back seat. Context-driven recommendation is made possible by a confluence of developments:

- Huge amounts of data generated by users in a wide range of contexts are available
- New sources of context-data are provided by sensors (smartphones, Internet of Things)
- The computational power to process these data is within our reach.

This *Contextual Turn* is valuable because instead of providing personalization for specific individuals, a context-driven recommender system *personalizes* to users context states by decoupling the users from their historical behavior, giving users room to develop beyond their past needs and preferences. Thus, users receive recommendations based on what is going on around them in the moment (situation) and on what they are trying to accomplish (intent).

Conclusions

Recommender systems have become ubiquitous and are an essential tool for information filtering and e-commerce. Over the years, collaborative filtering has emerged as the currently dominant approach to recommender systems. The amount of data are growing exponentially worldwide due to the explosion of digital data, for example, social networking sites, search and retrieval engines, media sharing sites, stock trading sites, and news sources. Big Data has become the new area for scientific data research and for business applications. Big Data and Recommendation engines have already proved an extremely useful combination for big corporations. But Big Data tools and technologies are affordable for smaller companies as well. Product recommendations are extremely important to provide a good user experience from the customer's viewpoint. Moreover, from the company's viewpoint, it takes into account unknown factors that can make a customer buy products which might seem unlikely.

In the current chapter, we discussed the issues and challenges related to Big Data in the field of recommender systems and the new technologies developed. For the tools discussed here, for batch-only workloads that are not time-sensitive, Hadoop is a good choice for less-expensive scalable applications than some other solutions. For mixed workloads, Spark provides high-speed batch processing and micro-batch processing for streaming. It has wide support, integrated libraries and tooling, and flexible integrations. Flink provides true stream processing with batch processing support. It is heavily optimized, can run tasks written for other platforms, and provides low latency processing, but is still in the early days of adoption.

The problems and limitations that recommender systems are facing in the Big Data era are essentially the same as those in the era before. The data sparsity is a growing problem that still needs to be faced. Both the number of users and items are continuously growing. Thus, the need for fast and scalable computation is important. Nowadays, recommendations are expected to be produced extremely fast in order for a recommender system to be able to function properly online. We believe that in the future, great attention will be devoted to the development of efficient and scalable algorithms. Other challenges important in recommender systems' research are the integration of methods to cope with long- and short-term preference changes and the evaluation of recommender systems. Evaluating recommender systems under a common framework has been proved a hard task. Although some metrics are preferred to most of the existing approaches, questions still remain on how recommender systems should be evaluated. The improvement of recommender systems will bring a benefit to organizations by better targeting of products to the right person and thereby probably increasing the conversion rate and the user experience. For consumers, it will become even easier to find the product that they are looking for. Currently, more advanced techniques from Artificial Intelligence such as Deep learning are becoming available and eventually applied to recommender systems. These do not only play a role in improving algorithms but also new interactions paradigms. In the future, it could be possible to analyze not just the transactions of users but also patterns of interaction (e.g., mouse movement, keystrokes, facial expressions). These ultimately lead to new research questions for new adaptive interfaces and how the user controls these recommender systems.

References

[1] W. Hill, L. Stead, M. Rosenstein, and G. Furnas, Recommending and evaluating choices in a virtual community of use, in *Proceedings of the SIGCHI Conference on Human Factors in Computing Systems*, Denver, CO, May 7–11, 1995.

[2] P. Resnick, N. Iakovou, M. Sushak, P. Bergstrom, and J. Riedl, Grouplens: An open architecture for collaborative filtering of netwews, in *Proceedings of the Computer Supported Cooberative Work Conference*, Chapel Hill, NC, October 22–26, 1994.

[3] U. Shardanand and P. Maes, Social information filtering: Algorithms for automating word of mouth, in *Proceedings of the SIGCHI Conference on Human Factors in Computing Systems*, CHI'95, pp. 210–217. New York: ACM Press/Addison-Wesley Publishing, 1995.

[4] D. Goldberg, D. Nichols, B. M. Oki, and D. Terry, Using collaborative filtering to weave an information tapestry, *Communication of the ACM*, 35, 61–70, 1992.

[5] J. B. Schafer, D. Frankowski, J. Herlocker, and S. Sen, Collaborative filtering recommender systems, in *The Adaptive Web*, P. Brusilovsky, A. Kobsa, and W. Nejdl (Eds.), pp. 291–324. Berlin, Germany: Springer-Verlag, 2007.

[6] J. Delgado and N. Ishii, Memory-based weighted-majority prediction for recommender systems, 1999.

[7] G. Adomavicius and E. Tuzhilin, Toward the next generation of recommender systems: A survey of the state-of-the-art and possible extensions, *IEEE Transactions on Knowledge and Data Engineering*, 17, 734–749, 2005.

[8] M. Pazzani and D. Billsus, Content-based recommendation systems, *Lecture Notes in Computer Science*, 4321, 325–341, 2007.

[9] R. Baeza-Yates and B. Ribeiro-Neto, *Modern Information Retreival.* New York: Addison-Wesley, 1999.

[10] N. Belkin and B. Croft, Information filtering and information retrieval, *Communication of the ACM*, 35(12), 29–37, 1992.

[11] T. Zhou, J. Ren, M. Medo, and Y. C. Zhang, Bipartite network projection and personal recommendation, *Physical Review E*, 76, 046115, 2007.

[12] M. Blattner, B-rank: A top n recommendation algorithm, in *Proceedings of the International Multi-Conference on Complexity, Informatics and Cybernetics (IMCIC 2010)*, Orlando, FL, 2010.

[13] T. Zhou, Z. Kuscsik, J. G. Liu, M. Medo, J. R. Wakeling, and Y. C. Zhang, Solving the apparent diversity-accuracy dilemma of recommender systems, *Proceedings of the National Academy of Sciences*, 107, 4511–4515, 2010.

[14] K. Goldberg, T. Roeder, D. Gupta, and C. Perkins, Eigentaste: A constant time collaborative ltering algorithm, *Information Retrieval*, 4, 133–151, 2001.

[15] T. Hofmann, Latent semantic models for collaborative filtering, *ACM Transactions on Information Systems*, 22, 89–115, 2004.

[16] Y. Koren, R. Bell, and C. Volinsky, Matrix factorization techniques for recommender systems, *Computer*, 42, 30–37, 2009.

[17] Y. Koren, Collaborative filtering with temporal dynamics, *Communications of the ACM*, 53, 89–97, 2010.

[18] S. L. J. Bennett, The netflix prize, *Proceedings of KDD Cup and Workshop*, 2007, 35, 2007.

[19] B. Sarwar, G. Karypis, J. Konstan, and J. Riedl, Analysis of recommendation algorithms for e-commerce, in *ACM E-Commerce 2000 Conference*, Minneapolis, MN, October 17–20, 2000.

[20] E. Vozalis and K. Margaritis, Analysis of recommender systems' algorithms, in *The 6th Hellenic European Conference on Computer Mathematics & its Applications* (*HERCMA*), pp. 732–745. Athens, Greece: LEA, 2003.

[21] E. Savitz, Gartner: 10 critical tech trends for the next five years, *Forbes*, October 22, 2012.

[22] D. Laney, 3-d data management: Controlling data volume, velocity and variety, Application Delivery Strategies by META Group Inc., p. 949, February 2001.

[23] A. Gandomi and M. Haider, Beyond the hype: Big data concepts, methods, and analytics, *International Journal of Information Management*, 35(2), 137–144, 2015.

[24] H. Chen, R. H. L. Chiang, and V. C. Storey, Business intelligence and analytics: From big data to big impact, *MIS Quarterly*, 36, 1165–1188, 2012.

[25] O. Kwon, N. Lee, and B. Shin, Data quality management, data usage experience and acquisition intention of big data analytics, *International Journal of Information Management*, 34(3), 387–394, 2014.

[26] Y. Demchenko, C. de Laat, A. Wibisono, P. Grosso, and Z. Zhao, Addressing big data challenges for scientific data infrastructure, in *Proceedings of the 2012 IEEE 4th International Conference on Cloud Computing Technology and Science*, pp. 614–617. Washington, DC: IEEE Computer Society, 2012.

[27] C. Lynch, Big data: How do your data grow? *Nature*, 455(7209), 28–29, 2008.

[28] A. S. Szalay, Extreme data-intensive scientific computing, *Computing in Science & Engineering*, 13(6), 34–41, 2011.

[29] C. Hagen, H. Evans, M. Ciobo, J. Miller, D. Wall, and A. Yadav, Big data and the creative destruction of today's business models, A. T. Kearney Report, 2013.

[30] J. Manyika, M. Chui, B. Brown, J. Bughin, R. Dobbs, C. Roxburgh, and A. H. Byers, Big data: The next frontier for innovation, competition, and productivity, McKinsey Global Institute, 2012.

[31] D. Agrawal, P. Bernstein, E. Bertino, S. Davidson, U. Dayal, M. Franklin, J. Gehrke et al., *Challenges and Opportunities with Big Data.* Cyber Center Technical Reports, West Lafayette, IN, 2011.

[32] R. T. Kouzes, G. A. Anderson, S. T. Elbert, I. Gorton, and D. K. Gracio, The changing paradigm of data-intensive computing, *Computer*, 42(1), 26–34, 2009.

[33] M. Dehmer, F. Emmert-Streib, S. Pickl, and A. Holzinger, Eds., *Big Data of Complex Networks.* Boca Raton, FL: Chapman & Hall/CRC Big Data Series, CRC Press, 2017.

[34] O. Tene and J. Polonetsky, Big data for all: Privacy and user control in the age of analytics, *Northwestern Journal of Technology & Intellectual Property*, 11, 239–247, 2013.

[35] E. Curry, A. Freitas, A. Thalhammer, A. Fensel, A. Ngonga, I. Ermilov, K. Lyko et al., Big data public private forum. Big data technical working groups white paper, pp. 13–26, Technical Report, Springer, 2014.

[36] R. Zhao, W. Ouyang, and X. Wang, Unsupervised salience learning for person re-identification, in *IEEE Conference on Computer Vision and Pattern Recognition (CVPR)*, pp. 3586–3593. IEEE, 2013.

[37] W. S. Zheng, S. Gong, and T. Xiang, Person re-identification by probabilistic relative distance comparison, in *IEEE Conference on Computer Vision and Pattern Recognition (CVPR)*, pp. 649–656. IEEE, 2011.

[38] M. Zimmer, More on the "anonymity" of the facebook dataset—it's harvard college, Internet Research Ethics, Privacy, Social Media, October 3, 2008.

[39] K. Lewis, J. Kaufman, M. Gonzalez, A. Wimmer, and N. Christakis, Tastes, ties, and time: A new social network dataset using facebook.com, *Social Networks*, 30(4), 330–342, 2008.

[40] G. D. Acquisto, J. Domingo-Ferrer, P. Kikiras, V. Torra, Y.-A. de Montjoye, and A. Bourka, Privacy by design in big data. An overview of privacy enhancing technologies in the era of big data analytics, *European Union Agency for Network and Information Security*, 2015. https://www.enisa.europa.eu/publications/big-data-protection.

[41] S. F. Oliveira, K. Fuerlinger, and D. Kranzlmuller, Trends in computation, communication and storage and the consequences for data-intensive science, in *Proceedings of the 2012 IEEE 14th International Conference on High Performance Computing and Communication & 2012 IEEE 9th International Conference on Embedded Software and Systems*, HPCC'12, pp. 572–579. Washington, DC: IEEE Computer Society, 2012.

[42] H. Jing, E. Haihong, L. Guan, and D. Jian, Survey on nosql database, in *6th International Conference on Pervasive Computing and Applications* (*ICPCA*), Port Elizabeth, South Africa, October 26–28, 2011.

[43] G. A. Liebchen and M. Shepperd, Software productivity analysis of a large data set and issues of confidentiality and data quality, in *11th IEEE International Symposium Software Metrics*, March 14–16. New York: Columbia University, 2005.

[44] N. Tang, Big data cleaning, in *Web Technologies and Applications*, L. Chen, Y. Jia, T. Sellis, and G. Liu (Eds.), pp. 13–24. Cham, Switzerland: Springer International Publishing, 2014.

[45] H. H. Mohamed, T. L. Kheng, C. Collin, and O. S. Lee, E-clean: A data cleaning framework for patient data, in *2011 First International Conference on Informatics and Computational Intelligence* (*ICI*), pp. 63–68. IEEE, 2001.

[46] J. I. Maletic and A. Marcus, Data cleansing: A prelude to knowledge discovery, in *Data Mining and Knowledge Discovery Handbook*, O. Maimon and L. Rokach (Eds.), pp. 19–32. Secaucus, NJ: Springer, 2010.

[47] S. García, S. Ramírez-Gallego, J. Luengo, J. M. Benítez, and F. Herrera, Big data preprocessing: Methods and prospects, *Big Data Analytics*, 1(9), 1–22, 2016.

[48] M. Deshpande and G. Karypis, Item-based top-n recommendation algorithms, *ACM Transactions on Information Systems* (*TOIS*), 22(1), 143–177, 2004.

[49] B. Chandramouli, J. J. Levandoski, A. Eldawy, and M. F. Mokbel, Streamrec: A real-time recommender system, in *Proceedings of the 2011 ACM SIGMOD Conference*, pp. 1243–1246. ACM, 2011.

[50] P. Domingos and G. Hulten, Mining high-speed data streams, in *Proceedings of the 6th ACM SIGKDD Conference*, pp. 71–80. ACM, 2000.

[51] Apache hadoop, https://hadoop.apache.org/.

[52] Spark, https://spark.apache.org/.

[53] Y. Zhou, D. Wilkinson, R. Schreiber, and R. Pan, Large-scale parallel collaborative filtering for the netflix prize, in *Proceedings of the 4th International Conference on Algorithmic Aspects in Information and Management*, AAIM'08, pp. 337–348. Berlin, Germany: Springer-Verlag, 2008.

[54] G. Takács, I. Pilászy, B. Németh, and D. Tikk, Scalable collaborative filtering approaches for large recommender systems, *Journal of Machine Learning Research*, 10, 623–656, 2009.

[55] Mahout, http://mahout.apache.org/.

[56] H.-F. Yu, C.-J. Hsieh, S. Si, and I. Dhillon, Scalable coordinate descent approaches to parallel matrix factorization for recommender systems, in *2012 IEEE 12th International Conference on Data Mining (ICDM)*, Brussels, Belgium, December 10–13, 2012.

[57] C. R. Aberger, Recommender: An analysis of collaborative filtering techniques, http://cs229.stanford.edu/proj2014/Christopher%20Aberger,%20Recommender.pdf.

[58] Apache flink, https://flink.apache.org/.

[59] S. Schelter and S. Owen, Collaborative filtering with Apache Mahout, in *Proceedings of ACM RecSys Challenge*, September 9–13. Dublin, Ireland, 2012.

[60] S. Shahrivari, Beyond batch processing: Towards real-time and streaming big data, *Computers*, 3(4), 117–129, 2014.

[61] J. Dean and S. Ghemawat, Mapreduce: Simplified data processing on large clusters, in *Proceedings of the 6th Conference on Symposium on Operating Systems Design & Implementation—Volume 6*, OSDI'04, p. 10. Berkeley, CA: USENIX Association, 2004.

[62] Mllib, https://spark.apache.org/mllib/.

[63] Flink-ml, https://github.com/apache/flink/tree/master/flink-staging/flink-ml.

[64] Dato core. https://github.com/dato-code/dato-core.

[65] S. Landset, T. M. Khoshgoftaar, A. N. Richter, and T. Hasanin, A survey of open source tools for machine learning with big data in the hadoop ecosystem, *Journal of Big Data*, 2(1), 24, 2015.

[66] S. Chalmers, C. Bothorel, and R. Picot-Clemente, Big data—state of the art, Technical Report, Telecom Bretagne, 2013.

[67] C. Lemnaru, M. Cuibus, A. Bona, A. Alic, and R. Potolea, A distributed methodology for imbalanced classification problems, in *Proceedings of the 2012 11th International Symposium on Parallel and Distributed Computing*, ISPDC'12, pp. 164–171. Washington, DC: IEEE Computer Society, 2012.

[68] K. Hammond and A. Varde, Cloud based predictive analytics: Text classification, recommender systems and decision support, in *2013 IEEE 13th International Conference on Data Mining Workshops*, Dallas, TX, December 7–10, pp. 607–612, 2013.

[69] C. Zeng, Y. Jiang, L. Zheng, J. Li, L. Li, H. Li, C. Shen et al., Fiu-miner: A fast, integrated, and user-friendly system for data mining in distributed environment, in *Proceedings of the 19th ACM SIGKDD International Conference on Knowledge Discovery and Data Mining*, pp. 1506–1509. ACM, 2013.

[70] R. M. Esteves, R. Pais, and C. Rong, K-means clustering in the cloud—a mahout test, in *2011 IEEE Workshops of International Conference on Advanced Information Networking and Applications*, pp. 514–519. IEEE, 2011.

[71] X. Geng and Z. Yang, Data mining in cloud computing, in *Proceedings of the 2013 International Conference on Information Science and Computer Applications (ISCA 2013)*, November 8–9. Changsha, China, 2013.

[72] R. D. Souza, R. Chiky, and Z. Aoul, Open source recommendation systems for mobile application, in *Workshop on the Practical Use of Recommender Systems, Algorithms and Technologies (PRSAT 2010)*, Barcelona, Spain, September 30, pp. 55–58, 2010.

[73] J. Lin and A. Kolcz, Large-scale machine learning at twitter, in *Proceedings of the 2012 ACM SIGMOD International Conference on Management of Data*, pp. 793–804. ACM, 2012.

[74] J. Miller, Recommender system for animated video, *Issues in Information Systems*, 15(2), 321–327, 2014.

[75] D. Wegener, M. Mock, D. Adranale, and S. Wrobel, Toolkit-based high-performance data mining of large data on mapreduce clusters, in *2009 IEEE International Conference on Data Mining Workshops*, pp. 296–301. IEEE, 2009.

[76] M. Zaharia, M. Chowdhury, M. Franklin, S. Shenker, and I. Stoica, Spark: Cluster computing with working sets, in *Proceedings of the 2nd USENIX Conference on Hot Topics in Cloud Computing*, Boston, MA, June 22–25, 2010.

[77] M. Zaharia, M. Chowdhury, T. Das, and A. Dave, Fast and interactive analytics over hadoop data with spark, *USENIX Login*, 37(4), 45–51, 2012.

[78] Z. Ni, *Comparative Evaluation of Spark and Stratosphere.* PhD thesis, KTH Royal Institute of Technology, 2013.

[79] D. Singh and C. Reddy, A survey on platforms for big data analytics, *Journal of Big Data*, 2, 8, 2014.

[80] N. Katsipoulakis, Y. Tian, B. Reinwald, and H. Pirahesh, A generic solution to integrate sql and analytics for big data, in *18th International Conference on Extending Database Technology (EDBT)*, Brussels, Belgium, March 23–27, pp. 671–676, 2015.

[81] M. Alber, *Big Data and Machine Learning: A Case Study with Bump Boost.* PhD thesis, Free University of Berlin, 2014.

[82] A. Alexandrov, R. Bergmann, S. Ewen, J. Freytag, F. Hueske, A. Heise, O. Kao et al., The stratosphere platform for big data analytics, *VLDB Journal—International Journal on Very Large Data Bases*, 23(6), 939–964, 2014.

[83] M. Boehm, A. V. Evfimievski, N. Pansare, and B. Reinwald, Declarative machine learning—A classification of basic properties and types, *CoRR*, abs/1605.05826, 2016.

[84] Systemml, https://systemml.apache.org/.

[85] J. Herlocker, J. Konstan, L. Terveen, and J. Riedl, Evaluating collaborative filtering recommender systems, *ACM Transactions on Information Systems*, 22(1), 5–53, 2004.

[86] F. Garcin, B. Faltings, O. Donatsch, A. Alazzawi, C. Bruttin, and A. Huber, Offline and online evaluation of news recommender systems at swissinfo.ch, in *Proceedings of the 8th ACM Conference on Recommender Systems*, pp. 169–176. ACM, 2014.

[87] S. McNee, J. Riedl, and J. Konstan, Being accurate is not enough: how accuracy metrics have hurt recommender systems, in *Conference on Human Factors in Computing Systems*, pp. 1097–1101. New York: ACM, 2006.

[88] L. Terveen and W. Hill, *Beyond Recommender Systems: Helping People Help Each Other.* Reading, MA: Addison Wesley, 2001.

[89] S. M. McNee, I. Albert, D. Cosley, P. Gopalkrishnan, S. K. Lam, A. M. Rashid, J. A. Konstan, and J. Riedl, On the recommending of citations for research papers, in *Proceedings of the 2002 ACM Conference on Computer Supported Cooperative Work*, pp. 116–125. New York: ACM, 2002.

[90] A. Maksai, F. Garcin, and B. Faltings, Predicting online performance of news recommender systems through richer evaluation metrics, in *Proceedings of the 9th ACM Conference on Recommender Systems*, pp. 179–186. New York: ACM, 2015.

[91] R. Kohavi, Online controlled experiments: Introduction, learnings, and humbling statistics, in *Proceedings of the Sixth ACM Conference on Recommender Systems*, pp. 1–2. New York: ACM, 2012.

[92] A. R. Damasio, *Descartes Error: Emotion, Reason and the Human Brain.* New York: Penguin Group (USA), 1994.

[93] A. Pak and P. Paroubek, Twitter as a corpus for sentiment analysis and opinion mining, *LREC*, 10, 2010.

[94] C. Strapparava and R. Mihalcea, Learning to identify emotions in text, *SAC*, pp. 1556–1560. New York: ACM, 2008.

[95] P. Covington, J. Adams, and E. Sargin, Deep neural networks for youtube recommendations, in *Proceedings of the 10th ACM Conference on Recommender Systems.* New York: ACM, 2016.

[96] 10th acm conference on recommender systems, https://recsys.acm.org/recsys16/.

[97] Y. Bengio and Y. LeCun, Scaling learning algorithms towards AI, in *Large Scale Kernel Machines*, L. Bottou, O. Chapelle, D. DeCoste, and J. Weston (Eds.), pp. 321–360. Cambridge, MA: MIT Press, 2013.

[98] I. Arel, D. Rose, and T. Karnowski, Deep machine learning-a new frontier in artificial intelligence research, *IEEE Computational Intelligence Magazine*, 5, 13–18, 2010.

[99] A. van den Oord, S. Dieleman, and B. Schrauwen, Deep content-based music recommendation, in *Proceedings of the 26th International Conference on Neural Information Processing Systems*, NIPS'13, December 5–10, pp. 2643–2651. Curran Associates, 2013.

[100] R. Salakhutdinov, A. Mnih, and G. Hinton, Restricted boltzmann machines for collaborative filtering, in *Proceedings of the 24th International Conference on Machine Learning*, ICML'07, pp. 791–798. New York: ACM, 2007.

[101] S. Sedhain, A. K. Menon, S. Sanner, and L. Xie, Autorec: Autoencoders meet collaborative filtering, in *WWW 2015 Companion*, Florence, Italy, May 18–22, 2015.

[102] H.-T. Cheng, L. Koc, J. Harmsen, T. Shaked, T. Chandra, H. Aradhye, G. Anderson et al., Wide & deep learning for recommender systems, *CoRR*, 7–10, abs/1606.07792, 2016.

[103] P. Y. Simard, D. Steinkraus, and J. C. Platt, Best practices for convolutional neural networks applied to visual document analysis, in *Proceedings of the Seventh International Conference on Document Analysis and Recognition (ICDAR 2003)*, Washington, DC: IEEE Computer Society, 2003.

[104] D. Cosley, S. Lam, I. Albert, J. Konstan, and J. Riedl, Is seeing believing how recommender system interfaces affect users opinions, in *CHI03*, pp. 585–592. ACM, 2003.

[105] A. Ballatore, G. McArdle, C. Kelly, and M. Bertolotto, Recomap: An interactive and adaptive map-based recommender, in *25th ACM Symposium on Applied Computing (ACM SAC 2010)*, pp. 887–891. ACM, 2010.

[106] Y. Ding and X. Li, Time weight collaborative filtering, in *Proceedings of the 2005 ACM CIKM International Conference on Information and Knowledge Management*, Bremen, Germany, October 31–November 5, 2005.

[107] D. Yin, L. Hong, Z. Xue, and B. D. Davison, Temporal dynamics of user interests in tagging systems, in *AAAI'11 Proceedings of the Twenty-Fifth AAAI Conference on Artificial Intelligence*, San Francisco, CA, August 7–11, 2011.

[108] D. Zhang, R. Mao, and W. Li, The recurrence dynamics of social tagging, in *Proceedings of the 18th International Conference on World Wide Web, WWW 2009*, Madrid, Spain, April 20–24, 2009.

[109] S. Chang, Y. Zhang, J. Tang, D. Yin, Y. Chang, M. A. Hasegawa-Johnson, and T. S. Huang, Streaming recommender systems, *CoRR*, abs/1607.06182, pp. 381–389, 2016.

[110] R. Pagano, P. Cremonesi, M. Larson, B. Hidasi, D. Tikk, A. Karatzoglou, and M. Quadrana, The contextual turn: From context-aware to context-driven recommender systems, in *Proceedings of the 10th ACM Conference on Recommender Systems*, RecSys'16, pp. 249–252. New York: ACM, 2016.

[111] G. Adomavicius and A. Tuzhilin, *Context-Aware Recommender Systems*, pp. 191–226. New York: Springer, 2015.

Chapter 10

Preprocessing in Big Data: New challenges for discretization and feature selection

Verónica Bolón-Canedo

Noelia Sánchez-Maroño

Amparo Alonso-Betanzos

Introduction ... 286
The advent of Big Data ... 287
The need for preprocessing ... 288
  Discretization ... 289
    Discretization process ... 289
    Popular discretization methods ... 291
  Feature selection ... 291
    Feature selection process ... 292
    Popular feature selection methods ... 294
Challenges ... 295
  Millions of dimensions ... 296
  Stability of feature selection ... 297
  Scalability ... 298
  Distributed feature selection ... 300
  Real-time processing ... 303
  Visualization and interpretability ... 305
Case studies ... 306
  A parallel implementation of the minimum description length-based discretizer ... 306
  Redesign of an algorithm for feature selection for its use in parallel platforms ... 308
  Other distributed and incremental feature selection approaches ... 314
Conclusion and future research directions ... 315
References ... 316

Introduction

Nowadays, human society collects and stores vast amounts of information about every subject imaginable and is archiving this information in attempts to use it for scientific, utilitarian (e.g., health), and business purposes. In this scenario, the term *Big Data* appears. Giving a proper definition of this term is not easy, and it is usually defined by its properties, as it will be presented in the next section. A useful definition of *Big Data* is data that is too big to process comfortably on a single machine, either because of processor, memory, or disk bottleneck. To deal with Big Data, the classical approximations of machine learning are not enough and new methods are being developed. Not only is it necessary to design new classification algorithms able to tackle large volume of data, but also to cover all stages of the classification process, including preprocessing techniques. In this chapter, we will focus on two of them: discretization and feature selection (FS).

Feature discretization is an extremely important preprocessing task used for classification in data mining and machine learning as many classification methods require that each dimension of the training dataset contains only discrete values [1]. Roughly speaking, discretization translates quantitative data into qualitative data, procuring a nonoverlapping division of a continuous domain. It also ensures an association between each numerical value and a certain interval. The specialized literature gathers a huge number of proposals for discretization [2,3], and they can be classified according to many different criteria (global vs. local, supervised vs. unsupervised, splitting vs. merging, etc.) [2]. Despite the great impact of discretization as data-preprocessing technique, few elementary approaches have been developed in the literature for Big Data, so it poses new challenges for the scientific community.

Large volume is one of the properties of Big Data; it may refer not only to a large number of instances but also to a large number of features. To confront the problem of the large number of features, dimensionality reduction techniques are indispensable and may help one to improve learning performance. FS is a dimensionality reduction technique based on discarding the irrelevant inputs while maintaining the relevant ones. It has been deeply studied by the machine learning community in the last few years, and there are many FS methods available (see Chapter 2 in Reference 4). These methods can be grouped into three categories: (1) filter, (2) embedded, and (3) wrappers, according to its interaction with the classifier used afterwards (from totally independent of using the classifier as a subroutine of the selection process) [5]. Another categorization divides FS methods based on their output, turning to two different groups: feature subset selection or feature ranking [6]. As the name suggests, the former returns a subset of relevant features, whereas the latter returns an ordered list of features. Some rankers may also indicate the weight assigned to each feature based on the internal metric used. Despite the large amount of FS methods available, when it comes to mining over high-dimensional data, the search space from which an optimal feature subset is derived grows exponentially in size, leading to an intractable demand in computation for many of these methods. Distribution, parallelization, and streaming are common techniques to tackle this issue in which new approaches are constantly appearing, and this chapter will present the most recent advances and different cases of study.

The current chapter is structured as follows. Section "The advent of Big Data" briefly introduces the concept of Big Data and how it opens important challenges for machine learning researchers. To extract useful information from this large amount of data, some preprocessing techniques are required. As previously mentioned, in this chapter, we focus on two of them: discretization and FS, both are presented in section "The need for preprocessing." Then, section "Challenges" explains the open challenges that Big Data brings, centered in FS and discretization. Section "Case studies" is devoted to present different case studies, specifically, a parallel implementation of the minimum description length (MDL)-based discretizer and a redesign of the mRMR (minimum redundancy maximum relevance) algorithm for its use in different parallel platforms, and, finally, section "Conclusion and future research directions" concludes this chapter.

The advent of Big Data

In recent years, an important number of organizations and enterprises have stored large amounts of data to be analyzed at some point in the near future, but without a clear idea of its potential usefulness. Moreover, recent advances in technology have enabled data to be generated not only from many different sources—systems, sensors, mobile devices, and so on—but also in many different formats—text, multimedia, and so on. Some studies have attempted to determine the size of this digital universe, that is, the amount of bits created, replicated, and consumed per year. One of these studies [7] affirms that the digital universe is doubling in size every two years. This means that, by 2020, it is expected to reach 44 zettabytes ($10^{(21)}$ bytes).

In this scenario, a new term is coined: *Big Data*, which was used for the very first time in 1997 referring to the area of scientific visualization, in which the datasets are usually very large. Specifically, the authors said "When datasets do not fit in main memory (in core), or when they do not fit even on local disk, the most common solution is to acquire more resources." This definition is related with one of the main characteristics of Big Data: *volume*. However, this concept was rapidly expanded to include two more properties: *velocity* and *variety* [8]. *Velocity* refers to the speed of data creation, whereas *variety* is related to the richness of data representation (text, multimedia, etc.). These first properties were called the three Vs to define Big Data. Then, it turned into the five Vs, adding *veracity* (data are virtually worthless, if those are not accurate) and *value* (data have to be turned into value, otherwise it is useless). Finally, nowadays people refer to Big Data as the seven Vs, by further including *variability* (data, the meaning of which is constantly changing), and *visualization* (it is necessary to present the data—which can contain dozens of variables and parameters—in a readable and accessible way).

According to Hashem et al. [9], Big Data can also be classified based on five different aspects: (a) data sources, (b) content format, (c) data stores, (d) data staging, and (e) data processing. Data staging (cleaning, transformation, and normalization of the data) and data processing (batch or real time) are usually faced with machine learning algorithms. However, machine learning is still in its early stages of development [10]. Many algorithms have been developed years ago and are not able to deal with Big Data. This opens an important challenge for machine learning researchers, who are interested now not only in developing accurate algorithms but also scalable algorithms that can be applied in real-world situations with datasets of trillions of elements.

For this reason, new scalable distributed techniques and frameworks have recently appeared, to deal with Big Data. MapReduce [11] and its open-source version Apache Hadoop [12,13] were the first distributed programing techniques to face this problem. Apache Spark [14,15] is one of these new frameworks, designed as a fast and general engine for large-scale data processing based on in-memory computation. Through this Sparks ability, it is possible to speed up iterative processes present in many machine learning problems. Similarly, several machine learning libraries for Big Data have appeared as support for this task. The first one was Mahout [16] (as part of Hadoop), subsequently, followed by machine learning library(MLlib) [17] that is part of the Spark project. Although many state-of-the-art machine learning algorithms have been implemented in MLlib, preprocessing techniques have not received the same amount of interest.

The need for preprocessing

To be able to extract useful information from all these data generated from the advent of Big Data, we require new analysis and processing tools [18]. Most of these data have been generated in the last few years—as we continue to generate quintillions of bytes daily. The growing size of datasets raises an interesting challenge for the research community; to cite Donoho et al. [19] "our task is to find a needle in a haystack, teasing the relevant information out of a vast pile of glut."

In this scenario, preprocessing techniques are more necessary than ever—yet more difficult to apply. In this section, we will focus on two of the most popular preprocessing techniques: discretization and FS.

Discretization

The process of discretization has aroused general interest in recent years and has become one of the most effective data preprocessing techniques in machine learning. Discretization translates quantitative data into qualitative data, procuring a nonoverlapping division of a continuous domain. It also ensures an association between each numerical value and a certain interval. Actually, discretization is considered a data reduction mechanism because it diminishes data from a large domain of numeric values to a subset of categorical values [2].

Many machine learning algorithms can only work with discrete attributes. In fact, three of the ten methods pointed out as the top ten in data mining [20] require a data-discretization process in one form or another: C4.5 [21], Apriori [22], and naive Bayes [23]. Among its main benefits, discretization causes that the learning methods show remarkable improvements in learning speed (more important than ever in the era of Big Data) and also in accuracy. Moreover, some decision tree-based algorithms produce shorter, more compact, and accurate results when using discrete values [24].

There are a huge number of methods for discretization, and the election of one or another usually depends on the type of data to deal with. Notice that this is an important decision, as it will imply the success of the subsequent learning phases, such as FS and/or classification. To help the user decide among the broad suite of discretization methods, a new taxonomy has been recently proposed by Ramírez et al. [2].

However, classical discretization methods are not expected to scale well when managing huge data—both in number of features and instances—so their application can be undermined or even become impracticable [25]. As mentioned before, a recent solution to this problem is the use of distributed frameworks, such as Hadoop or Spark. However, few attempts have been made to parallelize standard discretization methods in these Big Data platforms, trying to boost both performance and accuracy. Recently, a distributed implementation of one of the most well-known discretizers based on information theory has been proposed [2], obtaining better results than the entropy minimization discretizer proposed by Fayyad and Irani [26]. This method will be explained in detail in section "A parallel implementation of the minimum description length-based discretizer."

Discretization process

Suppose that we have a supervised learning problem, or, more specifically, a classification problem. Let S be a dataset consisting of N examples, M attributes, and c class labels. A discretization scheme D_A would exist on the continuous attribute $A \in M$, which partitions this attribute into k discrete and disjoint intervals: $\{[d_0, d_1], (d_1, d_2], ..., (d_{k_A-1}, d_{K_A}]\}$, where d_0 and d_{K_A} are,

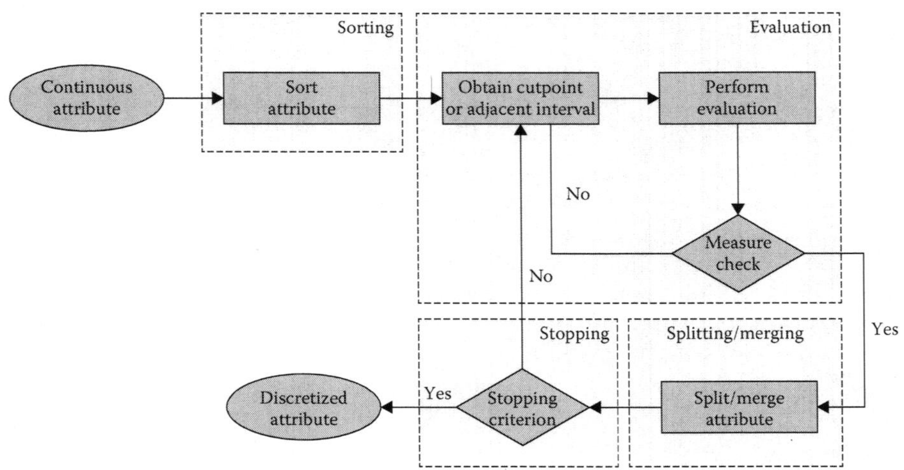

FIGURE 10.1: Discretization process.

respectively, the minimum and maximal value, and $P_A = \{d_1, d_2, ..., d_{k_A-1}\}$ represents the set of cut points of A in ascending order [2].

The basic discretization process consists of four steps: (i) sorting the continuous values of the attribute to be discretizer, (ii) either evaluating a cut point for splitting or adjacent intervals for merging, (iii) splitting or merging intervals for continuous values according to some defined criterion, and (iv) stopping at some point. This process can be seen in Figure 10.1.

- *Sorting*: The continuous values for an attribute are sorted in either descending or ascending order. It is important to use an efficient sorting algorithm for this task.

- *Selection of a cut point*: After sorting, the best cut point or the best pair of adjacent intervals should be found in the attribute range to split or merge in a following required step. It is necessary to determine the correlation, gain, improvement in performance, or any other benefit according to the class label, by means of an evaluation measure of function.

- *Splitting/merging*: Depending on the operation method of each discretization algorithm, intervals can be split or merged. For splitting, the possible cut points are the different real values present in the feature. For merging, the discretization algorithm tries to find the best adjacent intervals to merge in each iteration.

- *Stopping criteria*: It specifies when to stop the discretization process. Usually, it assumes a trade-off between a lower number of intervals, good comprehension, and consistency.

Popular discretization methods

The description of four popular discretization methods (included in the popular Weka tool [27]) are provided in the following. For more information about discretization methods, see Ramírez et al. [2].

- *Entropy minimization discretization, EMD*: This popular method was created by Fayyad and Irani [26]. It evaluates as a candidate cut point the midpoint between each successive pair of the sorted values. For evaluating each candidate cut point, the data are discretized into two intervals and the resulting class information entropy is calculated. A binary discretization is determined by selecting the cut point for which the entropy is minimal amongst all candidates. The binary discretization is applied recursively, always selecting the best cut point. A MDL criterion is applied to decide when to stop discretization.
- *Proportional k-interval discretization, PKID*: This method was proposed by Yang and Webb [23]. The idea behind PKID is that discretization bias and variance relate to interval size and interval number. This strategy seeks an appropriate trade-off between the bias and variance of the probability estimation by adjusting the number and size of intervals to the number of training instances. The following compromise is adopted: given a numeric attribute, supposing we have N training examples with known values for the attribute, we discretize it into $\sqrt{N}$ intervals, with $\sqrt{N}$ instances in each interval. Thus, we give equal weight to both bias and variance management. Further, with N increasing, both the number and size of intervals increase correspondingly, which means discretization can decrease both the bias and variance of the probability estimation. This is very desirable, because if a numeric attribute has more instances available, there is more information about it. PKID has greater capacity to take advantage of the additional information inherent in large volumes of training data.
- *Equal width discretization*: This simple method divides the number line between the minimum and maximum values of an attribute into k intervals of equal width; in which k is a user predefined parameter.
- *Equal frequency discretization*: This method divides the sorted values into k intervals so that each interval contains approximately the same number of training instances. Thus, each interval contains N/k (possibly duplicated) adjacent values. Again, k is a user predefined parameter.

Feature selection

In the new era of Big Data, machine learning methods need to be able to deal with the unprecedented scale of data. Analogous to Big Data, the term

Big Dimensionality has been coined to refer to the unprecedented number of features arriving at levels that are rendering existing machine learning methods inadequate [28].

This ultrahigh dimensionality not only implies massive memory requirements and a high computational cost for training but also affects to generalization capacities. According to Donoho et al. [19], Bellman coined the term *curse of dimensionality* in 1957 to describe the difficulty of optimization by exhaustive enumeration on product spaces [29]. This term refers to various phenomena that arise when analyzing and organizing data in high-dimensional spaces (with hundreds or thousands of dimensions) that do not occur in low-dimensional settings. A dataset is usually represented by a matrix in which the rows are the recorded instances (or samples) and the columns are the attributes (or features) that represent the problem at hand. To tackle the dimensionality problem, the dataset can be summarized by finding *narrower* matrices that in some sense are close to the original. As these narrower matrices have a smaller number of samples and/or features, they can be used much more efficiently than the original matrix [18]. One of the most popular methods to reduce the dimensionality is called *FS*.

FS is defined as the process of detecting relevant features and discarding irrelevant and redundant features with the goal of obtaining a subset of features that accurately describe a given problem with a minimum degradation of performance [5]. Theoretically, having a large number of input features might seem desirable, but the *curse of dimensionality* is not only an intrinsic problem of high-dimensionality data, but more a joint problem of the data and the algorithm being applied. For this reason, researchers usually select features in a preprocessing phase in an attempt to convert their data into a lower dimensional form.

Traditionally, FS is applied in a centralized manner, that is, a single learning model is used to solve a given problem. However, most existing FS methods are not expected to scale efficiently when dealing with millions of features; indeed, they may even become inapplicable. A possible solution might be to distribute the data, run FS on each partition, and then combine the results [30,31].

As happens with discretization, although MLlib includes a number of learning algorithms, there is not much effort made in the field of FS. Recent cases in points include the parallelization of mRMR [32] (both in Spark and using graphic processing units [GPUs], see section "Redesign of an algorithm for feature selection for its use in parallel platforms") and of several popular FS algorithms in Spark and with a multithread version [33].

Feature selection process

Formally, we can define FS as follows: Let e_i be an instance such that $e_i = (e_{i1}, ..., e_{iN}, e_{iy})$, where e_{ir} corresponds to the rth feature value of the ith sample, and e_{iy} corresponds to the value of the output class Y. Suppose that

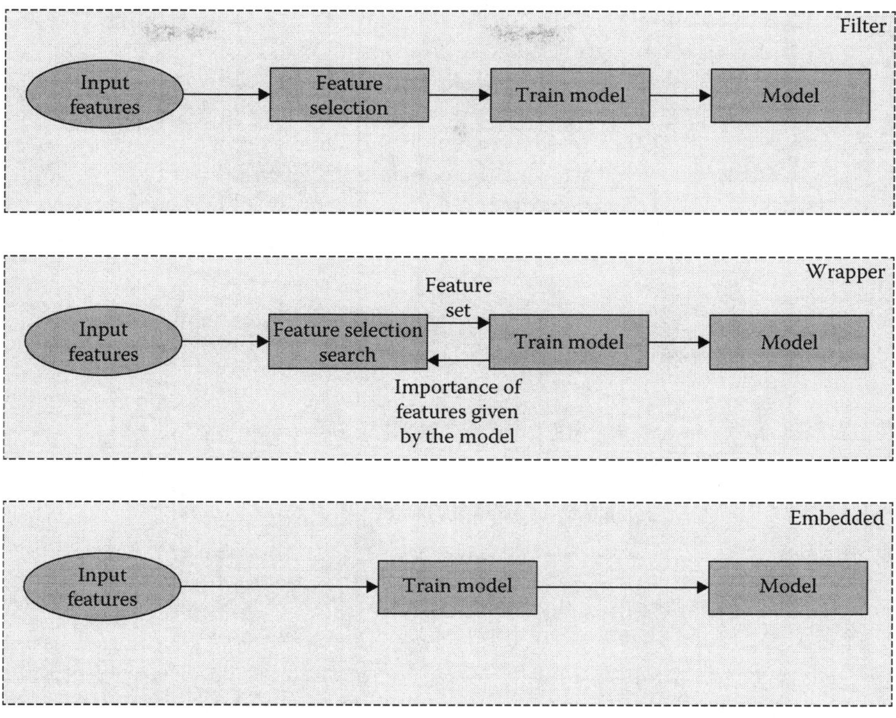

FIGURE 10.2: Different feature selection schemes.

we have a training set S with N examples, whose instances e_i are formed by a set X of M features. Then, $F_\theta \in X$ is the subset of selected features yielded by a FS algorithm.

With regard to the relationship between a FS algorithm and the inductive learning method used to infer a model, three major approaches (Figure 10.2) can be distinguished [34]:

- *Filters*, which rely on the general characteristics of training data and carry out the FS process as a preprocessing step with independence of the induction algorithm. This model is advantageous for its low computational cost and good generalization ability.

- *Wrappers*, which involve a learning algorithm as a black box and consist of using its prediction performance to assess the relative usefulness of subsets of variables. In other words, the FS algorithm uses the learning method as a subroutine with the computational burden that comes from calling the learning algorithm to evaluate each subset of features. However, this interaction with the classifier tends to give better performance results than filters.

- *Embedded methods*, which perform FS in the process of training and are usually specific to given learning machines. Therefore, the search for an optimal subset of features is built into the classifier construction and can be seen as a search in the combined space of feature subsets and hypotheses. In other words, ensemble methods learn which features best contribute to the accuracy of the model while the model is being created. This approach is able to capture dependencies at a lower computational cost than wrappers.

Popular feature selection methods

The description of seven popular FS methods (included in the popular Weka tool [27], except mRMR) are provided in the following. For more information about FS methods, see Bolón-Canedo et al. [4].

- *Correlation-based FS*: This is a simple multivariate filter algorithm that ranks feature subsets according to a correlation-based heuristic evaluation function [35]. The bias of the evaluation function is toward subsets that contain features that are highly correlated with the class and uncorrelated with each other. Irrelevant features should be ignored because they will have low correlation with the class. Redundant features should be screened out as they will be highly correlated with one or more of the remaining features. The acceptance of a feature will depend on the extent to which it predicts classes in areas of the instance space not already predicted by other features.

- *Consistency-based filter*: This subset filter [36] evaluates the worth of a subset of features by the level of consistency in the class values when the training instances are projected onto the subset of attributes.

- *INTERACT*: This algorithm [37] is a subset filter based on symmetrical uncertainty and the consistency contribution, which is an indicator about how significantly the elimination of a feature will affect consistency. The algorithm consists of two major parts. In the first part, the features are ranked in descending order based on their symmetrical uncertainty values. In the second part, features are evaluated one by one starting from the end of the ranked feature list. If the consistency contribution of a feature is less than an established threshold, the feature is removed, otherwise it is selected. The authors stated that this method can handle feature interaction, and efficiently selects relevant features.

- *Information gain*: This is one of the most common attribute evaluation methods [38]. This univariate filter provides an ordered ranking of all the features and then a threshold is required. In this work, the threshold will be set up selecting the features that obtain a positive information gain value.

- *ReliefF*: This filter [39] is an extension of the original Relief algorithm. The original Relief algorithm works by randomly sampling an instance from the data and then locating its nearest neighbor from the same and opposite class. The values of the attributes of the nearest neighbors are compared with the sampled instance and used to update relevance scores for each attribute. The rationale is that an useful attribute should differentiate between instances from different classes and have the same value for instances from the same class. ReliefF adds the ability of dealing with multiclass problems and is also more robust and capable of dealing with incomplete and noisy data. This method may be applied in all situations, has low bias, includes interaction among features, and may capture local dependencies that other methods miss.
- *minimum Redundancy Maximum Relevance (mRMR)*: This filter [40] selects features that have the highest relevance with the target class and are also minimally redundant, that is, it selects features that are maximally dissimilar to each other. Both optimization criteria (maximum-relevance and minimum-redundancy) are based on mutual information (MI).
- *Recursive feature elimination for support vector machines (SVM-RFE)* was introduced by Guyon et al. [41]. This embedded method performs FS by iteratively training a support vector machines (SVM) classifier with the current set of features and removing the least important feature indicated by the SVM.
- *WrapperSubsetEval*: This wrapper [27] evaluates attribute sets by using a learning scheme. Cross validation is used to estimate the accuracy of the learning scheme for a set of attributes. The algorithm starts with the empty set of attributes and searches forward, adding attributes until performance does not improve further.

Challenges

In a context in which datasets are becoming larger everyday, a critical step to obtain a good model is determining which features should be included in it. In addition, to exhibit a proper behavior, some of these FS methods demand discrete inputs. As previously commented, there are many discretization and FS methods. However, there are still an important number of emerging challenges that researchers need to deal with. In this section, we will discuss the most relevant ones, some of them extracted from Reference 18.

Millions of dimensions

Our capability for data generation has never been so powerful and enormous ever since the invention of the information technology in the early nineteenth century. For example, on October 4, 2012, the first presidential debate between President Barack Obama and Governor Mitt Romney triggered more than 10 million tweets within 2 hours [42]. Another example is Flickr, a public picture sharing site, which received close to 2 million photos per day, on average, during 2015 [43]. These examples demonstrate the rise of Big Data applications in which data collection has grown tremendously and is beyond the ability of commonly used software tools to capture, manage, and process within a *tolerable elapsed time* [25]. The most fundamental challenge for Big Data applications is to explore the large volumes of data and extract useful information or knowledge for future actions [44].

This increase in the volume of data has been reflected in the repositories that are commonly used by the machine learning community. Considering the number of samples, there are 17 and 9 datasets at the widely used University of California Irvine (UCI) Machine Learning Repository [45] and the popular library for support vector machines (LIBSVM) Database [46], respectively, that have more than 1 million instances. Similarly, if we focus on the number of attributes of the UCI Machine Learning Repository, 19 datasets have more than 5000 features and most have a samples/features ratio below 0—a level that potentially hinders any learning process—; for example, the *twin gas sensor arrays* dataset has $480,000$ features but only 640 instances. Analogously, in the LIBSVM Database, 20 of the existing 99 datasets have more than 5000 features, and 11 datasets have many more features than samples. Apart from these generic repositories, there are others with specific high-dimensionality problems, such as the aforementioned DNA microarray classification [47] or single-nucleotide polymorphism datasets [48] both in the field of bioinformatics.

In this scenario, existing state-of-the-art discretization and FS methods are confronted by key challenges that potentially have negative repercussions on performance. For example, Ramirez et al. [2] indicate that it takes more than $5,000$ seconds to completely discretize a dataset formed by $500,000$ instances and $2,000$ features. Similarly, Zhai et al. [28] pointed to more than a day of computational effort by the state-of-the-art SVM-RFE and mRMR feature selectors to crunch the data for a psoriasis single-nucleotide polymorphism dataset composed of *just* half a million features.

Moreover, many state-of-the-art FS methods are based on algorithm designs for computing pairwise correlation. The implications when dealing with a million features are that the computer would need to handle a trillion correlations. This kind of issue poses an enormous challenge for machine learning researchers that still remain to be addressed.

Stability of feature selection

Stability is an important measure when evaluating the adequacy of a FS algorithm. Stability is defined as the sensitivity of the FS procedure to small perturbations in the training set. This issue is of course extremely relevant with small training samples, for example, in bioinformatics applications. If the alteration/exclusion of just one training example results in a very different choice of features, we cannot justifiably say the FS is doing a reliable job [49].

Then, stable FS methods are desirable because, if the features are consistent among models created from different training data, the confidence of the users in the analysis results is strengthened [50]. Although the study of He and Yu [51] is centered on biomarker discovery, they identify three sources of instability that may occur in other areas:

- Algorithm design without considering stability. Most FS algorithms are focused on obtaining a reduced set of features maintaining an adequate level of accuracy in the posterior classification task. Then, stability is ignored in the algorithm design.
- The existence of multiple sets of true markers, that is, true features. It is possible that there exist multiple sets of potential true features in real data. It could be due to the existence of highly correlated features but, even without correlation, it is possible to obtain different sets of true features.
- Small number of samples in high-dimensional data. It has been experimentally verified that the relatively small number of samples in high-dimensional data is one of the main sources of the instability problem in FS [52,53].

In addition, the discretization process may cause side effects such as assigning a large number of features with a single value because of the low variability of these features [50], especially in cases with reduced number of samples. Therefore, FS methods discard these features.

To deal with the first item, a proper stability measure is needed. Nowadays, there are many different measures used to quantify stability [50,54,55]. Recently, Nogueira and Brown [49] have analyzed the desirable properties of a stability measure deriving that Pearson's correlation has most of them.

Several stable FS methods can be found in the literature, a comprehensive survey of the first few works can be checked in Reference 51. A general technique was presented by Meinshausen and Bühlmann [56] based on subsampling in combination with (high dimensional) selection algorithms. Authors demonstrated its applicability for variable selection in regression and Gaussian graphical modeling. The basic idea is that, instead of applying one's favorite algorithm to the whole dataset to determine the selected set of features, one instead applies it several times to random subsamples of the data of size $\lfloor n/2 \rfloor$ (n being the number of samples) and chooses those variables that are selected most frequently on the subsamples [57]. Shah and Samworth [57] introduce a variant to this technique, called complementary pairs stability selection. Recently, in Reference 58, a class of stable FS algorithms called feature weighting as regularized energy-based learning is studied. Despite the importance of stability, many recent FS methods do not contemplate it, so there is still work to be done in this regard.

Scalability

Most existing learning algorithms were developed when dataset sizes were much smaller, but nowadays, different solutions are required for the case of small-scale versus large-scale learning problems. Small-scale learning problems are subject to the usual approximation–estimation trade-off, but this trade-off is more complex in the case of large-scale learning problems, not only because of accuracy but also due to the computational complexity of the learning algorithm. Moreover, as most algorithms were designed under the assumption that the dataset would be represented as a single memory-resident table, these algorithms are useless when the entire dataset does not fit in the main memory. Dataset size is therefore one reason for scaling up machine learning algorithms. However, there are other settings in which a researcher could find the scale of a machine learning task daunting [59], for instance, (a) model and algorithm complexity, (b) inference time constraints, (c) prediction cascades, or (d) model selection and parameter sweeps.

For all these reasons, scaling up learning algorithms is a trending issue. Cases in point are the workshop "PASCAL Large Scale Learning Challenge" held at the 25th International Conference on Machine learning (2008) and the more recent "Large-Scale Kernel Learning Workshop" held at International Conference on Machine learning (2015). Scaling up is desirable because increasing the size of the training set often increases the accuracy of algorithms [60]. In scaling up learning algorithms, the issue is not so much one of speeding up a slow algorithm as one of turning an impracticable algorithm into a practical one. Today, there is a consensus in machine learning and data-mining communities that data volume presents an immediate challenge pertaining to the scalability issue [28]. The crucial point is seldom how fast you can run on a particular problem, but rather how large a problem you can deal with [61].

Scalability is defined as the impact of an increase in the size of the training set on the computational performance of an algorithm in terms of accuracy, training time, and allocated memory. Thus, the challenge is to find a trade-off among these criteria—in other words, to obtain *good enough* solutions as *fast* and as *efficiently* as possible. As explained before, this issue becomes critical in situations in which there are temporal or spatial constraints as happens with real-time applications dealing with large datasets, unapproachable computational problems requiring learning, and initial prototyping requiring rapidly implemented solutions.

The complexity of most discretization methods is in terms of the number of training samples (n). For instance, the complexity of the methods PKID, equal width discretization, and equal frequency discretization commented in section "Popular discretization methods" is $\mathcal{O}(n \log n)$ [23], whereas EMD is $\mathcal{O}(cn \log n)$, c being the number of classes. However, there are discretization methods that are even more computational demanding, such as lazy discretization—$\mathcal{O}(nt)$, t is the number of test samples—that takes days to try to discretize a dataset with more than half a million samples [3]. Then, scalable discretization methods are appearing such as the method presented in Reference 62 that introduces a GPU-based implementation of the class-attribute interdependence maximization (CAIM) algorithm—CAIM, one of the state-of-the art-algorithms for discretizing—that significantly speeds up the discretization process. In Reference 1, authors present a supervised high-dimensional data discretization method that learns the intrinsic geometry of the data to derive the lower representative dimensions by proposing a novel local linear embedding algorithm for dimension reduction. This method has been successfully applied to computer vision and image classification. In the consulted literature, there are not many more works that address this issue, so it can be an interesting line of research.

Similarly, when dealing with a dataset containing a huge number of both features and samples, the scalability of the FS method also assumes crucial importance. As most existing FS techniques were designed to process small-scale data, their efficiency is likely to be downgraded, if not reduced totally, with high-dimensional data.

Few studies have been published regarding filter behavior in small training sets with a large number of features [63–66] and even fewer on the issue of scalability [67]. What studies do exist are mainly focused on scalability in particular applications [68], modifications of existing approaches [69], combinations of instance and FS strategies [70], and online [71] and parallel [72] approaches. A recent paper by Tan et al. [73] describes a new adaptive feature-scaling method applied to several synthetic and real big datasets; based on group FS and multiple kernel learning, it enables scalability to Big Data scenarios. In the area of fuzzy-rough set theory, Jensen and Parthaláin [74] present two different novel ways to address the problem of the complexity of the subset evaluation metric using a neighborhood approximation step and attribute grouping to alleviate the processing overhead and reduce complexity. They conducted a series of experiments on benchmark datasets, including microarray, which demonstrate that much computational effort can be avoided.

Broadly speaking, although most classical univariate FS approaches (with each feature considered separately) have an important advantage in terms of scalability, they ignore feature dependencies and thus potentially perform less well than other FS techniques. Multivariate techniques, in contrast, may improve performance, but at the cost of reduced scalability [75]. The scalability of a FS method is thus crucial and deserves more attention from the scientific community.

One of the solutions commonly adopted to deal with the scalability issue is to distribute the data into several processors, discussed in the following section.

Distributed feature selection

Traditionally, preprocessing techniques and classification are applied in a centralized manner, that is, a single learning model is used to solve a given problem. However, as data may be distributed nowadays, these techniques can take advantage of processing multiple subsets in sequence or concurrently. There are several ways to distribute this task [76] (note: real-time processing will be discussed in section "Real-time processing"):

1. *The data are together in one very large dataset*: The data can be distributed on several processors, an identical FS algorithm can be run on each and the results combined.
2. *The data may be in different datasets in different locations* (e.g., in different parts of a company or even in different cooperating organizations): As for the previous case, an identical FS algorithm can be run on each and the results combined.
3. *Large volumes of data may be arriving in a continuous infinite stream in real time*: If the data are all streaming into a single processor, different parts can be processed by different processors acting in parallel. If the data are streaming into different processors, they can be handled as earlier.
4. *The dataset is not particularly large but different FS methods need to be applied to learn unseen instances and combine results* (by some kind of voting system). The whole dataset may be in a single processor, accessed by identical or different FS methods that access all or part of the data.

As mentioned in section "Scalability," most existing FS methods are not expected to scale efficiently when dealing with millions of features; indeed, they may even become inapplicable. Analogously, some discretization methods may become unfeasible. A possible solution is the one presented at the previous item 1, that is, to distribute the data, run FS on each partition using discretization, if necessary, and then combine the results. The two main approaches to partitioned data distribution are by feature (vertically) or by sample (horizontally). Distributed learning has been used to scale up datasets that are too large for batch learning in terms of samples [77–79]. Although not very common, there have been some developments regarding data distribution by features [80,81]. Even less common, there is a proposal in which data partitioning is both vertical and horizontal [82]. In Reference 31, several methodologies for distributing the FS process based on data complexity measures [83] have been proposed. These novel procedures were able to reduce significantly the runtime while maintaining or even improving classification performance. However, when dealing with big-dimensionality datasets, researchers, of necessity, have to partition by features. In the case of DNA microarray data, the small sample size combined with big dimensionality prevents the use of horizontal partitioning. However, the previous mentioned vertical partitioning methods do not take into account some of the particularities of these datasets, such as the high redundancy among features, as is done in the methods described by Sharma et al. [84] and Bolón-Canedo et al. [30], the latter at a much lower computational cost. As most discretization methods are univariate, vertical partitioning is not a challenge for this issue; however, in gene expression data analysis, the discretization of the data plays a major role in the outcomes of the analysis, and the choice of a suitable discretization scheme may improve the performance of predictive models by reducing the noise inherent to the experimental data [85].

The second approach, which means different data at different locations, implies both horizontally and vertically partitioned data. To the knowledge of the authors, apart from the mentioned paper by Banerjee and Chakravarty [82], there are no other works dealing with this issue; therefore, it is an open challenge for the scientific community. On the contrary, streaming FS has taken great attention, and it will be considered in section "Real-time processing."

The last approach, known as *ensemble learning*, has recently been receiving a great deal of attention [86]. The interest in this approach is due to the fact that high variance, such as commented in section "Scalability," is a problem of FS methods, even when discretization is previously applied. One possible solution is to use an ensemble approach based on combining methods [87,88]. The individual selectors in an ensemble are known as base selectors. If the base selectors are all of the same kind, the ensemble is termed homogeneous. Ensemble FS is accomplished in two steps. First, a set of different feature selectors are applied, on the principle that there is no universally optimal technique and that there may be more than one subset of features that discriminate data similarly. Second, each feature selector produces outputs that are subsequently aggregated via consensus feature ranking, choosing the most frequent features selected, and so on [89].

In spite of being one of the more studied distribution methods, new works constantly appear in this area. For instance, in Reference 90, authors present an ensemble of wrappers based on a forward sequential selection strategy using nearest neighbors as base classifier over a bootstrapped sample and using a majority voting scheme to arrive at predictive results. This approach uses an iterative procedure to automatically select the most compact feature set which consists of features that are strongly bound together. Another ensemble technique that aggregates the consensus properties of various FS methods to develop a more optimal solution is proposed in Reference 91. Authors demonstrate that the ensemble nature of this technique makes it more robust across various classifiers. An integrated algorithm for simultaneous FS and designing of diverse classifiers using a steady-state multiobjective genetic programing is presented in Reference 92. An homogeneous distributed ensemble is presented in Reference 93, which tries to reduce the computational time by parallelizing the task of training the model, improving considerably the training times.

A big concern while sharing data is data privacy. When the data are horizontally partitioned, each party involved in data sharing has information about all the features but for different sets of samples, whereas when the data are vertically partitioned, each party has partial information about all the samples [82]. Although scarce in literature, some approaches of the type are described: in Reference 94, a local distributed privacy preserving algorithm for FS in large peer-to-peer environment is described. Jafer et al. [95] propose a privacy-aware filter-based FS method in which users define a trade-off measure for controlling the amount of privacy and efficacy using filter-based FS techniques. In Reference 96, an iterative approach to minimize sensitive data disclosure by focusing on privacy-aware FS is introduced. Apart from these efforts, it is necessary to develop methods that will allow FS for multiple parties without revealing the data. In References 80 and 81, vertical distributions are used in a novel ensemble approach, with results comparable with centralized approaches, while reducing the amount of communication required between sites and allowing each node to maintain privately its raw data.

As commented at section "The advent of Big Data," several paradigms for performing distributed learning have emerged in the last decade, such as MapReduce [11], Hadoop [13], or Apache Spark [14]. Machine learning researchers are using these paradigms to enhance the FS methods, such as in Reference 97. Developed within the Apache Spark paradigm was MLlib [17], created as a scalable machine learning library containing algorithms. Although it already includes a number of learning algorithms such as SVM and naive Bayes classification, k-means clustering, and so on, as yet, it includes no FS algorithms. This poses a challenge for machine learning researchers, as well as offering an opportunity to initiate a new line of research.

Another open line of research is the use of GPUs to distribute and thus accelerate calculations made in FS and discretization algorithms such in Reference 62. With many applications to physics simulations, signal processing, financial modeling, neural networks, and countless other fields, parallel algorithms running on GPUs often achieve up to 100× speedup over similar CPU algorithms. The challenge now is to take advantage of GPU capabilities to adapt existing state-of-the-art FS and discretization methods to be able to cope effectively and accurately with millions of features. An example will be presented in section "Redesign of an algorithm for feature selection for its use in parallel platforms."

Real-time processing

Data are being collected at an unprecedented fast pace and, correspondingly, need to be processed rapidly. What distinguishes current datasets from earlier ones is automatic data feeds. We do not have just people who are entering information into a computer. Instead, we have computers entering data into each other, examples of applications are web mining, network monitoring, and so on [98]. Then, we need sophisticated methods that are capable of dealing with vast amounts of data in real time, for example, for spam detection and video/image detection [28].

Classical batch learning algorithms cannot deal with continuously flowing data streams, which require online approaches. Online learning [99], which is the process of continuously revising and refining a model by incorporating new data on-demand, has become a trending area in the last few years, because it solves important problems for processes occurring in time (e.g., a stock value given its history and other external factors). The mapping process is updated in real time, as more samples are obtained. Online learning can also be useful for extremely large-scale datasets, as a possible solution might be to learn data in a sequential fashion.

Although discretization is a well-known topic in data analysis and machine learning, most of the works refer to a batch discretization in which all the examples are available for discretization. Although using the title of Reference 100, and contrary to popular belief, Incremental Discretization can be sound, computationally efficient and extremely useful for streaming data. However, there are very few works that refer to incremental discretization [101–103] or similar approaches, such as online discretization, suggesting an interesting line of research. The work in Reference 101 reimplemented three classical methods—the k-means discretizer, the χ^2 filter, and a one-layer artificial neural network—to be able to tackle online data, showing promising results on both synthetic and real datasets. In Reference 102, Gama and Pinto propose a new method to perform incremental discretization based on two layers. The first layer receives the sequence of input data and keeps some statistics on the data using many more intervals than required. Based on the statistics stored by the first layer, the second layer creates the final discretization using any base discretization method: *equal frequency, recursive entropy discretization, chimerge,* and so on. A novel incremental discretization method for naive Bayes (NB), incremental flexible frequency discretization, is presented in Reference 103. Incremental flexible frequency discretization discretizes values of a quantitative attribute into a sequence of intervals of flexible sizes.

Similarly, online FS (OFS) has not received the same attention as online learning [99]. Nonetheless, a few studies exist that describe attempts to select relevant features in a scenario in which both new samples and new features arise. Zhang et al. [104] proposed an incremental feature subset selection algorithm that, originating in the Boolean matrix technique, efficiently selects useful features for the given data objective. Nevertheless, the efficiency of the

FS method was not tested with an incremental machine learning algorithm. Katakis et al. [105] proposed the idea of a dynamic feature space, whereby features selected from an initial collection of training documents are subsequently considered by the learner during system operation. However, features may vary over time and an initial training set is often not available in some applications. Katakis et al. [105] combined incremental FS with what they called a feature-based learning algorithm to deal with online learning in high-dimensional data streams. This same framework was applied to the special case of concept drift [106] inherent to textual data streams (i.e., the appearance of new predictive words over time). The problem with this approach is that features are assumed to have discrete values. Perkins et al. [107] described a novel and flexible approach, called grafting, which treats the selection of suitable features as an integral part of learning a predictor in a regularized learning framework. What makes grafting suitable for large problems is that it operates in an incremental iterative fashion, gradually building up a feature set while training a predictor model using gradient descent. Perkins and Theiler [108] tackled the problem of features arriving one at a time rather than being available from the outset; their approach, called OFS [109], assumes that, for whatever reason, it is not worthwhile waiting until all features have arrived before learning begins. They thus derived a *good enough* mapping function from inputs to outputs based on a subset of features seen to date. The potential of OFS in the image-processing domain was demonstrated by applying it to the problem of edge detection [110]. A promising alternative method, called online streaming FS, selects strongly relevant and nonredundant features [111]. In yet another approach, two novel OFS methods use relevance to select features on the fly; redundancy is only later taken into account, when these features come via streaming, but the number of training examples remains fixed [112]. Finally, the literature contains a number of studies referring to OFS and classification. One is an online learning algorithm for feature extraction and classification, implemented for impact acoustics signals to sort hazelnut kernels [113]. Another, by Levi and Ullman [114], proposed classifying images by ongoing FS, although their approach only uses a small subset of the training data at each stage. Yet another describes OFS performed on the basis of the weights assigned to each classifier input [115]. A special and interesting case is OFS, which is especially useful in those cases in which concept-drift situations may appear, producing changes in the relevance of selected features over time.

As can be seen, OFS has been dealt with mostly on an individual basis, that is, by preselecting features in a step independent of the online machine learning step, or by performing OFS without subsequent online classification. Therefore, achieving real-time analysis and prediction for high-dimensional datasets remains a challenge for computational intelligence on portable platforms. The question now is to find flexible FS methods capable of modifying the selected subset of features as new training samples arrive, and it becomes even a more difficult issue if these features have to be discretized.

Visualization and interpretability

In recent years, several dimensionality reduction techniques for data visualization and preprocessing have been developed. However, although the aim may be better visualization, most techniques have the limitation that the features being visualized are transformations of the original features [116–118]. Thus, when model interpretability is important, FS is the preferred technique for dimensionality reduction.

A model is only as good as its features, for which reason features have played and will continue to play a preponderant role in model interpretability. Users have a twofold need for interpretability and transparency in FS and model creation processes: (i) They need more interactive model visualizations in which they can change input parameters to better interact with the model and visualize future scenarios and (ii) they need more interactive FS processes in which, using interactive visualizations, they are empowered to iterate through different feature subsets rather than be tied to a specific subset chosen by an algorithm.

Some recent works describe using FS to improve the interpretability of models obtained in different fields. One example is a method for the automatic and iterative refinement of a recommender system, in which the FS step selects the best characteristics of the initial model to automatically refine it [119]. Yet another is a generative topographic mapping-based data visualization approach that estimates feature saliency simultaneously as the visualization model is trained [120]. Krause et al. [121] describe a tool in which visualization helps users develop a predictive model of their problem by allowing them to rank features (according to predefined scores), combine features, and detect similarities between dimensions. In *Prospector* [122], data scientists can understand how features affect the prediction overall because it provides interactive partial dependence diagnostics. In the context of *feature ideation*, that is, thinking of new features, Brooks et al. [123] present FeatureInsight, an interactive visual analytics tool for building new dictionary features (semantically related groups of words) for text classification problems.

However, data are everywhere, continuously increasing, and heterogeneous. We are witnessing a form of Diogenes syndrome referring to data: organizations are collecting and storing tonnes of data, but most do not have the tools or the resources to access and generate strategic reports and insights from their data. Organizations need to gather data in a meaningful way, so as to evolve from a data-rich/knowledge-poor scenario to a data-rich/knowledge-rich scenario. As illustrated at the "2016 Workshop on Human Interpretability in Machine Learning," the latest trend in machine learning is to use very sophisticated systems involving deep neural networks with many complex layers, kernel methods, and large ensembles of diverse classifiers. Although such approaches produce impressive, state-of-the-art prediction accuracies, they give little comfort to decision makers, who must trust their output blindly because very little insight is available about their inner workings and the provenance of how the decision was made. Then, the challenge is to enable user-friendly visualization of results so as to enhance interpretability and so, it is in this way that machine learning methods can have impact on consequential real-world applications. The complexity implied by Big Data applications also underscores the need to limit the growth in visualization complexity. Thus, even though FS and visualization have been dealt with in relative isolation from each other in most research to date, the visualization of data features may have an important role to play in real-world high-dimensionality scenarios. However, it is also important to bear in mind that, although visualization tools are increasingly used to interpret and make complex data understandable, the quality of associated decision-making is often impaired due to the fact that the tools fail to address the role played by heuristics, biases, and others in human–computer interactive settings. Therefore, interactive tools similar to that described by Krause et al. [121] are an interesting line of research.

Case studies

As stated earlier, data preprocessing is necessary as real data might be, and frequently are, affected by inconsistency, incompleteness, noise, redundancy, and so on, and thus, it is necessary to carry out a previous data cleansing and conditioning step that might integrate cleaning, integration, discretization reduction, FS, and so on to be able to obtain quality data that can be used in data-mining processes to derive knowledge of interest for a given field (Figure 10.3). Several preprocessing techniques have been receiving attention lately for their capacity in data reduction, critical in the present scenarios of Big Data. In the following, we will briefly describe some approaches in discretization and FS for confronting the high dimensionality of data.

A parallel implementation of the minimum description length-based discretizer

As a brief reminder, discretization is a process that groups continuous values in a number of discrete intervals, thus reducing data sizes, and allowing to prepare it for further analysis. Besides, some algorithms for classification or FS, for example, only accept categorical attributes as input. Furthermore, discretization allows in general for a more accurate and quick learning process [124]. In the process of discretization, several decisions, such as how many continuous values should be grouped in an interval, how many intervals are adequate for a given problem, or where should the cut-points be established in the scale of values, are far from trivial. Several discretization algorithms have been developed in accordance [2,124–126], such as those mentioned in section

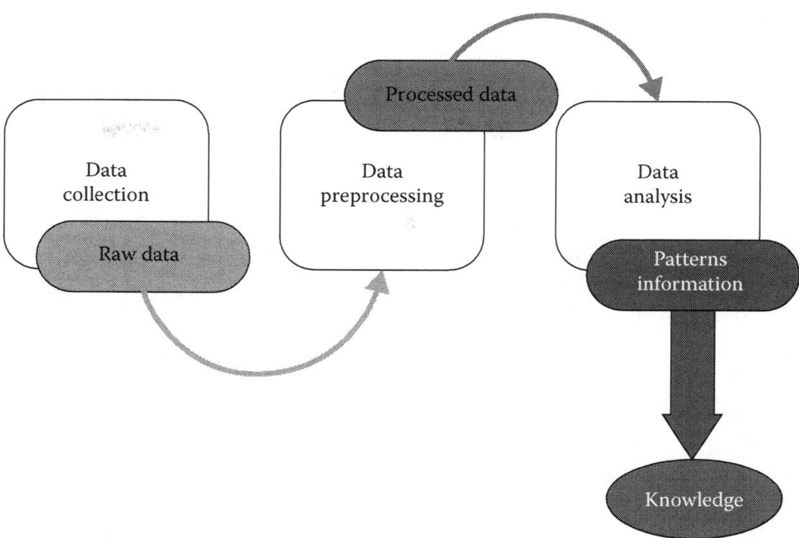

FIGURE 10.3: Data preprocessing.

"Popular discretization methods." Among them, it is worth mentioning the entropy-based developed by Fayyad and Irani [26], which is a global, static, and supervised method that has become very popular, and it is in fact the discretization method used by default in the popular Weka learning platform [27]. This method will be described briefly here, as it has been one of the first discretization algorithms adapted to distributed environments [2], something that could appear to be simple but in fact it is not, due to the recursive nature of the method and the high dependence among threshold candidates. The main problem of discretization consists in finding the thresholds that determine in which intervals should be grouped the different possible values of the variables. The process followed for each variable to be discretized is the following:

- The values of each attribute, together with their corresponding class, are ordered.
- The candidate points are to be determined and sorted. A candidate point is the middle point between two different values of the attribute, the classes of which are also different. The sorting operation is a time-consuming operation.
- The candidate values are evaluated, and this operation is the most time consuming, as in the worst case, it implies a complete evaluation of entropy for all points. The evaluation of each point implies calculating the entropy of the classes in both sides of the point; thus, each candidate point depends on the other candidates. Once all candidate points are evaluated, the best is chosen and the values are partitioned accordingly.

- The algorithm is executed recursively until the stop criteria are met. In our implementation, to the original stop criteria of MDL principle, it has been added a limitation in the maximum number of intervals per variable.

Detailed descriptions of the procedures used and the algorithms designed to adapt the original discretization method to the Spark platform [14] are available in Ramírez et al. [2], in which it is shown that the transformation of the original iterativity of the algorithm in a single-step computation by a complete redesign enhances its performance, making it around 270 times faster while improving accuracy, thus, paving the way for discretization in large-scale online problems. Two binary datasets were employed to test the efficiency of the proposed redesign: ECBDL and Epsilon (Table 10.1). The first one is highly imbalanced, and thus a previous oversampling method has to be applied to equalize the number of samples for both classes. Epsilon dataset contains only numerical, whereas ECBDL contains both numerical and categorical attributes.

The evaluation criterion used was the efficiency of the discretization process (Table 10.2). Moreover, accuracy and time efficiency of posterior classification step were checked, showing [2] that both improve using the previous discretization algorithm proposed.

Redesign of an algorithm for feature selection for its use in parallel platforms

FS is another preprocessing technique that has gained prominence lately, due to its capacity to reduce dimensionality on datasets while maintaining the original attributes, and thus permitting better explanations of the retained variables in fields such as bioinformatics. There are several FS algorithms available [4,5,34], but mRMR is one of the most well-known and used in several fields as it obtains highly accurate results [40]. The counterpart is its

TABLE 10.1: A Summary of the characteristics of the two datasets used in the experimental study

Dataset	Attributes	Training samples	Testing samples
ECBDL14	631	65,003,913	2897,917
Epsilon	2000	400,000	100,000

TABLE 10.2: Time (in seconds) of the discretizer implementation for the two datasets used in the experimental study

Dataset	Sequential	Distributed	Speed-up
ECBDL14	295.51	1087	271.9
Epsilon	5764	476	12.1

computational complexity, thus requiring important computation times in complex high-dimensional domains [34]. mRMR scales quadratically with the number of features, and linearly with the number of samples. The method relies on finding the maximum dependency between the set of features and the class using MI. However, implementation of MI criterion is not straightforward for high-dimensional spaces, as the estimation of multivariate density implies expensive computations. Alternatively, the maximum relevance criterion could be used, but this solution comes with another problem, as its use might imply appearance of redundant features, and thus the minimum redundancy criteria should be added. The combination of both criteria leads to mRMR. In Reference 32, an extension of the method, named fast-mRMR, which allows boosting its performance through several optimizations is described. In Reference 127, a package is provided including the following:

1. A sequential version in C++. Several optimizations were made to improve performance of the original method:

    - First, the implementation of it as a greedy search, as it will not affect the final result, whereas the original complexity will be transformed into an iterative process (linear order), limited by a small number of iterations (the number of features selected).
    - Accumulating the redundancy in each iteration, and thus avoiding computing the MI between each pair of features, and needing only to calculate it between the nonselected features and the last selected feature.
    - Caching marginal computations to avoid computing marginal probabilities in each iteration.
    - Change the data access pattern from the original feature-wise to a row-wise version.

    The results obtained by the method are the same as those of the original one, as it was to be expected, but the time reduction is considerable. For more details, see Reference 32. The comparison between this new implementation, Fast-mRMR, and the original mRMR was performed using the datasets in Table 10.3, which were previously employed in the original mRMR article validation [40].

TABLE 10.3: Datasets used in the experimental comparison

Dataset	Samples	Features	Speedup
Lung	73	326	387.83
Lymphoma	96	4027	53.48
Leukemia	72	7071	28.83
Colon	62	2001	108.76
NCI	60	9173	19.51

As mRMR is a ranker method, it returns an ordered ranking of the features, and thus a threshold needs to be established, and the authors have opted for retaining the top 50, 100, 200, and 400 features. For space reasons, only the two extreme values are shown in Figure 10.4. As can be seen, fast-mRMR obtained much better performance results for the 5 datasets, with an average improvement of 20 times faster for 50 features, 50 for 100 features, 116 for 200 features, and 159 for 400 features. In terms of complexity, as the number of features grows, the time

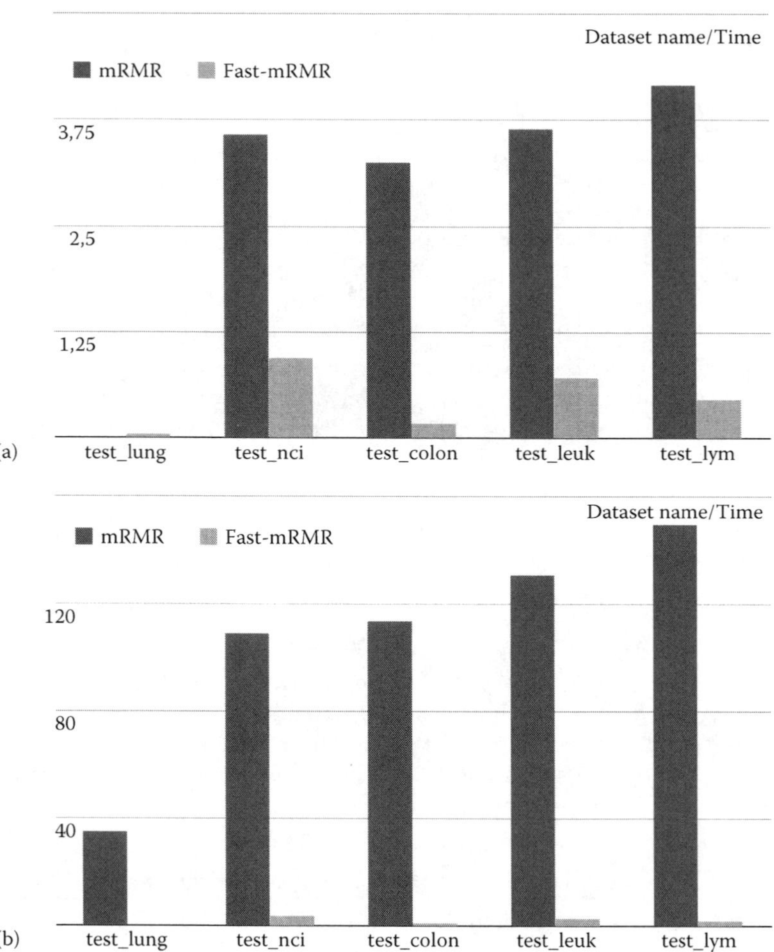

FIGURE 10.4: Time versus number of selected features between the proposed implementation and the original mRMR. (a) 50 Features selected, (b) 400 Features selected.

increases linearly in the case of the fast-mRMR, whereas in the original mRMR, time increases polinomically. Beside performance, scalability was also tested in terms of number of different values for the features, number of samples, and number of features, using synthetic datasets. The results that can be checked at Reference 32 showed that the complexity of Fast-mRMR increases linearly, whereas that of mRMR does it polinomically regarding the number of possible values for a feature. Similar results were obtained for the scalability regarding the number of patterns. As a result of this, finer discretizations can be made on the original data when using the proposed implementation, without degrading the performance in terms of time and accuracy.

2. A parallel version in GPU-CUDA (Graphic Processing Unit-Compute Unified Device Architecture) [128].

   The use of GPUs for rendering is well known, but their power for general parallel computation has only recently been explored [129–131]. Parallel algorithms running on GPUs can often achieve up to 100% speedup over similar CPU algorithms, with many existing applications for physics simulations, signal processing, financial modeling, neural networks, and countless other fields. For that reason, it is worthwhile to adapt mRMR to be executed in GPU, so as to be employed when data size exceeds the size in which the CPU algorithm does not behave adequately. CUDA is a parallel computing platform and programing model created by Nvidia and implemented by the GPUs that they manufacture [132]. CUDA gives direct access to the virtual instruction set and memory of the parallel computational elements in GPUs. In CUDA, the computation is distributed in a grid of thread blocks, with all blocks containing the same number of threads, that execute a special program called kernel on the device. A kernel is designed to be executed in parallel on multiple threads that are grouped in blocks. Only threads in the same block can communicate directly and synchronize each other.

   A kernel can make use of registers, shared memory, and global memory to make its calculations and communicate with other threads. The first two levels have very fast access but, unfortunately are very scarce. If you were to use too much of these resources, many processing units are to remain unemployed during a kernel execution due to a lack of resources. On the other hand, global memory is usually not limited for practical purposes, but its access is too slow, degrading the overall performance. Thus, the kernel must be carefully designed to balance (a) the use of shared memory and registers, (b) active processing units, and (c) reducing the number of global memory accesses and optimizing these access patterns. In fast-mRMR, a hybrid approach for MI and marginal probability calculations based on previous studies has been adopted.

TABLE 10.4: Synthetic datasets for testing GPU scalability

Dataset	Samples	Features	Values
a-samples	50	1000	251
b-samples	500	1000	251
c-samples	5000	1000	251
d-samples	50,000	1000	251
f-samples	500,000	1000	251

This hybrid strategy uses a different kernel depending on the number of possible outcomes, in three different intervals: (i) below 64 different outcomes, as current GPUs can make use of the full set of processing units without making use of global memory; (ii) for the interval 64–256, as a lack of shared memory would produce a sharp decrease in processing units usage; and (iii) if the number of possible outcomes exceeds 256, then shared memory is no longer an option by itself, so the calculations should be partitioned, and a different strategy should be followed. For more detailed information, please see Reference 32. To test the GPU performance regarding the number of possible values, synthetic datasets (Table 10.4) were used, discretized in 30 and 200 possible values. Moreover, two real datasets, Knowledge Discovery and Data Mining (KDD) Tools Conference Cup 99 and Higgs, were employed to test the algorithm under real conditions. The KDD Cup 99 dataset [133] is a dataset derived from the DARPA dataset that has about 5 million samples and 41 features and was used for the KDD Cup 99 Competition. Each record represents a Transmission Control Protocol/Internet Protocol (TCP/IP) connection that is composed of 41 features that are both qualitative and quantitative in nature. The Higgs dataset, available on the UCI repository [45], contains 11 million samples with 28 features containing physical data produced using Monte Carlo simulations. The first 21 features are kinematic properties measured by the particle detectors in the accelerator. The last seven features are functions of the first 21 features; these are high-level features derived by physicists to help one discriminate between two classes.

Figure 10.5 shows the time complexity versus the number of patterns for the case in which the dataset has a high number of possible values (200, which is the worst case for GPU implementation, see Figure 1.5a), and the case in which the dataset has a small number of possible values (30, which is the best case for GPU implementation, see Figure 1.5b). These figures show that it is worth using the GPU implementation from a million patterns on.

Finally, and to show the benefits of using the GPU implementation with real datasets, in Figure 10.6, we show the time needed for both fast-mRMR implementations (GPU and CPU) for KDD Cup dataset

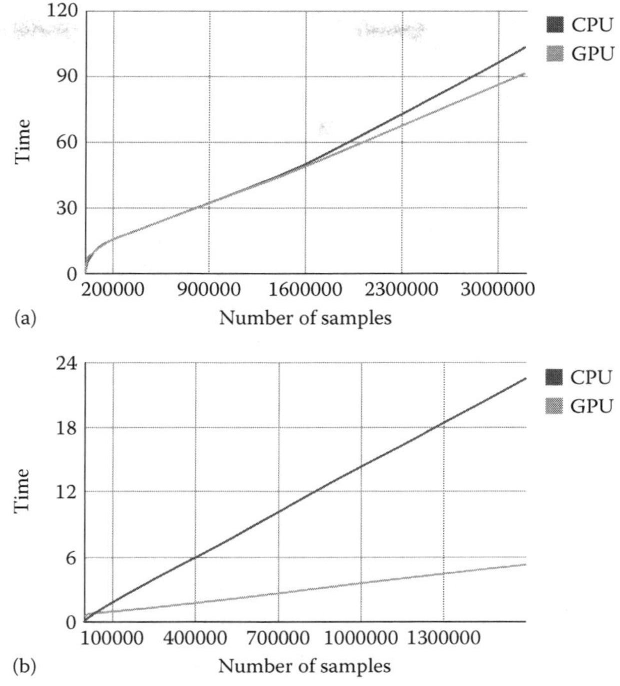

FIGURE 10.5: Results of comparing GPU and CPU implementations of fast-mRMR for the worst and best cases, regarding GPU. (a) Worst situation, near 256 possible values and (b) best situation, low number of possible values.

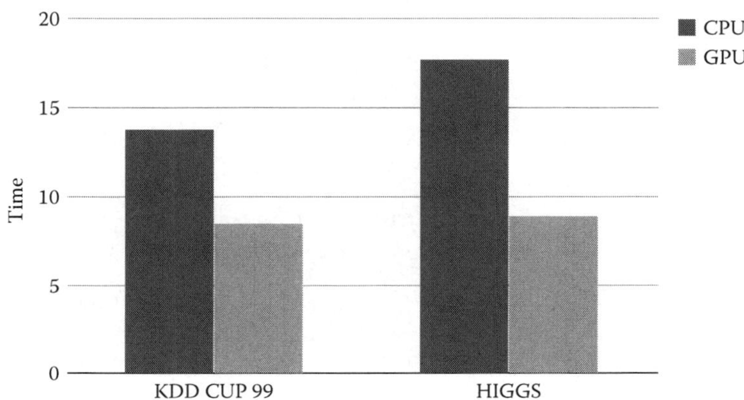

FIGURE 10.6: Times for CPU and GPU implementations for KDD Cup 99 and Higgs datasets.

TABLE 10.5: Datasets for testing Spark versus CPU versions of mRMR

Dataset	Features	Samples	CPU time (s)	Spark time (s)	Speedup
ECBDL14	631	65,083,913	11,281.27	2420.94	4.65
Epsilon	2000	400,000	2553.79	542.05	4.71
Kddb	29,890,095	19,264,097	—	2789.55	—

Source: C. Chang and C. Lin, LIBSVM data: Classification, regression, and multi-label, https://www.csie.ntu.edu.tw/cjlin/libsvmtools/datasets/. Accessed: November 2016; C. Chang and C. Lin, *ACM Trans. Intell. Syst. Technol.*, 2, 1–27, 2011.

and Higgs dataset. In those cases, the GPU version runs around 1.6 times faster than the CPU optimized implementation, thus accelerating up to 600 times the original algorithm in the best case.

3. A distributed Apache Spark version

   Maintaining the main ideas, mRMR was also adapted for its use under the Spark paradigm [14]. To do so, three new operations are needed to be incorporated. First, the local matrix provided by each partition of the original data was transposed with the aim of caching it (in memory) in this new format, and reuse it in the following steps (leveraging for data locality). Afterward, new matrices in each block/partition with one row per feature, instead of one row per instance, are produced. Then, all the blocks for the same feature are grouped in the same set of partitions. Once data are in a columnar format, the histograms for all the candidate features are computed in a such a way in which data locality is preserved, and thus each feature has all the information needed to compute the relevance or redundancy independently. Finally, the final histograms are obtained by aggregating all partial matrices. Then, MI values should be calculated to rank the final features. The detailed procedure can be read in Reference 32, and the results are shown in Table 10.5. As can be seen, the reduction of time is very important, an indispensable factor in the nowadays Big Data scenario.

Other distributed and incremental feature selection approaches

Another set of interesting approaches for scaling up FS methods are those based on adopting distributed, incremental, or ensemble solutions. Regarding the distributed approaches, two different situations can be confronted using this framework, as was described in section "Distributed feature selection": (i) Data might be already distributed in origin, and it might be illegal or antieconomic to gather all data at a single, central node, or privacy concerns are to be considered, as mentioned before, and (ii) as most FS methods do not scale well, the data might be distributed into several different processors, do the FS and learning in parallel, and then combine the several results obtained. Therefore, data are partitioned in both cases, and two different situations can take place (if already distributed) or can be done: vertical or horizontal partitioning. Some distributed approaches [30,31,80–82,94] and some others based on ensembles or parallel platforms [33,93,97] that have shown satisfactory results were already described in more detail in section "Distributed feature selection." A special and interesting case is OFS and is also described in detail in section "Real-time processing." Although most works face the problem of FS and classification separately [109,112], as after an online (and not online) FS process the set of relevant features might change not only in its content but also in its number, and thus the learning model should have the capacity of updating itself both to new samples and new features. In Reference 101, an original online pipeline is proposed in which both FS (with previous online discretization) and classification are achieved. Experimental results showed that classification error decreases over time, adapting to the appearance of new data. Besides, the number of features is reduced, whereas classification accuracy is maintained.

Conclusion and future research directions

The need for preprocessing techniques has increased dramatically in recent years to deal with Big Data scenarios, in which it is necessary to cope with an unprecedented large number of features and samples. Therefore, to be able to extract useful information from all the data generated, preprocessing techniques are more needed than ever, although the enormous size of data makes them, in some cases, inapplicable.

The current chapter analyzed two of the most popular preprocessing techniques: discretization and FS. Although there exist a wide number of methods in the literature, the choice of an appropriate one for a given problem is important. For example, it is necessary to bear in mind that the use of one or another discretization method prior to FS—as some FS methods were developed to work with discrete data—affects the results of the FS process [135,136].

Moreover, we have revealed the new challenges that researchers need to face, as there is still a lack of studies dealing with the evolution of data dimensionality. However, these challenges must be also seen as new opportunities for machine learning researchers. The need for scalable yet efficient preprocessing techniques is obvious, as the existing methods are sometimes inapplicable. Specifically, the society has expressed new necessities, such as in the areas of distributed learning and real-time processing, in which an important gap that still needs to be filled is developing.

Finally, we have presented several case studies in which new approaches in discretization and FS have been developed to confront the high dimensionality of the data. There is no doubt that the explosion in data dimensionality points to a number of hot spots for machine learning researchers to launch new lines of research.

References

[1] Y. Sang, H. Qi, K. Li, Y. Jin, D. Yan, and S. Gao. An effective discretization method for disposing high-dimensional data. *Information Sciences*, 270:73–91, 2014.

[2] S. Ramírez-Gallego, S. García, H. Mouriño-Taln, D. Martnez-Rego, V. Bolón-Canedo, A. Alonso-Betanzos, J. M. Benítez, and F. Herrera. Data discretization: Taxonomy and big data challenge. *Wiley Interdisciplinary Reviews: Data Mining and Knowledge Discovery*, 6(1):5–21, 2016.

[3] Y. Yang and G. I. Webb. A comparative study of discretization methods for naive-Bayes classifiers. In *Proceedings of PKAW*, Vol. 2002. Citeseer, 2002.

[4] V. Bolón-Canedo, N. Sánchez-Maroño, and A. Alonso-Betanzos. *Feature Selection for High-Dimensional Data*. Heidelberg, Germany: Springer, 2015.

[5] I. Guyon. *Feature Extraction: Foundations and Applications*. Berlin, Germany: Springer, 2006.

[6] L. Yu and H. Liu. Efficient feature selection via analysis of relevance and redundancy. *The Journal of Machine Learning Research*, 5:1205–1224, 2004.

[7] V. Turner, J. F. Gantz, D. Reinsel, and S. Minton. The digital universe of opportunities: Rich data and the increasing value of the internet of things. Boston, MA: IDC Analyze the Future, 2014.

[8] D. Laney. 3d data management: Controlling data volume, velocity and variety. *META Group Research Note*, 6:70, 2001.

[9] I. A. T. Hashem, I. Yaqoob, N. B. Anuar, S. Mokhtar, A. Gani, and S. U. Khan. The rise of big data on cloud computing: Review and open research issues. *Information Systems*, 47:98–115, 2015.

[10] R. E. Bryant, R. H. Katz, and E. D. Lazowska. Big data computing: Creating revolutionary breakthroughs in commerce, science and society. *A white paper prepared for the Computing Community Consortium committee of the Computing Research Association*, 2008.

[11] J. Dean and S. Ghemawat. MapReduce: Simplified data processing on large clusters. *Communications of the ACM*, 51(1):107–113, 2008.

[12] T. White. *Hadoop: The Definitive Guide.* Sebastopol, CA: O'Reilly Media, 2012.

[13] Apache Hadoop Project. https://hadoop.apache.org/. Accessed: November 2016.

[14] Apache Spark: Lightning-fast cluster computing. http://spark.apache.org/. Accessed: November 2016.

[15] H. Karau, A. Konwinski, P. Wendell, and M. Zaharia. *Learning Spark: Lightning-Fast Big Data Analysis.* Sebastopol, CA: O'Reilly Media, 2015.

[16] Apache Mahout Project. http://mahout.apache.org/. Accessed: November 2016.

[17] Machine Learning Library (MLlib) for Spark. https://spark.apache.org/docs/1.2.0/mllib-guide.html. Accessed: November 2016.

[18] V. Bolón-Canedo, N. Sánchez-Maroño, and A. Alonso-Betanzos. Recent advances and emerging challenges of feature selection in the context of big data. *Knowledge-Based Systems*, 86:33–45, 2015.

[19] D. L. Donoho. High-dimensional data analysis: The curses and blessings of dimensionality. In *AMS Math Challenges Lecture-Math Challenges of the 21st Century*, pp. 1–32. Providence, RI, 2000.

[20] X. Wu, V. Kumar, J. R. Quinlan, J. Ghosh, Q. Yang, H. Motoda, G. J. McLachlan et al. Top 10 algorithms in data mining. *Knowledge and Information Systems*, 14(1):1–37, 2008.

[21] R. Agrawal and R. Srikant. Fast algorithms for mining association rules. In *Proceedings of the 20th International Conference on Very Large Data Bases, VLDB*, 1215, pp. 487–499, 1994.

[22] J. R. Quinlan. *C4. 5: Programs for Machine Learning.* San Francisco, CA: Morgan Kaufmann, 1993.

[23] Y. Yang and G. I. Webb. Discretization for naive-bayes learning: Managing discretization bias and variance. *Machine learning*, 74(1):39–74, 2009.

[24] H.-W. Hu, Y.-L. Chen, and K. Tang. A dynamic discretization approach for constructing decision trees with a continuous label. *IEEE Transactions on Knowledge and Data Engineering*, 21(11):1505–1514, 2009.

[25] X. Wu, X. Zhu, G-Q. Wu, and W. Ding. Data mining with big data. *IEEE Transactions on Knowledge and Data Engineering*, 26(1):97–107, 2014.

[26] U. Fayyad and K. Irani. Multi-interval discretization of continuous-valued attributes for classification learning. In *Proceedings of the 13th International Joint Conference on Artificial Intelligence* (*IJCAI*), pp. 1022–1029, 1993.

[27] M. Hall, E. Frank, G. Holmes, B. Pfahringer, P. Reutemann, and I. H. Witten. The weka data mining software: An update. *ACM SIGKDD Explorations Newsletter*, 11(1):10–18, 2009.

[28] Y. Zhai, Y. Ong, and I. Tsang. The emerging big dimensionality. *Computational Intelligence Magazine, IEEE*, 9(3):14–26, 2014.

[29] R. Bellman. *Dynamic Programming*. Princeton, NJ: Princeton University Press, p. 18, 1957.

[30] V. Bolón-Canedo, N. Sánchez-Maroño, and A. Alonso-Betanzos. Distributed feature selection: An application to microarray data classification. *Applied Soft Computing*, 30:136–150, 2015.

[31] L. Morán-Fernández, V. Bolón-Canedo, and A. Alonso-Betanzos. Centralized vs. distributed feature selection methods based on data complexity measures. *Knowledge-Based Systems*, 117:27–45, 2017.

[32] S. Ramírez-Gallego, I. Lastra, D. Martínez-Rego, V. Bolón-Canedo, J. M. Benítez, F. Herrera, and A. Alonso-Betanzos. Fast-mRMR: Fast minimum redundancy maximum relevance algorithm for high-dimensional big data. *International Journal of Intelligent Systems*, 32(2):134–152, 2017.

[33] C. Eiras-Franco, V. Bolón-Canedo, S. Ramos, J. González-Domnguez, A. Alonso-Betanzos, and J. Touriño. Multithreaded and Spark parallelization of feature selection filters. *Journal of Computational Science*, 17:609-619, 2016.

[34] V. Bolón-Canedo, N. Sánchez-Maroño, and A. Alonso-Betanzos. A review of feature selection methods on synthetic data. *Knowledge and Information Systems*, 34(3):483–519, 2013.

[35] M. A. Hall. Correlation-based feature selection for machine learning. PhD thesis, The University of Waikato, 1999.

[36] M. Dash and H. Liu. Consistency-based search in feature selection. *Artificial Intelligence*, 151(1):155–176, 2003.

[37] Z. Zhao and H. Liu. Searching for interacting features. *IJCAI*, 7:1156–1161, 2007.

[38] J. R. Quinlan. Induction of decision trees. *Machine learning*, 1(1): 81–106, 1986.

[39] I. Kononenko. Estimating attributes: Analysis and extensions of relief. In F. Bergadano and L. De Raedt (Eds.), *Machine Learning: ECML-94*, pp. 171–182. Berlin, Germany: Springer, 1994.

[40] H. Peng, F. Long, and C. Ding. Feature selection based on mutual information criteria of max-dependency, max-relevance, and min-redundancy. *IEEE Transactions on Pattern Analysis and Machine Intelligence*, 27(8):1226–1238, 2005.

[41] I. Guyon, J. Weston, S. Barnhill, and V. Vapnik. Gene selection for cancer classification using support vector machines. *Machine Learning*, 46(1–3):389–422, 2002.

[42] Twitter Blog, Dispatch from the Denver Debate. http://blog.twitter.com/2012/10/dispatch-from-denver-debate.html. Accessed: November 2016.

[43] F. Michel. How many photos are uploaded to flickr every day, month, year? https://www.flickr.com/photos/franckmichel/6855169886/. Accessed: November 2016.

[44] J. Leskovec, A. Rajaraman, and J. D. Ullman. *Mining of Massive Datasets.* Cambridge, UK: Cambridge University Press, 2014.

[45] A. Asuncion and D. J. Newman. 2007. UCI machine learning repository. http://archive.ics.uci.edu/ml/index.php. Accessed: June 2017.

[46] C. Chang and C. Lin. LIBSVM data: Classification, regression, and multi-label. https://www.csie.ntu.edu.tw/cjlin/libsvmtools/datasets/. Accessed: November 2016.

[47] V. Bolón-Canedo, N. Sánchez-Maroño, A. Alonso-Betanzos, J. M. Bentez, and F. Herrera. A review of microarray datasets and applied feature selection methods. *Information Sciences*, 282:111–135, 2014.

[48] National center for biotechnology information. https://www.ncbi.nlm.nih.gov/snp. Accessed: November 2016.

[49] S. Nogueira and G. Brown. Measuring the stability of feature selection. In P. Frasconi, N. Landwehr, G. Manco, and J. Vreeken (Eds.), *Joint European Conference on Machine Learning and Knowledge Discovery in Databases*, pp. 442–457. Cham, Switzerland: Springer, 2016.

[50] A. Kalousis, J. Prados, and M. Hilario. Stability of feature selection algorithms: A study on high-dimensional spaces. *Knowledge and Information Systems*, 12(8):95–116, 2007.

[51] Z. He and W. Yu. Stable feature selection for biomarker discovery. *Computational Biology and Chemistry*, 34(4):215–225, 2010.

[52] S. Y. Kim. Effects of sample size on robustness and prediction accuracy of a prognostic gene signature. *BMC Bioinformatics*, 10(1):1, 2009.

[53] S. Loscalzo, L. Yu, and C. Ding. Consensus group stable feature selection. In *Proceedings of the 15th ACM SIGKDD International Conference on Knowledge Discovery and Data Mining*, pp. 567–576. ACM, 2009.

[54] L. I. Kuncheva. A stability index for feature selection. In *Proceedings of the 25th IASTED International Multi-Conference Artificial Intelligence and Applications*, Innsbruck, Austria, pp. 421–427, 2007.

[55] L. Yu, C. Ding, and S. Loscalzo. Stable feature selection via dense feature groups. In *Proceedings of the 14th ACM SIGKDD International Conference on Knowledge Discovery and Data Mining*, pp. 803–811. ACM, 2008.

[56] N. Meinshausen and P. Bühlmann. Stability selection. *Journal of the Royal Statistical Society: Series B (Statistical Methodology)*, 72(4): 417–473, 2010.

[57] R. D. Shah and R. J. Samworth. Variable selection with error control: another look at stability selection. *Journal of the Royal Statistical Society: Series B (Statistical Methodology)*, 75(1):55–80, 2013.

[58] Y. Li, J. Si, G. Zhou, S. Huang, and S. Chen. Frel: A stable feature selection algorithm. *IEEE Transactions on Neural Networks and Learning Systems*, 26(7):1388–1402, 2015.

[59] R. Bekkerman, M. Bilenko, and J. Langford. *Scaling Up Machine Learning: Parallel and Distributed Approaches*. Cambridge, UK: Cambridge University Press, 2011.

[60] J. Catlett. Megainduction: Machine learning on very large databases. PhD thesis, University of Sydney Australia, 1991.

[61] F. Provost and V. Kolluri. A survey of methods for scaling up inductive algorithms. *Data Mining and Knowledge Discovery*, 3(2):131–169, 1999.

[62] A. Cano, S. Ventura, and K. J. Cios. Scalable CAIM discretization on multiple GPUs using concurrent kernels. *The Journal of Supercomputing*, 69(1):273–292, 2014.

[63] G. Brown, A. Pocock, M. Zhao, and M. Luján. Conditional likelihood maximisation: A unifying framework for information theoretic feature selection. *The Journal of Machine Learning Research*, 13(1):27–66, 2012.

[64] A. Fahad, Z. Tari, I. Khalil, I. Habib, and H. Alnuweiri. Toward an efficient and scalable feature selection approach for internet traffic classification. *Computer Networks*, 57:2040–2057, 2013.

[65] G. Gulgezen, Z. Cataltepe, and L. Yu. Stable and accurate feature selection. In W. Buntine, M. Grobelnik, D. Mladenić, and J. Shawe-Taylor (Eds.), *Machine Learning and Knowledge Discovery in Databases*, pp. 455–468. Berlin, Germany: Springer, 2009.

[66] D. Dernoncourt, B. Hanczar, and J. D. Zucker. Analysis of feature selection stability on high dimension and small sample data. *Computational Statistics & Data Analysis*, 71:681–693, 2014.

[67] D. Peteiro-Barral, V. Bolón-Canedo, A. Alonso-Betanzos, B. Guijarro-Berdiñas, and N. Sánchez-Maroño. Scalability analysis of filter-based methods for feature selection. *Advances in Smart Systems Research*, 2(1):21–26, 2012.

[68] D. Luo, F. Wang, J. Sun, M. Markatou, J. Hu, and S. Ebadollahi. Sor: Scalable orthogonal regression for non-redundant feature selection and its healthcare applications. In *Proceedings of the 2012 SIAM International Conference on Data Mining*, pp. 576–587, 2012.

[69] Y. Sun, S. Todorovic, and S. Goodison. A feature selection algorithm capable of handling extremely large data dimensionality. In *Proceedings of the 2008 SIAM Internactional Conference in Data Mining*, pp. 530–540, 2008.

[70] N. García-Pedrajas, A. de Haro-García, and J. Pérez-Rodrguez. A scalable memetic algorithm for simultaneous instance and feature selection. *Evolutionary Computation*, 22(1):1–45, 2014.

[71] S. C. H. Hoi, J. Wang, P. Zhao, and R. Jin. Online feature selection for mining big data. In *Proceedings of the 1st International Workshop on Big Data, Streams and Heterogeneous Source Mining: Algorithms, Systems, Programming Models and Applications*, pp. 93–100. ACM, 2012.

[72] Z. Zhao, R. Zhang, J. Cox, D. Duling, and W. Sarle. Massively parallel feature selection: an approach based on variance preservation. *Machine Learning*, 92(1):195–220, 2013.

[73] M. Tan, I. W. Tsang, and L. Wang. Towards ultrahigh dimensional feature selection for big data. *The Journal of Machine Learning Research*, 15(1):1371–1429, 2014.

[74] R. Jensen and N. Mac Parthaláin. Towards scalable fuzzy–rough feature selection. *Information Sciences*, 323:1–15, 2015.

[75] A. Alonso-Betanzos, V. Bolón-Canedo, D. Fernández-Francos, I. Porto-Díaz, and N. Sánchez-Maroño. Up-to-date feature selection methods for scalable and efficient machine learning. In B. Igelnik and J. M. Zurada (Eds.), *Efficiency and Scalability Methods for Computational Intellect*, pp. 1–26. Hershey, PA: IGI Global, 2013.

[76] M. Bramer. *Principles of Data Mining.* Heidelberg, Germany: Springer, 2007.

[77] V. S. Ananthanarayana, D. K. Subramanian, and M. N. Murty. Scalable, distributed and dynamic mining of association rules. In M. Valero, V. K. Prasanna, and S. Vajapeyam (Eds.), *High Performance Computing HiPC 2000*, pp. 559–566. Berlin, Germany: Springer, 2000.

[78] P. K. Chan and S. J. Stolfo. Toward parallel and distributed learning by meta-learning. In *AAAI Workshop in Knowledge Discovery in Databases*, pp. 227–240, 1993.

[79] G. Tsoumakas and I. Vlahavas. Distributed data mining of large classifier ensembles. In *Proceedings Companion Volume of the Second Hellenic Conference on Artificial Intelligence*, pp. 249–256, 2002.

[80] S. McConnell and D. B. Skillicorn. Building predictors from vertically distributed data. In *Proceedings of the 2004 Conference of the Centre for Advanced Studies on Collaborative Research*, pp. 150–162. Indianapolis, IN: IBM Press, 2004.

[81] D. B. Skillicorn and S. M. McConnell. Distributed prediction from vertically partitioned data. *Journal of Parallel and Distributed computing*, 68(1):16–36, 2008.

[82] M. Banerjee and S. Chakravarty. Privacy preserving feature selection for distributed data using virtual dimension. In *Proceedings of the 20th ACM International Conference on Information and Knowledge Management*, pp. 2281–2284. ACM, 2011.

[83] T. K. Ho and M. Basu. *Data Complexity in Pattern Recognition.* London: Springer, 2006.

[84] A. Sharma, S. Imoto, and S. Miyano. A top-r feature selection algorithm for microarray gene expression data. *IEEE/ACM Transactions on Computational Biology and Bioinformatics (TCBB)*, 9:237–252, 2012.

[85] C. A. Gallo, R. L. Cecchini, J. A. Carballido, S. Micheletto, and I. Ponzoni. Discretization of gene expression data revised. *Briefings in Bioinformatics*, 17:758–770, 2015.

[86] L. I. Kuncheva and C. J. Whitaker. Measures of diversity in classifier ensembles and their relationship with the ensemble accuracy. *Machine Learning*, 51(2):181–207, 2003.

[87] V. Bolón-Canedo, N. Sánchez-Maroño, and A. Alonso-Betanzos. An ensemble of filters and classifiers for microarray data classification. *Pattern Recognition*, 45:531–539, 2012.

[88] V. Bolón-Canedo, N. Sánchez-Maroño, and A. Alonso-Betanzos. Data classification using an ensemble of filters. *Neurocomputing*, 135:13–20, 2014.

[89] A. Ben Brahim and M. Limam. Robust ensemble feature selection for high dimensional data sets. In *2013 International Conference on High Performance Computing and Simulation (HPCS)*, pp. 151–157. IEEE, 2013.

[90] C. H. Park and S. B. Kim. Sequential random k-nearest neighbor feature selection for high-dimensional data. *Expert Systems with Applications*, 42(5):2336–2342, 2015.

[91] C. Sarkar, S. Cooley, and J. Srivastava. Robust feature selection technique using rank aggregation. *Applied Artificial Intelligence*, 28(3): 243–257, 2014.

[92] K. Nag and N. R. Pal. A multiobjective genetic programming-based ensemble for simultaneous feature selection and classification. *IEEE Transactions on Cybernetics*, 46(2):499–510, 2016.

[93] B. Seijo-Pardo, I. Porto-Díaz, V. Bolón-Canedo, and A. Alonso-Betanzos. Ensemble feature selection methods: Homogeneous and heterogeneous approaches. *Knowledge-Based Systems*, 118: 124–139, 2017.

[94] K. Das, K. Bhaduri, and H. Kargupta. A local asynchronous distributed privacy preserving feature selection algorithm for large peer-to-peer networks. *Knowledge and Information Systems*, 24(3):341–367, 2010.

[95] Y. Jafer, S. Matwin, and M. Sokolova. Privacy-aware filter-based feature selection. In *Big Data (Big Data), 2014 IEEE International Conference on*. IEEE, 2014.

[96] E. Pattuk, M. Kantarcioglu, H. Ulusoy, and B. Malin. Privacy-aware dynamic feature selection. In *2015 IEEE 31st International Conference on Data Engineering*, pp. 78–88. IEEE, 2015.

[97] D. Peralta, S. del Río, S. Ramírez-Gallego, I. Triguero, J. M. Benitez, and F. Herrera. Evolutionary feature selection for big data classification: A MapReduce approach. *Mathematical Problems in Engineering*, 501:246139, 2015.

[98] J. Gama. *Knowledge Discovery from Data Streams.* Boca Raton, FL: CRC Press, 2010.

[99] O. Fontenla-Romero, B. Guijarro-Berdiñas, D. Martinez-Rego, B. Pérez-Sánchez, and D. Peteiro-Barral. Online machine learning. In B. Igelnik and J. M. Zurada (Eds.), *Efficiency and Scalability Methods for Computational Intellect*, pp. 27–54. Hershey, PA: IGI Global, 2013.

[100] G. I. Webb. Contrary to popular belief incremental discretization can be sound, computationally efficient and extremely useful for streaming data. In *2014 IEEE International Conference on Data Mining*, pp. 1031–1036, IEEE, 2014.

[101] V. Bolón-Canedo, D. Fernández-Francos, D. Peteiro-Barral, A. Alonso-Betanzos, B. Guijarro-Berdiñas, and N. Sánchez-Maroño. A unified pipeline for online feature selection and classification. *Expert Systems with Applications*, 55:532–545, 2016.

[102] J. Gama and C. Pinto. Discretization from data streams: Applications to histograms and data mining. In *Proceedings of the 2006 ACM Symposium on Applied Computing*, pp. 662–667. ACM, 2006.

[103] J. Lu, Y. Yang, and G. I. Webb. Incremental discretization for naive-bayes classifier. In X. Li, O. R. Zaïane, and Z. Li (Eds.), *International Conference on Advanced Data Mining and Applications*, pp. 223–238. Berlin, Germany: Springer, 2006.

[104] C. Zhang, J. Ruan, and Y. Tan. An incremental feature subset selection algorithm based on Boolean matrix in decision system. In *Convergence Information Technology*, pp. 16–23. South Korea: Advanced Institute of Convergence Information Technology Research Center, 2011.

[105] I. Katakis, G. Tsoumakas, and I. Vlahavas. Dynamic feature space and incremental feature selection for the classification of textual data streams. In *Knowledge Discovery from Data Streams*, pp. 107–116. Berlin, Germany: Springer, 2006.

[106] A. Tsymbal. The problem of concept drift: Definitions and related work. Computer Science Department, Trinity College Dublin, 106, 2004.

[107] S. Perkins, K. Lacker, and J. Theiler. Grafting: Fast, incremental feature selection by gradient descent in function space. *The Journal of Machine Learning Research*, 3:1333–1356, 2003.

[108] S. Perkins and J. Theiler. Online feature selection using grafting. In *Machine Learning* -International Workshop then Conference-, Vol. 20, p. 592, 2003.

[109] J. Wang, P. Zhao, S. C. Hoi, and R Jin. Online feature selection and its applications. *IEEE Transactions on Knowledge and Data Engineering*, 26(3):698–710, 2014.

[110] K. Glocer, D. Eads, and J. Theiler. Online feature selection for pixel classification. In *Proceedings of the 22nd International Conference on Machine Learning*, pp. 249–256. ACM, 2005.

[111] X. Wu, K. Yu, H. Wang, and W. Ding. Online streaming feature selection. In *Proceedings of the 27nd International Conference on Machine Learning*, Haifa, Israel, 2010.

[112] X. Wu, K. Yu, W. Ding, H. Wang, and X. Zhu. Online feature selection with streaming features. *IEEE Transactions on Pattern Analysis and Machine Intelligence*, 35(5):1178–1192, 2013.

[113] H. Kalkan and B. Çetisli. Online feature selection and classification. In *2011 IEEE International Conference on Acoustics, Speech and Signal Processing (ICASSP)*, pp. 2124–2127. IEEE, 2011.

[114] D. Levi and S. Ullman. Learning to classify by ongoing feature selection. *Image and Vision Computing*, 28(4):715–723, 2010.

[115] V. R. Carvalho and W. W. Cohen. Single-pass online learning: Performance, voting schemes and online feature selection. In *Proceedings of the 12th ACM SIGKDD International Conference on Knowledge Discovery and Data Mining*, pp. 548–553. ACM, 2006.

[116] K. Bunte, M. Biehl, and B. Hammer. A general framework for dimensionality-reducing data visualization mapping. *Journal Neural Computation*, 24:771–804, 2012.

[117] P. Flach. *Machine Learning: The Art and Science of Algorithms that Make Sense of Data*. Cambridge, UK: Cambridge University Press, 2012.

[118] S. Shalev-Shwartz and S. Ben-David. *Understanding Machine Learning: From Theory to Algorithms*. New York: Cambridge University Press, 2014.

[119] A. Bellogn, I. Cantador, P. Castells, and A. Ortigosa. Discerning relevant model features in a content-based collaborative recommender system. In *Preference Learning*, pp. 429–455. Springer, 2010.

[120] D. M. Maniyar and I. T. Nabney. Data visualization with simultaneous feature selection. In *2006 IEEE Symposium on Computational Intelligence and Bioinformatics and Computational Biology, CIBCB'06*, pp. 1–8. IEEE, 2006.

[121] J. Krause, A. Perer, and E. Bertini. Infuse: Interactive feature selection for predictive modeling of high dimensional data. *IEEE Transactions on Visualization and Computer Graphics*, 20(12):1614–1623, 2014.

[122] J. Krause, A. Perer, and K. Ng. Interacting with predictions: Visual inspection of black-box machine learning models. In *Proceedings of the 2016 CHI Conference on Human Factors in Computing Systems*, pp. 5686–5697. ACM, 2016.

[123] M. Brooks, S. Amershi, B. Lee, S. M. Drucker, A. Kapoor, and P. Simard. Featureinsight: Visual support for error-driven feature ideation in text classification. In *2015 IEEE Conference on Visual Analytics Science and Technology (VAST)*, pp. 105–112. IEEE, 2015.

[124] S. Garcia, J. Luengo, and F. Herrera. *Data Preprocessing in Data Mining*. Berlin, Germany: Springer, 2015.

[125] J. Dougherty, R. Kohavi, and M. Sahami. Supervised and unsupervised discretization of continuous features. In *Proceedings of the Twelfth International Conference on Machine Learning, ICML-95*, pp. 194–202. San Francisco, CA: Morgan Kaufmann, 1995.

[126] D. Janssens, T. Brijs, K. Vanhoof, and G. Wets. Evaluating the performance of cost-based discretization versus entropy-and error-based discretization. *Computers & Operations Research*, 33(11):3107–3123, 2006.

[127] Fast-mRMR package. https://github.com/sramirez/fast-mRMR. Accessed: November 2016.

[128] NVIDIA accelerated computing, CUDA platforms. https://developer.nvidia.com/additional-resources. Accessed: November 2016.

[129] P. Du, R. Weber, P. Luszczek, S. Tomov, G. Peterson, and J. Dongarra. From CUDA to OpenCL: Towards a performance-portable solution for multi-platform GPU programming. *Parallel Computing*, 38(8):391–407, 2012.

[130] D. Tarditi, S. Puri, and J. Oglesby. Accelerator: Using data parallelism to program GPUs for general-purpose uses. *ACM SIGARCH Computer Architecture News*, 34(5):325–335, 2016.

[131] S. Che, M. Boyer, J. Meng, D. Tarjan, J. W. Sheaffer, and K. Skadron. A performance study of general-purpose applications on graphics processors using cuda. *Journal of Parallel and Distributed Computing*, 68(10):1370–1380, 2008.

[132] CUDA Nvidia. *Programming Guide*. 2008.

[133] The UCI KDD Archive. KDD cup 1999 data. https://kdd.ics.uci.edu/databases/kddcup99/kddcup99.html. Accessed: November 2016.

[134] C. Chang and C. Lin. LIBSVM: A library for support vector machines. *ACM Transactions on Intelligent Systems and Technology*, 2(27):1–27, 2011.

[135] V. Bolón-Canedo, N. Sánchez-Maroño, and A. Alonso-Betanzos. A combination of discretization and filter methods for improving classification performance in KDD Cup 99 dataset. In *International Joint Conference on Neural Networks (IJCNN 2009)*, pp. 359–366. IEEE, 2009.

[136] V. Bolón-Canedo, N. Sánchez-Maroño, and A. Alonso-Betanzos. On the effectiveness of discretization on gene selection of microarray data. In *International Joint Conference on Neural Networks (IJCNN 2010)*, pp. 1–8. IEEE, 2010.

Chapter 11

Causation, probability, and all that: Data science as a novel inductive paradigm

Wolfgang Pietsch*

Introduction: A new empiricism 329
Arguments concerning inductivism 331
Causation 335
The principal argument for causation 336
Methods of variational induction 338
An adequate causal methodology 340
Probability 343
Objective interpretations of probability 344
Probability, symmetries, and independence 346
Correlations and causation 348
Wrapping up: The novel inductivism of data science 349
References 350

Introduction: A new empiricism

Is data science genuine science? Or is it merely some inferior practice that can at best contribute to the scientific enterprise but cannot stand on its own? A brief survey of the literature suggests that there is anything but a consensus on this and related issues concerning the foundations of data science. In fact, the extent of disagreement is outright astonishing.

Some authors see a novel empiricism on the rise, a new paradigm of doing science [1], whereas others insist that faced with Big Data, it will be even more important to stick to the old ways [2]. Some proclaim *the end of theory* [3], whereas others argue that, to the very contrary, theoretical reflection and guidance are indispensable as science increasingly drowns in data [4]. Some

*Wolfgang Pietsch is a philosopher of science and technology at the Munich Center for Technology in Society of Technical University Munich.

celebrate a novel era, in which patterns and correlations replace the age-old search for causation [5], whereas others maintain that science by definition requires causal explanation of the phenomena [6]. Some urge to let the data speak by itself [3], whereas others stress that when taken out of context, data loses its meaning and that bigger data are not always better data [7].

In the recent success story of data science, the technical apparatus has been developed to impressive sophistication. Many powerful algorithms exist that have led to novel and often ground-breaking results in a diverse range of scientific fields. However, a robust conceptual framework that would be required to resolve the above-mentioned controversies is still largely missing. For example, the role of causation in data science can only be meaningfully explored given an adequate definition of causation. Or, the usefulness of correlations can only be assessed on the basis of a sound understanding of probability. Certainly, such conceptual questions are anything but trivial as for example a considerable number of interpretations both of causation and of probability exist.

Thus, one of the crucial frontiers in data science is to develop its conceptual and methodological foundations—to establish whether a strongly data-based, relatively theory-free approach is feasible at all that allows for reliable prediction and effective manipulation of the phenomena. Some preliminary considerations in this regard are presented in this essay.

In section "Arguments concerning inductivism," several standard arguments concerning inductivism are reviewed, that is, concerning the idea that scientific laws and theories can be derived inductively from statements of facts. Some have suggested that data science is impossible as inductivism has allegedly long been refuted. However, the almost universal rejection of inductivism in contemporary science is undermined by other periods in the history of science, in which inductivism was the dominant view. Indeed, some of the most influential scientists and methodologists in the past, including Francis Bacon, Isaac Newton, Antoine Lavoisier, or John Stuart Mill, advocated inductivism. Data science, as I will argue in this essay, stands in this old and venerable empiricist tradition.

In section "Causation," I turn to a discussion of inductive methodology. The fundamental distinction between enumerative and eliminative induction is briefly introduced, the former focusing on the mere repetition of phenomena, the latter on the variation of phenomena. In line with most inductivists, I argue that eliminative induction provides a much more plausible and realistic picture of actual scientific practice. Moreover, an account of causation is outlined that corresponds to eliminative induction and that allows establishing the crucial distinction between relationships that are purely accidental and those that allow for prediction and manipulation. This disentangles the conceptual muddle behind the claim that correlation replaces causation in data science, which is often held to be one of the central tenets of this discipline.

The methodological framework sketched in section "Causation" relies on the assumption of determinism, which certainly cannot be upheld for most applications of data science. The notion of probability therefore is considered in section "Probability." I sketch an objective, nonfrequency interpretation of probability that relies on symmetries in the causal structure of probabilistic phenomena to establish probability values. Thus, far from being replaced by correlation, the notion of causation and a causal perspective on probability constitute the main conceptual tools to single out those correlations in data science that are meaningful and useful.

Arguments concerning inductivism

Before the advent of Big Data, science in the twentieth century has largely been under the spell of deductivism, maintaining that it proceeds from hypothesized theory to facts rather than in the opposite direction as according to inductivism. Indeed, many contemporary scientists and methodologists doubt, whether strongly data-driven, theory-sparse approaches are feasible at all. However, although there are sophisticated arguments against inductivism, its outright rejection in much of today's science is surprising. After all, in other periods of the history of science, inductivism appears to have been just as universally accepted as it is nowadays rejected. It is hard not to conclude from this situation that the debate on scientific method is to a considerable extent governed by fashion rather than reason. Of course, this does not imply that all antiinductivist arguments are wrong or that deductivist methodology is mistaken. But surely, one should not turn an alleged refutation of inductivism into an argument against data science.

Indeed, some of the most influential scientists and methodologists of the past, including such luminaries as Francis Bacon, Isaac Newton, Antoine Lavoisier, Jean-Marie Ampère, or John Stuart Mill, have endorsed inductivism, whereas admittedly just as many scientists of no less standing have leaned toward deductivism. Some of the core tenets of an inductivist approach are as follows: (1) scientific laws should be proven from the phenomena, that is, from experiment and observation; (2) these laws can be considered true or at least highly probable in the sense that only one correct set of laws adequately describes a certain range of phenomena; (3) this implies an aversion against hypotheses, which by definition are always preliminary and never proven beyond doubt. As many authors in the inductivist tradition stress, hypotheses may be and are formulated in the beginning of the scientific process, but eventually scientific knowledge should move beyond the merely hypothetical; (4) it is often assumed that scientific laws are derived by a methodology of varying the circumstances; (5) this process continuously improves the knowledge about the phenomena, at least in the long run; (6) finally, inductivism establishes a hierarchy of laws of increasing universality, starting with simple observation statements that are combined into low-level phenomenological laws, and then into laws of increasing generality and abstractness slowly ascending until the highest level of generality.

Evidence for these tenets can be found with a wide variety of inductivist writers. Isaac Newton's scientific methodology is a case in point, as briefly summarized in his celebrated "rules of reasoning in philosophy" in the very *Principia Mathematica Philosophiae Naturalis*, in which he also laid the foundations of modern physics [8]. Rule 1 states what has later been called the doctrine of *verae causae* that science has to look for those causes that are "both true and sufficient to explain [the] appearances." Rule 4 summarizes his inductivist credo: "In experimental philosophy we are to look upon propositions inferred by general induction from phenomena as accurately or very nearly true, notwithstanding any contrary hypotheses that may be imagined, till such time as other phenomena occur by which they may either be made more accurate or liable to exceptions." Many of the aspects mentioned before can be identified in this brief statement. Most importantly, for Newton science starts with the facts and from there proceeds to theory and universal laws. He also claims that the inductive process can at least approximate truth and that further evidence, rather than refuting established knowledge, always improves it by "making it more accurate or liable to exceptions." Finally, Newton is critical of the role of hypotheses in science—as also famously expressed in his dictum "hypotheses non fingo" from the General Scholium of the third book of the *Principia*.

Jean-Marie Ampère, who has been called *the Newton of electromagnetism*, largely follows Newton's empiricist spirit. Indeed, Ampère calls his masterpiece that lays the foundations of modern classical electrodynamics the "mathematical theory of electro-dynamic phenomena *uniquely derived from experiments*"* (my italics) [9]. In the introduction, he summarizes his method as follows:

> First observe the facts, while varying the conditions to the extent possible, accompany this first effort with precise measurement in order to deduce general laws based solely on experiments, and deduce therefrom, independently of all hypotheses regarding the nature of the forces which produce the phenomena, the mathematical value of these forces, that is to say, the formula which represents them, this was the path followed by Newton. This was the approach generally adopted by the scholars of France to whom physics owes the immense progress which has been made in recent times, and similarly it has guided me in all my research into electrodynamic phenomena. I have relied solely on experimentation to establish the laws of the phenomena and from them I have derived the formula which alone can represent the forces which are produced; I have not investigated

* "théorie mathématique des phénomènes électrodynamiques uniquement déduite de l'expérience"

> the possible cause of these forces, convinced that all research of this nature must proceed from pure experimental knowledge of the laws [...]*

This statement is a textbook description of an inductivist approach, again containing all the elements listed at the beginning of this section. Note in particular that Ampère stresses the importance of varying the circumstances as widely as possible to experimentally derive the laws from experience—this focus on a *rationale of variation* [10] is not as prominent in Newton's comments on methodology. Furthermore, Ampère rejects hypotheses and believes that science can discover the one true theory, "the formula which alone can represent the forces which are produced."

Inductivism, which according to Ampère was "generally adopted by the scholars of France to whom physics owes the immense progress which has been made in recent times," then came under attack in the second half of the nineteenth century. A number of crucial debates followed in which all important arguments for and against inductivism can be found. Notably, there is a famous exchange between John Stuart Mill and William Whewell, the former siding with inductivism, the latter arguing for a deductivist approach stressing the indispensable role of hypotheses in science. Several decades later, the controversy is continued between the empiricists of the Vienna Circle and Karl Popper taking the opposing view of deductivism.

Some of the objections against inductivism that are raised in these debates are answered relatively easily. For example, a standard argument is that inductivists allegedly overlook that hypotheses are formulated at every corner of the scientific enterprise. But this amounts to attacking a strawman, because, as pointed out previously, inductivists by no means deny that hypotheses can play a fruitful role in the early stages of the scientific process. What sets them apart is the belief that the truth or approximate truth of some propositions can be empirically established, that is, that at some point science moves beyond the preliminary status of mere hypotheses.

Furthermore, deductivists usually stress the so-called problem of induction, which can be traced back chiefly to the Scottish empiricist David Hume [11]. According to this epistemological riddle, inductive inferences cannot

* "Observer d'abord les faits, en varier les circonstances autant qu'il est possible, accompagner ce premier travail de mesures précises pour en déduire des lois générales, uniquement fondées sur l'expérience, et déduire de ces lois, indépendamment de toute hypothèse sur la nature des forces, c'est-à-dire la formule qui les représente, telle est la marche qu'a suivie Newton. Elle a été, en general, adoptée en France par les savants auxquels la physique doit les immenses progress qu'elle a faits dans ces derniers temps, et c'est elle qui m'a servi de guide dans toutes mes recherches sur les phénomènes électrodynamiques. J'ai consulté uniquement l'expérience pour établir les lois de ces phénomènes, et j'en ai déduit la formule qui peut seule représenter les forces auxquelles ils sont dus; je n'ai fait aucune recherche sur la cause même qu'on peut assigner à ces forces, bien convaincu que toute recherché de ce genre doit être précédée de la connaissance purement expérimentale des lois [...]"

be justified. Consequently, from particular observations of fact, no matter how numerous they may be, one can never reliably infer general laws. In the words of Whewell, the process of induction necessarily "includes a mysterious step" [12]. And Popper emphasizes at the very beginning of his influential *Logic of Discovery* that "the various difficulties of inductive logic here sketched are insurmountable" [13]. Until today, the problem of induction is held to be unsolved and unsolvable by most epistemologists and philosophers of science.

But although it is certainly true that induction to universal laws involves some steps beyond the purely empirical, deductivists have invariably overstated their case. One important aspect is that, already starting with Hume's classic treatment, most analyses have focused on the wrong kind of induction, namely enumerative induction based on the mere repetition of phenomena, as opposed to eliminative induction based on variation of circumstances that was favored by major inductivists such as Bacon, Herschel, or Mill. As a consequence, it remains unclear whether standard arguments for the problem of induction, including the reasoning given by Hume, apply to eliminative induction as well.

Some of the most sophisticated arguments against inductivism can be found in the work of Pierre Duhem, in particular in his book on *The Aim and Structure of Physical Theory* [14]. One crucial point is the so-called theory-ladenness of observation and experiment, which supposedly undermines the inductivist idea that in the scientific process one can strictly ascend step by step from particular statements of fact to increasingly general laws. According to the doctrine of theory-ladenness, such a clean hierarchical ordering of scientific propositions is impossible, as every experiment and observation always presuppose considerable theoretical background knowledge. Consequently, there are no basic, theory-independent statements of fact. Note especially that this objection is often brought forward against the inductivism of data science, in which, without doubt, all sorts of theoretical commitments play a role in both the collection and the processing of data [2,4].

However, just pointing to theory-ladenness cannot decide the quarrel between inductivism and deductivism. Instead, one has to look carefully at the details, how much and what kind of theory must be presupposed in various contexts. And indeed, although no observation is entirely theory-free, for example, all statements of fact presuppose a stable and robust language, certainly the underlying theory can exhibit different levels of sophistication. Some observations, for example, regarding the color of a tree or the smell of some food, can be stated by merely relying on primary sensory categories, whereas others presuppose the latest most abstract physical theories, for example, when a physicist reports on the latest experiment at Conseil Européen pour la Recherche Nucléaire, European Organization for Nuclear Research (CERN). Indeed, already Duhem introduced a crucial distinction between phenomenological sciences such as physiology and theoretical sciences such as physics, according to him theory-ladenness troubles chiefly the latter. This indicates that some observation statements, notably those that mostly rely on primary sensory qualities, presuppose little and simple theory and, thus, can serve as a relatively stable basis for induction. Furthermore, as we will see in section "Causation," it is possible to derive causal knowledge from the comparison of such basic observation statements, which may then serve as the lowermost level of phenomenological laws in the inductive hierarchy.

Besides theory-ladenness of observation, maybe the most challenging argument against inductivism is the thesis of *confirmational holism*: "the physicist can never subject an isolated hypothesis to experimental test, but only a whole group of hypotheses; when the experiment is in disagreement with his predictions, what he learns is that at least one of the hypotheses constituting this group is unacceptable and ought to be modified; but the experiment does not designate which one should be changed" [14]. This thesis contradicts the inductivist idea that observations and experiments can directly confirm general laws. However, we will see in Section "Causation" that at least at a level of phenomenological laws of little abstractness, it is possible to confirm certain causal hypotheses directly from statements of fact. And again, this does not necessarily contradict Duhem's account. After all, he largely confined the idea of confirmational holism to abstract sciences such as physics.

Inductivism is supposedly further undermined by arguments concerning the *underdetermination of theory by evidence*, that is, there are always several theories that can account for certain phenomena, never only a single true theory, or concerning the *impossibility of crucial experiments* deciding between competing, mutually contradictory hypotheses. These arguments are closely intertwined with the other points that we discussed before and thus again, Duhem mostly restricts them to theoretical or abstract sciences such as physics. Consequently, Duhem's perspective is compatible with the view that we develop in the course of this essay arguing for an inductivism regarding the level of phenomenological laws as distinct from the theoretical constructs of abstract sciences. Note that data science, thus far, mostly remains on such a phenomenological level as well.

In summary, I hope to have shown that although there are many interesting and sophisticated arguments against inductivism, none of them is really decisive. For all of them, plausible rejoinders from the inductivists exist. Disproving or mitigating the major arguments against inductivism, of course, does not relieve us from tackling the positive task of developing a sound conceptual framework and methodology for inductivism. To this, we will turn now.

Causation

One of the major frontiers for data science is developing adequate concepts underlying its mainly inductivist methodology. After all, claims concerning the *end of causation* or that *correlation replaces causation* are without meaning, unless such extremely complex and controversial notions as causation or probability are explicated in sufficient detail. With respect to causation, there are at least four major interpretations: the regularity view, the interventionist theory, counterfactual accounts, and finally mechanistic or process views. I will pursue a counterfactual approach in this essay, so let me briefly explain, why the other accounts are not suitable for data science.

According to the classic *regularity view*, causal relationships consist in the constant conjunction of certain events or properties [11]. If one finds after a sufficient number of observations that the light is always on when a switch is on, then we may conclude that the latter is the cause of the former. The main and ultimately unsolvable problem for the regularity view is that it cannot distinguish between causal relations and merely accidental correlations. This renders regularity views of causation useless in the context of data science.

The currently popular *interventionist view* construes causal relationships in terms of possible interventions [15]. Broadly speaking, there is a causal relationship between two variables, if an intervention on one variable leads or would lead to a change in the other. For example, the switch is a cause for the light, because an intervention on the variable *switch* leads to a change in the variable *light*. However, this approach does not satisfy the requirements of data science, as there one is often faced with the task of deriving causal relationships from mere observations, that is, in the *absence* of explicit interventions.

Finally, *process or mechanistic accounts* trace back causation to the fundamental physical mechanism or process linking cause and effect (e.g., Wesley Salmon [16]). According to this perspective, the causal relation between switch and light could only be established if the physical process is known leading from one phenomenon to the other. The main problem for process accounts in the context of data science is that the details of the processes leading from cause to effect are mostly unknown and thus, causal relationships must be established without such knowledge.

The remaining counterfactual approach to causation does not suffer from the shortcomings and flaws that have been pointed out above. We will see in the following that it can at least in principle distinguish causal relationships from accidental correlations, that it can reason from mere observations, and that it can establish causal relationships by difference making without explicitly relying on a mechanism or process that links cause and effect.

The principal argument for causation

Many have suggested that with data science, the age-old quest for causal knowledge is coming to an end and is being replaced by just keeping track of correlations [3,5]. Even though these claims are widespread, they can easily be refuted. The core of a rejoinder is already contained in a well-known quote by the philosopher of science Nancy Cartwright, in which she makes the case for the indispensability of causal notions in science: "I claim causal laws cannot be done away with, for they are needed to ground the distinction between effective strategies and ineffective ones" [17]. Now, as data science is all about effectively intervening in the world, for example, to achieve better search results, to sell more products in an internet store, or to develop efficient medicine for treating complex diseases, the underlying relationships must to some extent be causal. In other words, the distinction between causal and non-causal relationships is crucial because only the former can be effectively put to use.

Even when data science only aims at reliable predictions rather than effective interventions, causality remains an indispensable concept. In some cases, predictions are reliable, because there is a direct causal link between the considered variables, that is, the corresponding relationships could also have been used for effective interventions. In the absence of a direct causal link, a common cause for two variables may also establish why predictions of one of the variables based on the values of the other turn out reliable. Arguably, this second situation is more prevalent in data science and some of the more notorious applications are of this type, for example, that vegetarians miss fewer flights or that Mac-users book expensive hotels [18]. Plausibly, there are no direct causal connections between the variables in both cases. Owning a MacBook does not causally increase travel budgets. However, it is plausible that a common cause structure makes this correlation robust and reliable for prediction. A factor such as wealth or fondness of luxury may be common to both Mac-users and travelers with a taste for staying in fancy hotels. If that is the case, then taking into account that someone owns a MacBook will indeed on average increase the probability for expensive hotel bookings. By contrast, a purely accidental correlation that does not arise due to a direct causal link or at least a common cause, but merely by chance, cannot be used either for reliable prediction or for effective intervention. Therefore, according to the argument just given, both successful prediction and intervention need to be justified in terms of causal relationships. A direct causal link allows for both intervention and prediction, a common cause structure only for prediction.

When in some of the literature on Big Data and data science it is claimed that causality is being replaced by correlations, presumably these authors are referring to the role of causation in scientific explanation. After all, data science seems mainly interested in predicting rather than in explaining phenomena. Then, if one considers explanation as the main task for causation in the sciences, as these authors presuppose at least implicitly, it follows that causation does not play an important role in data science. But such an argument crucially overlooks Cartwright's point that—although admittedly also important for explanation—causation is indispensable for establishing reliable prediction and effective intervention, which constitute core tasks for data science.

Methods of variational induction

Certainly, the novel inductivism proclaimed by data science is only feasible, if there exists a scientific method fulfilling the requirements sketched in section "Arguments concerning inductivism": (1) This method should be able to establish causal relationships with some confidence; (2) it should reason more or less directly from the facts presupposing little theory; (3) further relevant evidence stemming from observations and experiments should continuously improve the causal knowledge about a phenomenon, at least in the long run; (4) the method should allow for a hierarchy of laws of increasing generality.

The main inductive method is still widely held to be Aristotelian *enumerative induction* according to which general laws are inferred from the observation of invariable regularities between properties or events. If one observes a sufficient number of swans and finds that all of them are white, then according to this inductive rule it is justified to assume that all swans are white or at least that the next swan will be white. However, this type of induction fares badly with respect to the requirements that we just stated. After all, it may always happen that a contrary instance occurs refuting the general law, even if it was previously confirmed by a very large number of observations—as the notorious black swan eventually discovered in Australia. Thus, it seems impossible to establish reliable causal knowledge by enumerative induction. Moreover, it is highly doubtful whether the quality of causal knowledge continuously improves when taking into account an increasing number of observations.

A further issue regarding enumerative induction is that it does not fit well with established scientific practice, most notably exploratory experimentation, which constitutes the most successful way to deduce causal relationships from the phenomena [19,20]. Exploratory experiments do not test the empirical consequences of a given theoretical framework. Rather, they attempt to inductively determine the dependencies between a newly discovered phenomenon and its circumstances. Exploratory experimentation proceeds by a methodology of varying the circumstances to find out their impact on the phenomenon—in contrast to the observation of mere regularities in enumerative induction involving no systematic variation. For example, when Röntgen by accident discovered a hitherto unknown type of rays, he set out to establish the laws governing this novel phenomenon by means of exploratory experimentation. To this purpose, he carefully changed various variables that he deemed important, for example, electric and magnetic fields, to see whether they had any impact on the properties of these rays.

Fortunately, there are powerful methods of induction that reflect much better than enumerative induction, the mentioned variational rationale underlying inductive inferences in scientific practice. Indeed, many major inductivists in history have expressed outright contempt for enumerative induction, for example, John Stuart Mill: "[Enumerative induction] is the kind of induction which is natural to the mind when unaccustomed to scientific methods. [...] It was, above all, by pointing out the insufficiency of this rude and loose conception of induction that [Francis] Bacon merited the title so generally awarded to him of Founder of the Inductive Philosophy" [21]. At the same time, methodologists such as Mill have outlined a so-called eliminative induction inferring from the variation of circumstances rather than from the mere repetition of phenomena. Presumably, the most influential accounts in history were those of the English philosopher and statesman Francis Bacon [22], the polymath and methodologist John Herschel [23], and the mentioned Scottish philosopher and economist John Stuart Mill [21]. On detailed inspection, it turns out that all these accounts are closely related.

Francis Bacon, for example, proposed a methodology based on collections of instances covering the widest possible variety of phenomena. The first step of induction, which Bacon calls *first vintage*, consists in a comparison of these different collections or tables of instances: "the problem is, upon a review of the instances, all and each, to find such a nature as is always present or absent with the given nature, and always increases and decreases with it; and which is, as I have said, a particular case of a more general nature" [22]. It can be argued that this brief statement already contains predecessors of most commonly accepted rules of eliminative induction.

Today, Mill's exposition of eliminative induction is almost universally considered to be the clearest and most precise. He formulates several methods, his so-called *canons of induction* [21]. Of these, he considers the *method of difference* as the most important to reliably determine causal relationships:

> If an instance in which the phenomenon under investigation occurs, and an instance in which it does not occur, have every circumstance save one in common, that one occurring only in the former; the circumstance in which alone the two instances differ, is the effect, or cause, or a necessary part of the cause, of the phenomenon.

Using an example by Mill, if someone is full of energy and then from one moment to the other is dying with a bullet in his heart, it is plausible that the bullet was the decisive change in circumstances and thus, the cause for death.

All these approaches of eliminative induction, from Bacon's first vintage to Mill's canons of induction, share a number of crucial features: (1) they all rely on a variational rationale examining what happens to a phenomenon under a change in circumstances; (2) they reason directly from singular statements of facts, for example, the method of difference in an ideal situation infers from only two instances; (3) they employ relatively simple rules; (4) in contrast to enumerative induction, these rules can be formulated in a logically consistent way, that is, if a prediction does not materialize, it can always be blamed on the premises not being fulfilled rather than on the failure of the employed inductive rule.

Let me finish this section by stressing that many methods of data science directly stand in the tradition of the simple but powerful rules of eliminative induction. In particular, they invariably rely on a variational rationale trying to determine the impact of a typically large number of circumstances when considering a comparably large number of instances. More specifically, I have argued elsewhere that popular Big Data algorithms such as decision trees proceed in close analogy to the method of difference [24]. For other machine-learning algorithms, the connection may be somewhat more difficult to see. For example, neural nets seem at first sight quite distinct given their usually complex structure of hierarchically linked neurons. But although the modeling technique in this case is peculiar, the underlying logic again is one of difference making. In the end, neural nets aim to determine—just like decision trees—on the basis of a large number of instances the most useful difference makers among the circumstances.

An adequate causal methodology

Although eliminative induction has historically been considered the most effective inductive methodology and also plays an important role in data science, the crucial problem is that most formulations of eliminative methods, including the influential framework due to Mill, are rather sketchy and open to all kinds of objections. Maybe the most important worry concerns applicability. For example, with respect to Mill's version of the method of difference, it generally seems impossible to change only a single one of the circumstances. Rather, with the change in cause variable, numerous other variables will vary besides the considered effect variable. Relatedly, the method of difference in Mill's formulation is incapable of identifying complex causal structures such as causal factors, that is, circumstances that require the presence of other circumstances to produce a phenomenon.

In the following, I will briefly outline both a concept and a corresponding methodology of causation that essentially develops the method of difference into a more rigorous inductive rule by taking into account the above-mentioned objections (for more details cf. Reference 25). As already indicated at the beginning of section "Causation," let me define the fundamental causal concepts in counterfactual terms:

CAUSAL RELEVANCE: In a context B, in which a condition A and a phenomenon C occur, A is causally relevant to C, if and only if the following counterfactual holds: if A had not occurred, C would also not have occurred.

CAUSAL IRRELEVANCE: In a context B, in which a condition A and a phenomenon C occur, A is causally irrelevant to C, if and only if the following counterfactual holds: if A had not occurred, C would still have occurred.

Consider again the light switch. The switch is causally relevant to the light, because first, we observe that the light is on with the switch in a certain position and second, it is plausible to assume that if the switch were in the opposite position the light would be off. The idea to define causation in terms of counterfactuals can already be found in the writings of David Hume: "We may define a cause to be *an object followed by another, and [...] where, if the first object had not been, the second never had existed*" [11]. Counterfactual accounts can easily justify why causal relationships allow for effective intervention—which we identified as the core function for causation in science (see section "The principal argument for causation"). After all, from the truth of the counterfactual statement in the definition of causal relevance, one can immediately infer that by changing the cause variable the effect variable must change as well.

Although counterfactual accounts are thus able to reproduce central intuitions about the role of causation in the sciences and everyday life, their main challenge consists in determining the truth values of counterfactual statements. Obviously, by definition these are *contra the facts* and, thus, cannot be directly observed. Several frameworks have been proposed in this regard, most notably Nelson Goodman's metalinguistic framework [26] and David Lewis's highly influential semantic approach [27]. The main problem of both these frameworks is that vagueness and subjectivity play a substantial role—which is difficult to reconcile with the largely objective function of causation in the sciences. After all, it should not be a matter of subjective perspective, whether the switch causes the light to illuminate.

The most promising way to deal with counterfactuals, which best can account for the objective role of causation in the sciences, relies on the notion of *homogeneity* [28,29]. The underlying idea is to construct a class of homogeneous, that is, sufficiently similar, instances that all have the same truth value. Furthermore, this class should include both the counterfactual instance in which one is interested as well as another instance that can be directly observed. Therefore, by observing the latter instance, the truth value of the former can be determined.

More exactly: *"If A were not the case, C would not be the case" is true with respect to an instance in which both A and C occur in a context B, if* (1) *at least one instance is realized in the actual world in which neither A nor C occurs in the same context B and* (2) *if B guarantees homogeneity.*

As a next step, *homogeneity* needs to be defined: *Context B guarantees homogeneity, if and only if only conditions that are causally irrelevant to C (and $\neg C$) can change,* (i) *except for A and* (ii) *conditions that are causally relevant to C in virtue of A being causally relevant to C.*

Essentially, homogeneity holds if only irrelevant circumstances may change as well as circumstances that mediate between cause and effect or are themselves causes for the considered cause variable. For example, we know that if the switch were in the opposite position, the light would be off, because (1) we observed that the light was off before the switch was flipped and (2) we can exclude that any other potentially relevant circumstances changed except of course (i) the switch variable itself as well as (ii) variables that mediate between switch and light, e.g. the electric current passing through the switch.

This resolves the problem mentioned at the beginning of this section that Mill's formulation of the method of difference is unrealistic in presupposing that only *one* circumstance may change—by specifying exactly which types of circumstances may vary. For this, introducing the notion of causal irrelevance turns out crucial. The approach also explains how causal knowledge can be slowly improved by accumulating further empirical evidence, for example, by showing that other circumstances are causally irrelevant and thereby rendering causal laws more general, while tracking exceptions. Causal knowledge that was once established by the described method cannot be falsified, as any counter-instance can always be blamed on the context B, that is, on an erroneous assumption regarding the irrelevance of certain circumstances.

With this basic inductive methodology, we can now tackle the second problem that we had pointed out for Mill's method of difference, namely how complex causal relationships can be identified using a methodology of difference making. Indeed, further concepts such as causal factors or alternative causes can be defined on the basis of the fundamental notions of causal relevance and causal irrelevance.

> *CAUSAL FACTOR: A is a causal factor for phenomenon C with respect to background B, if and only if there exists an X such that* (i) *A is causally relevant to C with respect to $B \wedge X$, and* (ii) *irrelevant to $\neg C$ with respect to $B \wedge \neg X$ (i.e. C is always absent in $B \wedge \neg X$).*

Here, $B \wedge X$ denotes a background that requires besides the circumstances subsumed under B that an additional variable x is in state X. As an example, the main fuse x of the power supply must be intact, that is, in state X, in order for the light switch to function. In other words, (1) the switch is causally relevant to the light only if the fuse is intact and (2) it is causally irrelevant if the fuse is broken. Therefore, according to the above-mentioned definition, the switch is a causal factor for the light, requiring the intactness of the fuse.

> *ALTERNATIVE CAUSE: A is an alternative cause to C with respect to background B if and only if there exists an X such that* (i) *A is causally relevant to C with respect to a background $B \wedge \neg X$, but* (ii) *causally irrelevant to C with respect to a background $B \wedge X$ (i.e., C is always present in $B \wedge X$).*

An example for alternative causes would be two switches A and X that are wired in parallel: (1) if the switch X is off, then switch A is causally relevant to the light; (2) if the switch X is on, A is causally irrelevant, because no matter what the state of A, the light will always be on due to X.

On the basis of these two concepts, we can now proceed to define an INUS-condition, which was proposed by John Mackie as the most general notion of cause when dealing with the presence or absence of circumstances [30,31]. The acronym INUS stands for "*I*nsufficient but *N*on-redundant part of a condition that is itself *U*nnecessary but *S*ufficient." For example, a match inadvertently dropped in a forest will cause a fire only under certain further conditions, for example, hot weather and no rain. The match is thus nonredundant but also insufficient, as it depends on these further conditions whether a fire will occur. The U.S.-part then points out the possibility of alternative causes for the fire, for example, lightning or a meteor.

INUS-CONDITION: A factor X is an INUS-condition for C with respect to a background B, if and only if X is a causal factor in a condition A that is causally relevant to C with respect to a background (B plus absence of all alternative causes for C, of which there must be at least one).

In a deterministic world, that is, in a world in which all phenomena are fully determined by their circumstances—and that is a considerable limitation that we will address in the next section—all causal relationships regarding the presence or absence of circumstances* can be stated in terms of INUS-conditions. The sketched account thus furnishes the conceptual and methodological basis for a sound inductivist methodology, how the variation of circumstances allows one to determine causal relevance and irrelevance, and therefrom INUS-conditions that can be employed to predict and change empirical phenomena. With respect to the epistemology of data science, the fundamental challenge remains to establish a connection between the outlined eliminative induction and the underlying logic of various successful machine-learning algorithms [24,34].

Probability

From a conceptual viewpoint, the account formulated in section "Causation" clarifies why causation must play a central role in the epistemology of data science, plainly speaking because data science is all about reliable prediction and effective intervention. But as mentioned, the account presupposes determinism and in particular can only establish deterministic relationships—whereas, of course, the relationships in data science are almost all only statistical, that is, the considered circumstances never fully determine a phenomenon, but only a probability distribution over a range of phenomena. When an online store suggests a book, of course, it cannot be expected that

*A generalization to functional dependencies is straightforward but cannot be discussed here due to lack of space [32,33].

every customer will necessarily buy it. Rather, the suggestion just raises the probability of a purchase. Similarly, when an algorithm determines the most suitable cancer drug for a specific patient, she will not recover with absolute certainty, but only with some—hopefully large—probability. Therefore, the account of the previous section has to be generalized to include statistical relationships—to resolve what is maybe the central issue in the epistemology of data science, namely to distinguish between correlations that are meaningful, that is, that can ground prediction and manipulation, and merely accidental correlations. To tackle this problem, a conceptual analysis of probability is required—to that we turn now.

Objective interpretations of probability

The most fundamental distinction with respect to different interpretations of probability is between subjective and objective interpretations [35,36]. Given that the general purpose of probabilities in data science is to establish reliable prediction—if holding only on average—a notion of probability for data science should have as few subjective elements as possible since these would only undermine the reliability of predictions.

There are three main contenders for an objective interpretation of probability. The best known and most widely accepted, in particular among scientists and practitioners, is the *frequency interpretation* [37,38], which construes probability in terms of the relative frequency of an attribute occurring in a large number of similar instances, for example, the relative frequency with which a six shows in many subsequent throws of a die. An important distinction concerns whether probabilities are identified with the relative frequency in some finite sequence of events or with that in the infinite limit. In spite of their popularity, frequency views are not well suited to explicate probability in data science because these approaches are mostly incapable of drawing the distinction between correlations that are useful for prediction and manipulation and those that are merely accidental (cp. [39]). One may speculate whether the infinite limit could play a role in establishing the distinction, but in any case this limit is epistemically inaccessible and, therefore, the problem remains unsolved within frequency views.

Already since the end of the nineteenth century, doubts about the frequentist approach have led methodologists to develop alternative interpretations. For a long time, the main contender has been the so-called propensity theory with one of its most influential proponents being Karl Popper [40] (see also [41]). The propensity approach shifts the focus from considering the relative frequency in a large series of similar events toward examining the circumstances or conditions under which probabilistic phenomena occur—somewhat mirroring the distinction between enumerative and eliminative induction. More exactly, according to the propensity view, probability corresponds to the *strength of certain tendencies or dispositions* inherent in the circumstances to realize a certain type of event. Originally, propensities were proposed mostly for indeterministic contexts, in particular Popper initially conceived this interpretation to deal with probabilities arising in quantum mechanics, for example, the probability of an atom decay. The main objection against propensity interpretations is that the notion itself of a propensity has never been clarified in a satisfactory manner. This has led to the proliferation of several competing approaches, none of which has managed to become mainstream. In particular, the process how exactly probabilities arise from the circumstances has never been spelled out in sufficient detail.

A third interpretation, the history of which also reaches back to the late nineteenth century, has recently moved into focus due to work by Jakob Rosenthal [42], Michael Strevens [39], and Marshall Abrams [43]. This *SRA-approach,* the acronym resulting from the initials of the main contemporary proponents, is based on the so-called method of arbitrary functions as developed among others by Henri Poincaré (see [44] for an overview). The basic idea is to determine the full range of initial conditions that can lead to a probabilistic phenomenon and then ask for the relative measure of initial conditions that imply a certain type or outcome of this phenomenon. This relative measure yields the probability of the respective outcome. One of the classic examples, already discussed in much detail by Poincaré, is the roulette wheel. Red and black as outcomes are equally probable, as plausibly an equal number of initial conditions leads to black and to red. In addition, it can be shown that these probabilities are largely independent of the exact choice of measure over initial conditions—hence the term *arbitrary functions*—in which the measure basically denotes the relative frequencies with which certain initial conditions occur. This independence results because initial conditions leading to red and to black are equally and densely distributed over the whole range of initial states, that is, small changes in initial conditions can easily lead to a change in outcome.

As in the propensity interpretation, the circumstances (i.e., initial conditions) under which probabilities arise play a crucial role in the SRA-approach. But in contrast to the propensity interpretation, the SRA-approach is typically applied to deterministic contexts, in which each initial condition results in a definite outcome. Moreover, the SRA-approach is more specific about the concrete processes leading from initial conditions to probabilities. These processes are determined by laws of nature, for example, the laws of mechanics in the example of the roulette wheel linking all initial conditions with either the outcome black or red.

The main problem of the SRA-approach is how to interpret the measure over initial states—essentially designating the relative frequency, with which these states occur. Obviously, the danger looms that for the interpretation of this measure one has to recur again to relative frequencies—and that would lead back to a frequentist interpretation. The ultimately unconvincing solution within the SRA-approach is to argue that the probabilities are largely independent of the choice of measure; therefore, there is no need to give this measure a specific interpretation.

To sum up, when it comes to the epistemology of data science, frequentism is ruled out as a useful explication because it fails to make the distinction between meaningful and accidental correlations. More plausibly, both propensity theories and the SRA-approach focus on the circumstances under which probabilities arise corresponding to the various variables whose impact is assessed in data science—for example, when the best search result is determined by an algorithm relying on user profiles, past searches, and so on. The main problem with propensity theories is that data science requires a concrete picture of how the circumstances lead to probabilities, which these theories in general do not provide—referring instead to vague and metaphysically laden concepts such as tendencies or propensities. By contrast, the SRA-approach provides such a picture in terms of the laws of nature linking the initial conditions with certain outcomes. However, this approach only works if it can be shown that the probabilities are independent of the choice of measure over initial conditions. If at all, this premise can at best be fulfilled for very few highly idealized applications, certainly not for the typical applications of data science. I therefore propose in the following an interpretation of probability that, while drawing on ideas from all the above-mentioned accounts, is suitable for the explication of probabilities in data science and in particular can ground the distinction between meaningful and accidental correlations (a more detailed exposition can be found in Reference 45).

Probability, symmetries, and independence

In the following, I tackle the two fundamental issues identified in the previous section: first, that the crucial distinction between meaningful and accidental correlations cannot be established by means of relative frequencies and second, the question by what mechanism or process the circumstances of a probabilistic phenomenon lead to probabilities. For this purpose, an interpretation of probability is developed that is based on *symmetries in the circumstances* as generative for probabilities rather than on *relative frequencies of events*. It has of course long been noted that symmetries play at least as fundamental a role as relative frequencies in the determination of probabilities. For example, the physical and mechanical symmetries of a die allow determining the respective probabilities and the relative frequencies that follow from these probabilities by the law of large numbers.

Let us once more start from the assumption of determinism that in principle phenomena are fully determined by their circumstances or conditions. Thus, even events that look completely chancy, for example, the toss of a die, are assumed to be determined by minute details in the circumstances. The assumption of determinism can be considerably weakened, but this issue cannot be addressed here due to lack of space (cp. [46]). In deterministic contexts, probabilistic phenomena arise, when not all circumstances are considered fix but some are allowed to vary.

Let us introduce some useful terminology in that regard. Those circumstances that are held constant shall be called *collective conditions*, borrowing a term from Richard von Mises [38]. Those that are allowed to vary are termed *range conditions*—with reference to Johannes von Kries' concept of a *Spielraum* or range of circumstances [46]. Furthermore, every possible combination of range conditions shall be associated with exactly one of a number of labels or *attributes*. The ultimate goal is to determine the probability of these attributes.

For example, when playing roulette one might be interested in the probability of the attributes *red* and *black* (omitting the zero for reasons of simplicity). The collective conditions, that is, the conditions that remain the same in all trials include the specific roulette-wheel and ball that are used as well as some general instructions how the wheel is turned, how the ball is thrown, when the wheel is stopped, and so on. Examples of range conditions are the exact velocity and angle with which the ball is thrown or the velocity with which the wheel turns at the outset. Again, these range conditions can vary from trial to trial within certain bounds. Obviously, the probability distribution of the attributes depends on the probability distribution over the range conditions. And this leads directly to a crucial problem of the approach—namely that for interpreting the probability distribution over attributes one needs to refer to the probability distribution over range conditions, which immediately raises the threat of circularity.

The proposed solution is that the probability distribution over range conditions results from *symmetries in the collective conditions*. Such symmetries can be defined in terms of invariances:

> *CAUSAL SYMMETRY: A causal symmetry of a probabilistic phenomenon exists if the probability distribution over the attributes is invariant under a permutation of the attribute space—corresponding to a mere relabeling while the collective conditions determining the causal structure of the probabilistic phenomenon remain unchanged.*
>
> → *If and only if such a causal symmetry exists, then the permuted labels must have the same probabilities.*

A generalization to continuous attribute spaces and also to attributes with unequal weights is fairly straightforward but cannot be discussed here due to lack of space [45].

Let us consider once more the roulette wheel as an example. Although the collective conditions determining the causal structure of the setup remain unchanged, the labels on the wheel are permuted, for example, the numbers of the fields are all increased by one turning red fields into black ones and vice versa. Plausibly, both situations are indistinguishable under such a relabeling and therefore black and red must have the same probability.

Let us simplify things a bit, by assuming that the wheel is spinning with constant velocity, that it is stopped at a certain moment by a blindfolded person, and that the ball is then placed in the pocket at the top of the wheel. It is clear that this procedure treats all areas on the roulette wheel equally and therefore, all pockets should be ascribed equal weight, that is, the measure over possible initial conditions should be equally distributed. Now, to establish this measure as a probability measure, the random nature of the attribute sequence must also be proven, for example, by establishing the independence of subsequent trials. Following a widespread intuition [47], such independence can result from the absence of causal influences from one trial to the next. Thus, a sufficient condition for independence is as follows:

PROBABILISTIC INDEPENDENCE: Two trials are probabilistically independent, if the range conditions in one trial are causally irrelevant for the collective conditions in the other trial and thereby for the probability distribution of range conditions in the other trial.

In our example, the key feature is that the person stopping the wheel is blindfolded, that is, he or she has no information at all about the current state of the wheel. In particular, whatever the result of the previous draw was, that is, the actual range conditions that were realized in the previous trial cannot influence in a relevant way her decision when to stop the wheel. Therefore, the collective conditions of the following trial remain unaffected by the result of the previous trial and consequently the probability distribution.

In sum, we derived the probability measure over range conditions without referring to relative frequencies but only in terms of causal symmetries and of probabilistic independence following from causal irrelevance. In principle, this line of reasoning is always possible for probabilistic phenomena and therefore an interpretation of probabilities based on causal symmetries is feasible.

Correlations and causation

The conceptual framework sketched above provides the means to solve what is arguably the fundamental epistemological problem of data science, namely to distinguish between meaningful and accidental correlations. Let me stress once more that causation is indispensable for drawing that distinction. Essentially, we have meaningful probabilities only in the case that we are dealing with genuine probabilistic phenomena, that is, there must be stable collective conditions that determine a probability distribution over the range conditions. Note further that the collective conditions in combination with the actual range conditions that are realized in a certain instance determine the attribute in that instance.

In accordance with the concept of causation delineated in section "Causation," a correlation between two variables A and B that allows for both reliable prediction and effective intervention—of course, only on average—results if one of the variables, A, is a collective condition and the other, B, an attribute of a probabilistic phenomenon. For example, A could be the number of sides on a fully symmetric die, e.g., 4, 6, 8, 12, or 20, and B the result of a toss of that die. Clearly, there is a correlation between the number of sides of the die and say the probability of throwing the number one. As this correlation results from a direct causal link between the collective condition and the attribute, it can be used both for prediction and manipulation. After all, if the geometry of the die is changed, this will immediately have an impact on the probability of getting a one. Note, finally, that this correlation inherits the asymmetry of causation, in that a manipulation of the effect variable would certainly not imply a change in the cause variable.

Obviously, many correlations *cannot* be employed for manipulation, but only for prediction. In those cases, there is no direct causal link between A and B, but rather a common cause structure, where A and B are both effects of a common cause C (as discussed already in section "The principal argument for causation"). As an example, consider a die, which besides numbers also has different colors on its sides. Now, when throwing several of these dice, the coloring of the sides may be such that stable correlations between certain colors A and certain numbers B result. Then, colors can be used to *predict* numbers, but certainly not to manipulate them—because the color, in contrast to the geometrical shape considered earlier, is not a cause for the number, but merely a proxy or symptom. In particular, the overall probability of the numbers cannot be manipulated by changing the coloring of the sides. Note, finally, that reliable prediction on the basis of proxies or symptoms is again only possible, when the corresponding probabilistic phenomenon is fully specified in terms of collective conditions determining probability distributions both of colors and of numbers. It is this quite demanding premise that draws into doubt the predictive reliability of many correlations in data science. As just one example, Google flu trends stopped working, when this premise was no longer satisfied [48].

Still, the conceptual and methodological framework proposed in this essay allows establishing one of the crucial desiderata for an epistemology of data science, namely to draw within an inductive methodology the crucial distinction between three types of correlations, (1) those that are due to a direct causal link and allow for both prediction and manipulation, (2) those that are due to a common cause structure and only allow for prediction, and finally, (3) accidental correlations that can neither be used for prediction nor for manipulation.

Wrapping up: The novel inductivism of data science

Many discussants in the debate on the epistemology of data science allege that inductivism does not work and therefore, genuine data science is not feasible. Nothing could be further from the truth. It is widely known that some of the greatest scientists in history claimed to be inductivists, including such luminaries as Newton or Ampère. A typical rejoinder has been that either these scientists were trying to let their theories look more true than they actually were or that maybe there was a curious discrepancy between their intuitive mastery of scientific method and their purportedly crude and naïve depiction of what they were doing. However, it is much more plausible to assume that these scientists reflected in depth on the virtues and limits of the scientific method, but arrived at a different conclusion than today's standard lore. And curiously, some of the most effective inductive methods like the method of difference do not figure prominently in contemporary debates, whereas the obviously defective enumerative induction is widely and wrongly held to be at the core of inductive methodology. Arguing against enumerative induction, as many epistemologists do, thus amounts to an attack on a strawman. Indeed, inductivist practices such as exploratory experimentation remain immensely productive and data science has already lived up to some of its promises as well, although it is still largely a heuristic approach. In this essay, I sketched a conceptual framework that could underlie an inductivist epistemology of data science. The main challenge for future work on the conceptual frontier of data science is to reflect on specific algorithms from the perspective of such an epistemological framework.

References

[1] Gray, J. 2007. Jim Gray on eScience: A transformed scientific method. In T. Hey, S. Tansley, and K. Tolle (Eds.). *The Fourth Paradigm. Data-Intensive Scientific Discovery.* Redmond, WA: Microsoft Research. http://research.microsoft.com/en-us/collaboration/fourthparadigm/4th_paradigm_book_jim_gray_transcript.pdf.

[2] Callebaut, W. 2012. Scientific perspectivism: A philosopher of science's response to the challenge of big data biology. *Studies in History and Philosophy of Biological and Biomedical Science* 43(1):69–80.

[3] Anderson, C. 2008. The end of theory: The data deluge makes the scientific method obsolete. *WIRED Magazine* 16/07. http://www.wired.com/science/discoveries/magazine/16-07/pb_theory.

[4] Leonelli, S. 2014. What difference does quantity make? On the epistemology of big data in biology. *Big Data & Society* April–June 2014:1–11.

[5] Mayer-Schönberger, V., and K. Cukier. 2013. *Big Data.* London: John Murray.

[6] Mainzer, K. 2014. *Die Berechnung der Welt. Von der Weltformel zu Big Data.* München, Germany: C.H. Beck.

[7] Kitchin, R. 2014. Big data, new epistemologies and paradigm shifts. *Big Data & Society* 1:1–12.

[8] Newton, I. 1726/1999. *Mathematical Principles of Natural Philosophy.* Berkeley, CA: University of California Press.

[9] Ampère, J.-M. 1826/2012. *Mathematical Theory of Electro-dynamic Phenomena Uniquely Derived from Experiments.* Transl. M. D. Godfrey. Paris, France: A. Hermann. https://archive.org/details/AmpereTheorieEn.

[10] Russo, F. 2009. *Causality and Causal Modelling in the Social Sciences. Measuring Variations.* New York: Springer.

[11] Hume, D. 1777. *An Enquiry Concerning Human Understanding.* Oxford, UK: Clarendon Press.

[12] Whewell, W. 1860. *On the Philosophy of Discovery, Chapters Historical and Critical.* London: John W. Parker and Son.

[13] Popper, K. R. 1934/2002. *Logic of Scientific Discovery.* London: Routledge.

[14] Duhem, P. 1914/1954. *The Aim and Structure of Physical Theory.* Princeton, NJ: Princeton University Press.

[15] Woodward, J. 2003. *Making Things Happen: A Theory of Causal Explanation.* Oxford, UK: Oxford University Press.

[16] Cartwright, N. 1979. Causal laws and effective strategies. *NOÛS* 13: 419–437.

[17] Salmon, W. 1984. *Scientific Explanation and the Causal Structure of the World.* Princeton, NJ: Princeton University Press.

[18] Siegel, E. 2013. *Predictive Analytics.* Hoboken, NJ: John Wiley & Sons.

[19] Burian, R. 1997. Exploratory experimentation and the role of histochemical techniques in the work of Jean Brachet, 1938–1952. *History and Philosophy of the Life Sciences* 19:27–45.

[20] Steinle, F. 1997. Entering new fields: Exploratory uses of experimentation. *Philosophy of Science* 64:S65–S74.

[21] Mill, J. S. 1886. *System of Logic.* London: Longmans, Green & Co.

[22] Bacon, F. 1620/1994. *Novum Organum.* Chicago, IL: Open Court.

[23] Herschel, J. F. W. 1851. *Preliminary Discourse on the Study of Natural Philosophy.* London: Longman, Brown, Green, and Longmans.

[24] Pietsch, W. 2015. Aspects of theory-ladenness in data-intensive science. *Philosophy of Science* 82:905–916.

[25] Pietsch, W. 2016. A difference-making account of causation. http://philsci-archive.pitt.edu/11913/.

[26] Goodman, N. 1983. *Fact, Fiction, and Forecast.* Cambridge, MA: Harvard University Press.

[27] Lewis, D. 1973. Causation. *Journal of Philosophy* 70:556–567.

[28] Baumgartner, M., and G. Graßhoff. 2004. *Kausalität und kausales Schließen.* Norderstedt, Germany: Books on Demand.

[29] Holland, P. W. 1986. Statistics and causal inference. *Journal of the American Statistical Association* 81(396):945–960.

[30] Mackie, J. L. 1965. Causes and conditions. *American Philosophical Quarterly* 12:245–265.

[31] Mackie, J. L. 1980. *The Cement of the Universe.* Oxford, UK: Clarendon Press.

[32] Skyrms, B. 2000. *Choice and Chance.* Belmont, CA: Wadsworth.

[33] von Wright, G. H. 1951. *A Treatise on Induction and Probability.* New York: Routledge.

[34] Pietsch, W. 2016. The causal nature of modeling with big data. *Philosophy & Technology* 29(2):137–171.

[35] Galavotti, M. C. 2005. *Philosophical Introduction to Probability.* Stanford, CA: CSLI.

[36] Gillies, D. 2000. *Philosophical Theories of Probability.* London: Routledge.

[37] Reichenbach, H. 1935/1971. *The Theory of Probability.* Berkeley, CA: University of California Press.

[38] von Mises, R. 1928/1981. *Probability, Statistics and Truth.* New York: Dover.

[39] Strevens, M. 2011. Probability out of determinism. In C. Beisbart and S. Hartmann (Eds.). *Probabilities in physics.* Oxford, UK: Oxford University Press.

[40] Popper, K. R. 1959. The propensity interpretation of probability. *British Journal for the Philosophy of Science* 10:25–42.

[41] Berkovitz, J. 2015. The propensity interpretation of probability: A re-evaluation. *Erkenntnis* 80:629–711.

[42] Rosenthal, J. 2012. Probabilities as ratios of ranges in initial-state spaces. *Journal of Logic, Language, and Information* 21:217–236.

[43] Abrams, M. 2012. Mechanistic probability. *Synthese* 187(2):343–375.

[44] von Plato, J. 1983. The method of arbitrary functions. *The British Journal for the Philosophy of Science* 34:37–47.

[45] Pietsch, W. 2015. Causal interpretations of probability. http://philsci-archive.pitt.edu/12513/.

[46] von Kries, J. A. 1886. *Die Principien der Wahrscheinlichkeitsrechnung.* Tübingen, Germany: Mohr Siebeck.

[47] Strevens, M. 2015. Stochastic independence and causal connection. *Erkenntnis* 80 (Supplement 3):605–627.

[48] Butler, D. 2013. When Google got flu wrong. *Nature* 494:155–156.

Chapter 12

Big Data in healthcare in China: Applications, obstacles, and suggestions

Zhong Wang*

Xiaohua Wang

Introduction 356
Source and features of healthcare data 356
Data from hospitals and primary-level medical and healthcare institutions 356
Data from specialized public health institutions 357
Data from regional health-service platform 357
Medical insurance data 358
Data from personal-use healthcare terminal 358
Applications of healthcare Big Data 359
Health management 359
Monitor and prediction of infectious diseases 360
Efficiency and cost controlling of health insurance 361
Efficiency of drug consumption 362
Obstacles of Big Data application in healthcare 364
New challenge to privacy protection 364
Low-level of openness and sharing of healthcare Big Data 365
Urgent need of the perfection of law system in healthcare Big Data 366
Suggestions to healthcare Big Data application 367
Regulation of healthcare data acquisition 367
Cross-border flows of healthcare data regulation 367
Perfection of privacy disclosure relief system 368
Establishment of sharing and opening mechanisms for healthcare Big Data resource 368
References 368

*Zhong Wang is a Research Associate Professor from the Institute of Economics at Beijing Academy of Social Sciences in China. Xiaohua Wang is a Research Associate Professor from Technology and Engineering Center for Space Utilization, Chinese Academy of Sciences. E-mail: wz.0@hotmail.com, saloty@sina.com

Introduction

Healthcare data cover many fields such as disease treatment and medical research. Throughout the human lifecycle, medical data are the important strategic resources of fundamental as well as the treasure of personal health and disease control. According to *Interpretation on Population Health Information Management Measures* (*Trial Implementation*) enacted by National Health and Family Planning Commission of the People's Republic of China (PRC) in 2014, the term *population health information* refers to the basic population, medical, and health services information produced in the process of service and management provided by medical, health, and family-planning institutes at various levels in accordance with national laws and regulations and their responsibilities. Based on this definition, the term *healthcare data* mainly refer to the data generated by personal immunity, physical examination, outpatient service, hospitalization, and other activities. With the popularity of wearable devices, the general *healthcare data* involve the data generated by personal-use healthcare intelligent terminal and mobile applications. This chapter discusses the source, features, application, and obstacles of current healthcare data in China and puts forward relevant proposals. The main contribution of the chapter is proposing regulation criterions for healthcare data acquisition, as well as the supervision means on cross-border flows of healthcare data. In addition, we tackled the perfection of privacy disclosure relief system, and the sharing and opening mechanisms for healthcare Big Data resource.

Source and features of healthcare data

Healthcare data have a lot of sources that are mainly from medical institutions. By the end of 2015, the total number of medical institutions in China has reached 983,528 of which 27,587 are hospitals, 920,770 are primary-level medical and healthcare institutions, and 31,297 are specialized public health institutions. Furthermore, the data generated by personal-use healthcare intelligent terminal and mobile applications have exploded in recent years. This section is a brief explanation of the different sources and features of healthcare data.

Data from hospitals and primary-level medical and healthcare institutions

The generation of data from hospitals and primary-level medical and healthcare institutions is in the process of routine clinical treatment, research, and management, including not only the record of outpatient and emergency, hospitalization, medical-imaging, laboratory, medications, surgery, and follow-up but also Medicare data. Most of the data, formatting in a medical professional manner and in a natural randomness of clinical practice, are the most primitive clinical record [8]. From the perspective of clinical management and research, the data are actual record on medical treatment and clinical practice. It is valuable. Although some data remain to be improved and revised, it still contains important medical information for future exploring and utilizing. The data have a large number of professional medical terms. There are more than 30,000 kinds of disease, thousands of titles of operation, and names of diagnosis and medicine. As a server of clinical care in various stages, the relationship among the data is complicated and impressionable that some data show bias. Hospitals differ in many ways, such as the level of diagnosis and treatment, the level of recording and coding medical data, the personal characteristics of the patient, and the extent of the disease. Thus, if the researcher ignores those differences, a conclusion error may be led. If healthcare Big Data has errors, clinical practice will be greatly impaired. Furthermore, in addition to patients' private information, healthcare Big Data also involves large amounts information such as hospital running, treatment methods, drug efficacy, and so on, which may be commercially sensitive. Therefore, if the interpretations are not rigorous, though the data have fulfilled analysis, it is still controversial and even legally disputed.

Data from specialized public health institutions

There are many specialized public health institutions in China, whose data are derived from medical research or disease surveillance specifically dedicated to large population. For example, in 2013, the major project *Large Cohort Studies on Influence of Environmental and Genetic Factors and Interactions on Coronary Heart Disease and Ischemic Stroke* supported by National Natural Science Foundation of China, covering more than 500,000 natural population in cities and rural areas of northeast, northwest, east, south, and southwest, uses large amounts of data to assess the influence of genetic and environmental risk factors and complicated interactions on coronary heart disease and ischemic stroke. This project not only includes the data of respondents and regions but also involves a variety of the data of nationwide sample survey and disease surveillance.

Data from regional health-service platform

Some regional health-service platforms have been established in a part of provinces and cities in China, such as Sichuan Province, Jiangsu Province (Nanjing), assembling and integrating many healthcare data of hospitals and medical institutions in those regions. Data on the platforms have been scientifically demonstrated and planned in advance, featuring more standardized than the original data, which embody the developing direction of healthcare data in the future. In China, regional health-service platforms can be established by two ways: Government administration section authorizes platforms, or IT companies offer to set up platforms. Both of them aim to realize data circulation by integrating the treatment data from various hospitals. IT companies, offering third-party services for more reasonable and more practical medical data, are more creative. For example, they try to create the individualized treatment based on medical circle as well as the health management and improvement based on health circle. Data from health-service platform show regional representation, of which results are more suitable for the local people, but the difference among the hospitals and the individual characteristics of the patients still exists, and it should not be neglected.

Medical insurance data

Medicare insurance: data, mainly from China's *Gold-insurance project*, are in accordance with national policy of medical insurance. The data are produced from computer information systems for the personnel to enjoy the supervisory service of basic insurance, which includes managing insurance information, endowing and allocating fund, paying for consultant charges by individual account, reimbursing risk-pooling fund reimbursement, settling accounts online, and so on. Medicare data have four features: First, the data are massive due to the large coverage of Chinese medicare, uninterrupted clinical observation, complicated results of medical examination, and other characteristics. Second, the data are heterogeneous that come from medical facilities, individuals, clinics, funds, and so on, covering number, characters, date, and other types. Third, the data are flexible, whose fluctuation may depend on policy changes. Fourth, the data are shared among different departments and operations. Medicare information system is commonly applied in China. Medicare data, however, are still in the initial stage of application. There is an increasing cause for concern to link the data in order and delve those deeper for clinical supports as well as scientific decision-making.

Data from personal-use healthcare terminal

The heterogeneous multidata, collected by the intelligent hardware in terms of physical states, diagnosis, clinic, and so on, involve personal health, medical service, and other respects. If organically integrated, it can effectively control and prevent the disease of patients and patients with predisposition, improving their health.

Applications of healthcare Big Data

Healthcare is a data-intensive industry, and healthcare data are the wealth of medical resources to improve health services, promote medical efficiency, and increase medical resources. Thus, healthcare Big Data has become an important driver of reducing medical cost-effectiveness. In the medical field, the applications of the Big Data include prevention and control of chronic disease, monitor and prediction of infectious diseases, efficiency and cost controlling of health insurance, and rationalization of drug consumption.

Health management

As an important part of social life, healthcare is related to national health and disease control, extensively concerned by the government and residents. Medical expenses in China show a growth year by year in the share of GDP, that is, 4.6% in 2000, 5.0% in 2010, 5.1% in 2011, 5.4% in 2012, and 5.6% in 2013. China has a big population base. In recent years, elderly population and chronic disease population have kept growing rapidly. Therefore, the demand for healthcare has skyrocketed, coming with a series of problems such as shortage and waste of medical resource, low quality of service, weak development of commercial insurance, irrational layout of medical resource, and fragmentation of data system. Meanwhile, medical efficiency needs to be improved, and medical cost remains to be reduced.

Chronic diseases have the largest proportion of medical expenses and the highest mortality rate all over the world. In 2016, according to the study of *The Lancet*, referring to 142 nations and 93.2% of population in the world [19], the healthcare cost for chronic diseases is more than $53.8 billion [13]. In China, there are massive numbers of people suffering chronic diseases. The *2015 Report on Chinese Nutrition and Chronic Disease* indicates that Chinese residents with chronic diseases accounted for 86.6% of total deaths [14]. Therefore, chronic disease prevention and control have become a significant and urgent task of Chinese society [15]. To obtain comprehensive, favorable treatment and extensive, high-quality medical resources, more investment is necessary. Meanwhile, the reasonable use of resources and right incentives is important to ensure greater value for medical expenses. Using Big Data for effective allocation of resources will bring larger magnitude of effect. If chronic diseases, for example, those for which population requires much more needs than other types of diseases, can effectively be prevented and controlled, not only the disease risk but also the medical costs can be markedly reduced [16]. As McKinsey's forecast, using Big Data in medical field will generate $70 billion to $100 billion a year. In China, for instance, if 5% of patients of diabetes without complications can be prevented from complications every year, medical expenses can be saved about 86 billion yuan [9].

Applications of Big Data in this field have these following key functions:

To control the predisposition group in advance: The comparison and analysis of user's behavior, sensory and demographic database can identify the high-risk group, who will be helped with health education and reminder of diet or physical activity to achieve the prevention of diseases.

To prevent the predisposition individual early: The use of genetic testing can predict the types of individuals with predisposition, who will receive the general education in disease prevention to achieve precise prevention.

To clearly manage patients for improving treatment compliance: The data of patient's body can be combined with the Big Data for reminding on time treatment of patients, which can prevent disease aggravation caused by late treatment and reduce disease risk [17]. By using social disease management, patients can share data with their relatives and friends. With their encouragement, treatment compliance can be improved to prevent disease progression caused by noncompliance.

To equitably distribute limited medical resources: Different diseases, especially chronic diseases, have the fluctuations of severity for an extended period. For example, the patient may have serious illness that needs immediate treatment, or the patient's disease may change for the better so that can stop the treatment. By analyzing the Big Data, a reasonable allocation is available to arrange referral time, prescription, and medication for more effectively configuring the medical resources.

In China, the website xywy.com tailored an integration service for obese people [18], referring to "Smart physique analyzer + Medical app + personalize guide of weight-loss." By using smart physique analyzer to measure the 10 healthy-body indicators for the users, this service can recommend suitable sports, diet, and lifestyle program for users according to the results of the Big Data analysis. What is more, it adds interesting and inspiring practices to customize the healthy weight loss for users.

Monitor and prediction of infectious diseases

The outbreaks of infectious diseases not only directly threaten people's life and health but also seriously impact social, economy, and national security. With the extensive urbanization and rapidly developing global communication network, many infectious diseases such as Ebola, cholera, and meningitis have a tendency of resurgence that still have high prevalence, causing public health emergencies. Thus, accompanying with the development of information technology, the monitoring and prediction of infectious diseases based on the Big Data play an increasingly important role in preventing and controlling infectious diseases.

Based on the Big Data, through reasonable mathematical model, spreading process can be simulated, qualitatively analyzed, and quantitatively analyzed, which can help one reveal the cause, elements, and development progress of infectious diseases outbreak, predict its epidemic dynamics and development trend, and formulate appropriate strategies of disease prevention and control. Applications of Big Data in this field have these following key functions:

To monitor and predict infectious diseases based on internet Big Data: With the development of the internet and search technology, people often search the relevant information online when certain diseases break out. The work such as tracking keywords and frequency, data filtering, statistics, and analysis can predict the incidence of disease to establish disease warning.

To monitor and predict infectious diseases based on Big Data of society and environment: Social and natural elements, such as transportation, human behavior, meteorology, and geological conditions, can affect the occurrence of the disease. The analysis of those elements is also an effective way to monitor and predict infectious diseases.

To monitor and predict infectious diseases based on clinical Big Data: This is mainly through the continuous and systematic analysis of collected clinical data to discover instantly abnormal aggregated diseases in the time and the space, so that the detection, prediction, and rapid response can be made in the early outbreak of disease.

Chinese center for disease control and prevention has set up China Infectious Disease Automatic-alert and Response System, on the basis of the Internet to improve the early identification of infectious diseases for their outbreak and epidemic, which has a good overall effect since 2008.

Efficiency and cost controlling of health insurance

China's health insurance is primarily basic health insurance led by government, supplemented by commercial medical insurance. China's system of basic health insurance has been approximately completed and realized the full coverage of national residents, but it is still inadequate in the coverage of major disease and protection of serious illness, and commercial insurance also does not provide an effective supplement. Nowadays in China, among over 100 insurance companies, there are only four of them having business of health insurance. Furthermore, because the compensation rate is too high and the business costs such as agent fees and managerial fees are high, most of the health insurance runs at a loss.

Both basic health insurance and commercial insurance are extensive in business, management, and other aspects. They lack of depth analysis of treatment cost and scientific assessment of risk cost for those insured groups, weak in actuarial and pricing bases. They lack of judgment of clinical rationality in medical services and monitoring of loss, fraud, and unreasonable medical behavior. They lack of technical means to reasonably assess the medical quality and cost of the hospital, ineffective in long-term cost-control. They also lack of the marketing and sales analysis based on the data, causing market stagnation with price competition problem and low yields.

Applications of Big Data in this field can provide a better protection of payment, reduce the burden on patients, and promote the development of the industry. The key functions are as follows:

To deeply analyze the data of medical fee: By combing with the incidence among different age groups and disease evolution information, the support can be provided for designing and actuarial pricing of claims-based illness insurance, which can enrich the types of commercial medical insurance and make up for the lack of major disease insurance.

To analyze multiple types of data for timely detecting the cost risks of fraud, waste, abuse, and others: Through analyzing the data of hospitalization, medical examination program, high-value medical consumables, drugs indicators of diagnosis and prescriptions, etiological factor, and medicine measurement et al., the risks of improper using insurance costs can be discovered very soon.

To determine the different medical behaviors in disease management according to clinical data: Through data analysis of drug dose and drug response, the medical processes can be evaluated. Through data analysis of adverse event rates in operation, readmission rates and other rates, medical effects can be assessed. Through the assessment of medical expenses and quality, the treatment cost can be controlled on the basis of the healthcare quality.

To analyze the health conditions of customer and driving factors of cost by using the Big Data: Optimizing the protection of design will win customers' trust on the professionalism of the insurance company.

The company, Kuaimayiliao.com, uses Big Data technology to implement real-time monitoring on the key aspects of the formation of medical risks. By reviewing prescriptions, handling drug claims, and assisting in the draft of drug catalogs, they monitor the risk of health insurance, under the premise of no prejudicing to the quality of healthcare, to reduce costs and improve the efficiency of health insurance funds.

Efficiency of drug consumption

With technological advances, new drugs continue to spring up, providing patients with better treatment opportunities but increasing the cost of medicine. Drugs are essential in medical field, ranking the third largest expenditure program of healthcare expenses after hospitalization and outpatient. The rationalization of drug costs needs to balance the relationship between over the counter drug (OTC) and receptor x, i.e, prescription drug (RX), ensure higher cost-efficiency of citizen medications and medicine expenses. Moreover, it needs policy maker to balance the relationship between new drug and limited health budgets and correctly stimulate the development of a new generation of drugs. The Big Data plays an important role in reducing medical cost-effectiveness.

China is the world's largest emerging pharmaceutical market and one of the countries in which drug consumption is fastest growing in the world. IMS Institute for Healthcare Informatics predicts that in 2020 the global drug spending will reach $1.4 trillion and as a key driver, China's drug spending will reach from $160 billion to $190 billion [20]. One reason of China's mounting drug spending is that the expansion of basic medical insurance covers almost all 1.4 billion people, whose medicine consumption is growing. Another reason is that the new drugs with higher costs are put into service.

Compared with other medical costs, the proportion of personal drugs investment is larger. In-patient and out-patient account for 21% of the total personal expenses, whereas drug spending reaches 37%. Although China has established a universal basic medical insurance, patients still have to pay a lot of money by themselves for medicine, such as in most of nations in the world. Some newly developed drugs create more opportunities to cure the patients, but they add to the treatment cost. Although China will exceed the United States in the total amount of drugs, its average dosage of new drugs is very limited.

In the future, with the newly developed high-cost drugs assessing into the market as well as the arrival of aging problem, the increase of drug consumption is expected to reach over 50% of the growth of medical expenditure. IMS predicts that, in 2020, global drug consumption will be 29%–32% higher than that in 2015.

Applications of Big Data in this field will make personal drug spending and medicare investment more reasonable, make medication effective, and make the development of new drugs convenient to service economy. The key functions are as follows:

To promote the rational use of drugs in hospitals, which is an important field of clinical research and application: Through the analysis of data, including drug types, consumption, sales amount, usage amount, treatment course, and frequency of medication in various hospitals, the characteristics, experience, and problems of drug utilization can be found to promote the rational use of drugs. For example, medical school of Chinese PLA has already studied on the survey and comprehensive evaluation of the use of essential drugs.

To promote the rationalization of the drug catalog of medical insurance: To control reasonably the medical expenses and make good balance between the public and individual expenditure, China has formulated the basic drug catalog of medical insurance. If its range is too small, the protection level will be lower, which cannot effectively reduce the burden of the insured group. If its range is too large, the public expenditure will be higher, which brings unbearable burdens for the countries. Therefore, the rationalization of the drug catalog of medical insurance is the key point of medicare reimbursements. By using the Big Data to deeply analyze the medicare details can make more scientific and rational catalog of medical insurance. University of Science and Technology of China has already implemented some research.

To develop new drugs effectively. In developing new drugs, the consensus of many countries is that all the drug innovations should be affordable and accessible. Traditional drug developing faces an increasing challenge of mounting costs and risks. By using the Big Data to develop drugs can relocate drugs and expand indications, through the association analysis of the whole genome, the connection of gene expression profiling, the biologic criteria of drug side effects, and other analysis methods, which has become the crucial strategy for many international pharmaceutical companies to avoid risks in research and development, lower costs, and accelerate the process of putting new drugs into the market.

China's TaiMei Technology, using cloud computing and intelligent algorithm for the Big Data, helps pharmaceutical enterprises to analyze medical data by collecting clinical research data, managing drugs, managing clinical trials, and so on.

Obstacles of Big Data application in healthcare

From a macropolicy perspective, the state encourages and assists the development of healthcare Big Data. In terms of policy implementation, various actual obstacles need to be overcome, the following aspects are included.

New challenge to privacy protection

With the development of technology and social progress, the concept of privacy was generated, which changes constantly along with the development [1]. Privacy disclosure may cause discrimination, fraud, harassment, personal injury, and so on, which has serious implications for social stability and personal security [2]. To have a better application of healthcare Big Data, the relationship between data usage and privacy protection should be well balanced. Medical privacy is closely related to sociology, law, and information technology, which is hard to define clearly. Privacy protection not only faces the challenge of protecting unclear content, but also multiple challenges such as difficult anonymization [3], the possibility of previous safe database may be used to analyze personal sensitive information in the era of Big Data [4–6], and so on. Specific performances are as follows:

Anonymization is harder. In the age of Big Data, the scale and size of data continue to expand. One party published an anonymous data, personal and privacy may be relearned on the basis of the data released elsewhere [10]. In the 1990s, Massachusetts Commission of Insurance announced the healthcare data of government employee to promote PubMed research. To avoid the privacy disclosure, all the sensitive information were deleted and anonymized such as name, home address, and so on before the release of healthcare data. Sweeney from Massachusetts Institute of Technology (MIT), however, succeeded in realizing *deanonymization* and identifying the medical record of specific people. Sweeney further explored and found that 87% American will be identified by viewing gender, birthday, and zip code as a set of characteristic to characterize someone [11].

Metadata are sensitive. Metadata are data of characterization, which are applied to describe the contents, features, and properties. Through managing and structuring, metadata help people better understand, realize, and describe the contents, features, properties, and development of data. Metadata are an important vehicle for data management and control widely existing in daily life, for example, the file metadata that include author, company, time, length, number and size, and so on. In the age of Big Data, due to the even more sophisticated dataset, the related metadata become more and more complicated. Metadata maybe meaningless on its own, but the collection of a large number of metadata combined with the analytical techniques of Big Data may trace personal sensitive information and behavior fully.

In the age of Big Data, the rapid development of data scale, data types, and analysis techniques has made previous privacy protection technology not robust enough, which requires new techniques and approaches to assure privacy and at the same time better guide dataflow among medical institutions and give full play to healthcare Big Data.

Low-level of openness and sharing of healthcare Big Data

Medical and health institution is the main force of collecting and storing healthcare Big Data [12]. Compared with data produced by mobile health application, data from medical and health institution have a higher accuracy and commercial development value. Nevertheless, under the current healthcare system, different degrees of data barrier exist in different medical and health institutions, also between medical and health institutions and social public, and medical and health institutions have no motivation to share data. Isolated data island not only results in duplicate patient data and waste of medical resources but also hampers the systematic development and construction of healthcare Big Data.

With the deepening reform of medical system and the improved degree of hospital informatization, data barrier is expected to break among hospitals. In the *circular regarding application and development of Big Data in the health and medical sectors*, the General Office of the State Council indicated a centralized establishment of a healthcare data-sharing mechanism cooperated closely by interdepartment. The *Healthy China 2030 blueprint* has mentioned the elimination of data barriers, a centralized establishment of a healthcare data-sharing mechanism cooperated closely by interdepartment, the realization of the collection, integration and sharing, and business coordination of data on application information system in public health, family planning, medical services, medical security, drug supply, integrated management, and so on.

In the future, under the leadership of government and multisectorial coordination and cooperation, healthcare Big Data may be systematically developed and applied, and the isolated data island is expected to improve or break radically. Nevertheless, the establishment of a national integration and sharing platform of healthcare data involves various regulators and participators, which is difficult to implement and far from the completion, development, and utilization of the platform. Besides, the openness of the medical data resources in the private enterprises and foreign-funded enterprises is still unknown. During the construction of the platform, private enterprises and foreign-funded enterprises can only, through bilateral cooperation, use data resource and explore the development and application of healthcare Big Data.

Urgent need of the perfection of law system in healthcare Big Data

Recently, Chinese law still cannot well explain and define the ownership of healthcare data, particularly the ownership right, which results in disputes in the healthcare data whether it belongs to the patient or the hospital in practice. Some people argue that hospital and patient are both involving the formation of healthcare data, so that the data are common, whereas others believe that the ownership of data belongs to the patient himself; the control power goes to the hospital and the management rights lie in the government. The blur ownership of healthcare data blocks the authorized use of data and poses a huge hazard to the protection of personal information right.

Under the current legal frame, healthcare data serve as a kind of information assets; protection can be divided into two categories: If the data are processed by medical institution or authorized by third party with intellectual achievement and economic value quality, the data are protected under the frame of intellectual property or business secrets; if the raw data associated with personal medical health are collected by medical institution or medical operator, the date belong to the scope of personal information and privacy and should be protected from the perspective of personal rights. With the increased awareness of personal information rights, the legislature may accelerate the process of the legislation and introduction of personal information protection single law. The general provisions of civil law are currently under consideration, which is expected to separate the personal information protection from right to privacy and be protected specially.

Suggestions to healthcare Big Data application

Regulation of healthcare data acquisition

The European Union had been agreed for the *General Data Protection Regulation* known for its strictness in April 2016, which regulates the transparency of personal data processing and the principle of minimum data collection and endows data subject with right to withdraw consent, right to be forgotten, right to carry, and so on [7]. Although China has not yet passed the law clearly regulating similar principles and rights, with the development of personal information protection legislation and economic globalization, it should learn the lessons and consult the experience of the developed countries in the practice of the legislation of personal information protection and take the following measures: First, adhering to the overall principle of legality, justification, and necessity, data are collected through nonmedical institutions platform, and through privacy terms or other ways; the purpose, method, and scope of the gathering and using information are presented and agreed by the collectors. Second, if the data shared by the medical institutions are used, data protection should be set through effective desensitization, so that data are unable to identify specific person and recover.

Cross-border flows of healthcare data regulation

At present, the regulation of the overseas output of healthcare Big Data and personal information has not been prohibited in China at the legal field. In the *Interpretation on Population Health Information Management Measures* (*Trial Implementation*), the National Health and Family Planning Commission expressly forbids population health information from storing in overseas servers. Population health information refers to the basic population information and medical service information created by various types of medical health family planning services in the process of service and management. With the development of the Big Data technology, these regulations need to be improved; first, protection should be extended to health information for individuals collected by medical mobile application. Second, after desensitization of data on population health, information should be allowed across borders; by means of technology, the data no longer have the characteristics of *citizen's personal information*, which is beneficial to the development of innovation. Third, safety assessment mechanism and standard system will be established, through the safety valuation, healthcare data-processing platform can output the citizen's personal information collected and stored by the platform overseas.

Perfection of privacy disclosure relief system

In 2011, Ministry of Health in the notice of *Guidance on the Level of Information Security in Health Industry* had pointed that classification protection system for information security would be divided into five levels; the level of vital health information system security should not be lower than level three [21]. Current law has put forward complete requirements to security protection; however, the criteria of relief and compensation have not been clarified. The healthcare Big Data platform providers should apply technologies and other necessary measures to ensure the security of the information and prevent personal information data collection in the business activities from leaking, damaging, and losing [22]. When the earlier happens or is likely to, effective remedies should be adopted instantly to compensate the loss of personal.

Establishment of sharing and opening mechanisms for healthcare Big Data resource

In September 2015, the State Council issued *the Policy Outline of the Promotion of Big Data*, which has put the openness of government data as one of the key projects for the development of China's Big Data. Actually, healthcare data are the weakest and most difficult type of data in the opening of data. Regional health-service platform is a very good exploration; platform function should be further extended to establish a healthcare data-sharing mechanism well coordinated and unified by the departments of health and family planning, traditional Chinese medicine and education, science and technology, industry and information technology, public security, civil affairs, human resources and social security, environmental protection, agriculture, commerce, safety supervision, quarantine and inspection, food and drug supervision, statistics, sports, tourism, meteorology, insurance regulation, federation of disabled persons, and so on.

References

[1] Warren, S. D. and Brandeis, L. D. The right to privacy. *Harvard Law Review* 1890, 4: 193–220.

[2] Prosser, W. L. Privacy. *California Law Review* 1960, 48: 383–423.

[3] Pedersen, D. M. Model for types of privacy by privacy functions. *Journal of Environmental Psychology* 1999, 19(4): 397–405.

[4] Wong, R. C. Big data privacy. *Journal of Information Technology & Software Engineering* 2012, 2: e114.

[5] Schadt, E. E. The changing privacy landscape in the era of big data. *Molecular Systems Biology* 2012, 8(1): 11–23.

[6] Jeffrey, R. *The Unwanted Gaze: The Destruction of Privacy in America.* New York: Random House LLC, 2011.

[7] Chaobing, Y. The system construction for the protection of personal credit information privacy–Inspirations from the rational experiences of the EU and the USA. *Information Studies: Theory & Application* 2013, 3: 20–24 (in Chinese).

[8] Brian, H. and Boris, E. *Expand Your Digital Horizon With Big Data.* Washington, DC: Forrester Research, 2011.

[9] McKinsey Global Institute. *Big Data: The Next Frontier for Innovation, Competition and Productivity.* Chicago: McKinsey Global Institute, 2011.

[10] Bryant, R. E., Katz, R. H., and Lazowska, E. D. Big-Data Computing: Creating revolutionary breakthroughs in commerce, science, and society: A white paper prepared for the Computing Community Consortium committee of the Computing Research Association. 2008. http://cra.org/ccc/resources/ccc-led-whitepapers/

[11] Agrawal, D., Bernstein, P., Bertino, E. et al. *Challenges and Opportunities with Big Data-A Community White Paper Developed by Leading Researchers across the United States.* 2012.

[12] Gantz, J. and Reinsel, D. Extracting value from chaos. IDC research report (Vol. 19, p. 11). Framingham, International Data Corporation, 2011.

[13] OECD. *Health at a Glance 2015: OECD Indicators.* Paris, France: OECD Publishing, 2015. doi:10.1787/health_glance-2015-en. ISBN 978-92-64-24351-4.

[14] Binghua, Z., Ligui, W., Yansong, S., Hongbin, S. Progress in researches on surveillance and early warning of infectious diseases based on big data. *Chinese Journal of Public Health* 2016, 9: 1276–1279 (in Chinese).

[15] Wilson, K. and Brownstein, J. S. Early detection of disease outbreaks using the internet. *Canadian Medical Association Journal* 2009, 180: 829–831.

[16] Mykhalovskiy, E. and Weir, L. The global public health intelligence network and early warning outbreak detection: A Canadian contribution to global public health. *Canadian Journal of Public Health* 2006, 97: 42–44.

[17] Wall, M. Ebola: Can big data analytics help contain its spread? October 15, 2014. http://www.bbc.com/news/business-29617831.

[18] Li, X., Xuhui, Y., Jing, W. et al. Residual early warning of influenza-like illness based on the OTC sales volume. *Chinese Preventive Medicine* 2014, 15(8): 724–728 (in Chinese).

[19] Ding, D., Lawson, K. D., Kolbe-Alexander, T. L. et al. The economic burden of physical inactivity: A global analysis of major non-communicable diseases. *Lancet* 2016, 388: 1311–1324.

[20] IMS Institute for Healthcare Informatics. *Global Medicines Use in 2020 Outlook and Implications*. Norwalk: IMS Institute for Healthcare Informatics, 2015.

[21] Weizhong, Y., Yajia, L., Zhongjie, L. Review and outlook of studies on infectious disease alarming. *Chinese Preventive Medicine* 2014, 48(4): 244–247 (in Chinese).

[22] Wang, K. J., Shi, L. M., He, L. et al. New opportunity for Chinese pharmaceutical R & D: Systematic drug repurposing based on big data. *Chinese Science Bulletin* (*Chin Ver*) 2014, 59: 1790–1796 (in Chinese).

Index

Note: Page numbers followed by f and t refer to figures and tables, respectively.

A

Ability, mass communication, 176
A/B testing, 269
Accountability principles, data protection regulation, 12
Activity approach, information usage by, 56–64
  collection, 57–58
    affected rights, 57
    automated, 57
    characteristics, 57
    legal issues, 57–58
  physical devices automation, 61–64
    affected rights, 62
    automation and autonomy, 62
    characteristics, 61
    legal issues, 62–64
    in mechanical engineering, 62
  processing, 58–59
    affected rights, 59
    automated, 58
    characteristics, 58
    legal issues, 59
  storage and distribution, 59–61
    affected rights, 60
    automation, 59
    characteristics, 59
    legal issues, 60–61
AdChoices Icon, 175
Ad hoc ethics committee, 27
Ad hoc public authority, 5
Akaike Information Criterion, 238
Allocation problem, 123
Alternating least squares (ALS) technique, 260
  for matrix factorization, 262–263, 267
Ampère, Jean-Marie, 332
Apache Hadoop, 264–266
Apache Hive, 200
Apache Mahout, 261, 266
Apache Spark, 314
Application programming interfaces (APIs), 197
Arendt, Hannah, 89
Article 24 GDPR, 11–12
Article 32 GDPR, 11
Article 35(7) GDPR, 13
Article 35 GDPR, 11–12
Article 39(2) GDPR, 15–16
Article 58 GDPR, 14
Artificial intelligence in Big Data, 223–248
  machine learning for, 229–231
    deep learning, 229–230
    ensemble learning, 230–231
    RL, 230
  methodological framework, 231–239
    optimal wavelet decomposing algorithm, 236–239
    RL, 231–232
    thresholding, 235–236
    wavelet transform, 234
  overview, 223–225

Artificial intelligence in Big Data (*Continued*)
X 4.0 era, 225–228
BI&A 4.0, 228–229
Industry 4.0, 225–226
Web 4.0, 226–228
Audiovisual data, 148
Automated collection of information, 57
Automated data-collection processes, 255
Autonomy, 62

B

B2C relationship, 19
Bag-of-words technique, 152, 154
Bandura's SCT framework, 180
Batch processing, computer infrastructure, 264
Bayesian Information Criterion, 238
Bayesian RL (BRL) technique, 233
Behavioral incentives, 178
Bellman equation, 232
Benevolence, mass communication, 176
BI&A 4.0. *See* Business intelligence and analytics 4.0 (BI&A 4.0)
Big Data, 2, 9, 17, 48, 54, 75, 148, 255–260, 286–315
advent of, 287–288
analytics, 2–3, 8, 13, 21, 23, 147, 200
personal data protection, Council of Europe guidelines on, 25–29
risk-assessment, 23–24
balancing of interests, 76
for business decisions, 212
CCTV cameras, 76
challenges, 258, 295–306
distributed FS, 300–302
millions of dimensions, 296
real-time processing, 303–304
scalability, 298–300
stability of FS, 297–298
visualization and interpretability, 305–306
characteristics, 48, 192–193, 193f, 256, 287–288
of Council of Europe, 16
for data-driven medical decision-making, 213–214
definition, 192, 286
deriving value from, 195–207
different aspects, 288
discretization, 289–291
methods, 291
process, 289–290
era, 8, 104
EU reform on, 35–36
fighting crime, 212
FS, 291–295
methods, 294–295
process, 292–294
generation in smart device, 61
harmed initiative, 71
in heart arrhythmia research, 207–209
impact on decision making, 192–216
case study, 207–215
deriving value from. *See* decision-making process, deriving value from Big Data
need for, 288
power imbalance in, 22
prediction, 29–36
preprocessing, 259–260
and privacy protection, 76
and social surveillance, 31–34
stock market fluctuations prediction, 214–215
storage, 259
structured, 195–196
unstructured, 196
usage in
industries, 257f
investigation, 30–31
veracity, 48

Big dimensionality, 292
Big Five personality factors, 182
Bipartite user-item network, 254
Birgé–Massart thresholding, 235
Blackmun, Judge, 97
Block thresholding, 236
Blueprints, data ownership right, 125–129
  contractual rights, 128–129
  intellectual property rights, 126–127
  neighboring rights, 127
  property rights, 125–126
  torts, 128
BRL technique. *See* Bayesian RL (BRL) technique
Brundtland Report, 157
Burners-Lee, Tim, 226
Business intelligence and analytics 4.0 (BI&A 4.0), 228

C

CAIM algorithm. *See* class-attribute interdependence maximization (CAIM) algorithm
Cartesian automata, 96
Categorical data analysis, 17, 20
Causation, data science, 335–343
  methodology, 340–343
  methods of, 338–340
  principal argument, 336–337
CCTV cameras, 76, 104
Celestrak, 56
c-function, 234
Characteristics, data ownership, 120–134
  publicity, 134
  right holder, 123–125
    collective ownership, 124–125
    contract, 124
    data subject, 124
    investment, 124
    scripture, 123–124
  scope of protection, 125–133
    potential data ownership right elements, 129–133
    right blueprints, 125–129
  subject matter of protection, 120–123
    data, information, and knowledge, 120–121
    public good/private good/club good, data as, 122
    unitary/commodity asset, data as, 123
    volunteered, observed, and inferred data, 122
Class-attribute interdependence maximization (CAIM) algorithm, 299
Clean Air Act, 163
Cloud (storage), 59
Coase theorem, 118
Cold start problem, 255
Collaborative filtering techniques, 254, 260
Collective data protection, 18
  non-aggregative, 20
Commercial and industrial sector, information security in, 52–54
Commodity
  asset, 127, 135
  protection approach, data ownership, 123
Communication privacy management (CPM) theory, 176–177
Communications Assistance for Law Enforcement Act of 1994, 32
Communications Capabilities Development Program, 33
Complementary pairs stability selection, 298
Computational linguistics analysis, 155
Computer-mediated communication (CMC), 176

The Concept of Law, 71–70, 82–84, 90, 94–95
Conflicting interests, 21–22
Congressional corpus, 156
Consequential prediction, Big Data, 30
Consistency-based filter, 294
Consumer law, 23
Content analysis, 153
Content-based recommender systems, 254
Context-aware recommender systems, 273
Context-dependent notions, 21
Context-driven recommender system, 273
Contextual Turn, 273
Contractual rights, 128–129
Contrario claims, 73
Convention 108, 25
Copernican revolution, 5
Copyright protection, 126
Corpus linguistics, 155
Correlation-based FS, 294
Cost function, 261–262
Costs and benefits misallocation, 117–118
Council of Europe
    guidelines on personal data protection, Big Data, 25–29
    Recommendation No. R (87) of, 36
Counter geospatial intelligence (counter geo-int), 50
CPM theory. *See* communication privacy management (CPM) theory
Crash, text, 149
Crawford, Kate, 18
Credit score systems, 20–21
Critical Discourse Analysis, 154
Critical Text Analysis, 153
Curse of dimensionality, 292
Cyberattacks, 60–61
Cyber-physical systems, 226

D

D3 visualization. *See* Data-driven documents (D3) visualization
DaaS. *See* Data as a Service (DaaS)
Data
    cleaning, 198
    collection, 4–6
        purposes of, 9
    consent, 7
    controllers, 10–11, 28–29
    EU model, 6–10
    exploration in decision-making, 200–203
        challenges in, 202–203
        tools for illustration, 201–202
    extraction, 195–197
    challenges, 197
    in healthcare. *See* healthcare, data in
    integration, 195
    mart, 194
    monitoring, 172–173
    ownership, 111–136
        characteristics. *See* characteristics, data ownership
        implementation, 134–136
        overview, 112–113
        proponents, 119
        rationale, 113–120
        standardization, 116
    portability, 131–132
    preprocessing, 259, 307f
        cleaning, 259
        integration, 259
        reduction, 259–260
        transformation, 260
    processing, 4–6
        large scale, 12
        necessity and proportionality principle, 13–14
        negative impact of, 12
        origins, 9
        risk management in, 10

protection
accountability principles, 12
authorities, 10, 12, 15, 24
collective, 18
collective interests, 23–25
conflicting interests, 21
flawed, 19
fundamental elements, 5
impact assessment, 12–14
initial core of, 6
laws, fourth generation of, 3–4
notion of, 5
regulations, 4–6, 11
risk-assessment, 10–16, 21
social control, 31–34
socio-ethical impacts, 21–25
risk-analysis, 10–16
science, 329–350
causation. *See* causation, data science
overview, 329–331
probability, 343–349
space debris population in orbit, 55
use, 10–16
for decision-making purposes, 17–29
purpose of, 3
in social network, 10
visualization, 2
warehouse, 194, 199
Data as a Service (DaaS), 226
model, 197
Data-centered approach, 21–23
Data-driven documents (D3) visualization, 204, 205f
Data-driven economy, 7
Datafication, 172
DataFrames, 267
Data Protection Directive, 10, 52
Dataset, 292
Dataveillance, 172
Data-visualization tools, 204–207
D3, 204, 205f
datawrapper, 204
Dygraphs, 204, 206f
fusion charts suite XT, 205
Google charts, 205–206, 206f
Tableau, 206–207
Datawrapper, 204
Dato GraphLab, 268
Debt, 214–215
Decisional privacy, 97–98
Decision-making process, 194–195, 194f
case study, Big Data in, 207–215
for business decisions (Netflix), 212
data-driven medical decisions, 213–214
for economic competitiveness analytics, 210–212
fighting crime, 212
heart arrhythmia, 207–209
stock market fluctuations, 214–215
for weather prediction, 212–213, 213f
deriving value from Big Data, 195–207
exploration, 200–203
extraction, 195–197
loading, 199–200
transformation, 198
using visualization for data incorporation in, 204–207
ways for, 207
Declarative large-scale machine learning, 268
Deep learning technique, 202, 229–230, 270–271
De minimis rule in convention, 73
Democratization process, 9
Denoising performances, 247f, 248f
Descriptive metadata, 55
Devlin, P., 70–71, 79–83, 86–89, 91, 94–95, 98–103
Devlin–Hart debate, 70–71, 81–83, 99–101
Digital Advertising Alliance, 174–175

Digital universe, 172
Directive 95/46/EC, 7, 12
Direct marketing, 6
Discourse analysis, 154
Discrete wavelet transform (DWT), 240
Discretization, 289–291
 methods, 291
 process, 289–290, 290f
Discrimination, 18–19
Dougherty, Dale, 227
Dygraphs, 204, 206f

E

ECBDL dataset, 308
Echelon Interception System, 32
ECHR. *See* European Convention on Human Rights (ECHR); European Court of Human Rights (ECHR/ECtHR)
ECtHR. *See* European Court of Human Rights (ECHR/ECtHR)
Electronic Information Privacy Center, 175
Electronic marketspace, 173
Embedded methods, FS, 294
EMD. *See* Entropy minimization discretization (EMD)
Emotion recognition, 270
Endowment effect, 118
The Enforcement of Morals, 81
Ensemble learning, 230–231, 301
Entity resolution, 198
Entropy minimization discretization (EMD), 291
Enumerative induction, 334, 338–339
Environmental Response, Compensation, and Liability Act of 1980, 163
Equal frequency discretization, 291
Equal width discretization, 291
Erga omnes rights, 134
ETL process. *See* Extract, Transform, and Load (ETL) process
EU. *See* European Union (EU)
EU General Data Protection Regulation (GDPR), 4, 9, 11, 35, 52, 131
 Article 24, 11
 Article 35, 11–12
 Article 35(7), 13
 Article 58, 14
 risk-based model by, 12
 risk-mitigation approach by, 16
European Chart of Fundamental Rights of the European Union, 13
European Convention, 72
European Convention on Human Rights (ECHR), 72, 89
 Article 5, 31
 Article 8, 73–75, 77–78
European Court of Human Rights (ECHR/ECtHR), 34, 72–73
 Article 9, 75
 Article 10, 75
 Article 11, 75
 Article 14, 78
 Article 18, 78
 Article 33, 75
European data protection
 laws, 7
 regulations, 5
European Union (EU), 34, 52
 model, 6–10
European Union's General Data Protection Regulation, 49
Extract, Transform, and Load (ETL) process, 195, 196f

F

FADP. *See* Federal Act on Data Protection (FADP)
Feature-based learning algorithm, 304
Feature discretization, 286
Feature selection (FS), 286, 293f

Federal Act on Data Protection (FADP), 119
Federal Trade Commission (FTC), 173
Filters, FS, 286, 293
  consistency-based, 294
FISA. *See* Foreign Intelligence Surveillance Act (FISA) of 1978
Flawed data processing, 19
Flink, 265f, 267–268
Flink-ML, 267–268
Foreign Intelligence Surveillance Act (FISA) of 1978, 32
Formatting, information, 58
Fourth generation of data protection laws, 3–4
Fourth industrial revolution, 225–226
Four Vs, Big Data. *See* Big Data, characteristics
Framing privacy, 103
Frobenius norm, 261
FS. *See* feature selection (FS)
FTC. *See* Federal Trade Commission (FTC)
Fuller, Lon L., 70, 79–80, 85, 93, 98, 103, 106
Fuller's qualities of legal orders, 90

G

GDPR. *See* EU General Data Protection Regulation (GDPR)
Gelly API, 268
Generalized optimal wavelet decomposing algorithm (GOWDA) system, 225, 240
Geofeedia software, 34
Geolocation, 58
Global Information Technology Report (2014), 171–172
Global memory, 311
Goodness-of-fit of RL-GOWDA$_{\mathrm{DWT}}$, 243t–244t
Goodness-of-fit of RL-GOWDA$_{\mathrm{MODWT}}$, 244t–246t
Google AdSense, 18
Google charts, 205–206, 206f
Government and military
  information security in, 50–52
  science information in, 55
GOWDA system. *See* generalized optimal wavelet decomposing algorithm (GOWDA) system
GPU scalability, 312t
Grafting, 304
Graphic Processing Unit-Compute Unified Device Architecture (GPU-CUDA), 311
Graphic processing units (GPUs), 302, 311–312
Grubbs test, 237
Grudge informer case, 84–85

H

Hadoop, 266
Hart, H.L.A., 71, 79
  Devlin–Hart debate, 70–71, 81–83, 99–101
  Hart–Fuller debate, 70, 79–81
  law and morality, 70, 79–81
  opposes Devlin's thesis, 101–102
  position as legal positivist, 79–80
  and right to privacy, 79
  rule of adjudication, 83–88
  rules of change, 70–71, 81–83
  utilitarianism and fundamental rights, 98–99
Hart–Fuller debate, 70, 79–81
Healthcare, data in, 355–368
  applications, 359–364
    drug consumption, 362–363
    efficiency/cost, 361–362
    health management, 359–360
    monitoring and prediction, 360–361

Healthcare, data in (*Continued*)
obstacles, 364–367
Big Data, 364
law system, 366–367
openness/sharing, 365–366
privacy protection challenge, 364–365
source and features, 356–358
hospitals/primary-level medical/healthcare, 356–357
medical insurance, 358
personal-use healthcare terminal, 358
regional health-service platform, 357–358
specialized public health institutions, 357
suggestions, 367–368
cross-border flows, 367–368
data acquisition, 367
disclosure relief system, 368
resource, 367
sharing/opening mechanism, 368
Heart arrhythmia, Big Data in, 207–209
Higgs dataset, 312
Home computers, 6
Homosexual conduct, criminalization of, 79–80, 91, 95, 101–102
Homosexuality, 86, 91
Hyper-targeted message delivery, 173–174
Hypothetical claims, 73

I

In abstracto claims, 72–73, 76–78, 104
Incentives, 174
Inferred data, 122
Information
authentication, 58
collection, 57–58
affected rights, 57
automated, 57
characteristics, 57
legal issues, 57–58
formatting, 58
gain method, 294–295
processing, 58–59
affected rights, 59
automated, 58
characteristics, 58
legal issues, 59
science, 48
legal and policy aspects, automated environments, 48–64
usage by
activity approach, 56–64
sectoral approach, 50–56
Informations and communications technology (ICT) market, 115
Inner/outer morality, 70
Integrity, mass communication, 176
Intellectual property rights, 126–127
Intelligent recommendation systems, 270
INTERACT algorithm, 294
Internet Advertising Revenue Report (2015), 173
Internet of Things, 49, 61
Interpretability, FS, 305–306

K

Kernel, 311
KNIME, 197, 201
Knowledge Discovery and Data Mining (KDD) Tools, 312

L

Labor law, 22
Latent factor models, 261–262
Law, Liberty, and Morality, 79, 82, 91, 95, 99
Law and morality, 70, 79–81
Legal positivists, 70, 78. *See also* Hart, H.L.A.

Leistungsschutzrechte, 127
Lenev v. Bulgaria, 105
Library for support vector machines (LIBSVM) Database, 296
Linguistic relativity, 154

M

Machine learning
algorithms, 288
for artificial intelligenc, 229–231
deep learning, 229–230
ensemble learning, 230–231
RL, 230
toolkits, 263–269
Mahout, 266–267
MapReduce, 264–266, 265f, 288
Market failure
in narrow sense, 115–116
in wider sense, 116–118
costs and benefits misallocation, 117–118
transaction costs, 116–117
Markov decision process, 231
Markovian dynamic system, 231
Markov-switching multifractals, 240
Massachusetts Talent, Technology, and Reporting System (MATTERS), 210
Matrix factorization, 260
algorithms, 255
ALS algorithm for, 262–263
latent factor models, 261–262
MATTERS. *See* Massachusetts Talent, Technology, and Reporting System (MATTERS)
Maximal overlap discrete wavelet transform (MODWT), 240
Mediator-based data integration, 199
Memory-based collaborative filtering algorithm, 254
Metadata, 54–55
Millian harm principle, 80, 86
minimum Redundancy Maximum Relevance (mRMR), 295
MIT-BIH Arrhythmia database, 207–208
Mobile commerce and consumer information paradox, 171–182
communication privacy management theory, 176–177
data monitoring, 172–173
motivational models, 177–180
convenient information seeking, 178
monetary benefits, 179–180
personal and social status, 179
overview, 171
personalized advertising, 173–174
privacy
management and trust, 175–176
paradox and AdChoices icon, 174–175
research agenda, 180–182
generational differences, 181
grounding, 180–181
personality traits, 182
Model-based collaborative filtering algorithm, 254
Monte Carlo simulations, 239, 312
The Morality of Law, 79
mRMR. *See* minimum Redundancy Maximum Relevance (mRMR)
Multivariate techniques, 299–300
My Debut as a Literary Person, 69

N

Naive Bayes (NB), 302–303
Narrower matrices, 292
National Information Infrastructure Task Force, 175
National legal systems, 51
National public laws, 52
National security, 50

National Security Agency (NSA), 32, 71
  data collection, 76
Natural language processing (NLP), 151–152
Necessity and proportionality principle, data processing, 13–14
Negative attitudes, personalized advertising, 174
Negotiation costs, 116
Neighboring rights, 127
Netflix, 212
Netflix Prize competition, 260, 268
Neural networks, 229–230
Newton of electromagnetism, 332
Nonauthenticated information, 57
Nonrivalrous goods, 115
Notice and consent model, 3–4, 8–10, 16, 26, 29
Not only SQL (NoSQL) database, 200, 259
Numeric data, 148
Numerus clausus principle, 116

O

Observed data, 122
Occupy Wall Street movement, 34
Online FS (OFS), 303
Online identity, 177
Online streaming FS, 304
Optimal wavelet decomposing algorithm, 236–239
Orthodox economic theory, 118

P

People v. Harris, 34
Personal control, privacy boundary management, 177
Personal information, protection of, 51
Personalized advertising, 173–174
Persuasion knowledge model, 175
PESIA. *See* Privacy, Ethical, and Social Impact Assessment (PESIA)
Physical devices automation, 61–64
  affected rights, 62
  automation and autonomy, 62
  characteristics, 61
  legal issues, 62–64
Physical embodiment, information, 121
Policymakers, 17, 21, 23
Positive freedom, 97–103
Positivism and the Separation of Law and Morals, 84
Potential data ownership right elements, 129–133
  additional powers and limitations, 132–133
  core powers and limitations, 129–132
    access to data, 129–130
    copying of data, 130–131
    data portability, 131–132
    use and integrity, 132
Pragmatic level, 121
Predictive policing, 33
  solutions, 17
PredPol, 17, 33, 212
Preemptive prediction, Big Data, 30
Preferential prediction, Big Data, 30
Price discrimination, 18–19
Privacy, 51
  boundary management, 177
  infringements, 104
  intrinsic limit on legal orders, 88–103
    individual autonomy, 92–97
    necessities of life, 89–92
    positive freedom, 97–103
  management and trust, 175–176
  paradox and AdChoices icon, 174–175
  as secondary rule, 103–107
Privacy, Ethical, and Social Impact Assessment (PESIA), 11, 26
Private use, data ownership right, 133

Probability, 343–349
correlations and causation, 348–349
objective, 344–346
symmetries, independence and, 346–348
Problems of Philosophy of Law, 96
Property rights, 125–126
Proportional k-interval discretization (PKID), 291
Pseudonymization, 55
Public good, 122

Q

Q-function, 232

R

Rapid Miner, 201
RDD. *See* Resilient Distributed Datasets (RDD)
Real-time data processing processing, computer infrastructure, 264
Real-time processing, 303–304
Reasonable suspicion, 30–31
Recital 75 GDPR, 11
Recital 77 GDPR, 12
Recital 84 GDPR, 14
Recital 91 GDPR, 12
Recommendation systems, 268–269
Recommender systems, 254
with Big Data, challenges, 258–259
heterogeneity, 258
incompleteness, 258
privacy, 258–259
scale and complexity, 258
timeliness, 258
in Big Data era, 260–263
ALS for matrix factorization, 262–263
latent factor models and matrix factorization, 261–262
Big Data frameworks and machine-learning toolkits, 263–269
Apache Mahout, 266
Dato GraphLab, 268
declarative large-scale machine learning, 268
evaluation, 268–269
Flink, 267–268
MapReduce paradigm and Apache Hadoop, 264–266
Spark, 266–267
future of, 269–273
context-aware to context-driven recommendation, 272–273
deep learning, 270–271
emotion recognition, 270
streaming, 272
user experience, 271
intelligent, 270
offline evaluation, 269
online evaluation, 269
Recursive feature elimination for support vector machines (SVM-RFE), 295
Regularity view, 336
Reinforcement learning (RL), 225
Relational database management system, 199
ReliefF, 295
Resilient Distributed Datasets (RDD), 266–267
Retroactive law, 85
Right holder, 123–125
collective ownership, 124–125
potential attribution criteria, 123–124
contract, 124
data subject, 124
investment, 124
scripture, 123–124
Right to data portability, 131
Right to privacy, 72, 74, 75
Risk-assessment, 24, 27
based on risk-based approach, 28
Big Data analysis, 23–24
data protection, 10–16, 21

Risk-based approach, 11
aspect of, 14
risk assessment based on, 28
Risk-mitigation approach, 16
RL. *See* reinforcement learning (RL)
Roessler, Beate, 93
Roe v. Wade, 97
Rotaru vs. Romania, 34
R Studio, 202
Rule of adjudication, 83–88
Rules of change, 70–71, 81–83

S

Samsara, 266
Sapir-Whorf hypothesis, 154
Scalability, 298–300
Scaling up learning algorithms, 298
Scientific use, data ownership right, 133
SCT. *See* social cognitive theory (SCT)
Sectoral approach, information usage by, 50–56
commercial and industrial, 52–54
government and military, 50–52
science, 54–56
Self-determination, 6
in data processing, 8
Semantic level, 121
SGD technique. *See* stochastic gradient descent (SGD) technique
Shaw v. Director of Public Prosecutions, 87
Smartphone, 57
Social cognitive theory (SCT), 178
Social control, data protection, 31–34
Social science research, methodologies, 147
Social Solidarity and the Enforcement of Morality, 94
Social surveillance, Big Data and, 31–34
Spark, 265f, 266–267
MLlib, 267
vs. CPU versions of mRMR, 314t
Spark Streaming, 267
Specification problem, 120
SPSS Modeler, 202
Stable FS methods, 297
State-of-the-art FS methods, 296
Stemming, 152
Stochastic gradient descent (SGD) technique, 260
Stratosphere, Flink, 267
Streaming processing, computer infrastructure, 264
Streaming recommender systems, 272
Stream processing engines, 197
Structured data, 148, 195–196
Structured Query Language (SQL), 199
Sui generis right, 112
Supervised machinelearning algorithms, 3
SURE thresholding, 235
Sustainable transportation, 157
methodology, 158–164
SVM-RFE. *See* recursive feature elimination for support vector machines (SVM-RFE)
Swiss Debt Enforcement and Bankruptcy Act, 119
Symbiotic web, 227
Syntactic level, 120–121
Szabó & Vissy (case), 77

T

Technical expertise, 148
TEMPORA program, 33
Territorial dimensions, data, 12
Text
corpus, 155
data, 148
data analytics, 147–164, 150f

language context and content coupled, 153–155
methodology, 158–164
mining, 151–153
using linguistics, 156
words as data technique, 151–153
data mining, 151–153
content analysis, 153
linguistic methodologies, 155
NLP, 152
purpose of, 152
tools of, 152
tokenized, 151
Theory-ladenness of observation, 334–335
Three Vs, Big Data. *See* Big Data, characteristics
Thresholding, 235–236
Time limitation, data ownership right, 133
Torts, 128
Total Information Awareness program, 32
Transaction costs, 116–117
Transmission Control Protocol/Internet Protocol (TCP/IP) connection, 312
Trust, 175

U

Ultra-intelligent electronic agent, 227
Unstructured text data, 148
linguistic complexity, 149
technical complexity of, 149
U.S. Congress, 156
Use-by-use case, 180–181
Uses and gratifications (U&G), 176
assumptions, 178
paradigm, 177–178
Utilitarian approach, 114, 123
Utilitarianism and Natural Rights, 98

V

Value, Big Data, 256
Variability, Big Data, 256
Variety, Big Data, 192, 193f, 256, 287
Velocity, Big Data, 193, 193f, 256, 287
Veracity, Big Data, 48, 192–193, 193f, 256
V-function, 232
Visualization, 305–306
Big Data, 256
Volume, Big Data, 192, 193f, 256
Volunteered data, 122

W

Waikato Environment for Knowledge Analysis (Weka), 204
Warehousing-based data integration, 199
Wavelet transform, 234
Web 3.0 technologies, 227
Web-crawling process, 197
Web-scraping process, 197
Weka. *See* Waikato Environment for Knowledge Analysis (Weka)
Westin, Alan, 93
Wolfenden report, 79
Words as data technique, 151–153
World Economic Forum (WEF), 122
Wrappers, 293
WrapperSubsetEval, 295

X

X 4.0 era, 225–229
BI&A 4.0, 228–229
Industry 4.0, 225–226
Web 4.0, 226–227
X-KEYSCORE, 32

Z

Zakharov (case), 77
Zero-mean Gaussian distribution, 234